SEATTLE IN THE GREAT DEPRESSION

Edwin Hill tending his Hooverville shack, Seattle, 1939. Seattle Post-Intelligencer Collection, PI22393, Museum of History & Industry, Seattle. Used with permission.

SEATTLE IN THE GREAT DEPRESSION

A History of Business, Labor, and Politics Drawn from Local Chronicles

Bruce A. Ramsey

Washington State University Press
Pullman, Washington

Washington State University Press
PO Box 645610
Pullman, Washington 99164–5910
Phone: 800-354-7360
Email: wsupress@wsu.edu
Website: wsupress.wsu.edu

© 2025 by the Board of Regents of Washington State University
All rights reserved
First printing 2025

Printed and bound in the United States of America on pH neutral, acid-free paper. Reproduction or transmission of material contained in this publication in excess of that permitted by copyright law is prohibited without permission in writing from the publisher.

Library of Congress Cataloging-in-Publication Data
Names: Ramsey, Bruce A., author.
Title: Seattle in the Great Depression : a history of business, labor, and politics drawn from local chronicles / Bruce A. Ramsey.
Description: Pullman, Washington : Washington State University Press, 2024. | Includes bibliographical references and index.
Identifiers: LCCN 2024026606 | ISBN 9780874224320 (paperback)
Subjects: LCSH: Depressions—1929—Washington (State)—Seattle. | Seattle (Wash)—History—20th century. | BISAC: HISTORY / United States / State & Local / Pacific Northwest (OR, WA) | HISTORY / United States / 20th Century
Classification: LCC HB3754.S34 R36 2024 | DDC 330.9797/772—dc23/eng/20241101
LC record available at https://lccn.loc.gov/2024026606

The Washington State University Pullman campus is located on the homelands of the Niimíipuu (Nez Perce) Tribe and the Palus people. We acknowledge their presence here since time immemorial and recognize their continuing connection to the land, to the water, and to their ancestors. WSU Press is committed to publishing works that foster a deeper understanding of the Pacific Northwest and the contributions of its Native peoples.

Cover design by Jeffry E. Hipp

For my family: Annie, Helen, and Morgan

Contents

ACKNOWLEDGMENTS	ix
Introduction	1
1. Top of the World, 1929	5
2. Denial, 1930	23
3. Bankers, 1931–1932	39
4. The Bottom, 1931–1932	55
5. Homeless, 1931–1941	71
6. Relief, 1931–1935	87
7. Hope, 1932–1936	101
8. The Blue Eagle, 1933–1935	117
9. The Left Rises, 1932–1935	131
10. The Labor Push, 1934–1937	145
11. Dave Beck, 1931–1938	161
12. John Dore, 1932–1938	173
13. J. D. Ross, 1930–1939	187
14. The Popular Front, 1936–1938	201
15. The Front Shatters, 1937–1939	215
16. The Great Builder, 1930–1939	231
17. Up, Down, and Up Again, 1936–1939	237

18. Enterprise, 1933–1939	249
19. Forward from Hard Times	263
Appendix: Seattle Dailies and Their Biases	275
Endnotes	281
Principal Works Consulted	327
Index	333
About the Author	343

Acknowledgments

Research for this book took five years, principally in the Suzzallo and Allen Libraries at the University of Washington, and through the Internet services of the Seattle Public Library. Help also came from archivists at state, county, city, and the National Archives, and at the Seattle Room of the Seattle Public Library; also from sports historian David Eskenazi and the keepers of files at the Anacortes Museum, the American Plywood Association and the Washington Athletic Club. Thanks also to Lorraine McConaghy, who got me started reading old papers, to Pam McGaffin and Mark Funk, who read an early version, to my son, Morgan, who made many valuable suggestions, and to my wife, Annie, for her untiring support and honest criticism.

Seattle's view of itself. Seattle Post-Intelligencer, *10-6-1929, p. 1C.* © *Hearst Communications Inc.*

Introduction

It seems that all my life I have been preparing to write a book about the Great Depression.

I grew up hearing about it from my parents. They were married in March 1933, in the week Franklin Roosevelt closed the banks. The Depression was a big part of their lives. It affected where they lived, what they wore, and what they ate. They recalled eating cucumber sandwiches, and restaurants serving "vegetable plates" for 25 cents. Thirty years later, my father still wouldn't eat macaroni and cheese. He'd had his fill of cheap food in the 1930s.

In October 1979, when I was a 28-year-old business reporter at the *Seattle Post-Intelligencer* (*P-I*), I interviewed my father, G. G. Ramsey, and my aunt, Alverna Kavanaugh, for a feature story on the Depression at the 50th anniversary of the crash. It was the only time I ever quoted my family in the newspaper. In the story, my father recalled his days as an insurance salesman, driving out into rural Oregon and Washington to seek out workers who were still employed. "Sawmill workers were getting 28 cents an hour," he said. "Loggers got 40 cents. It was a 10-hour day, six days a week. It wasn't much, even in those days, but those men were damn glad to have a job."

My aunt told of losing her job as a high-school music teacher in Ridgefield, Washington, because she was a married woman. She explained it: "The attitude was, 'You're married. You don't need the job. Let some single girl take it.'" It didn't matter that her husband had left her and she was supporting herself. She was fired.

Alongside my story in the *Post-Intelligencer* was a column by Miner Baker, the retired chief economist for the Seattle-First National Bank. He recalled the radicalism of the 1930s, when he was a student. Baker said that in 1932, had he been old enough to vote, he would have voted for the Socialist, Norman Thomas. "A few of my friends, or a number of my acquaintances, were Communists or became Communists," he wrote. "The difference was partly emotional, partly rational. I might have been one of them, but I didn't want to risk that much. I also wasn't all that certain they were right."

2   *Seattle in the Great Depression*

Newspaper art from the author's 1979 look back at the Great Depression: John D. Rockefeller and Herbert Hoover. *David Horsey*, Seattle Post-Intelligencer, *10-7-1979, p. 1 © Hearst Communications Inc.*

Baker suggested that someday he would write a column to "trace the course which took me from the brink of Communism in the 1930s . . . to a position in the state's largest bank." He never did, but in researching this book, I found out that in 1933, at 19, he got in trouble at the University of Washington as an officer of a club that invited a Communist to speak on campus. She was Jessie London Wakefield, the wife of Seattle's Red journalist, Lowell Wakefield. She had recently been jailed in Harlan, Kentucky, for stirring up the coal miners. The university's president, Hugo Winkenwerder, didn't allow speakers like that on campus. He ordered the club's officers to cancel her talk. When they refused, he suspended them all. Baker was readmitted, and later was voted student body president.

As a business reporter at the *Post-Intelligencer*, and an editorial writer and book reviewer at the *Seattle Times*, there was a limit to what I could write about history. Approaching retirement, I joined a group of volunteers to read local newspapers from the 1860s to compile a database about the

Civil War. We skimmed through old papers on the internet and on microfilm, stopping to read relevant stories and making notes.

That was a way of doing history from the bottom up. By reading journalism of the 1860s, I was hearing the voices of the people—the words they used and the thoughts and feelings they had. When I retired, I undertook to write a book of local history using the same method. The book was *The Panic of 1893: The Untold Story of Washington State's First Depression* (Ramsey, 2018).

Writing *Panic* took three years. Using the same technique, I took more than five years to write *Seattle in the Great Depression*. Looking through several hundred reels of old microfilm is not an efficient way to research a book. No one could make a living that way. But to research the history of a city during a decade of the 20th century, it is the best way.

Newspapers have their weaknesses. They cover public things—public documents, public events, and the acts of public officials—better than private things. During hard times, people tended to keep their troubles to themselves. At the bottom of the Depression, newspapers covered unemployment as a public problem, but until late in the decade they rarely told stories of a family's struggle or an individual out of work.

One exception was a series by Lidablanche Robe printed in the *Seattle Post-Intelligencer* in January 1932. Robe donned ratty clothes and posed as a down-and-outer in order to experience life on the street. Some of her stuff was graphic. She wrote, "I found men and even women searching through the street refuse cans in the lower part of town, and saw them eat withered vegetables and partly spoiled fruit." This was good journalism, though probably not the coverage that middle-class newspaper publishers were eager to put on readers' breakfast tables. Robe was a freelancer, meaning that she was outside the newspaper hierarchy. Probably she came up with the story idea herself. It is also notable that she was a woman. Later in the Depression, when the newspapers started writing more about the lives of the unemployed, most of the work was by women.

Newspapers cover events a day at a time, which is both a strength and a weakness. Some stories are big only in hindsight. For example, in September 1931, the bond market crashed. The Seattle papers ran wire stories about it on the business pages. In hindsight, the bond crash should have been page-one news. It meant, for example, that Seattle City Light would have to stop work on Diablo Dam for several years. Three months later, the newspapers saw the meaning of it when City Light stopped work and began laying off engineers.

Another only-in-hindsight story was the closure of the Ford Motor Company plant. The plant was big news in Seattle when it opened in 1932, in the darkest time of the Depression. The plant had been designed by the greatest industrial designer in the world and was the most modern industrial plant in the city. Seven months later, the newspapers reported that Ford was temporarily suspending operations because of a supply problem. That story stood as the public statement on the plant for more than seven years. Only when it was sold to the government did the newspapers acknowledge that Ford had never reopened it.

For all of their faults, newspapers tell the story of a city better than any other source. They cover the issues at the level of detail that such a story needs: local, but not too individual. Over time, facts once ignored come out. They bubble up in editorials, opinion columns, letters to the editor, and even the ads. They come out in lawsuits, public hearings, and official reports. Later in the Depression, when officials boasted about how much better things were, they revealed how bad they had been before.

For more about the biases and limitations of Seattle's newspapers, see the appendix on page 275.

Research on this book also included histories and academic papers, which are listed at the back. But I offer no apologies for using newspapers more. To an old newspaperman, academic work often tastes overprocessed, like industrial food. Newspaper stories are first impressions, fresh takes. Because I wasn't there, I want to listen to the people who were.

A final note. I have written this account in the present tense. It's a style I picked up at *Asiaweek* magazine in Hong Kong, which ran long pieces we called "good reads." I hope the reader will think of this book as one.

Bruce A. Ramsey
Seattle, April 2025

1
Top of the World, 1929

On October 16, 1929, an odd-looking aircraft from Russia swoops down into Lake Washington. The plane is named *Land of the Soviets*. In the welcoming crowd at Seattle's Sand Point, a girl in Russian costume offers the four aviators an old-country welcome of flowers, bread, and salt.

The crowd includes a group called Friends of the Soviet Union. A year hence, the Hoover administration will try to deport its spokesman, a Russian tailor named Leon Glaser, as an alien Communist. Because the United States has no diplomatic relations with Josef Stalin's government, the effort will fail. On the day the aviators arrive, the U.S. government sends no one to greet them.

Officially, the United States still recognizes the old Russian government, which has been dead for 12 years. That government still has a consulate in downtown Seattle in the Lyon Building, complete with an Imperial flag and a portrait of Czar Nicholas II. Consul Nicholas Bogolawlenski has been receiving his pay through the sale of goods the old government bought in America during World War I. The Union of Soviet Socialist Republics has no consulates in the United States, but it does own Amtorg Trading Corporation in New York. And Amtorg has a Seattle office in the Smith Tower.

Seattle's welcome for the Russians is commercial. Leading the welcome at Sand Point is William O. McKay, head of the Aviation Division of the Seattle Chamber of Commerce. McKay is also Seattle's largest Ford dealer— and Henry Ford has recently taken an interest in Russia by offering to help industrial designer Albert Kahn set up a tractor plant in Stalingrad.

After the flowers and photographs, the Russian fliers are whisked under police escort to a suite in the Olympic Hotel. The next day, the chamber hosts a banquet at which an Amtorg man assures the Seattle audience that his country wants their business. Siberia needs American investment, and Seattle is closer to Russia than any major port in the United States.

As the Americans talk, the Russian aviators smile and eat. The next day they climb into *Land of the Soviets*, now equipped with wheels instead of pontoons. They set off for Chicago, where they see a football game; Detroit, where they meet Henry Ford; and New York, where they are greeted by aviator Charles Lindbergh.

Trade with the Soviet Union will blossom—for a while. America's big import during the 1930s, however, will not be Soviet goods. It will be Soviet ideas.

On September 3, 1929, the Dow Jones Industrial Average closes at 381. The stock market will not beat this mark for 25 years.

Life is good. Americans are enjoying automobiles, washing machines, refrigerators, electric ranges, radios, talking pictures, bootleg liquor, baseball, and hot dogs. In September 1929, Seattle people have their first chance to buy factory-sliced bread.

Labor is at peace. American wages are the highest in the world. The work week, which in living memory was 60 hours, has dropped to 44 hours,

Greeting the Russian aviators at Sand Point, October 1929. Seattle Post-Intelligencer Collection, PI20262, Museum of History & Industry, Seattle. Used with permission.

Russian plane with wheels (above), and with pontoons in Lake Washington (below). Image above: *Author's collection*. Image below: Seattle Post-Intelligencer *Collection, PI20261, Museum of History & Industry, Seattle. Used with permission.*

and in a few industries to 40 hours. Back East, General Electric makes news by offering paid vacations, with one week off after three years' service and two weeks off after ten years. B. C. Forbes, the Scotsman who founded *Forbes* magazine, thinks it's a fine idea. "Surely American civilization—and its prosperity—have reached a stage where citizens should not have to work from January 1 to December 31 without any release from the daily grind," he writes in his column for the Hearst newspapers.

Women have made big strides. Few compete with men for top jobs, but more are earning money as telephone operators, secretaries, sales clerks, nurses, and schoolteachers. They are driving cars, and they are coming to the brokerage houses to invest their money. They vote, and in 1926 they helped elect Bertha Landes for a two-year term as mayor of Seattle. At the University of Washington, coeds are not allowed to smoke, on campus or off, but at the illegal speakeasies young women sit at the bar. Hemlines, which a decade ago were at the floor, have risen to the knee. Women do not yet wear pants.

For Seattle's commerce, a milestone comes in mid-September 1929. More than 10,000 spectators gather on the earthen runway of Boeing Field to witness the city's first air-mail flight. They cheer as pilot Kenneth Neese lifts off in a single-engine biplane, circles the field, and heads for Portland. In 36 hours, his sack of mail will arrive in New York. To celebrate this day, banks and investment houses take out an ad in the *Seattle Times* to herald the new "wings to Seattle's financial progress."

On October 6, 1929, the *Seattle Post-Intelligencer* imagines the city's fabulous future. On a Sunday section front, it runs full-page art of a 500-foot giant looming behind skyscrapers and holding reins on ships in Elliott Bay (see page x). Flying at the giant's shoulder is a three-engine, fabric-wing biplane, a Boeing Model 80. Above are the words: "SEATTLE: *Gateway to the Pacific.*"

The 1920s have been a time of building bigger and showier. You can see it in Seattle's downtown theaters, which have been adorned in what one writer calls "Arabian Nights splendor."

In 1926, the almost 3,000-seat 5th Avenue opens in the new Skinner Building. Done in a Chinese motif, the 5th Avenue is one of the most lavishly appointed theaters on the West Coast. In 1927 comes the 2,700-seat

Orpheum, done in Spanish Renaissance. In 1928 the nearly 4,000-seat Paramount (initially called the Seattle Theatre) opens, done in rococo-French Renaissance with gaudy chandeliers and wall medallions encrusted with gold leaf. And in April 1929 comes the 2,600-seat Fox (later renamed the Music Hall) done in Spanish Baroque.

In a few years, Seattle's entertainment palaces will be emptied out. But in 1929, each is alive with vaudeville: comedians, dancers, and live music, followed by a newsreel, cartoons, and one of the new talking pictures.

The 1920s have also brought a hotel boom. The Claremont (later the Andra) is built in 1925, the Vance and the Camlin in 1926, the Bergonian (later the Mayflower Park) in 1927, the Hungerford (later the Executive Pacific) in 1928, and the Benjamin Franklin in 1929. Seattle's grandest hostelry, the Olympic, built in 1924, is given a new wing in 1929.

The new hotels push aside the old. In 1929, the Rainier Grand at First and Madison is slated for demolition to make room for the Federal Building (now the Old Federal Building). At the Butler Hotel at Second and James, a court order shuts down the restaurant for violating the Prohibition law. In May 1929, the Butler declares bankruptcy. Once the gathering place for prospectors returning from the Klondike, it will become a parking garage.

In the retail world of the 1920s, shoppers ride the streetcars downtown to buy groceries at the Pike Place Market. They also shop at the multilevel department stores: Rhodes, Frederick & Nelson, MacDougall-Southwick, Cheasty's, Fraser-Paterson, and the Bon Marché. In August 1929, at the peak of the boom, the Bon opens its air-conditioned department store, which will last into the 21st century. Designed by Seattle architect John Graham, the store takes up an entire block. Also in 1929, the Bon begins offering 30-day charge accounts.

The great passion of downtown developers is the office tower. Seattle's signature skyscraper of the 1920s is the 27-story Northern Life Tower, designed by Abraham Albertson and opened in March 1929. Called the Seattle Tower today, the building is an Art Deco beauty, with its bricks dark brown at the bottom rising to a light gray at the summit to create a "sunrise effect."

Between the rounded top of the Northern Life Tower and the arrowhead top of the Smith Tower (see pages 16–17) lies most of downtown Seattle. Its buildings are of brick, many of them built in the 1890s or the

10   *Seattle in the Great Depression*

Seattle's Art Deco tower of the 1920s. *Image from display ad in* Seattle Post-Intelligencer, *2-18-1929, p. 19.*

early 20th century after the gold rush to the Yukon. In the 1920s, new towers have risen: the 12-story Dexter Horton Building in 1922, the 11-story Terminal Sales Building in 1923, the 18-story Medical Dental Building in 1925, the 8-story Skinner Building in 1926, and the 14-story Joseph Vance Building in 1929. None is as tall as the 42-story Smith Tower, built in 1914, but together they add up.

In September 1929 the *Argus*, Seattle's establishment weekly, writes: "New buildings are being erected on every hand and almost before they are created space is at a premium ... New capital is pouring into the city."

Bringing much of that capital is young Ben Ehrlichman, who is said to have Seattle's sharpest financial mind. The name Ehrlichman will become famous decades later when John Ehrlichman will be counsel to President Richard Nixon during the Watergate affair in the 1970s. Ben is his uncle. He will never be nationally known, but in 1929, at age 34, he is a force in Seattle business.

His father was a clothing merchant who immigrated from Russia in 1881. His mother immigrated from Romania. Ben was their third child, born in the depression year 1895.

From the start, Ben Ehrlichman is ambitious. He peddles newspapers. According to one story, at age 17 he is downtown, cold and wet, when he spots a well-dressed man at First and Cherry. Ehrlichman buttonholes him, asking for work. The man says, "What do you know how to do?" Ehrlichman replies, "I don't know how to do anything." The man says, "You're just the fellow I'm looking for." The man is Henry Carstens, one of the city's principal bond brokers. Ehrlichman drops out of high school to go to work for him. The boy has a fast mind and within a short time is able to quote detailed bond tables from memory.

In 1915, Ehrlichman is put in charge of the bond department at the new Guardian Trust & Savings Bank. Because he is only 20, the bank needs a special dispensation from the state legislature to entrust him with the work. During World War I, he joins the Army as a flight instructor. After the war, he and a partner open a bond firm, first in Tacoma then Seattle.

Ben Ehrlichman. Seattle Post Intelligencer, 3-25-1929, p. 17. © Hearst Communications Inc.

A newspaper story on Ehrlichman, which calls him a "youthful genius," notes that he does not play golf. He works. In the 1920s, he and his partner build their firm into one of the principal bond houses in Seattle. By 1928, three partners have several financial companies under a holding company, United Corporation. Its central role is to attract Eastern capital to the Pacific Northwest.

United goes public in July 1928, and its stock soars. Ehrlichman is conscientious; in June 1929, he warns investors that United's stock is selling far above book value. At the market's peak in September, he advises investors not to hold stocks on margin.

Still, like almost everyone, Ehrlichman errs on the side of optimism. In Seattle, his misstep is the United Shopping Tower at Third and Pike. The building is a stand-up shopping center of 12 stories, some with only one shop to a floor. On the 11th floor is a tearoom, in the basement a bargain counter, and on the sidewalk a footman in livery. The idea of 27 shops under one roof is a good one. The modern woman will want convenience like that.

Shopping Tower, Seattle, 1929: Twelve stories of shops and no parking. *Pemco Webster & Stevens Collection, 1983.10.4122, Museum of History & Industry, Seattle. Used with permission.*

The mistake is to make the experience vertical rather than horizontal and to provide no parking.

The Shopping Tower opens in November 1929. It is not a success. The bargain basement does all right, as do the first two floors, but the high-rise space ends up being filled with cut-rate shops. Many of them fail. Pinched by the Depression, the building management eventually curtails the elevator service and lays off the footman. In 1932, the building defaults on its 99-year ground lease. It evicts its remaining tenants and leases to an insurance company. (The Shopping Tower is now the Olympic Savings Tower Condominium.)

In the fall of 1929, Ben Ehrlichman has a bigger project in his sights. The 23-story Exchange Building is to be the home for the Seattle Stock Exchange, an institution Ehrlichman helped create in 1926. The building is to have a huge amount of floor space. To finance it, Ehrlichman's company, renamed United National Corporation, is selling bonds. In the 1920s, most of Seattle's big office buildings, apartments, and hotels are financed with bonds, typically at 6 to 6.5 percent interest. The buildings themselves will weather the Depression, but in a few years most of the bonds will default.

In 1929 another of Seattle's financiers is William D. Comer. Born in 1869, Comer was raised in a Quaker family in Indiana. In Seattle, he will be one of the founders of the Pilgrim Congregational Church.

Comer begins his career as an inspector for a farm lender. In his twenties he moves to Seattle, and in 1897 he goes north to the Klondike in search of gold. After a taste of the North, he decides the city has better diggings.

Comer builds up two companies. One is the Mutual Savings and Loan Association, which he takes over in 1916 when it has barely a thousand dollars in deposits. He doesn't own the Mutual; it is owned by its depositors. He does own W. D. Comer & Co., a bond-underwriting house he starts in 1921. He begins with an office and a desk. Its income statement from 1923 shows that more than a third of his expenses are newspaper ads—"No investor with us has ever lost a single dollar," they say—and his salary. Most of the remaining expenses are commissions to bond salesmen.

W.D. Comer, c. 1930. *Author's collection.*

Comer's business is to buy up building bonds at 90 cents on the dollar and retail them at full value. In this way he finances buildings all over the Northwest. Notable are two of his 1928 deals, the 11-story Marcus Whitman Hotel in Walla Walla, which will survive into the 21st century, and the 14-story Benjamin Franklin Hotel in Seattle, which will be torn down to make room for the Westin.

In 1928, Comer also arranges Eastern financing for the mile-and-a-half-long bridge across the Columbia River at Longview. As a private toll bridge, the project will be a disappointment. During the 1930s it will default on its bonds, and in the 1950s it will be sold to the state for 37.5 cents on the dollar. But it is a solid bridge, and in 1928 it is a triumph for W. D. Comer.

The Seattle financier also rescues the struggling project to build the Washington Athletic Club. He becomes the club's president. In 1929 he provides the land for the club's 21-story Art Deco building, which will be designed by architect Sherwood Ford.

A high-school man, Comer has married Vassar-educated Cornelia Atwood Pratt, a writer of novels and, for a time, the literary editor of the *Seattle Post-Intelligencer*. In 1927 he builds her a 12-room mansion in Washington Park, but she falls ill and in 1929 she dies, leaving him with his work.

A history written in the 1920s says Comer has managed his companies so carefully "that they have the distinction of having foreclosed but one mortgage in the city of Seattle." He is past president of the state association of savings bankers. He is a member of the Chamber of Commerce, the Rainier Club, and the Seattle Auto Club. But trouble is coming to Comer's world. On September 5, 1929, one day after the bear market begins on Wall Street, the advertising man at W. D. Comer & Co. jumps off the sixth floor of the Leary Building (now the Insurance Building) onto the sidewalk of Madison Street.

Comer assures the press that the dead man, Fred H. Henry, 33, was not involved in any financial trouble. Comer is lying. Henry had borrowed $180,000 from Comer, and his half-secured note is three months past due. After Henry's death, Comer pledges the note to his savings and loan as part of the security for an $800,000 loan.

Comer is pushing his luck.

Around the world, risk is rising. Before World War I, Britain was the world's great lender; since then, the Americans have taken on the job. They are not yet good at it.

Americans have been buying German bonds, lending Germany the money to pay the war reparations demanded by Britain and France. Those countries, in turn, have been using Germany's money to pay war debts owed to the U.S. Treasury. This neat circle of finance assumes that Americans will keep buying German bonds. In 1929 their appetite slackens, bringing on a financial crisis in Germany. On August 30, Britain and France agree to reduce Germany's reparations by a little, but not enough. On September 8 the *Post-Intelligencer* reports that in Germany, "Capital is growing scarce and the stock markets are hysterical." This is the beginning of the Great Depression. It begins in Germany, the loser of World War I.

The debt problem is not only there. During the 1920s, other governments borrow heavily on Wall Street. For example, in September 1929 the *Seattle Times* runs "tombstone" ads for the 6.5-percent bonds of the Brazilian state of Minas Geraes. The bonds are for buying equipment for the South Minas Railway and the Paracatu Railway, for funding the Banco Credito Real of Belo Horizonte, and to repay Minas Geraes' short-term debt.

Are these safe investments? How would Seattle readers know? Probably they have never heard of Minas Geraes. It might reassure them that the bonds are offered by the First National City Bank of New York—Citibank. Also, the Seattle investor is paying only 87.5 cents for every 100 cents of bond. The banks are skimming off another 4 cents, so it is a deal for them, too. For each dollar it owes, the state of Minas Geraes is borrowing 83.5 cents. For thirty years, Minas Geraes promises to pay interest on the full 100 cents out of its tax receipts on coffee. It will not stick to this promise. In March 1932, with the price of coffee having collapsed, Minas Geraes will default on the interest. Its bonds will fall to 22 cents on the dollar.

In 1929 Seattle's newspapers are loaded with tombstones for bonds of such distant debtors as the State of Rio de Janeiro, the Republic of Panama, the National Hotel of Cuba, the Kingdom of Romania, and the Roman Catholic Archbishop of Manila. Salesmen are peddling exotic offshore paper all across the Pacific Northwest, from Seattle to Hoquiam to the tiny First National Bank of Sedro-Woolley.

The American president inaugurated in March 1929, Herbert Hoover, should be just the right man for such a situation. Educated at Stanford University, Hoover is a self-made international businessman. He has worked in Australia and China, and as a mining consultant in London. During the Great War, he was appointed U.S. "food czar" and was so effective that a new word, *hooverize*, meaning economize, entered the American vocabulary. After the war, he headed the American Relief Administration, which provided food aid to Europe and Russia. Then Hoover was secretary of commerce under Warren Harding and Calvin Coolidge. No other modern president has had Hoover's depth of global experience, and no other secretary of commerce has ever been elected president.

Hoover is not the right man. In the summer and fall of 1929, he should be reining in the senators of his own party, who have gone wild on a bill offered by Senator Reed Smoot of Utah and Representative Willis Hawley

The *Seattle Times* imagines a causeway using dirt and rock fill to cross Lake Washington from Seward Park to Mercer Island. Seattle Times, *10-13-1929, p. 5.* © *The* Seattle Times.

Downtown Seattle looking south, with the Northern Life Tower at left (now the Seattle Tower) and the Smith Tower in the distance, 1929. *Photograph by Edwin Pierson, Pierson Photo Co., 1929. Author's collection.*

FILL, WOULD MAR LAKE WASHINGTON'S BEAUTY

h average-sized steamboats and sailing craft that cannot slip a causeway to be built just east of the park to match the one rcer Island.

the proposed toll bridge, with its 1,700 feet of solid earthen built under the proposed franchise, a fifty-year grant would

be given the concessionaires, and the lake residents and lake business of the district that extends out as far as Renton would be handicaped and an unsightly barrier similar to a sandspit would affront the artistic tastes of lake visitors. Whatever artistic features there are to the causeway are abandoned in the earth fill.

of Oregon. The Smoot-Hawley bill is supposed to raise tariffs on a few agricultural goods to help out the farmers. But other interests have piled on and demanded barriers against their foreign competitors. Hoover has done nothing to stop them.

The Smoot-Hawley bill is bad medicine for all the foreign borrowers that need dollars to pay off bonds they sold in the United States. It is also bad for the American bondholders who expect to be repaid.

In 1929, shares that once sold at 8 to 10 times earnings are selling at 20 to 35 times. A few voices attempt to raise an alarm about this. One is from the man the *Post-Intelligencer* calls "the dean of Seattle bankers," Manson F. Backus, chairman of Seattle's National Bank of Commerce (later Rainier Bank). Backus, 75, is old enough to remember the depression of the 1890s. Returning from a meeting at the Federal Reserve Bank of San Francisco, Backus says he has been badgered about the stock market by an office worker, a barber, and a headwaiter. "Everywhere I went it was like that," he says. "I have lived through many such periods, although this seems to be the longest exuberant stock market splurge I can remember." All of those booms, he says, led to "long periods of depression."

Manson Backus, 1928. *Image from* Gold Horizon: The Life Story of Manson F. Backus, Forty-five Years a Banker in the Pacific Northwest, *by Neil Roy Knight, Dogwood Press, 1937.*

There are other warnings. One of them comes on October 4, 1929. Police arrest unlicensed "financial wizard" John E. Dimond, who does business out of his house in La Jolla, California, his cabin on Mercer Island, and various hotel rooms. Dimond has been dealing in securities without a state license. His accusers, May and Madge Morrill, owners of the Coffee Cup Restaurant in downtown Seattle, say Dimond promised them a 50 percent return on their money.

Investigators seek out other Dimond clients. On October 15, Gardner Wood of the *Seattle Star*, the city's other afternoon daily, interviews several of them waiting to be interviewed at the King County Courthouse. "An expression of bewilderment clouded the faces of many of the waiting witnesses," he writes. "They could not understand why they had been called, or why anyone should want to investigate the man who had been making money for everyone. There was not one among the waiting group but who had the highest praise for John E. Dimond and 'the wonderful work' that he has been doing."

Within three months Dimond will vanish. Creditors will claim he owes them $2 million, but the only asset they can find is his automobile. His wife will divorce him and take back her maiden name. The man will never be found.

All through October 1929, the market drifts down. On the day Dimond is arrested, *Post-Intelligencer* financial editor L. E. Hill writes that brokerage offices in Seattle are "thronged with quiet men" watching the ticker tell the tale of their shrinking assets.

On October 24, America's investors panic. Prices fall on huge volume, but late in the day New York bankers step in, and the market comes back. Still, many investors are burned, and the next day the market continues down.

On Saturday morning, October 26, Arthur Bastheim, 56, secretary-treasurer of the North Pacific Finance Company, Seattle, retires to his Second Avenue office and shoots himself in the head. The next day the *P-I* reports that Bastheim was said to be in ill health and feared a stroke. The *Star* reports that his colleagues "ridiculed reports that Bastheim had been playing the stock market." The *Times* reports that he *had* been playing the market, but had assured his friends that he'd "cleaned up" and got out. A vice president of the loan company says, "We have carefully checked the books and have found everything satisfactory."

It's another lie. Bastheim has been playing the market with the company's money and has lost it. The company soon suspends its dividend to stockholders and in 1930 is broken up.

On Monday, October 28, 1929, panic returns to Wall Street. This time, there is no rescue. The Dow Jones Industrials plunge 12.8 percent. On October 29, Black Tuesday, the Industrials sink another 11.7 percent. Volume hits a staggering 16 million shares, a record that will not be broken for almost 40 years.

This is the crash of 1929.

On November 13, 1929, two weeks and a day after Black Tuesday, the Industrials bottom at 198. From the high of September 3, the index is down 48 percent. The most-traded stock on the Seattle Stock Exchange, Ben Ehrlichman's United National Corporation, drops to $31. From its high of $50.75 on October 18, it is down 39 percent.

At the bottom of the Depression, United National stock will be down 99 percent.

Four months later, the *Seattle Times* will recall this moment as a time when the country was "close to the verge of panic." At the time of the crash, the newspapers say no such thing. No banks fail. There is no run on the Treasury's gold. "None of the actual money lost in the market has left the country," writes Paul Lovering, financial editor of the *Times*.

President Hoover is determined to keep up the people's spending. He pushes a tax cut through Congress. He calls in the heads of industry and has them promise not to cut wages. Henry Ford, who famously raised wages to $5 a day in 1914, seizes the spotlight by raising the standard wage from $6 a day to $7. "Wages must not come down," declares Ford. "They must go up."

The *Seattle Star* argues that, now that the bubble has burst, people can work and invest at home rather than sending their money to New York. And it seems they are. In Seattle, Frederick Anhalt is putting up Norman-style brick apartment houses on Capitol Hill. Downtown, work is about to begin on the 19-story Roosevelt Hotel and the 21-story Washington Athletic Club. W. D. Comer is moving ahead with a 17-story building at Seventh and Olive called the Textile Tower. Its tenants are to be Seattle's producers and wholesalers of apparel, fur wraps, work clothes, neckties, gloves, boots, and shoes, which together employ more than 3,000 workers.

The public sector is busy. The city is building a drawbridge over the West Waterway of the Duwamish River at Spokane Street. Funded by the state, county, and city (but no federal grants), work has begun on the Aurora bridge over the Lake Washington Ship Canal. King County is building Harborview Hospital and Boeing Field. The federal government is building, or about to build, a new office complex on the site of the old Rainier Grand Hotel at First and Madison, an Immigration and Assay building on Sixth

Avenue South, a Marine hospital at the northern tip of Beacon Hill and an airfield at Sand Point.

The focus on projects moving forward takes eyes off the ones that don't. Some are fanciful. Charles M. Thomsen, son of Moritz Thomsen, founder of Centennial Mills (Krusteaz Flour), cooks up a scheme to bring 800 German families to farm corn, bananas, pineapples, and coconuts near Acapulco, Mexico. In October 1929 he offers stock in the German-Mexican company at $2.50 a share. In the wake of the crash, the state cancels his permit to sell the shares. Thomsen's Mexican partner pulls out, and the venture collapses.

Among more mainstream ventures is an insurance company set up during 1929 by investors that include Raymond Frazier of Washington Mutual Savings Bank and Clarance Blethen of the *Seattle Times*. Frank T. Jamieson, who has 22 drugstores in Seattle, announces a plan to have 200 stores across Washington and Oregon. Developer Harry Gowman announces plans for a 30-story hotel in downtown Seattle. And in October 1929, the United National Corporation announces that work will begin in 30 days on the second half of the Medical Dental Building.

After the crash, all these projects stop. The second half of the Medical Dental Building will not be built for 20 years.

In April 1929, the owners of the Seattle Indians baseball team proposed a 15,000-seat stadium at the site of the future Seattle Center Arena. The team had been playing at Dugdale Park, a 15,000-seat stadium in the Rainier Valley. After the crash, plans for the new stadium are heard no more. Seattle's baseball team will not get a new stadium for nine years.

An even bigger dream is a transit plan proposed by a downtown business group in January 1929. Elevated trains would run south and north of downtown, connected by a subway down Second Avenue. Branching out in a giant X, at-grade rail would run to Fremont and the University District in the north, and to West Seattle and the Rainier Valley in the south. Seattle's streetcars would remain as feeder lines. Financing is the problem: It would come from the property tax, and in 1929, that is not a widely accepted idea. Transit is expected to pay its own way. After the crash, the plan is dropped.

Most impressive of all is the plan to build a bridge across Lake Washington. In 1929, King County commissioners accept a proposal to build a two-lane causeway and drawbridge to Mercer Island from Seward Park (see pages 18–19). In 1930, Seattle and King County issue 35-year franchises to the Puget Sound Bridge and Dredging Company to build it as a private toll bridge.

The bridge is to be financed with bonds—and the bond market is headed for trouble.

2
Denial, 1930

In January 1930, *Seattle Times* publisher Clarance Blethen sells a stake in the family business to New York newspaper publishers Joseph, Victor, and Bernard Ridder. Blethen explains to *Times* readers that the work of putting out the paper has "become so great that no man can possibly face the task alone."

That is not the reason. The reason is Blethen's spending. He's building a new plant for the *Times* at Fairview and John. It has three stories and a much bigger footprint than the paper's triangle-shaped building at Fifth and Stewart. Blethen announces that the project ultimately will include a tower at least 20 stories high. The *Times* has been doing well, but not well enough to reassure its lenders at Seattle-First National Bank. They hand Blethen an ultimatum: raise capital or no more loans.

The Ridders have an obvious motive to take an equity interest in the *Times*. They are waiting for Blethen's next misstep so they can take control of the paper. Blethen's plan is to use the Ridders' money while frustrating their ends—which he does. His bankers approve the first major newspaper bond in the Pacific Northwest. It raises $2 million for him to buy out the 65 percent interest held by his mother, his two sisters, and his sister-in-law. Blethen sells some of these shares to the Ridders, keeping just enough for a majority. "I have retained absolute control and management," he tells *Times* readers, "and after me, it will remain with my family." The skyscraper is forgotten. Passing on the *Times* to his five sons matters more. Blethen does pass it on, and his heirs frustrate the Ridders' plan into the 21st century.

Publisher Clarance Blethen, 1929. *Author's collection*.

With new capital, the financial pinch on the *Times* is eased. Clarance Blethen gives his managers a raise. He sets his own salary at a fabulous $114,000 ($2.1 million in 2024 dollars). He has a $100,000 penthouse apartment built on the top of the Olympic Hotel. He also commissions a 96-foot yacht. He names it the *Canim*, Chinook dialect for "big chief canoe."

In the Depression, Blethen will cut his salary by more than two-thirds. In June 1932, he sells his yacht for 32 cents on the dollar. The buyer, Hollywood funny man Buster Keaton, renames it the *Natalie* in an attempt to placate his wife, who will divorce him anyway. The Blethens will keep the penthouse at the Olympic Hotel until the year of Clarance Blethen's death, 1941.

———

On February 26, 1930, the Communist Party holds demonstrations in several American cities to protest unemployment. In Seattle, hundreds of people march from Yesler Way to the County-City Building carrying signs saying, "We Demand Work or Wages" and "Down with Capitalism." They have no parade permit, and police disperse them with nightsticks.

In 1930 the Communists are a radical splinter that denounces all others on the left. Few take them seriously. Nor is unemployment taken that seriously. Not yet. Nationwide in 1930 it averages 8.7 percent—not good, but a figure that will be the lowest of the decade. Still, a writer to the *Seattle Times* tells of meeting a young man so depressed by his failure to find work that he walks in front of a moving truck. Another reports "hundreds of idle men hanging around on the streets and in the pool rooms south of Yesler Way." But *Times* editors see idle loggers and farmhands every winter. They are not alarmed.

The change in the economy after the crash is deceptive. Older people remember the Panic of 1893 and brace for a typhoon. They feel only a cold wind.

"In former times," writes B. C. Forbes, business columnist for the Hearst newspapers, "financial panics usually brought nationwide trouble immediately . . . the dismissal of hundreds of thousands of workers, the halting of construction work, numerous failures, demoralization in commodity markets." Forbes admits that railroad traffic, auto sales, bank clearings, steel orders, employment, and retail sales have all slowed—but not by a lot. "This fact," he writes, "is full of encouragement for the future."

Seattle's newspapers are upbeat. The *Star* sees "every reason" why good times should continue in 1930. And in the first week of January, *Times* financial editor Paul Lovering writes, "Another good year ... is just beginning."

Lovering allows that some readers accuse business of putting a happy face on bad news. Lovering has been making upbeat propaganda himself, and he will continue doing it into 1931. "Propaganda to inspire confidence in the country's future, if attempted, might be a dubious expedient," he writes, "but it would be understandable and certainly not be open to harsh criticism."

In another column, he writes, "A number of leading professional and semi-professional traders in this city are 'bears.' They distrust the market with a deep and abiding distrust." Lovering never explains why.

―――――

In the first third of 1930, the stock market sends a false signal. From mid-November 1929 through mid-April 1930, it goes up, recovering 40 percent of its losses since its peak of September 3.

On May 5, 1930, downtown Seattle celebrates the opening of the Exchange Building. The 22-story structure, designed by John Graham, has a black marble entrance hall with a gold ceiling and cast bronze elevator fronts. The building houses the Seattle Stock Exchange. In coverage brimming with fanfare and optimism, the newspapers report that its five acres of office space are already 60 percent leased. The *Post-Intelligencer* does not mention that before the Crash, its business editor predicted that the building would open fully leased because of all the investment firms being formed. Actually, it will not lease up for years. It will go through bankruptcy, and its bonds will eventually fall to 27 cents on the dollar. The Exchange Building will be the last big office tower built in downtown Seattle until the Norton Building almost 30 years later.

But in the spring of 1930, men of wealth continue to spend. William E. Boeing has his Vancouver, B.C., shipyard build a 127-foot yacht, the *Taconite*, made of Burmese teak. Boeing Air Transport's president, Philip G. Johnson, builds a house south of Edmonds with ten bedrooms, each with bath, on a ten-acre estate overlooking Puget Sound. And Donald E. Frederick, 69, who a year earlier sold the Frederick &

The Exchange Building: Last office tower of the 1920s. *Image from United Exchange Building, Inc. ad in* Seattle Post-Intelligencer, *5-15-30, p. 24.*

Optimism at the *Seattle Times*, March 1930. *Cartoon by Stuart Pratt, 3-23-1930, p. 6*
© *The* Seattle Times.

Nelson department store for $6 million, builds a mansion in The Highlands. The Frederick home, built on a 25-acre spread, has a stone exterior, slate roofs, marble and oak floors, hand-hewn doors, 11 bedrooms, and 8 bathrooms.

A more reliable sign of what's coming is an odd event at the other end of the social scale. In April, two blind beggars have a fistfight over use of a downtown Seattle streetcorner. The winner complains to the reporter from the *Star* that people these days are less generous with their coins. "We only get nickels and dimes now," the beggar says. "We used to get quarters and even half-dollars."

In mid-April, the stock market turns down again.

With jobs scarce, a feeling rises against Asians. Immigration is already low on account of the Immigration Act of 1924, a law written by a congressman from Washington state, Albert Johnson of Hoquiam. The law sets quotas that allow in Britons, Germans, and other Northern Europeans but few others. Asians are locked out except for Filipinos, because the Philippine Islands are a possession of the United States. Between 1920 and 1930, the Filipino population of the West Coast swells from 5,600 to more than 45,000.

As the Depression squeezes employers, they replace low-paid whites with Filipinos willing to work for less. One letter writer to the *Seattle Times* calls Filipinos "evils in the labor market," prompting P. L. Alisago to defend his people. "The Filipinos that are in America work for necessity alone; it is not their ambition to become servants," he says in a letter to the editor. "The Americans made them so. These islanders come here with high ambitions. But your cruel people have made them miserable."

The cruelty ramps up. On the night of May 6, 1930, a group of white men, some of them armed, swarm the bunkhouses of Filipino workers in farms around Auburn and Kent. The whites' complaint is that the Japanese-American truck farmers have hired the Filipinos at 25 cents an hour to replace whites who had been picking lettuce at 60 cents an hour. The vigilantes roust out the Filipinos, rough them up, force them into vehicles, and dump them several miles down the road in their underwear.

County sheriff Claude Bannick downplays the attack. "It looks like there might be a little race trouble down there," he tells the newspapers. "I hope it doesn't develop. It might be a bad thing."

It will get worse. Wages will drop from 25 cents an hour to 12 cents, and the violence will escalate. In January 1931, whites beat three Filipino farmworkers unconscious at a farm near Kent, beat the Japanese employer, and torch his farmhouse. In May 1932, after two more attacks, the farmers discharge the Filipinos and agree to hire whites only.

The *Times* condemns the violence but writes that Filipino immigration ought to be stopped. And it will be. In 1934, Congress will declare the Philippines a commonwealth. The law promises the territory its independence in ten years. In the meantime, the law limits immigration to 50 persons a year.

In the 1930s, worldwide immigration to the United States drops to the lowest level of the 20th century.

The urge to block foreign workers also applies to foreign products. By the summer of 1930, the Republicans in Congress are ready to pass the Smoot-Hawley bill, which will raise taxes on imports to the highest level in the 20th century. For Seattle, which is served by 60 different shipping lines, cutting off trade is bad medicine. But trade is not a popular cause. Says the *Seattle Times*, "The people generally haven't cared whether the bill passed or not."

The *Times*, a Republican paper, supports the bill because it raises tariffs on lumber and shingles from Canada. Governor Roland Hartley, Republican, owns a lumber and shingle mill in Everett. In a telegram to Congress, Hartley uses a racial argument to put tariffs up. British Columbia shingles, he says, are "products of labor which is 35 to 40 percent Oriental."

Seattle's two Democratic dailies oppose the bill. The *Star* slams Smoot-Hawley as a "big-business tariff." The *Post-Intelligencer* declares it "vicious legislation" that "will provoke a world-wide tariff war against the United States."

Herbert Hoover, 1932. Seattle Star, *6-16-1932, p. 1.*

After passing the House, the bill squeaks through the Senate 44 to 42. Washington's senators split. Republican Wesley Jones is the author of the Jones Act, the 1920 law that reserves the Alaska trade for U.S. ships. The tariff is similar policy: it aims to reserve the U.S. market for U.S. products. Jones votes yes. Clarence Dill, the state's Democratic senator, votes no.

Hundreds of economists petition President Hoover to veto the bill. But Hoover is chary of fighting his fellow Republicans. "He has no stomach for contests of that kind, partly because of lack of training in practical politics," writes the *Times*'s Washington correspondent, W. W. Jermane. When Hoover announces that he will sign the bill, the stock market plunges on heavy volume. Commodities fall to the lowest point in 13 years.

The *Post-Intelligencer* is right about Smoot-Hawley. By April 1931, 45 countries will raise tariffs against U.S. products. Most damaging is the reaction of America's number-one trading partner, Canada. In elections on July 28, 1930, Canadians turn to the Conservatives, a nationalist party that promises to orient Canada's trade toward the Commonwealth. The government of Premier R. B. Bennett quickly raises tariffs against U.S. goods. For years after this, British Columbia lumber will have an open door to the U.K. market and Washington's lumber will be shut out.

The foreign trade of the United States shrinks by more than half during the Depression. Smoot-Hawley is only one of several causes. Another is the drop in foreign borrowing, leaving foreigners with fewer dollars for buying U.S. goods. A further shrinkage will come when other countries go off the gold standard two years before the United States does. That will happen in 1931.

Amtorg Trading Corporation, owned by the Soviet government, has had offices in Seattle since April 1929. Amtorg's task is to support Josef Stalin's Five-Year Plan, which aims to industrialize the world's only Communist country through state ownership, forced investment, and forced labor. In January 1930, Amtorg buys the plans for 70-foot purse seiners from Seattle naval architect Harold C. Hanson. It also buys winches, propellers, and engines from suppliers in Seattle, so that a Russian shipyard in Vladivostok can build ten boats to catch salmon off the coast of Kamchatka.

In the first five months of 1930, the Soviet Union jumps to sixth place among countries buying U.S. products, up from 17th in 1929. The Soviets are eager to tap into American know-how. In January 1930 they send a delegation to Seattle to view the Boeing plant. In March they hire Norman L. Wimmler, Seattle's expert on Alaskan placer mining, to develop gold mining in Siberia. To get ideas for a tunnel through the Caucasus Mountains, they send a commissar to inspect the Great Northern's new tunnel at Stevens Pass.

In June 1930, the *Times* interviews James Frazier, 22, son of the president of Washington Mutual Savings Bank. Frazier has just returned from Russia. "So many American engineers were entering or leaving Russia," writes the *Times*, that Frazier "had difficulty obtaining hotel accommodations ... He gained the impression that the Soviet government is not satisfied with the importation of engineers alone, but is recruiting highly skilled American workmen to superintend operations in the new factories."

The American romance with Russia does not last. To pay for U.S. goods, the Soviets export wheat, manganese ore, pulpwood, and lumber. Soon U.S. producers complain that the Russians are flooding their markets. In July 1930 the Treasury bans Russian pulpwood as a product of slave labor. In February 1931, the ban is extended to Russian lumber.

Americans working in Russia quickly sour on Soviet life. Many of the engineers at the tractor plant in Stalingrad have brought wives and children. In September 1930, the Americans demand to go home. They are fed up with cramped quarters, sickness, bad food, and the lack of things to buy.

In America, attitudes also sour. Congressman Hamilton Fish, Republican of New York, holds hearings on Communist influence, including the role of Amtorg Trading. In October 1930, the Fish hearings come to Seattle, a city where Communists have a meeting hall and hundreds of supporters. In the spring of 1931, Seattle Police and federal immigration agents raid the Communist hall, looking for illegal aliens. In March 1931, Governor Roland Hartley signs a bill requiring all public schoolteachers and university professors to sign loyalty oaths to the state and the federal government. In May, the University of Washington bans Communist speakers on campus. The following month, Amtorg Trading closes up and leaves town.

In July 1930, Wylie Hemphill, president of the Seattle Chamber of Commerce, gives Seattle's business leaders a pep talk. He tells them he's tired of men "with faces as long as ladders" talking about cutting wages and laying off workers. "Now, I'm not any profound economist," he says. (He's a vice president at the National Bank of Commerce.) "I've learned most of my economic principles on Pike Street and Second Avenue." Hemphill urges each business in the city to hire one more person and cut no one's pay or hours. He dubs this "Siwash economics," a low-class reference to the Indian tribes. The *Seattle Times* puts Hemphill's sidewalk economics on page one, and in the following weeks, several big employers promise to impose no pay cuts.

Hearst columnist B. C. Forbes has a similar message. He does not deny the Depression. By mid-1930 the stock market is in the grip of a gloom so deep, he writes, "It has been hard to breathe." As always, Forbes looks for the upside. Noting the cutback in steel production, railroad traffic, stock and commodity prices, Forbes reaches for folk wisdom. "You cannot cut a dog's tail off twice," he writes. He adds, "There never yet was a panic that didn't end."

In July 1930 Forbes swings through Seattle. Speaking to the Chamber, he says, "You are standing up to it like men. You are going right ahead with your business, working rather than whining." In particular, he tells the lumbermen it's time to invest. But Forbes is not in the lumber business. In the summer of 1930, mills in the Douglas fir region are operating at less than half capacity. Three large fir producers have cut wages from $3.40 to $2.50 for an eight-hour day. In Everett, Governor Roland Hartley has just closed the Clough-Hartley lumber mill and laid off 300 men. Hartley says his mill has lost money during all six years he's been in Olympia and that the Smoot-Hawley tariff of $1 per thousand board feet is not high enough. Laying off hundreds of men is bad public relations for the governor, but in 1930 Hartley is not up for reelection.

———

In a gloomy year, a few investors make bold moves. In August 1930, hotel owners Frank Dupar, Severt Thurston, and Adolph and Peter Schmidt—the Schmidts of Olympia Brewing, which is disabled by Prohibition—form Western Hotels. In Seattle, Western Hotels secures contracts to manage the New Washington, the Benjamin Franklin, the Camlin, the Cambridge, the Waldorf, and the Roosevelt. It also manages several new hotels around the state, including the Morck in Aberdeen, the Leopold in Bellingham, the Cascadian in Wenatchee, and the Marcus Whitman in Walla Walla. Western Hotels will survive the Depression and eventually become Westin Hotels.

Also in August 1930, the Wallin & Nordstrom shoe store moves into larger quarters at Second and Pike, at the center of Seattle's streetcar network. Founders Carl F. Wallin and John W. Nordstrom have retired, leaving

The new Fraser-Paterson department store, October 1930. *Image from display ad in* Seattle Times, *10-6-1930, p. 27.*

the store in the hands of Nordstrom's sons Everett and Elmer. They change its name to Nordstrom's. Decades later, the company will become a nationwide chain.

The most visible investment in downtown Seattle is the new Fraser-Paterson store. Fraser-Paterson has had a department store at Second and University since 1912. In 1930 cofounder A.G.M. Fraser takes the fateful step of signing a 30-year lease on the southwest corner of Second and Pike. John Graham, the architect who designed the Bon Marché, designs a five-story building.

The new Fraser-Paterson—"Seattle-planned, Seattle-financed, Seattle-constructed," says the *Times*—opens October 6, 1930. "The interior of the store," writes the *Times*, "is a study in modern decoration: high-ceilinged, silvery, with a leaf motif reaching up the hexagonal pillars." The store offers everything from women's apparel and shoes to lamps, draperies, radios, and rugs. On opening day, says the *Times*, the throngs of shoppers show "no hint of depression, no echo of the stock market debacle."

A reporter finds a smiling A.G.M. Fraser is on the sales floor, attending to details. "Happy?" he says. "Indeed I am. Satisfied? Never quite. Our job now is to live up to what we've begun."

Fraser has made his move at the wrong time. His store will close in 1933. Two other retail groups will lease the building and fail. In 1939 the building will be taken over by J.C. Penney, which caters to price-conscious consumers. The downtown Penney's will last until the 1980s, when it is torn down to make way for condominiums.

In the popular mind, depressions begin with bank failures. But for month after month, not one bank in Seattle goes under.

In July 1930, trouble comes to the Continental Mutual Savings Bank. Opened in 1922 in Pioneer Square, the bank has done poorly. It's in the wrong part of town. Its first president, a mining man from Alaska, is useless as a banker. When he dies in 1928, the trustees lend the bank $60,000 to move uptown. The gamble doesn't pay, and by 1930, the Continental Mutual is for sale.

State regulators want the buyer to be someone they can trust. They call on Raymond Frazier, the president of Washington Mutual Savings Bank. Washington Mutual is a hundred times the size of Continental Mutual, and normally wouldn't concern itself with a tiny competitor. But Washington Mutual's newspaper ads have long claimed that mutual savings banks never fail. To keep that statement true, Frazier will make Washington Mutual's first acquisition in its 41-year history. After an all-night meeting, Frazier agrees to absorb the Continental Mutual. The depositors are saved, though the trustees who lent the $60,000 are not.

The newspapers make no mention of financial weakness at Continental Mutual—and there is no bank failure in Seattle.

On October 27, 1930, the First National Bank of Auburn fails. The bank, in suburban King County, is the first national bank in Washington to go down in the Depression.

The owners are Charles E. Walters and his middle-aged son Ralph. The Walters have a scheme for buying small-town banks. They target one in which the president and vice president own most of the stock. Through a holding company, the Walters borrow money and buy the stock. Once they get control, they instruct the bank's president and vice-president to sell stock in the Walters' holding company to the bank's depositors. This allows the Walters to repay the loans they used to buy the bank.

Father and son have bought control of four small banks this way, two of them in Auburn: the First National and the Auburn National. But to make their holding-company stock attractive, they have had to pay an 8-percent dividend. And to do that, they have had to use the money from selling new shares.

The new investors pay the old ones: it's a Ponzi scheme.

On October 10, 1930, a letter goes out to stockholders announcing that the dividend is suspended. The assistant cashiers at both Auburn banks have been embezzling funds. The letter sets off a run against both banks as fearful depositors pull their money out. Charles and Ralph Walters appeal to the Seattle banks for help. The National Bank of Commerce and the Pacific National agree to rescue the Auburn National but not the First National.

The failure of the First National Bank of Auburn makes hardly a ripple in the Seattle and Tacoma papers. In the Auburn paper, it is a page-one disaster. For Charles and Ralph Walters, it will mean conviction for grand larceny and minimum sentences of 2½ and 5 years, respectively, in the state penitentiary at Walla Walla. Charles Walters, 69, will die in prison in 1934.

The Auburn bank failure freezes more than $750,000 in deposits. This is before deposit insurance. Instead, all bank stock is double-liability. If the

Charles (left) and Ralph Walters, their bank-buying days over. *Washington State Archives.*

bank fails, the receiver can assess the stockholders—bill them—for an amount up to the par value of their shares. He can do this only once, however, and it's his job to collect the money. Since the Civil War, among all the national banks that have failed in the United States, receivers have collected about half of such assessments. At the First National Bank of Auburn, where the principal stockholder is the Walters' holding company, the receiver collects only 16 cents of every dollar assessed. The depositors will have to rely instead on the receiver to collect the bank's loans and sell its assets. He will not finish the job until March 1937. By then, depositors will have received 67 cents on the dollar.

Rancher S. H. Hall fares even worse. He is in his late seventies. Both of his legs have been amputated. Hall had $1,050 on deposit at the First National Bank of Auburn, but Ralph Walters talked him into putting it all in holding-company stock. Hall is no longer a depositor. He's a stockholder, and stockholders get nothing.

About $250,000 of this stock has been sold. In south King County it is a disaster. Still, there is no bank failure in Seattle.

On September 2, 1930, a Seattle investment man walks out of his office building at 814 Second Avenue and disappears.

August Mehlhorn, 54, is a small man, 5 feet 4 inches, 135 pounds. He is frugal of habit; he wears a five-year-old overcoat and shines his own shoes. He wears dark suits and only occasionally smokes a cigar. He is said to be cold and reserved, but on that day the man at the cigar stand in the Exchange Building describes him as unusually cheerful.

Mehlhorn leaves behind his wife and their three children in a fine home on Queen Anne's Highland Drive. "I am worried and nearly crushed by his absence," Else Mehlhorn says. "He left without giving me any idea that he intended to stay elsewhere."

August Mehlhorn, 1935. *ACME Newspictures image in author's collection.*

He also leaves behind his company, Osner & Mehlhorn, which deals with about

400 investors. He sells them real estate contracts under which the borrowers pay Mehlhorn and he turns over the money to the investors. When the contract calls for the borrower to pay off the remaining principal—which is the way mortgages work in 1930—Mehlhorn collects the lump sum and passes it on to the investor. Except that lately he has been collecting the lump sum and using it himself, telling the investor the contract has been extended. Actually, it is canceled and the investor is financing Mehlhorn.

Mehlhorn leaves behind a rat's nest of unpaid bills and uncashed checks. His clients become unsecured creditors of a corporate estate with a $250,000 shortage. Within days, Washington Mutual Savings Bank seizes the Mehlhorn Building. Early in 1931 the King County sheriff will put 25 to 30 Osner & Mehlhorn properties up for tax sale, but they are dumped on a weak market. Creditors of Osner & Mehlhorn will get no money until December 1937, and then only three-quarters of a cent on the dollar.

Why does Mehlhorn run? He is German-American. In the war year 1918, when all Germans were under suspicion, he was called as a juror in the high-profile sedition trial of Hulet Wells, who had denounced the draft. But because Mehlhorn was a co-owner of the *Seattle German Press*, the judge would not let him serve on the jury. The questioning of Mehlhorn's loyalty was a story in the next day's papers. Probably it left him with a deep fear of public shame.

August Mehlhorn disappears for five years. In 1935 he will be arrested in Oakland, California, where he is making a living by selling milk and eggs, and living under the name Larson. He occasionally sees old friends; probably it is one of them who betrays him. King County's young prosecutor, Warren Magnuson, will bring Mehlhorn back to Seattle on the coast steamship. Mehlhorn will plead guilty to grand larceny and serve four years in prison.

As a result of her husband's actions, Else Mehlhorn loses her $80,000 inheritance and is forced to sell the family home on West Highland Drive. In 1936 she will file for divorce, declaring that she has "lost all love and affection" for her deadbeat husband.

―――――

During 1930, several big buildings are completed, notably Harborview Hospital, the Exchange Building, the Roosevelt Hotel, and the Washington Athletic Club. Construction, writes the *Daily Journal of Commerce*, has been "the one bright ray that shone through the fog." The question is whether this light will stay on.

During 1930, developers announce new high-rises: the 17-story Edmond Meany Hotel in the University District, a 15-story addition to the New Washington Hotel, a nine-story expansion of the Insurance Building, and two 21-story apartment hotels in the Denny Regrade. "A city gripped by depression could not carry on these projects," the *Star* declares.

The *Star* is right, but not in the way it means. Of these, only the Edmond Meany (now the Graduate) will be built. Financed by locally sold stocks and bonds, it will default on the bonds and be in bankruptcy for years. The Meany will be the last high-rise hotel built in Seattle for a long time.

3
Bankers, 1931–1932

On October 23, 1931, the Pacific Commercial Bank of Seattle fails. It is a small bank. In 1929 it was the city's 12th largest; the *Seattle Times* doesn't even cover the failure. The *Star* gives it two inches on page 3. The *Post-Intelligencer* notes it in L. E. Hill's business column on page 15. Hill reassures his readers: "The bank's customers were almost exclusively Japanese residents, and no other banks are affected."

The Pacific Commercial is the only bank in the state run by Japanese Americans. Ten thousand persons have their savings in it.

The bank's president, Masajiro Furuya, came to America at age 28. During the depression of the 1890s, he built a business importing and selling silks, fine arts, and furniture. He worked long hours, dressed plainly, and lived frugally on the top floor of his boarding house. He opened stores in Tacoma, Portland, and Vancouver, B.C. Within a few years, Furuya became the top retailer of Asian goods on the Pacific Coast.

Like many of Washington's pioneer bankers, he slipped into banking because someone had to do it. He began by handling cash for immigrant Japanese. In 1907 he helped start the Japanese Commercial Bank. But Furuya is a merchant, and he relies on other men to run his banks. His choice of men is not good. In the 1920s, bank examiners note that his bank has been lending money to vegetable growers, produce sellers, and restaurant men who have "a way of disappearing without making payments." Two of Furuya's bank directors are white men whose only contribution, the examiners say, is to take out loans and "make little, if any, effort to pay them."

After bailing out two other banks founded by Japanese Americans, Furuya consolidates his interests in 1928 into the Pacific Commercial Bank. In their report of September 1930, state examiners George Jackson and O. Williams write that Furuya's banks have made a mess over the years and that "Mr. Furuya has exhausted his personal funds and fortune in trying to clean it up." He also is using his bank to finance his business, which is dangerous.

Masajiro and Hatsu Furuya with their daughter, years before the Depression. *Author's collection.*

On October 23, 1931, M. Furuya & Company goes under and takes the Pacific Commercial Bank with it.

Reporter Jay Esse of the *Japanese American Courier* describes a meeting of depositors: "Mothers pale from anxiety sat among serious-visaged men looking tired after a hard day's work." Masajiro Furuya comes before them, humbly refuses to stand on the raised podium, and makes a simple apology. Esse describes him as "a picture of humiliation."

Under state law, Furuya's bank has 90 days to raise the money to reopen. It tries to sell $250,000 in stock, but 1931 is no year for doing that. The effort falls two-thirds short, and the bank stays closed. Depositors will eventually get 66 cents on the dollar.

Defeated, Furuya leaves the state. He will die in Japan.

———

Like Masajiro Furuya, Adolph Frederik Linden is a Seattle banker with his mind on other things. Otherwise, his story is much different.

Linden is the son of Swedish immigrants. At 21, he marries Esther Anderson, whom he has met at the Swedish Baptist Church, where his father is pastor. Through her father, who is a trustee of the Puget Sound Savings and Loan Association, Linden gets a job there at age 22 as vice president. Later her father becomes president. When he dies, Linden becomes president of Puget Sound Savings at age 34, passing over Vice President Edmund Campbell, 53.

Photographs show Linden as a cherubic figure with slicked-down hair and a sharp suit. He is not a conservative savings-and-loan man. He is a risk-taker.

Adolph Linden, 1928. *Author's collection.*

In 1923, Linden and Campbell make an investment. With $20,000 in savings-and-loan funds ($363,000 in 2024 dollars), they buy an interest in the one-year-old Ford dealership of William O. McKay, who is one of the savings-and-loan's trustees. McKay's dealership at South Lake Union is a solid business, but it is too boring for Adolph Linden.

Next they invest in oil drilling in Oklahoma. They lose their shirts. In 1925, they decide to create their own project, local and under their control. They set out to build an 11-story hotel, the tallest in Seattle. They name it after themselves: the Camlin.

Linden and Campbell have funded all their investments with "loans" from Puget Sound Savings. They haven't told anyone about these loans. They've just taken the money. The Camlin loan is a million dollars ($17.7 million in 2024 dollars).

In 1926, Puget Sound Savings' attorney, Corwin Shank, finds out about this. Alarmed, he calls in state savings-and-loan supervisor Wallace L. Nicely and says that Adolph Linden should be fired. When Nicely refuses to issue the order, Shank pushes Linden to resign. When Linden refuses, Shank resigns.

Nicely has the authority to shut down Puget Sound Savings, and later a grand jury will suggest that he should have done it. But the Puget Sound is the largest savings and loan in Washington. Nicely is not going to shut it down. He is also indebted to Linden. When Nicely was a mere examiner, Linden recommended him for the state supervisor's job. At the time,

The Camlin, built with informal finance, circa 1927. *Pemco Webster & Stevens Collection, 1983.10.3408.1, Museum of History & Industry, Seattle. Used with permission.*

Linden also gave $500 to the state printer, an operative of Governor Roland Hartley—a payment that looks a lot like a bribe.

Nicely's answer for the missing million is to have Linden and Campbell sign over the Camlin to Puget Sound Savings. They sign it over. Adolph and Esther Linden also sign over their 5,040-square-foot house in Lake Forest Park. Linden signs over his library of rare books, said to include Abraham Lincoln's Bible, and Esther signs over all the assets inherited from her father.

Nicely writes a letter to Puget Sound Savings' trustees warning that if similar withdrawals occur again, it will "result in immediate and summary removal and prosecution of this officer and employee regardless of who it may be or what it may effect." Nicely writes this a year after he discovers the problem, and Linden pays no attention to it.

Linden has a new fascination: radio. He buys Radio KJR from Vincent I. Kraft, who started the station at home. In 1927 Linden forms Northwest Radio Service and buys KGA-Spokane, KEX-Portland, and KYA-San Francisco. He finances these purchases with bonds, which he sells to Puget Sound Savings and other savings-and-loans.

Through the winter of 1927–1928, Linden spends his time at Northwest Radio, returning to Puget Sound Savings to collect his salary and stuff cash into bags. When Nicely finds out about the leakage of cash, he is furious, but Linden talks him out of doing anything. Linden will insist later that he always intended to pay it back. "We expected ultimately to make a lot of money out of radio," he will say.

In 1928, Campbell takes over as president of Puget Sound Savings and moves into the Camlin's 11th-story penthouse suite. Freed from his duties at the savings-and-loan, Linden forms the American Broadcasting Company—no relation to today's ABC. His plan is to string together a nationwide network of other people's radio stations to compete with NBC and CBS. It's a bigger plan than can be funded from the tellers' cages at one savings-and-loan in Seattle.

Linden sets up a private sale of stock in the American Broadcasting Company. Right away he runs into a new regulator. Under the "Blue Sky" law passed in 1923, no stock offering can be sold in Washington unless the state determines that it is fair to investors. The decision on Linden's stock sale is up to the elected secretary of state, J. Grant Hinkle, Republican.

Under Linden's stock offering, the investors would put up all of American Broadcasting's cash and would get one-tenth of the stock. Linden would put up none of the cash and keep nine-tenths of the stock. Hinkle's securities examiner, J. G. Rake, reckons this is unfair and urges him to say no. In his letter to Linden, Hinkle lays out the reasons for saying no—and then he says yes, "due to the strong earning possibilities, and due to our desire to encourage such enterprises as much as possible."

Hinkle is known as a tough regulator. He has said no to so many stock offerings that his authority is under attack in the legislature. By saying yes to Linden, Hinkle is trying to head off this attack. (It doesn't work, and he soon loses his authority.) In supporting Linden, Hinkle is also favoring a media owner whose support he might need. During the 1928 elections, Linden provided free air time on KJR to Governor Roland Hartley, Republican.

Linden makes the most of Hinkle's big yes. After the private sale of ABC stock, Linden has a public sale. He has no underwriter to certify that the sale is within industry standards. He splits the stock 15-for-1 and offers 3.7 percent of it to ordinary investors. The price, $12.50 a share, implicitly values the American Broadcasting Company at $16,875,000—$306 million in 2024 dollars. On paper, this would make Linden, the majority owner of a company that has never made a nickel of profit, one of the richest men in Seattle.

Already Linden is a big shot. His 300 employees call him "Daddy," a reference to Daddy Warbucks from the *Orphan Annie* comic strip. For his radio broadcasts, Linden wants live music. "You can't believe how fabulous it was," recalls an employee years later. "We had a twelve- to fourteen-piece orchestra—they played a couple of hours a day." In the summer of 1929, Linden sets up 20 outdoor concerts in Husky Stadium with the 70-piece American Philharmonic Orchestra. The concerts are for network stations, away from Seattle; locally they are for paying customers. The highlight of these concerts comes June 12, with vocalist Marian Anderson. She gives a fine performance, but the concerts lose money.

Early in the summer of 1929, Wallace Nicely finally closes the cash pipeline from Puget Sound Savings. At the peak of the most fabulous stock boom of the 20th century, American Broadcasting's sale of stock comes up short. Linden has sold less than one-third of the shares. He is desperate for money; his company has too little local advertising. He is paying the bills by kiting checks.

On August 22, 1929, Linden's musicians, who haven't been paid, put American Broadcasting into bankruptcy. The telephone company, unpaid for the use of the phone lines that link ABC to the network's 20 stations, shuts them off. ABC and Northwest Radio Service go under. Creditors arrive to seize equipment and furnishings, including the cream-colored curtains in Linden's office.

Linden is in New York, trying to sell his radio network to entrepreneur William Fox, who has recently acquired Loews's Theatres and Metro-Goldwyn-Mayer. Linden returns to Seattle, packs his wife and teenage son into the family's big Lincoln, and begins the long drive to New York. By the time the Lindens arrive, the stock market has crashed and Fox's expansion is in ruins.

The assets of Northwest Radio Service are its four radio stations. The court-appointed receiver's job is to sell them. To do that, the receiver needs to keep them on the air so that the Federal Radio Commission won't give away their frequencies. The receiver, attorney Ralph Horr, does this at KJR by using his own money to buy a stack of records and playing them hour after hour. He saves the stations, but the unsecured creditors get nothing.

The employees of the American Broadcasting Company, many of them musicians, get 8 cents on the dollar of their unpaid wages. The stockholders get nothing. And Seattle loses its bid to become a center of America's new media industry.

Several months before savings-and-loan regulator Wallace Nicely cuts off ABC, he writes to Puget Sound Savings' trustees. He is "getting about a complete bellyful" of worry about the financial wound at the savings and loan. "The farther it goes," he writes, "the deeper it gets." He tells them they need to find a merger partner.

They find William D. Comer and the Mutual Savings and Loan Association. The Mutual is smaller than the Puget Sound but in better shape. In August 1929, the month that Linden's radio empire fails, the two savings associations merge. The combined company keeps the name and building of Puget Sound Savings, but Comer is at the helm, not Edmund Campbell. The financial damage is camouflaged, not repaired.

Over the next 16 months, Comer uses his position to borrow money to support his other enterprises. At the end of 1930, he issues a financial report that says the Puget Sound is in good shape. The report is false. It counts as assets unsecured "loans" of $1.2 million to Adolph Linden and Edmund Campbell that the two men are never going to pay back, plus the $180,000 note signed by Comer's employee, Fred H. Henry, who jumped out of a window and died on the sidewalk in 1929. A tough examiner would flag these loans, but the examiner is Wallace Nicely, and he sits on the board of trustees. He hasn't done an annual examination since 1927.

That was the year the Puget Sound opened its fine new building at 1414 Fourth Avenue and bragged in the press that its vault had the thickest

1414 Fourth Avenue. *Drawing from display ad in* Seattle Times, *9-2-1929, p. 11.*

doors of any bank vault on the Pacific Coast. Five days before its failure, it is still running ads in the newspapers saying, "*Your funds are safeguarded by sound laws.*"

In January 1931, Wallace Nicely is fired from his state job. The new savings-and-loan examiner, H. J. Hoffman, immediately starts an audit of Puget Sound Savings. He discovers a gaping hole. To bail itself out, the Puget Sound would have to pay depositors zero interest for two and a half years—and that's not possible. Perhaps a private bailout might be possible. Hoffman shows his audit to financial men at the Olympic Hotel. He asks for help and pleads that the men keep the bad news in confidence.

Someone blabs. The next morning, February 7, 1931, the Puget Sound's president calls state officials in a panic. "You'd better get down here," Comer pleads. A bank run is under way. Depositors are lined up on the sidewalk, waiting for their money. At noon, the state orders the doors closed. $14.5 million in people's savings—$296 million in 2024 dollars—are frozen.

The collapse of the Puget Sound Savings and Loan Association is Seattle's largest financial failure of the Great Depression.

On Monday, February 9, depositors mob all Seattle savings institutions. Several institutions freeze withdrawals. Home Savings, which pays 5 percent on deposits, takes out a newspaper ad to explain the freeze: "The law provides that during periods of financial stress and 'runs,' withdrawals may be discontinued, if necessary, for six months and may then be paid only from such funds as have been received from new deposits and repayments on loans."

A run also hits Washington Mutual Savings Bank. Legally a mutual savings bank is different from a savings and loan, but it is in the same business. Washington Mutual is bigger than Puget Sound Savings and pays savers only 4½ percent. "Be content with SAFETY, plus a good rate of interest," says one of its ads, "and the certainty that you can get your money IF you want it WHEN you want it." Washington Mutual's ads promise that mutual savings banks "DO NOT FAIL."

Now comes the testing.

Washington Mutual's president, Raymond Frazier, is determined not to freeze depositors' funds. Once a bank does that, it loses its depositors' confidence and opens itself to future runs. As fearful savers fill WaMu's office at Second and Spring, Frazier instructs the tellers to pay them and thank them for their business. He works the crowd, greeting friends and assuring savers the bank can pay. Depositors wait in line outside, hunched against the cold.

The doors close on time at 4 p.m., but Frazier keeps his tellers working until everyone inside is served. From the back office, he wires Chase National Bank in New York for $10 million in exchange for some of Washington Mutual's gilt-edged bonds.

The Chase—the same bank that will take over Washington Mutual 77 years later—wires the money. Seattle's commercial bankers also help, a

Raymond Frazier. Seattle Post-Intelligencer, 4-1-1929, p. 19. © Hearst Communications Inc.

tradition of quiet solidarity that goes back to the Panic of 1893. One journalist will recount the story of a Washington Mutual depositor asking an officer of Seattle-First National Bank whether he should move his money. His answer: "I cannot promise you that it will be any safer with us."

The run against Washington Mutual peaks on Tuesday, February 10, with depositors pulling out $400,000 in one hour. In Wednesday's newspapers appears the following display ad:

> "ANCEMENT
> *"Open Until 9 O'Clock Tonight.*
> *"In order to correct rumors, the Washington Mutual Savings Bank announces that it is NOT requiring notice of withdrawal of deposits. This Bank is paying all withdrawals on demand and will continue to pay on demand."*
> Raymond R. Frazier, President

Frazier's courage pays off. The run breaks, and by week's end it is over. The bank will suffer a second run on the day before the state banking holiday of March 1933. Again, it will honor all requests. Washington Mutual will survive the Depression and will suffer no more bank runs for the next 75 years.

Puget Sound Savings is closed. The state tells the 27,000 depositors—the legal owners—that if they don't make up the $2 million shortage in 20 days, it will stay closed. To reopen, the savings-and-loan's trustees offer a plan of sacrifice. Each depositor is asked to sign over 25 percent of his savings. If enough sign to make up the lost $2 million, the business can reopen. Those who sign will have access to 75 percent of their money and a share of the bad assets, which will fetch something by and by. The depositors who don't sign, however, will have access to all their money immediately.

The depositors are furious. They want *justice*. They hold angry meetings. They file lawsuits. But owners of only one-third of the deposits agree to the trustees' plan of sacrifice, and the plan is not adopted. The offer will never come again.

Puget Sound Savings will reopen in 1935 for new business. But the old depositors will have to wait while the state's receiver collects loans and sells assets. They will eventually receive the 75 cents on the dollar they could have had in 1931, but the final payment will be in 1945.

In 1931 the state responds to the demand for justice by going after Adolph Linden, who hasn't been president of Puget Sound Savings for three years. They find him with his wife and teenage son in a tiny apartment in New York City. Linden started up a small business called A Bunch of Grapes, which is variously described as a "restaurant," a "tearoom," and a "night club"—that is, a speakeasy. His wife got a job at Macy's. By the time the cops arrive, however, the job and the speakeasy are gone, and the Lindens are cooking their meals on a hotplate and doing their laundry in a bathtub.

Adolph Linden, Edmund Campbell, and Wallace Nicely are indicted in King County Superior Court for grand larceny. Comer is indicted for issuing the false financial report.

———

On Friday, July 3, 1931, Ahira "Hi" Pierce, the head of Seattle's Home Savings and Loan Association, gets a call from the state. The bank examiners are coming on Monday, July 6. Pierce is stunned. He contemplates suicide. He takes up a gun but can't bring himself to do it.

Instead, Hi and Kay Pierce throw a party in their fine Magnolia home. At a time when America is legally dry, the Pierces are known for their "wet" parties; in their basement is a vault stocked with cognac, vermouth, Canadian beer, and 500 bottles of home brew. Wearing bedroom slippers and an open shirt, Hi Pierce tells his guests that the party is a wake for his financial career.

Pierce, 42, is described as "the only and adored son of a doting mother." He took over Home Savings in 1927 after the death of his father, who was president. Kay was his secretary. He married Kay and built her the five-bedroom house on Magnolia Bluff.

Pierce is a longtime pal of Adolph Linden. In 1925, the two went together to Olympia to lobby for Wallace Nicely to be their regulator. Pierce provided Linden's KJR Radio with free space in the Home Savings building at Fourth and Westlake. Linden's Puget Sound Savings, in turn, took a mortgage on Pierce's new house.

Home Savings has required depositors to give six months' notice to make withdrawals. In June 1931 Pierce sends out a letter explaining that those who gave notice to withdraw their money will receive zero interest on it. "The directors feel it would be unjust for a dividend to be declared and paid to those members who have not indicated any loyalty to the institution," the letter says. The bank examiners have seen the letter, which is why they're coming.

The state closes Home Savings. The newspapers are much amused when some of the first assets examiners find are Pierce's bottles of Benedictine, gin, cognac, and rum. Some of the more important assets, however, are missing.

Two weeks later, when prosecutors have a clearer idea of Pierce's crimes, he is arrested. Always a dandy, Hi Pierce is booked into jail, the *Post-Intelligencer* reports, "wearing a natty brown suit and faultlessly groomed, save for a day's growth of beard." He is skinny to the point of gaunt and said to weigh just 109 pounds.

———

Like Adolph Linden, Hi Pierce has been using the depositors' money. One way is to dip into the accounts of out-of-state residents. If they show up, he puts their money back and takes it from someone else.

Like Linden, Pierce has a side venture, the Washington Loan & Securities Company. It's in the bond business. Pierce creates the bonds, and his salesmen sell them.

Over the years, people have sensed that something was off about Washington Loan. Several have asked Secretary of State J. Grant Hinkle, the regulator who approved Adolph Linden's stock sale, to investigate Washington Loan. But Hinkle's Securities Division employs only two men, and they do nothing.

Washington Loan advertises that its bonds are backed by first mortgages on improved real estate. This is a lie. The "mortgages" aren't real. Hi Pierce has been sitting in his office for 14 years, ginning them up out of his head. He has used investors' money to buy assets for himself: a shuttered brewery in Nanaimo, British Columbia, and when Adolph Linden's empire collapses, Northwest Radio Service. But most of Washington Loan's money has gone to pay interest to the earlier investors so that new investors will keep coming.

Another Ponzi scheme.

When it all collapses, Pierce offers to plead guilty. However, King County's prosecutor, Robert Burgunder, wants to wait until he's sure exactly what Pierce is guilty of. This gives Pierce time to hide assets. He has already put his home in his wife's name; now he deeds their two rental houses to a real estate firm in which he is a partner. He also deeds his and Kay's automobiles to his attorneys, who talk him out of pleading guilty.

Three years later, Warren Magnuson, 29, will be King County prosecutor. Magnuson makes it clear that he would not have let Pierce do this. "When Hi Pierce was arrested in July 1931, he was ready to plead guilty, but delay led him to change his mind," Magnuson will say. At the time the future senator says this, Home Savings will have paid its shareholder-depositors only 10 cents on the dollar. It will eventually pay 55 cents, but it will never reopen. Washington Loan will pay its creditors only two and a half cents on the dollar.

It will be two and a half years before Hi Pierce goes to prison.

In 1932, Adolph Linden is tried three times for grand larceny. There is no doubt that he took hundreds of thousands of dollars, much of it in cash, from the tellers' cages at Puget Sound Savings. The question is whether he was committing a crime.

Was it theft? When he was the company's president, he gave himself permission. When Edmund Campbell was president, Campbell gave him permission. Linden didn't act like a thief and run off with the money; he invested it in a Seattle business. He insists that he intended to pay the money back, and probably he did, eventually. How could he think otherwise?

Was it a loan? He hadn't applied for a loan or signed a contract. He hadn't put up any security. He hadn't made any payments. He hadn't told the board of trustees about the hundreds of thousands he was taking. When Nicely, the state regulator, found out, he warned Linden to stop—and Linden ignored him.

In 1931 two juries deadlock over whether Linden was borrowing or stealing. At Linden's third trial, which includes Campbell as well, the jury is on the brink of deadlock when Judge William J. Steinert calls them back. He tells them to forget Linden's intention. The issue, he says, is whether Linden took the money without the owners' permission.

Guilty, then. Campbell, too.

Judge Steinert finally gets to say what he thinks. "Nothing, I believe, in the history of this community has shocked the public as has the abuse by these men in trusted positions," he says. "The closing of the Puget Sound

Savings and Loan was one of the greatest shocks this city has ever had. It has shaken the public's confidence in such institutions to its foundations."

Campbell hobbles out of the courtroom to the elevator, wearing a leg brace. Despondent over his fate, he has attempted suicide by jumping out of a second-story window in his Capitol Hill house but has managed only to break his ankle and some bones in his feet. A woman in the elevator sees him and shouts, "Get out, you big millionaire crook! You can't ride on this elevator!"

"Hush, please," Campbell begs.

She pulls back her arm and slugs him. Seeing Linden, she says, "And *you* get out, too!"

These days, notes the *Argus*, bankers are as popular as boils.

At their trials, all of them argue that the money they took never ended up in their pockets. This is hard to believe. Except for Nicely, whose larceny

In Prison: (top, left to right) Adolph Linden/Edmund Campbell/ (bottom, left to right) Wallace Nicely/William Comer. *Washington State Archives.*

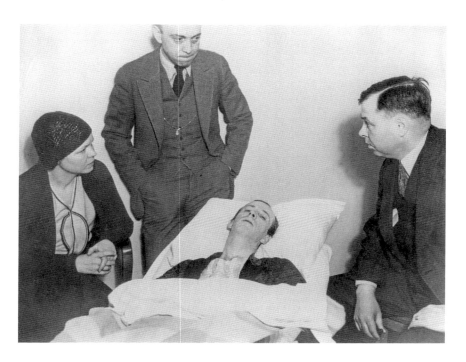

Ahira Pierce with his wife Kay and attorneys (*ACME Newspicture in author's collection*), and in prison *(Washington State Archives)*.

was small, they have been living high on the hog. Before his radio empire failed, Linden was living in the five-acre Wurdemann estate in Lake Forest Park. Campbell was living in the penthouse of the Camlin Hotel; when he moved out, he made off with the furniture, bedspreads, and curtains. Comer has a huge house in Madison Park that he will sell to the president of the Seattle-First National Bank. Pierce has the Magnolia property at 4515 W. Ruffner Street, which in 2021 will be assessed at $9 million.

Pierce is the last to be tried. After delaying trial for months on account of ill health, he appears in court on a stretcher, suffering from what the *Times* snidely calls "an alleged chronic ailment." Pierce is truly not well; in November 1931 he has an operation for rupture and abdominal strangulation, and at his trial in late 1932, he is wheeled into court weighing less than 100 pounds. The jury is not swayed and finds him guilty.

Linden, Campbell, and Comer are each sentenced to five to fifteen years, the maximum for grand larceny. Linden will serve the full five-year minimum. Campbell and Comer will each serve four years, Comer coming out at age 77. Nicely, who gets four to fifteen years, will serve three years and eight months. Pierce gets 20 to 65 years. Delayed by his illness, he will enter prison on February 10, 1934.

In a snide send-off to Pierce, *Argus* editor Harry A. Chadwick writes, "From now on Hi will lead a quiet and secluded life. There will be no more parties for Hi. He will get up in the morning at the appointed time, eat plain and wholesome food, do what he is told when he is told to do it . . . They will not hang him, but unless some weak-minded governor interferes, he will be carried out of the penitentiary feet-first."

And that is what happens. Pierce dies in prison of ulcerative colitis on January 16, 1935, at age 45, having served less than a year. His wife, Kay Pierce, sells their house on Magnolia Bluff. After she pays her husband's debts, she is left with just $400.

Linden gets out in 1938. He is a chastened man. He tells a reporter that he will no longer scramble for money, which is "only a small part of life."

4
The Bottom, 1931–1932

In Seattle commercial circles, the mood at the end of 1930 is dark. Stock prices are hitting new lows. So are the prices for sugar, silver, wheat, lumber, salmon, butter, and eggs. In December 1930 Seattle's union barbers drop the price of a man's haircut from 60 or 65 cents to 50 cents. The *Post-Intelligencer* reports that the price of moonshine has dropped from $8 or $9 a gallon to $3.

In late 1930 the Seattle Chamber of Commerce begins an effort to turn things around. Led by Ford dealer William O. McKay, the Chamber organizes what it calls the Committee of 59. At its first meeting, chamber president Wylie Hemphill, the promoter of "Siwash economics," challenges the committee to raise $100,000 to advertise Seattle and "harvest the tourist crop." Donald E. Frederick, the founder of Frederick & Nelson, contributes the first $3,000.

Advertising! The *Seattle Times* loves it. The editors hail the effort as the revival of the "Seattle Spirit" of frontier days. The editors paste mug shots of the Committee of 59 across several pages in the Sunday paper. The Committee, in turn, buys ads in the *Times*. Each side is showing off its civic-mindedness. In the paper's year-end business review, the *Times*' editors bubble with optimism, proclaiming that the 1930s "undoubtedly will see the greatest development the city has ever known."

The Committee of 59 buys a two-page spread in the *Saturday Evening Post* to promote Seattle to tourists. Having spent its money, the chamber then asks the Legislature to allow counties to raise property taxes for such campaigns. Legislators pass the bill, but Governor Hartley vetoes it. The newspapers say nothing.

Seattle banker Joshua Green and capitalist John W. Eddy offer an outlandish suggestion. Returning in December 1930 from a hunt in Africa in which each man bagged an elephant, they suggest a promotion by pachyderm. They offer to buy an elephant in New York, paint the word "SEATTLE" on its side in big white letters, and have it walked across America. The idea, notes the *Times*, is "that the elephant, thus marked, will attract attention at fifty places all along the line."

Probably it would have, but the idea goes nowhere, as does the Committee of 59. The year 1931 will bring problems far beyond the redemptive power of public relations.

Some warning signs are clear only in hindsight. On December 6, 1930, the *Seattle Times* runs an odd story out of Germany. A cinema in Berlin is showing *All Quiet on the Western Front*, a Hollywood movie based on Erich Maria Remarque's novel of World War I. At the point in the film when German soldiers in the trenches cower in fear, men in brown shirts stand up in the theater and yell, "A dirty film, made in America!" The brownshirts set off stink bombs and open a box of live mice. On their way out, they demand their money back, and when they meet resistance, they beat up the cashier. The leader of this demonstration, the story says, is a man named Joseph Goebbels.

The National Socialist German Workers' Party will not come to power for two years. But the Nazis are on the rise. In the September 1930 elections, they win 18.3 percent of the vote. Their aim is to tear up the Treaty of Versailles, give Britain and France nothing, and rebuild Germany's power. The Nazis detest the New York bankers and the financial world they represent.

For several years, Germany has been selling bonds in the United States. Already the value of those bonds has fallen. Late in 1930, James W. Gerard, the former U.S. ambassador to Berlin, warns American investors that Germany will default on its bonds within 18 months. In New York, Moody's Investors Service tells the bondholders not to worry. But they should. Seattle investors hold at least $800,000 in face value of German bonds—$14.9 million in 2024 dollars—and German paper is headed for the wastebasket.

Stock prices fall further in percentage terms in 1931 than in any year of the 20th century. In Seattle, shares in Ben Ehrlichman's United National Corporation, which sold at $50.75 at the market's peak, open in 1931 at $8. In

A men's apparel shop at 116 Pike Street quits in December 1936. *King County Archives.*

March the company omits the dividend and the shares fall to $5. By year-end they will trade at $1.50.

Nationally the unemployment rate nearly doubles in 1931, rising from 8.7 percent in 1930 to 15.9 percent. The Census Bureau measures it in Seattle in January 1931 at 17.7 percent. Unemployment will go higher but already is at depression levels.

Seattle's building permits plunge 69 percent in value from 1930 to 1931. In January 1931 more than half of Seattle's union carpenters and bricklayers are out of work. In March 1931, Frederick Anhalt, builder of the beloved Norman-style brick apartment houses on Capitol Hill, fails to pay contractors and is forced out of business.

In poor neighborhoods, people begin abandoning houses.

Bucking the trend, J.C. Penney opens a five-floor store at Second and Union. Anson A. Littler opens his first apparel shop at Fourth and Union. The new openings, however, are far outnumbered by business closures. In the Second and Third Avenue retail district, closures during the first half of 1931 include the big Cheasty's apparel emporium near the new Penney's, and also the Knettle's, Jordan's, and Florence shops in women's apparel;

Anhalt's Oak Manor. *Drawing by Anjl Rodee for* Colors of Capitol Hill *coloring book. Courtesy of Capitol Hill Historical Society.*

Browning King, Ray Bigelow, Stanley Blumenthal's, and Coplin's in men's apparel; and Dr. A. Reed's Shoes and Miller Trunk & Leather.

By mid-1931 the retail price level in Seattle has fallen 27.6 percent in two years. Businesses are struggling to pay old debts while selling merchandise at the new, lower prices. In May, the Olympic Hotel cuts the price of afternoon tea in the Palm Room to 75 cents—a sum still large enough to buy a full dinner elsewhere. Later in 1931 the Olympic's second-mortgage bonds default. In 1932 the Olympic's first-mortgage bonds default and fall to 20 cents on the dollar. Seattle's finest downtown hotel begins a fight with its bondholders that will not be resolved until 1936.

Another struggle comes at the new Washington Athletic Club. At the center of it is Darwin Meisnest. He is the son of a University of Washington professor of German who was dismissed during World War I after being accused in that hyper-patriotic time of sympathy with the enemy. The younger Meisnest lives down his father's (undeserved) reputation with a winning career in sports-related management.

He begins his rise as the student manager of the *Tyee*, the University yearbook. Since early in the century, the *Tyee*, the *Columns* monthly, the *Daily* student paper, and the University Bookstore have been managed by the Associated Students of the University of Washington. So have the university sports teams. The ASUW has grown into a real business. And that makes it the perfect spot for Darwin Meisnest, who, the *Seattle Times* says, "has been a businessman ever since he became old enough to wear trousers."

The *Tyee* is running at a loss. Meisnest straightens out the finances by having students sell the ads rather than paying a downtown agency to do it. On the strength of his success at the *Tyee* and his involvement in sports, Meisnest is named business manager for football. The UW's football team—then called the Sun Dodgers but soon to be renamed the Huskies—also runs at a loss. Meisnest puts it into the black, but he argues that it would do much better if he had a bigger stadium so that he could sell more seats. At age 23, he proposes building the grandest stadium on the Pacific Coast—the forerunner of today's Husky Stadium.

By this time, Meisnest is no longer a student but the paid manager of all ASUW sports. The university tells him to go ahead and raise the money for the stadium. He rents an office downtown and recruits 200 students to sell perpetual tickets to UW football games. In 1920, with the half million dollars his sales team raises, he builds the first version of Husky Stadium on the mud flats of Union Bay.

Darwin Meisnest, circa 1940. *David Eskenazi collection.*

In 1927, Meisnest has the ASUW build the Hec Edmundson Pavilion for indoor sports. The state and the university contribute to the project, but more than half of the money is from 5-percent bonds backed by the ASUW alone.

In building the "Hec Ed," Meisnest gets into political trouble. In 1928, the ASUW's president, law student Marion Zioncheck—more on him later—accuses Meisnest of turning the student government into a business. He is not wrong about that. Though the Seattle newspapers come to Meisnest's defense—they have been writing about him for nearly a decade—he soon leaves the university for a job at a cement company.

Meisnest does not confine his attentions to cement. As the Depression begins, he is active in the Seattle Chamber of Commerce. He also sells bonds to build the Edmond Meany Hotel. With a background in sports, management, and finance, he is a natural to be an officer in the brand new Washington Athletic Club.

The club opens in December 1930 in its 21-story tower downtown. It has a rocky start. The Depression is on in earnest, and by the spring of 1931, one-quarter of the club's 2,000 members have let their memberships lapse. The club's 200 employees are forced to take pay cuts that average 37 percent, and its bondholders take equal cuts in interest payments. Seattle financiers Victor Elfendahl, Gilbert Skinner, and William Edris buy the club's downtown building from club president William Comer, who has been disgraced in the failure of the Puget Sound Savings & Loan Association.

In April 1931, the Athletic Club's trustees hand over management to 33-year-old Darwin Meisnest. Under him, the club begins a membership drive. By temporarily dropping its initiation fee from $175 to $27.50 and its monthly dues to $7, it recruits 800 members. It also lowers prices inside the club. A haircut, which includes pressing a necktie, drops from 65 cents to 50 cents. The club begins offering services for women: swimming, tap-dancing, calisthenics, fashion shows, and classes in dramatics and interior decorating, in addition to the bowling, swimming, volleyball, handball, squash, badminton, and "smokers" for the men. "The whole atmosphere of the Club has been made more democratic than it was during its opening months," an April 1931 club circular boasts.

Meisnest's plan works and will keep the Washington Athletic Club alive through the Depression. Today's Washington Athletic Club, which is coming up on its 100th anniversary, honors his memory with a Meisnest Room.

With Meisnest gone and the Depression underway, trouble comes to the Associated Students of the University of Washington. Husky football has a poor season in 1931. Fewer fans are attending games, and sports revenues are down. For the interest payment due in January 1932 on the Hec Edmundson bonds, the ASUW sends bondholders one-year promissory notes.

In April 1932, the ASUW's cash runs out. The *Tyee*, the *Columns*, and the *Daily* are about to close. The Husky basketball team has no money to charter a bus for its game at Washington State College. The coaches line up six private cars, chip in to buy gas, and the players leave on the long drive to Pullman.

The ASUW beseeches Seattle bankers for a loan so it can keep paying salaries until fall, when football revenues kick in. The bankers have already lent the ASUW more than $100,000 and refuse to lend any more. But as a stand-alone business, the University Bookstore could support a loan. The ASUW quickly incorporates the Bookstore as a separate business, and four Seattle banks lend it $50,000. The Bookstore passes $30,000 to the ASUW, so that it can avoid a shutdown.

Its problem is not solved. At year-end 1932, the ASUW is unable to meet the next interest payment on the Hec Edmundson bonds or to redeem the one-year notes. The bankers insist that the university take responsibility for its finances.

Student leaders agree to give up their authority, but the change requires the student body's consent. A vote is held on February 23, 1933. The measure passes, and on April 1, the university appoints former Husky track star Charles Frankland as athletic director. Frankland, an officer of the Pacific National Bank, reports to the university president, not to the ASUW. He will remain as athletic director for three years before returning to the bank.

Frankland's appointment is not without a challenge. Three students file suit in King County Superior Court. Represented by a former justice of the Washington Supreme Court, the students allege that to meet the 25-percent turnout requirement in the ASUW voting, the university stuffed the ballot boxes with 427 fake ballots. The university's attorneys neither deny nor admit this, but they argue that student elections are none of the court's concern. The judge agrees and dismisses the case.

The matter is settled. The ASUW's bondholders are made whole with new bonds backed by Husky football receipts and 40 percent of student fees. The ASUW is reduced to the status of a student government, not a business. Never again will it have responsibility for university publications, the University Bookstore, or Husky football.

———

In 1931 the international financial system shatters. The collapse of the bond market is less famous than the 1929 crash in stocks, but it causes more damage. The smash-up in bonds is what puts the "Great" in the Great Depression.

The break begins in May 1931 with the failure the Kreditanstalt, a bank in Austria. The government of Austria is too small to bail out the bank. Panic spreads to Germany. Remembering the hyperinflation of 1923, Germans rush to exchange marks for foreign currencies and gold. In June 1931, U.S. president Herbert Hoover proposes a one-year standstill of sovereign debt, so that Germany can stop paying reparations to Britain and France, and Britain and France can stop paying on war debts to the United States. Germany quickly says yes, as does Britain. The French, who would come out behind, drag their feet. By the time they say yes, Germany has stopped redeeming marks in gold. Germany is off the gold standard.

The dominoes begin to fall. There is a run to exchange pounds for gold, and on September 20, 1931, the British Commonwealth goes off the gold standard. The pound drops from $4.86 to $3.88. Seattle streetcars stop accepting Canadian dimes, now worth only 8.6 U.S. cents. America has plenty of gold and stays on the gold standard. But the non-gold currencies now sell at a discount to the U.S. dollar, which means the products of those countries fall in price. America's exports shrink. The Dow Jones Industrials fall below 100. Stock in United National Corporation, which has been trading for months at $5, drops to $2.

Bonds issued by Germany, Hungary, Yugoslavia, and Bulgaria fall below 50 cents on the dollar. South American bonds plunge. Among them are the bonds of Brazil's state of Minas Geraes. Sold in September 1929 at 87 cents on the dollar, they have since defaulted. They drop to 11.

After the bond crash, money is not available on reasonable terms to any company or public agency in the state of Washington. For many, it is not available on any terms. In Seattle one casualty is the Puget Sound Bridge & Dredging Company, which holds a permit to build a private toll bridge across Lake Washington from Seward Park to Mercer Island. There is no market for the company's bonds, and the bridge will never be built.

———

In late December 1931, the *Post-Intelligencer* hires freelance writer Lidablanche Robe to pose as a homeless woman looking for a job. She dons old clothes and hits the streets for ten days. In January 1932, the *P-I* runs her stories. One of them describes spending the night at the Colonial Theatre, which charges 15 cents to watch movies play over and over. The Colonial is warm, and it is two-thirds full of people escaping the winter cold. "To try to sleep all night in a theatre is a nightmare," she writes. "You can shut your eyes but there is no way of keeping the talkies from your ears. When the theatre closed at 5, I went shivering to the cold streets to walk until daylight. Save for a few trucks there was no traffic and I met few people." She ends her walk at the employment office, where she is offered a job as a housemaid.

In 1932, Americans who still have work are hanging on to their jobs, afraid of what's next. Of the workforce, 24 percent are unemployed. Children are put to work. "More little boys are peddling from house to house the doughnuts and candy that mother makes," writes Mildred Masterson in the

Star. "More little schoolgirls are leaving their homes for others, where they do heavy housework in return for room and board."

In the Depression, life slows down. In 1932, marriages in King County are down 31 percent from 1929. Births are down. Divorces are down. In King County, suicides are up by half from 1928. Almost all the additional suicides are related to business reverses or idleness.

Capital is idle as well as labor. The disaster is quiet. There is no drama to it. The steam shovels and jackhammers are still. Newspapers shrink, their pages starved of advertising.

Architect's rendering of the Seattle Trust Tower, never built. *Drawing by John Graham, architect. Appeared in* Seattle Times, *10-30-1932, Brown Section, p. 8*.

In 1932, the *Seattle Times* runs a ten-part series on the building projects that are no more. The largest is a 33-story tower designed by John Graham for Seattle Trust and Savings Bank. The project is for a site next to the Exchange Building. In number of floors it would be second only to the Smith Tower. It will never be built.

In 1932, the city's building permits fall to 13 percent of their 1930 value. If it weren't for the Seattle Art Museum (now the Seattle Asian Art Museum), a gift to the city from Richard E. Fuller and his mother, Margaret MacTavish Fuller, the total would be even less. From February through July 1932, not one apartment house is built in Seattle. In 1932 one of every three apartments in the city is vacant, as people abandon their units and move in with others.

In the early 1930s the Ford Motor Company has 33 assembly plants around the United States. Its Seattle plant, in a five-story building at South Lake Union (now Public Storage), was built in 1914, the year Ford adopted the $5 daily wage. By 1930 the Lake Union plant is seriously out of date. In March of that year, during the false recovery, Ford announces plans for a modern low-rise plant south of downtown along the Duwamish River. The plant is designed by Albert Kahn, the Detroit architect who designed the Soviets' tractor plant at Stalingrad. Ford's Duwamish plant isn't as large as the one in Russia, but for Seattle, it's big. It opens in May 1932 at the bottom of the Depression.

The new plant incorporates the latest ideas. It has three miles of conveyor belts. The floors are of softwood blocks to dampen the sound of dropped tools. Overhead lights are mercury-vapor, with natural light from 100,000 square feet of windows. The windows are reversible so they can be cleaned from inside. The sinks in the washrooms have no handles, making them easier to clean; to turn on the water, you press a knob on the floor with your foot.

The plant is served by four different railroads for bringing parts and subassemblies from Detroit. For oceangoing ships, it has 500 feet of dock on the Duwamish Waterway. J. C. Donnelly, Ford's district manager, says, "In time, we expect to do most of the import and export business of the Pacific Coast from this plant."

In July 1932, the company opens its plant to the public, with fanfare that includes Governor Roland Hartley, Seattle mayor John Dore, and busloads of guests from the Seattle Chamber of Commerce. Already running at one-third capacity, the plant has 600 workers producing 75 to 100 cars a day. At full capacity, Ford expects to employ 1,600 men.

It is not to be. By 1932, Ford has fallen behind General Motors in the U.S. market, which is much shrunken by the Depression. Ford soon begins closing satellite plants and pulling the work back to Detroit. After operating for seven months, the company's state-of-the-art Seattle plant shuts down in December 1932. The newspapers run tiny stories saying that the plant will reopen in a few days. The stories are false. The assembly line will never run again. During the Depression, Ford will use the building for a showroom and for storage. In 1941, it will sell the property to the federal government for use as a warehouse to support the U.S. Army.

In future years, the Seattle area will have a Kenworth plant to assemble heavy trucks. The passenger-car industry will be gone.

———

Writers in the letters columns of Seattle's newspapers have been arguing for years that a married woman should be supported by her husband. Sent out to work, she will be tempted by other men. Being away from home, she will be less able to raise a child, or to have a child at all. And as the Depression deepens, men complain that married women are taking their jobs. "They cut down a man's chance to make a living," writes an unemployed timber rigger to the *Seattle Star*. "They ought to stay home and give us a break."

Dismiss the married women! The idea is simple, though the execution of it is not.

Married women push back. They don't accept blame for the Depression or the duty to give up their gains for men. "I never heard of a married woman working in a lumber mill [or] logging camp," writes one, arguing that it's wrong for loggers, mill workers, carpenters, and longshoremen to blame their troubles on women. Another woman tells the *Star* she and her husband need every penny she earns, but that she knows single girls who live with parents and fritter away their money on "a good time and pretty clothes." Lay *them* off, she says.

Women's defenders argue that a married woman might need to work to pay for a child's education or to help her husband out of debt. Writer J. Oakley asks why a woman seeking work should be required to list her needs at all. "People," she writes, "this is the United States yet, not Russia."

Architect's rendering of Ford Motor Company's Seattle plant, 1933. *Image from the Collections of The Henry Ford.*

Late in 1931, veterans of World War I, who already enjoy a preference in hiring for Seattle city jobs, push the city to dismiss its married women. The Seattle Central Labor Council agrees, as does the liberal *Star*. But when the City Council considers putting this on the ballot, professional women, led by former mayor Bertha Landes, fill the Council's chamber in protest. The councilmen back down.

The *Times* applauds. "Of course, if everything was right in the world, its work would all be done by men, and its women and girls would be adequately supported in the homes," the *Times*' editors write. "That was the old-fashioned way. But when so many men, for whatever reason, fail in that respect, women must carry on. Most of them make good in the things they undertake. Few employers, public or private, can be induced to believe it a duty to dismiss a competent woman solely to make a place for a man of unknown qualifications."

Mayor Bertha Landes, 1927. *Museum of History & Industry, Seattle, SHS2344. Used with permission.*

Some local governments and school districts dismiss married women, but Seattle does not. Thank Bertha Landes and also the fact that women vote. By 1931 they have had the vote in Washington for 21 years. Their political power now pays off in dollars and cents. Non-citizens, on the other hand, don't vote—and in 1933, Seattle and King County will dismiss them, including the graduates of Canadian medical schools working at Harborview Hospital.

The fight is not over. The accusation of married women taking jobs from men will come up again.

———

The City of Seattle is short of cash. It has been paying its employees in interest-bearing warrants stamped "not paid for want of funds." The employees cash the warrants at the banks, and the city redeems them when it has the money. In effect, the banks are giving the city a payroll loan. In May 1932, the banks announce that they are carrying too many warrants and want no more of them. Police, fire, and other city employees will have to sell their warrants to private brokers at a 5, 10, or 15 percent discount. For employees, this means a pay cut.

The warrant crisis is the first challenge for Seattle's new mayor, John F. Dore. To satisfy the banks, Dore and the city council impose pay cuts on city workers that average 16 percent. (More on this in chapter 12, "John Dore.") The council cuts the city's 1933 budget by 24 percent from the 1932 level, which itself is down 10 percent from 1931. Satisfied that the city has tightened its belt, the banks resume cashing warrants.

The crisis continues in 1933. That year, Seattle's rate of property tax delinquency hits a Depression high of 28 percent. By March 1933, the city is six months behind in redeeming pay warrants. After bankers once again refuse to cash any more, Mayor Dore closes nine of the city's 35 fire stations. By cutting work hours, he reduces Fire Department pay by 23 percent.

In 1933, Seattle's public-school teachers are cut again. A grade-school teacher with 12 years' experience is cut to $1,400 a year, a cumulative cut of one-third since the Depression began. And at the University of Washington, the professor earning $5,500 a year at the beginning of the Depression is cut a second time to $3,713, also a cut of one-third. For students, the legislature cuts tuition by one-third, from $15 a quarter to $10.

In November 1932, state voters okay a graduated income tax. In 1933, fearing that the tax will be struck down in the courts, the legislature passes a business gross-revenue (B&O) tax. Both taxes are challenged at the Washington Supreme Court. When Justice Emmett Parker, 74, is out sick, the court deadlocks 4–4 on each tax.

Justice Parker retires, and Governor Clarence Martin appoints James M. Geraghty to replace him. Irish-born "Jimmy" Geraghty, 63, first ran for the legislature in the wild year of 1896 as a Populist and only later became a Democrat. He votes yes on both taxes. Justice Oscar Holcomb, however, changes his vote to "no" on the income tax while leaving it at "yes" on the business revenue tax. And that is how Washington becomes one of the few U.S. states with no state income tax.

———

By mid-1932, few Americans have any interest in buying stock. People with spare cash are saving it, either at the bank or in coffee cans. Volume on the New York Stock Exchange shrivels to a dribble. The tiny Seattle Stock Exchange ends floor trading entirely, and will not reopen until September 1935.

In the midst of the gloom, a revival begins in the commodity markets. It's a small thing, and newspapers pay little attention to it. The upsurge starts in sugar and hogs. In June 1932, it moves to the beaten-down market for bonds. The rally spreads to German bonds. European leaders are negotiating at Lausanne, Switzerland, to reduce the war reparations imposed on Germany. On July 8, 1932, negotiators announce the deal: 97 percent of the Allies' war claim against Germany is forgiven. The Germans are off the hook. A surge of joy hits all foreign bonds, including Japanese bonds held in Seattle.

On the day of the Lausanne settlement, the Dow Jones Industrial Average closes at 41.22. For U.S. stocks, this is the bottom. The Dow will never be this low again. From its high of September 3, 1929, the Dow is down 90 percent. Stocks now move up; because prices are at rock-bottom, the percentage gains are huge. By mid-August, stock in United National Corporation doubles, from 50 cents bid to a dollar.

For the rest of the world, this is also the bottom for the economy. For the U.S. economy, a second bottom is yet to come.

5
Homeless, 1931–1941

The newspapers mostly ignore the struggles of people trying to save their homes. But in May 1931, one man's determination makes the public prints.

The *Seattle Times* knows Nicholas Oeconomacos. He lives alone in a little house near the newspaper's new building. An immigrant from Greece, Oeconomacos is "possibly the most gifted clarinetist in the Pacific Northwest," the *Times* says. Oeconomacos has been laid off by the Seattle Symphony and is three months behind on his house payments. His electricity has been cut off. Wearing his trademark black satin cape and broad-brimmed hat, he spends a day making music on downtown sidewalks, his hat out for dimes and quarters. "Music is my life," he says, "and I have no money."

His problem is more than the Depression. In a letter to the *Argus*, Oeconomacos writes, "Throughout America hundreds of thousands of us musicians are without employment because of the mechanical devices which have been in use in the theaters in the past three years." He's referring to movies with sound, which arrived in Seattle in 1928.

The Depression hurts the movie houses, especially the big theaters with big mortgages. Attendance falls. In downtown Seattle, the Blue Mouse, Fox, Paramount, and Orpheum close for months. Ticket prices fall from 50 cents to 35 cents and, in second-run houses at off-hours, as low as a dime.

Theaters that have been offering live vaudeville impose pay cuts on their musicians and stagehands. The cuts are not enough. In January 1933, the operator of the Fox, Fifth Avenue, Coliseum, and Paramount files for bankruptcy. The four theaters, which employed around 80 musicians and a score of stagehands to handle singing, gymnastics, juggling, and comedy acts, emerge under new owners as movie houses, each with a projectionist, a ticket taker, and a few ushers. During the decade, theater owners will attempt several times to revive vaudeville, but its heyday is over. And the silent movies are gone for good.

72   *Seattle in the Great Depression*

Nicholas Oeconomacos, 1931. Seattle Post-Intelligencer *Collection, 1986.5G.2241, Museum of History & Industry, Seattle. Used with permission.*

Making music on the sidewalk for one day, Oeconomacos picks up $503 (the equivalent of more than $10,000 in 2024 dollars). After that, Seattle's top commercial real estate man, Henry Broderick, picks up Oeconomacos in a car and takes him to a party hosted by Seattle businessmen. Later they put on a benefit concert for him at Meany Hall.

Oeconomacos's house is saved, and he gets his position in the symphony back for a while. But he borrows money from the symphony director and doesn't pay it back. He goes to California for work, and when he returns, he can get only occasional gigs. In January 1935 his house is again subject to a sheriff's sale. His friends try to help, but their help comes too late to save the house.

Oeconomacos goes on relief. He finds a house to rent and spends many hours festooning it with artwork, quotations, and old newspaper clippings. He takes in a few students but spends his last years mostly alone, decorating his house and eating three meals a day at a tavern on Aurora Avenue.

The Symphony never takes him back. He dies in 1945.

———

Humans are not the only creatures whose homes are at risk in the Great Depression. There is also an elephant.

In January 1933, Seattle mayor John Dore suggests that he might have to close the Woodland Park Zoo. Confining animals to cages, he says, "is a relic of the Dark Ages."

The problem is money. It costs the city $1,000 a month to feed the lions, bears, buffalo, coyotes, deer, and other animals. With all the people out of work, feeding zoo animals is becoming difficult to justify. In a jocular-but-serious vein, *Seattle Times* reporter Doug Welch writes, "There may be an elephant and a lion or two dropped from the payroll, and the rest of the animals may take a 10 percent cut in rations." The biggest appetite is that of a 12,500-pound Asian bull elephant named Tusko, who eats $2 in feed a day. Tusko also has a $4-a-day caretaker. "We've got to cut somewhere," Welch writes, "and Tusko looks like the place."

Tusko: 12,500 pounds and a fully exploited asset. *Author's collection*.

It looks like that to B. B. Lustig, president of the Seattle Board of Park Commissioners. In January 1933 he writes of Tusko to Mayor Dore: "We are perfectly willing to get rid of him, as he has been a constant source of worry to us, for the reason that it has been necessary to keep him chained."

And that is a problem for John Dore. Three months earlier, he became the hero to Seattle schoolchildren by saving Seattle's unemployed elephant.

Imported from Siam in 1902, Tusko earns his keep for years in private circuses. His owners keep him in chains, and several times he breaks free of them. In 1922 he runs amok in Sedro-Woolley in Skagit County, turning over cars and plowing through fences. In Portland, on Christmas Day, 1931, he breaks his chains and is nearly shot before being subdued.

Tusko is a depreciating asset. Bought by the Al G. Barnes Circus in 1922 for $6,000, he is sold in 1931 for $2,700, sold again at a sheriff's sale for $200, and sold a week later for one dollar. At age 42, Tusko is not clearly an asset at all. Still, in 1932 his owner, a Eugene, Oregon, dentist named Milton Bull, has him trucked to Seattle for Fleet Week, the forerunner of Seafair. He puts Tusko on display in South Lake Union in a tent under a sign, "See Tusko, Largest Living Creature on Earth," admission 10 cents.

Tusko changes hands again. After Fleet Week, his new owner, H. C. Barber of Kirkland, begins losing money on him. The Humane Society informs Mayor Dore that Barber plans to shoot the elephant at a public execution. After that, Tusko is to be tanned and stuffed, so that he will earn his keep without eating.

On October 8, 1932, Dore orders Tusko seized and trucked to the Woodland Park Zoo. The reason, he tells the press, is to save the animal's life. The legal excuse is that Barber hasn't paid the city's exhibitors' tax.

The zoo chains Tusko in a covered concrete pen. Because of his size and the drama of his rescue, Tusko quickly becomes the zoo's top attraction. And at a time when zoo director Gus Knudson is telling the Park Board he needs to cut back the number of creatures, and Mayor Dore talks of closing the zoo altogether, Tusko's popularity makes the zoo impossible to kill.

To save Tusko, Radio KOL begins a campaign to raise $8,000 to buy him from his owner and set him up in proper quarters. But 1933 is the worst possible time to ask the public for money. After several months, the nickels and dimes add up to only $79.13.

In June 1933 Tusko sickens and begins violently shaking. His handler, George Lewis, unchains him. Finally free, the elephant dies of a blood clot in the heart. His 40-pound heart is exhibited in the Olympic Hotel at a meeting of the state medical association.

Barber has never paid for Tusko, so ownership reverts to Dr. Bull. Through his Seattle lawyers, he demands that the city pay him $52,000 in compensation for taking his elephant. The city refuses. It sends him Tusko's hide and bones, including his 200-pound-skull. Bull has them put on display: 10 cents admission. He never pays his Seattle lawyers. In 1954, his son donates the bones to the Oregon Museum of Natural and Cultural History, where they still are.

Tusko's hide disappears for seven years. In 1940 a Port of Seattle employee discovers it in a cold-storage locker under the name of H. C. Barber. The cold-storage fees have been unpaid for five years. "Against our will, we find that we are the probable owners," says the Port's manager, Willis Bickford. "Without an elephant to fill it, the thing is practically useless as far as we are concerned." Unless the owner pays, Bickford says, "We'll have to get a court order to sell it to the highest bidder, bid it in for storage charges and then destroy it . . . Probably we'll tow it in the harbor and sink it."

And that is the last of Tusko.

For ordinary people trying to save their property, there is little hope of public rescue. People are on their own.

Bert Stuart, a 64-year-old widow, is a landlady. On the night of December 6, 1932, she pours three gallons of kerosene on the kitchen and bathroom floors of her rental house in West Seattle and sets it on fire.

Upon her arrest for torching her own house, she tells the newspapers that she has no money and no assets. For seven months, she has been sponging off a friend, trying to evict her tenants who won't pay the rent. When she tried to throw them out, they got some men from the food bank to stop her. She appealed to the mayor of Seattle, John F. Dore, but he told her there was nothing he could do.

The tenants finally moved out, but they left the house a ruin. She didn't have the money to fix it. "I was just discouraged," she says. "I finally decided to burn it." She hoped to collect the $1,000 insurance, pay off the $450 mortgage, and have some money back.

Before he was mayor, John Dore was a criminal defense attorney. He volunteers to take her case himself, pro bono. "I feel strongly for the property owners," he says. "I know such things are happening all over town." Bert Stuart is convicted of arson, but she gets a suspended sentence.

In the winter of 1932–1933, mortgage foreclosures are coming so fast that in January 1933 legislators in Olympia pass a moratorium on them. Bankers object; losing the power to foreclose on a nonperforming loan will further weaken the banks and put depositors at risk. It will also reduce the flow of new credit. By promising to go easier on borrowers, bankers persuade the state's new Democratic governor, Clarence Martin, to veto the bill. But he soon complains that bankers are demanding more collateral to make loans.

In the spring of 1933, a pitched battle erupts over the foreclosure of a house in Seattle's Columbia City district. The homeowner, Frank Frandsen, bought the house for $4,100 from Wilhelmina Peterson, a widow. He has paid off $2,900, but he lost his job as a lineman at Puget Power and has not made his $50-a-month house payment for 14 months. He also lost $1,000 in the failure of Ahira Pierce's Home Savings and Loan Association. Now Mrs. Peterson is foreclosing. Because the market is down, Frandsen will lose much of his equity.

Relief authorities line up a free house for his family to live in, but Frandsen refuses to move.

On April 26, 1933, sheriff's deputies arrive to evict the Frandsens. Several hundred men, some of them organized by the Communist Party, are standing guard. The deputies advance with nightsticks, and the defenders wield stones and clubs. A battle ensues. The defenders lose. The deputies arrest Frandsen, his 18-year-old son Orlan, and 14 others.

In June 1933, the 16 defendants stand trial in superior court for riot, assault, and resisting arrest. Two thousand protesters mass outside the court. After 95 hours of deliberation, the jury convicts 11 men and lets five go. Ten of them, including Frank and Orlan Frandsen, are sentenced to six months in jail. William Kominski, an immigrant from Yugoslavia, is convicted of second-degree assault for beating Deputy Sheriff August Buse with an iron shoe last, a foot-shaped form for making a shoe, while Orlan Frandsen held him around the legs. For this, Kominski is sentenced to 12 to 18 months in prison.

State welfare officials lease another house for the Frandsens. In 1935 the family will be evicted from that house for refusing to move at the end of the lease.

The spread of squatters' shacks begins early in the Depression. By the winter of 1930–1931, thousands of Seattle people are out of work, wandering the streets. On reclaimed land along the Duwamish at 14th Avenue South, a shanty town forms. "Near the railroad yards," writes the *Star*, "low, patchwork 'houses' of flattened tin cans, old packing cases and odds and ends of junk are rising daily." The first shantytowns are small, and the men get by. One tells the *Star*, "It isn't difficult to get food. You can get a sack of potatoes for 75 cents and [a bag of] bread for 25 cents. We don't have meat and butter much."

Seattle's leaders tolerate the shacks for the winter, but in May 1931, county health officer C. L. Dixon has them torn down.

As the next winter approaches, unemployment is worse. Out-of-work men and women panhandle for dimes. On skid road a dime will buy a beef sandwich with coffee or a plate of hotcakes with bacon. Those without dimes can get free meals from soup kitchens, but the free meals are not enough to stave off recurring hunger. Desperate men and women scrounge through garbage cans.

In the fall of 1931, homeless men swarm a nine-acre site on Elliott Bay that could be downtown Seattle's front porch. Decades later the site will be Terminal 46, stacked with shipping containers. In 1931 it is vacant land pocked with concrete machinery pits from the Skinner & Eddy Shipyard, which employed thousands of men during World War I. Squatters roof over the pits with gunnysacks and lumber. Some of the roofs are no more than two feet above ground.

Late in October, the city declares their huts a health hazard and burns them out. The *Post-Intelligencer* writes: "Fifty squatters, including wives and children, were driven from their shacks at the foot of Charles Street into the rain at 8 a.m. yesterday clutching pots, pans, coal oil lamps and bedrolls. A row more than three blocks long of huts made of box wood, driftwood and gunnysacks was set afire by five policemen using kerosene."

The squatters build again, and the police burn them out again. After that, the unemployed build unburnable hovels with old metal, brick, and

78   Seattle in the Great Depression

Hooverville, "the town that forgot the straight line," circa 1937. *University of Washington Libraries, Special Collections, UW2129.*

sand. The city lets them stay if they will agree to keep order, and they rebuild a third time.

On the waterfront rises what *American Architect* magazine describes as "the town that forgot the straight line"—a jumble of shacks, each one an expression of its builder's imagination and skill in construction, scrounging, and theft. The men who live there name it for America's president: Hooverville.

Seattle's waterfront squatter camp will last for ten years. Later in the Depression, University of Washington sociology student Donald Francis Roy will buy a shack for $15 and move in. Roy will write his department's most famous master's thesis, *Hooverville, A Study of a Community of Homeless Men in Seattle*.

By Roy's account, the men of Hooverville heat their shacks with woodstoves fashioned from bricks or five-gallon kerosene cans. They carry water from two public faucets. Few of the shacks have tubs; most of the men shower at the homeless shelters. Their latrines are built over Elliott Bay at the end of rickety catwalks and are for defecation only. Their urinal is the ground. You can smell it.

Roy conducts a census. Hooverville has more than 600 residents. Only seven are women, and none are children. More than 70 percent of the residents are white, most of them foreign-born, largely from Sweden, Norway, Finland, Russia, and Poland. Most are middle-aged and not schooled beyond eighth grade. There are Filipinos, most of them younger, and also African Americans. Most of the Hooverville men are loggers, miners, fishermen, farmers, or construction workers. Only half are on relief. Some scrounge from meat markets and bakeries. Some fish in the Sound. A few have low-level jobs. Some collect newspapers, worth 40 cents for 100 pounds, or hunt stray sawlogs in Elliott Bay. In the summer, the Filipinos leave for Alaska to work in the salmon canneries.

Roy finds the men "easy to approach, quick to pick up conversational cues and ever eager to share their humble fare." They are resigned to having no steady work, and maybe never having any, but most are not bitter about it. They have enough to eat. They gather to play cards and drink a homemade intoxicant called dehorn—denatured alcohol filtered through raw potatoes or bread. Their shacks afford them a level of privacy. They have access to cheap prostitutes and homosexual liaisons with their fellow men. The men of Hooverville are living day to day in what Roy describes as "a free and easy shanty life."

It is not an egalitarian life. The men of Hooverville are not equally poor. A *Star* reporter finds some of them living in "holes in the ground, like animals," and others in higher-quality hovels with scrap linoleum on the floor. In September 1932, *Post-Intelligencer* reporter Alice Elinor finds men repairing shacks made of boxes, broken planks, and tarpaper. She writes that the interiors appear to be tidy and clean. The men are living there, she writes, "because they are clinging to their thread of self-respect, too proud to seek shelter in the flophouses, too independent to ask for charity."

Another visitor to Hooverville is Selden Menefee, a University of Washington sociology student who will later join the teaching staff and become an outspoken radical. In an eight-part series for a weekly called the *Unemployed Citizen*, Menefee describes the typical Hooverville man: "He has a distaste for organized charity—breadlines and flophouses—so he decided to build a shack of his own and be independent." Menefee's series is called, "Studies in Rugged Individualism." The term is not one of approval. In the 1930s, "rugged individualism" is a pejorative, the name of a false ideal of a failed system.

Some property owners also live in shacks. In 1933 the *Seattle Times* runs a feature story on the family of an unemployed man living four miles east of Medina, near what is now downtown Bellevue. The man, Lester Spaulding, 44, has a daughter, Pervis, 11, and sons Buddy, 8, Billy, 7, and Donald, 5.

Lester Spaulding was a teamster. His last job, in 1928, was grading at Seward Park with a team of horses. Since then, he has put $75 down, with payments of $75 a year on 4½ acres of stumps. He has an unpainted two-room shack and a shanty for the animals: three calves and a skin-and-bones horse he got from a neighbor in exchange for two cords of firewood.

Spaulding's wife died shortly after the birth of their youngest. Caring for the kids has been tough, he says, but the daughter, Pervis, looks after little Donald. The reporter describes her as "a real-life Orphan Annie" who wears a thin, faded cotton dress and a cotton sweater. She's the one who keeps house. Buddy and Billy help with the animals and the growing of potatoes, corn, peas, and beans among the stumps. The family trades labor with the nearby farmers.

"I guess I'm one of those back-to-the-soil farmers you read about," Spaulding says. "I think I can make a go of it with a little good luck and a lot of hard work. The children and I are not afraid of hard work."

"We haven't starved yet, have we, father?" says little Buddy.

"No, and we're not going to," says the father, who says that when he has the money, he will add another room to the shack. He also plans to buy a pig.

Lester Spaulding and family, 1933: "I think I can make a go of it." 7-2-1933, p. 16.
© *The* Seattle Times.

The *Times* does not present the Spauldings as exceptional. The story is not news, nor is it an appeal for charity. The paper runs this story two days before the Fourth of July under the headline, "Family Poor, but Wealth Cannot Buy Their Spirit." Like Selden Menefee's series on Hooverville in *The Unemployed Citizen*, the *Times*' story on the Spauldings comes with a political point—but the opposite one. The *Times*' story is a celebration of American endurance. Whether the Spauldings are on relief it does not say.

In the gloomy days of February 1934, the *Seattle Times* runs a feature story on a "Modern Robinson Crusoe" living on an island in Union Bay. On its squishy surface, Martin Moen has laid down planks and built a shack. He has a tin stove, blankets, an axe, a water jug, and a rowboat to take him to shore.

A Norwegian immigrant, Moen says he has "been wandering around from place to place for nearly all of my 81 years." He was originally a carpenter and a painter but has been unemployed for a long time. He tells the reporter his savings ran out the previous November, and he has spent the winter in his rowboat. In a Seattle winter, a rowboat would be a grim abode. Now he has a roof over his head.

This is not a story to elicit sympathy for the poor. The *Seattle Times* is a conservative paper; it runs sympathy stories in December, to generate donations for its Christmas fund. It pictures Martin Moen as an independent, self-reliant man who isn't asking for help.

"I'm free here and I like it," he tells the reporter who paddled out to see him. "The landlord doesn't come around every month. I don't have any nosy neighbors, no solicitors, no boss of any kind. I come and go as I like, eat when I want to, sleep when I want to, catch fish now and then and just enjoy myself generally."

The story is notable in what it does not say: when Martin Moen last worked, where he last lived, how he ended up with only a rowboat, how he built his shack, how he gets his food, or how he keeps himself clean. It does not say whether he is on relief. In King County in 1934, 11 percent of the population is on some kind of public assistance.

Living alone on a tiny island is unusual, but living in a shack is not. During the month the *Times* runs this story—February 1934—sociology student Donald Francis Roy is making his famous study of Hooverville. There are other encampments, and they stay in Seattle for the rest of the decade. By the winter of 1938–1939, the city has another encampment on the land between Magnolia and Queen Anne, one in the industrial district south of downtown, and one on the slopes of Beacon Hill. A census finds 22,104 people living in Seattle's squatter camps.

By the late 1930s, the newspapers, particularly the *Seattle Star*, are paying the camps more attention. The *Star*'s waterfront columnist, H. E. Jamison, writes about the "dehorns," men addicted to denatured alcohol.

"A dehorn," he writes, is "a walking skeleton . . . His drooping shoulders will jerk, his shifty eyes are glazed with drink, his lips are blue and his nose has a purple tinge. His facial muscles have long since ceased to function and look like wax that has started to melt . . . The color of his face will vary from an unhealthy yellow to an equally unhealthy red. His gait is a furtive shuffle."

Most of the shack dwellers, however, are better than that.

"The shacks have kept many of us off the bread line and relief," writes Hooverville resident Martin Olson in a letter to the *Post-Intelligencer*. "Early in the morning and late at night a number of small pushcarts are pushed along the streets gathering paper and junk; others launch their tiny boats to go out fishing or gather driftwood, haul it to shore, cut it up for wood and sell it. Others again get short jobs, while some go to the logging camps, harvest, hop and berry picking, etc., which enables them by strictest economy to live through the winter."

Toward the end of 1938, the *P-I* sends reporter Doris McIlroy to talk to the shack people. McIlroy finds what Selden Menefee and Donald Francis Roy found years earlier. "Shacktown is the end of the road for many of its inhabitants," she writes. "They are the ones, usually the old men, who lost their jobs when they were too old to land other employment." One is Ralph Burrows, who gets by on food vouchers. Asked if he looks for work, he says, "I used to go out all the time. Not now. I know it's no use." Another is Ely Vojodich, 59, a former meat cutter. He scrounges lumber from Elliott Bay and cuts it for firewood at a dollar a cord.

At a camp on Empire Way (now Martin Luther King Way), McIlroy finds a young couple with a baby girl—a family of a type more familiar to the *P-I*'s readers. The man is Orlan Frandsen, 24, eldest son of Frank Frandsen, who fought sheriff's deputies in a failed attempt to save the family home in 1933. Orlan, then 19, was sentenced to six months in jail. Now he is married. He and his wife Edna have a baby daughter, Arlene.

McIlroy's story makes no mention of the battle over the family home in 1933, which happened years before she joined the *Post-Intelligencer*. Her story does mention what happened after the Frandsens lost their home the second time, in 1935. Frank and Orlan Frandsen walked the streets until they found an old house whose owner wanted it torn down. They used the lumber to build a two-room shack. "At first it was just a shelter," Frank Frandsen says. "Now it's a home." It has a stove, a refrigerator, and electric lights. The 1940 Census finds the family still living there and Orlan Frandsen still unemployed. The 1950 Census lists him as a plasterboard installer.

———

The late-1930s newspaper stories of shack dwellers reflect a growing public demand for the shacks to be gone. "The problem can be solved only by

Martin Moen on his swampy island, visible to the right of the shack, 2-25-1934. © *The Seattle Times*.

providing other and more suitable accommodations for these unfortunate people," says the state director of the Works Progress Administration (WPA), Don G. Abel. In 1939, the legislature passes a public housing bill to tap into federal loan money. The city council sets up the Seattle Housing Authority under Jesse Epstein, the public-housing advocate who had lobbied to create it.

The Housing Authority's first project is Yesler Terrace. The law requires that it be built on the site of a slum. The Authority chooses "Profanity Hill"—First Hill—a mixed-race area of old houses overlooking

the downtown. Of the 971 people forcibly displaced, 429 are Japanese. The project destroys 471 old units and builds 271 new ones—solid ones, built better than the housing that will be thrown up during the war.

Yesler Terrace opens in November 1941, a few weeks before the attack on Pearl Harbor. The project is a success. Under the federal housing law, it is the first project nationwide to be racially integrated, though the residents are mostly white, as is the city. The units are, however, reserved for families who are U.S. citizens. That knocks out immigrants from Japan, who are barred from citizenship by federal law. It also knocks out the

Moen preparing a meal of "duke's mixture." 2-25-1934. © *The* Seattle Times.

Hooverville men, most of whom are single and foreign-born. In any case, the Hooverville men are gone. Six months before Yesler Terrace opens, Hooverville is burned out to clear the site for use by the armed forces.

6
Relief, 1931–1935

Relief of the unemployed does not start with Franklin Roosevelt. In Seattle, the first big effort starts with two West Seattle socialists, Carl Brannin and Hulet Wells.

Carl Brannin is a Texan. Brannin comes to the socialist creed by reading the works of single taxers and social Christians. In World War I he declares himself a pacifist. Ruled unfit for the military, he is sent instead to investigate labor problems in the war industries. In 1919, Brannin reads of the Seattle General Strike and is inspired. He and his wife, Laura, move to Seattle and live in a shack that was built by an anarchist. He has no work but inherits some oil land in Texas. His oil income allows him to devote his time to the Seattle Labor College, a socialist institution founded in 1920.

Hulet Wells is from Skagit County. In 1909, he is fired by the Post Office for promoting a union. In 1912, he runs as a Socialist for mayor of Seattle and takes almost 22 percent of the vote in a five-way primary. After the U.S. entry into World War I, he is prosecuted under the Sedition Act for spreading propaganda against the draft. Convicted, he is sent to McNeil Island, where he is put into solitary confinement after refusing to do "slave labor." After his release, he travels to Russia to witness the Communist revolution.

In 1929, Brannin and Wells are among the members of Friends of the Soviet Union that meet the Russian aviators at Sand Point. The next year they create a monthly socialist paper. They name it *The Vanguard*—a riff on Lenin's slogan, "vanguard of the proletariat." Brannin and Wells admire the Soviet Union, but they are not members of the Communist Party.

In the summer of 1931, their focus is on unemployment. Tens of thousands of people are out of work in Seattle, and little is being done to help them. Writing in *The Vanguard*, Brannin and Wells call for a meeting of the jobless in West Seattle. Forty people show up, and the Unemployed Citizens League is born. Its long-term goal is a system of unemployment insurance. Its immediate effort is to provide food for the people out of work.

Brannin and Wells organize volunteers to pick strawberries for farmers and take their pay in berries. Volunteers harvest fruit that is worth too little for owners to pick. They catch fish. They chop down trees and cut firewood. They collect coal laying on the ground. They mend clothes and cobble shoes, donating their labor.

This private program is Seattle's first response to mass unemployment. Historian William H. Mullins writes that it fits Herbert Hoover's ideal of "cooperative individualism." That's not Brannin's and Wells's ideal. They are using private effort because it is what they have. When local government offers money, they will accept it—and the nature of their group will change.

———

Seattle has been receiving no state or federal money for people out of work, and in the winter of 1931–1932, the *Seattle Times* proudly declares that it doesn't need any. "Any fairly well-balanced community with a normal diversification of interests can take care of itself," the editors say. Following this line, King County and the City of Seattle agree to provide the destitute with food, clothing, fuel, and paid work.

To head the effort, Seattle mayor Robert Harlin appoints Irving F. Dix, the local manager for Pacific Telephone & Telegraph Company. Public service is part of his role. Dix is president of the Seattle Chamber of Commerce and the Seattle Community Fund.

To get a sense of his new task, Dix dons old clothes and mingles with the men on skid road. He sees what the Unemployed Citizens League is doing and asks them to staff the county-city food banks. He is given no money to pay them, but they are used to that.

In the fall of 1931, the city borrows money to pay the unemployed to clear land on Beacon Hill. The pay is based on need: $1.50 a day for single men, $2.50 for those with two to four dependents and $3.50 for those with larger families. City councilman Ralph Nichols, head of the council's finance committee, supports paying people this way. The city doesn't have the funds to pay $4.50 ($91 in 2024 dollars), the city's rate for common labor, he says. And to him, this isn't real work; real work, he says, is when "a person hires another capable of doing work the employer wants done. This is a case where work is created which otherwise would not be done at this time, and it is to be done by persons who may or may not be capable, but who are given it because of the urgency of their needs."

To the Unemployed Citizens' League, this *is* real work, the same as any other. The League insists that the city pay $4.50 a day. The Seattle Central Labor Council agrees. Union leaders don't want their members' wages undercut by the reliefers' cheap labor. The city council agrees with the unions and accepts the $4.50 wage. The city spreads the money by employing men for only two days a week. But Nichols is right about the funds. On the day after Christmas, the money runs out and the work ends.

―――――

In December 1931 the chamber of commerce in Tenino, Thurston County, prints scrip—unofficial money—to be redeemed later from the assets of a closed bank. In a flash of inspiration, it prints the 25-cent, 50-cent, and one-dollar scrip on cigar-box slabs of wood. Tenino's wooden money makes the news. Most of it is bought by tourists and never redeemed.

Taking a cue from Tenino, a group of architects and engineers led by Miles Clark and Charles Newhall offer the Seattle City Council a massive plan to fund street, sewer, and bridge projects with zero-interest, 20-year notes. To give the notes value, the city would accept them for the payment of taxes and to buy municipal bonds. What use the city would have for a pile of its own IOUs is not explained. The city council goes through the motions of considering this proposal and drops it.

Roy E. Furse, superintendent of the Seattle Municipal Street Railway, has a plan to pay laborers in streetcar tokens. He tells the city council that he has empty seats on the streetcars and plenty of tokens. Paying in streetcar rides would cost the system nothing. The councilmen know better. Men paid with bags of tokens would sell them at a discount to brokers, and the brokers would sell them to riders. And that *would* cost the system something. The council says no. Later in the Depression, streetcar riders will create an illicit market in one-hour transfers, with the same effect.

The council does allow the Water Department to put 500 unemployed men to work on a reservoir in West Seattle and pay them partly in credit on their water bills. But eight civil service workers file suit, arguing that the work belongs to them, and a judge orders the work stopped.

Relief workers don't want to be paid in water-bill credit or streetcar tokens. They want to be paid in money. Relief director I. F. Dix agrees; at Pacific Telephone, he pays his people in money, not in credit on their phone bills. Pacific Telephone never cuts pay rates in the Depression. But local government has a weaker revenue stream than the phone company. In mid-1932, Dix gives up as relief director and goes back to Pacific Telephone.

By tradition and law, the job of feeding the down-and-out falls to county governments. To do this, King County hands out food. "While it is true that the present so-called dole system is perhaps the worst for the individual," says Commissioner Don G. Evans, "it is the best for the taxpayer."

Food aid is reserved for people who have lived in the county six months and have no income. People who scam the system are subject to penalties. In 1932, Elmer M. Johnston, a man with a wife and two children, is sentenced to six months in jail for quitting his $80-a-month job and applying for free food.

Social workers police the relief system by questioning applicants about their work, income, and assets. This is intrusive, and people resent it. The *Vanguard*—Brannin's and Wells's socialist weekly—condemns the county's "inquisitorial social welfare methods." At a mass meeting of the Unemployed Citizens League in March 1932, unemployed men boo officials and demand that aid be given freely.

The county is barely able to give anything. It is buying food with warrants. When its outstanding warrants put it over the debt limit set in the state constitution, a citizen takes it to court, demanding that the warrants stop. The citizen loses. In June 1932 the Washington Supreme Court rules that to relieve hunger the county may issue all the debt it needs. The banks, however, are a stronger wall of no. They won't buy the county's warrants, and brokers will buy them only at a discount. The more warrants the county issues, the greater the discount. By November 1932, the discount on King County's warrants rises to 20 percent.

A more long-term solution would be to sell bonds, but state law caps bond interest at 6 percent. At that yield, investors don't want King County's bonds. The state could sell bonds, but the state's businessman-governor, Roland Hartley, has had the state pay down more than three-quarters of its debt during his two terms in office. Hartley refuses to soil the state's balance sheet. "Funds for relief should be raised and spent by local taxing units, where proper investigation of needs can be made," he says in July 1932. "There's nobody going to starve in Washington."

King County keeps providing food and paying in warrants.

In May 1932 the *Seattle Times* reports that Communists are promoting a "Red Utopia" at the food banks. The *Seattle Star* makes fun of the *Times*' story, but the story is not false. The League has been complaining about the Reds in its own paper. And years later, a former Communist Party man recalls the story in the *Star*. His fellow Communists, he writes, refused to catch fish and pick apples for the food banks because they believed in relief as a matter of right. To the Reds, by providing the food, the League was letting the capitalists off the hook. The Communists joined the League when it began receiving public money, because when it did that, it could no longer deny food to those who refused to work.

On July 4, 1932, a caravan of protesters from the Unemployed Citizens League converges on Olympia to demand state spending on relief. The protesters insist that Governor Hartley call a special session of the legislature. Hartley is out of town. It's Independence Day, and he's at his son's house in Everett having a picnic. As 600 protesters stake out the steps of the capitol, a brawl erupts. Challenging Carl Brannin and his League men is a group of Communists. The League men prevail, but back in Seattle a few weeks later, the Communists vote them out of League leadership. Under

On their way to Olympia. *Author's collection.*

its new leader, William H. Murray, the Unemployed Citizens League adopts a radical constitution that announces its "uncompromising hostility to all forms of professional philanthropy" and its aim to control the food banks. Murray will admit later to being a member of the Communist Party.

The radicals' first fight with King County is over meat. The county has been providing the Unemployed Citizens League with beef carcasses, which provide steaks as well as cheaper cuts. In August 1932 the county starts buying stew meat at a lower cost per pound. The League's new leaders reject the meat. William Beehe, manager of the White Center food bank, says, "I don't want my wife standing over a hot stove all day cooking stew. I'd rather take a little less meat and get a better cut so we could have a steak. This is the time of year when everybody who can is buying steaks. We have had to take what's left. I don't see why we shouldn't be able to have steak once in a while."

These are provocative words. County commissioners are not about to provide steak to men on relief. Nor will they take orders from men who demand it. In September 1932 the commissioners move to seize the food banks.

When the county's manager arrives at the food bank in Seattle's Georgetown district, workers refuse to accept him. By donating their labor, they feel they have earned the right to manage themselves. "We won't be slaves," declares Carl Tuber, the League's man there. "We worked here for months, running the commissary and saving the taxpayers money. We received no salaries ... We will not work under a paid boss." But in the end, they do. The county is buying the groceries, and it wins the argument.

The county has been paying in warrants instead of cash. It plans to pay back the warrants by selling bonds. In November 1932, county voters approve two bond issues: $1 million to redeem outstanding warrants and $2 million to fund the food banks going forward. But in the same election, statewide voters approve a cap on the property tax, which makes it impossible for the county to sell its bonds. Instead, the county borrows its relief money from the Hoover administration's Reconstruction Finance Corporation.

The Democratic victory of November 1932—more on this later—changes things for the unemployed. For the first time, federal grants, rather than loans, are available to the states for direct relief. In January 1933, legislators in Olympia pass the McDonald Act, which sets up county welfare boards to administer the money. The act keeps control of the money in the hands of the state, which means the radicals at the Unemployed Citizens League will not control it.

In February 1933 the League responds by sending 4,000 protesters to occupy the City-County Building in downtown Seattle. The protest is in the wrong place. Realizing its mistake, the League organizes a new protest. Two hundred cars, many of them from Whatcom, Skagit, and Snohomish counties, converge on Olympia.

On March 2, 1933, protesters meet with the state's new Democratic governor, Clarence Martin. They demand that he repeal the McDonald Act and permit them to parade through Olympia. Martin is no radical, and he takes umbrage at their "demands." He tells them he cannot repeal the law that he just signed and that he does not control the streets of Olympia. Like his Republican predecessor, Martin gives them nothing. The League's paper, *The Vanguard*, complains afterward that the protesters have been "blocked at every turn by Governor Martin and a legislature dominated by capitalist interests."

Under the McDonald Act, the state shuts down the food banks and replaces them with food vouchers. To qualify for relief, an unemployed person can keep his house and car, but will have to spend down any securities and cash. Under the new policies, 1,000 people are purged from the relief rolls in King County.

The Unemployed Citizens League is stripped of its public role. The Communists control the League, and the League controls nothing. Of the League's founders, Carl Brannin returns to Texas, where he will run for governor in 1936 as a socialist. Hulet Wells takes a relief job in a public park. Later he will go to work for Seattle congressman Marion Zioncheck.

In 1933, nationwide unemployment reaches 25.2 percent. This is slightly higher than in 1932 and is the highest rate of any year in the 20th century.

In King County, conflict continues over relief. For single men, the county pays a cafeteria near Pioneer Square to provide two meals a day. Before it did this, says county commissioner John C. Stevenson, "the men were largely patronizing Japanese places." Under the new system, he says, the men are getting "the best food they have ever had." The men don't think so. In

November 1933, the men at the welfare cafeteria boo Stevenson and fellow commissioner Wilmer Brinton. The *Times* reporter writes that the men "threatened to carry some of the kitchen's food to the commissioners and make them eat it."

In early 1934, the other commissioner, Louis Nash, agrees with the men. Nash writes that the welfare kitchen serves cheap, poor-quality food, much of it "wholly unfit for human consumption." He also accuses the county of paying an above-market price to the contractor, a pal of Stevenson's. The contractor replies that it's unfair to compare his price with restaurant prices, because the county pays him in warrants that aren't worth face value.

Work requirements also bring conflict. Most people agree that men on relief should have to work, but which men, and what kind of work? By mid-1933, only single men are required to work. At the county's farm near Boeing Field, they cultivate potatoes, corn, squash, pumpkins, turnips, celery, cucumbers, and cabbage.

The men resent that relief work pays less than regular work. J. C. Black, chairman of the King County Welfare Board, makes no apologies. "The Board has consistently felt that there is little, if any, connection between work done in exchange for relief and regular work for wages," he says in March 1933. In August, money runs short and relief payments are cut 20 percent. The Unemployed Citizens League complains that the single men get only 90 cents' worth of groceries for one day of work a week.

In October 1933, 500 single men refuse to work until they are paid in cash. After three weeks of giving them nothing, the state relents and gives them vouchers for food.

In mid-November the Civil Works Administration (CWA) begins offering cash for work. The CWA is the New Deal's "leaf-raking" agency. Within a few days, it has 1,100 at work in Seward Park, 950 at Fort Lawton, and 400 at Woodland Park. It pays unskilled labor 50 cents an hour—$12 an hour in 2024 dollars. It's a rate that beats anything the state can offer and is such good pay that it begins enticing men out of jobs in private industry. In King County, men who refuse CWA jobs continue to receive vouchers for food.

In 1934 the national unemployment rate falls to 21.7 percent. In 1935, it is stuck at 20.1 percent. Most Americans accept the need for relief in a social emergency, but the thought of millions of people on the dole year after year makes them uneasy.

In his State of the Union speech on January 4, 1935, President Roosevelt says: "The lessons of history, confirmed by the evidence immediately before me, show conclusively that continued dependence upon relief induces a spiritual and moral disintegration fundamentally destructive to the national fiber. It is inimical to the dictates of sound policy. It is in violation of the tradition of America. Work must be found for able-bodied but destitute workers."

"The federal government must and shall quit this business of relief," the president says. "I am not willing that the vitality of our people be further sapped by the giving of cash, or market baskets, [for] a few hours of weekly work cutting grass, raking leaves or picking up papers in the public parks. We must preserve not only the bodies of the unemployed from destitution, but also their self-respect, their self-reliance, courage and determination."

Franklin Roosevelt's enemies will throw these words back at him many times. Over the next few years, however, the New Deal does shift its relief spending to paid work. But creating meaningful work takes time. In February 1935 in King County, 56,433 men, women, and children—12.2 percent of the population—are on relief. Keeping them alive is a problem that won't wait.

To the Congress, Roosevelt proposes a $4.8 billion program—an immense sum in 1930s dollars—to create work. This is to be real work, not leaf-raking. The bill sails through Congress and becomes the Works Progress Administration (WPA). Of all the things the New Deal does, the WPA will be most fondly remembered. It will pay the idle to build things all across America. In Seattle it will build the northern and southern ends of the Ballard Bridge, replacing wood pilings with concrete. But in 1935 the WPA is still getting organized and employs few until late in the year.

Meanwhile, local authorities dole out grocery vouchers for people who have no money for food. In Washington state, applicants for relief must sign a "Declaration of Resources," attesting that they are paupers. But problems arise. What if a person with no money for food has a house worth thousands of dollars? You can't eat a house. From 1931 to 1933 Wynta Diana Meria of Seattle collects $175 in food relief while owning a house. In April 1935, the King County Superior Court rules that under the law, the state can claw back that money from the sale of her house after she dies.

A few persons are caught wrongly filing for relief. King County prosecutor Warren Magnuson charges Russian immigrant Sarah McFarland, 54, with taking $175 of state food coupons when she had $3,500. She saved the money while working as a charwoman in Alaska. Her husband doesn't know about her nest egg, but her banker does when she takes it out in cash. Confronted by police, she leads them to a roll of bills stuffed behind a shingle in the basement of her Seattle house.

In July 1935 Sarah McFarland is convicted of grand larceny in King County Superior Court. The court imposes the highest sentence, 15 years at the state penitentiary in Walla Walla. Reality is not so harsh: she will be paroled after six months.

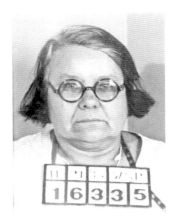

Sarah McFarland, chiseler.
Washington State Archives.

Relief for the unemployed—who should get it, how much, and whether work should be required—remains an issue all through the 1930s.

An alternative to relief is to set up the unemployed as farmers. It's an idea that speaks deeply to Americans, particularly the old people who can remember the 1870s, 1880s, and 1890s.

The conservative press loves it. "What could be better or more practical," the *Seattle Times* says, "than the settling of the unemployed on the soil, where they could become self-supporting, independent and taxpayers?"

To try out the idea, the New Deal creates the Resettlement Administration. In May 1935, it sends 133 farm families through Seattle on their way to settle the Matanuska Valley near Anchorage, Alaska. Seattle politicians greet them, and the newspapers run page-one stories about them.

The settlers are excited by the adventure. They are farm families that have lost their farms in Minnesota, Michigan, and Wisconsin—northern states—and are on relief. Instead of giving them money, the Federal Emergency Relief Administration is providing each family with 40 acres of Alaska bottomland, where the soil is said to be 14 feet deep. They are also given dairy cattle, tents, supplies, and lumber for houses. The growing season in Alaska is short, but during the long summer days, plants can grow fast.

Not all public voices are enthusiastic about the back-to-the-land idea. One Seattle left-wing weekly dismisses Matanuska as a "utopia of mosquitoes, hunger, malnutrition [and] disease." Another calls resettlement in general "a particularly vicious measure [that] would permanently stabilize the now-unemployed in poverty." On the liberal *Seattle Star*, journalist Jim Marshall dispenses advice to those who would try homesteading around Seattle. Clearing land of stumps and starting a farm requires "hard, muscular labor," he writes. "There is no such thing as 'starting from the ground up' with nothing." He adds, "Any man who goes to the land ought to have at least one year's living expenses—and preferably two—in his pocket or bank before he starts."

There are such men and women, and from 1930 to 1935 the number of farms in King County increases by 24 percent. But these are people choosing their land and risking their money individually. Designing a back-to-the-land project and recruiting settlers is a different thing. It depends on what the recruiter is trying to do—and on what the participants know, how much they risk, and how much they expect to be helped.

In King County several back-to-the-land projects make the news. One is Newhaven, a sweat-equity co-op on land around Lake Joy. Its newspaper ad in February 1934 begins: "Going to Profit by Mr. Roosevelt's New Deal? Low rate Gov't funds now available for income-bearing modern garden homes in model community ... No capital needed."

The promoter, Henry O. Zwarg, has no government funds. He and his associates sell 600 memberships at $5 and $10 each. The state denies them permission to sell bonds because of Zwarg's previous activities, but they sell the bonds anyway. Members are allocated five-acre tracts on land in the Cascade foothills—cut-over Weyerhaeuser land covered with stumps. The new pioneers are to clear the stumps, which will take several years. Their work will increase the value of the land. They are to keep some of the land, but not all of it.

The project fails. In 1936 Zwarg is sentenced to 20 months at the McNeil Island penitentiary for stealing the members' fees.

In early 1933 the King County Welfare Board begins a back-to-the-land project at Lake Forest Park. More than a dozen relief families are placed

Back to the land, as seen by the *Seattle Times*. *Cartoon by Stuart Pratt*, 1-22-1933. © *The Seattle Times*.

on 1¾-acre lots. Settlers are given lumber for houses and a few garden tools, with the cost to be deducted from their relief checks. The settlers will have to pay for the land, but their first payments are not due until 1935. When the day comes, however, only two of the 14 families make their payments of $10.

The settlers are unhappy. Lake Forest Park is 13 miles north of downtown Seattle, and most of the settlers have no outside work. Each week the Washington Emergency Relief Administration gives them vouchers and surplus food—meat, rice, vegetables, or milk. But the agency offers each family no gardening tools other than a mattock, a shovel, a rake, and a hoe. The settlers are on stump land with acidic soil that is poor for growing greens. They write a complaining letter to Federal Relief Administrator Harry Hopkins in which they say, "Few of us had any success because we had no fertilizer nor any way of getting any."

Federal aid is reserved for people on real farms, not 1¾-acre lots. The state offers to take the land back and relieve them of their debt—but they don't want to give up their homes.

For a few hardy folks, back-to-the-land is an idea that works, but for most urban people of the 1930s it is not. In the summer of 1935, John H. Shields, the head of Seattle's city employment office, complains that he can't fill all the openings for wood cutters, farm hands, and milkers. "A good many persons," he says, "would rather remain on relief and in the city than go to work in the country."

Grumbling comes from Alaska, too. All through the summer of 1935, families dribble back from the Matanuska Valley, complaining that the government didn't help them as promised. A Seattle doctor who visits the colony says the colonists expected too much. By 1940, more than half the families have gone, and by 1948, two-thirds have gone. The rest mostly stay. Decades later the project will be celebrated as a test of endurance. But for most Americans, back-to-the-land projects like Matanuska are not practical ways out of the Depression.

7
Hope, 1932–1936

On July 2, 1932, Democrats choose their nominee for president. The next morning, the *Seattle Post-Intelligencer* runs a page-one editorial. Publisher William Randolph Hearst declares, "Franklin D. Roosevelt will make a great President of the United States." To Hearst, Roosevelt is the man to make the Europeans pay their war debts. Day after day the *P-I* runs cartoons portraying Herbert Hoover as a weakling being bullied by Britain and France.

Hearst is a Democrat, and the *P-I*'s support is expected. Eyebrows rise when the Republican *Seattle Times* gives Roosevelt a page-one endorsement the same day. The *Times* has gone wet, and on Prohibition, Hoover remains stubbornly dry. Both the *Times* and *P-I* will turn against Roosevelt, but not in 1932.

None of Seattle's dailies see Roosevelt as an agent of big change. "There has been nothing in his public statements thus far to alarm the conservatives," reports W. W. Jermane, the *Times*' man in Washington, DC. Says B. C. Forbes, Hearst's business columnist, "Very few people in the financial world, even the most ardent Republicans, really fear that Franklin Roosevelt, if elected, would do anything very terrible."

Forbes will have a much different view in 1936.

The *Star*, Seattle's liberal daily, is not sure Roosevelt is liberal enough. The *Star* has been grumbling for months that America is ruled by the rich. Hoover is rich, but at least he earned his money. Roosevelt inherited his. But the *Star* cannot tolerate Hoover's aid to big business and his "insane building of higher and higher tariff walls." Late in the campaign, the *Star* endorses Roosevelt.

In the summer of 1932, thousands of veterans of World War I camp out in Washington, DC, to demand payment of a bonus they are supposed to receive in 1945. President Hoover gives the "Bonus Army" nothing. At the same time, protesters from the Unemployed Citizens League descend on Governor Roland Hartley in Olympia to demand that he support the unemployed. He also gives them nothing. Both Hoover and Hartley are making a stand for self-reliance, but history is against them. In Seattle, the newly elected mayor John Dore tells a crowd that neither man "has an understanding of what is confronting us, neither has sympathy for the little man who most needs help, and neither knows what to do."

In the primary election of September 1932, Governor Hartley loses the Republican nomination for a third term. His defeat is a warning to Republicans. A tsunami is coming.

As their nominee for governor, Democrats choose Clarence Martin, the mayor of Cheney in Spokane County. Martin's politics are centrist. Like Hartley, Martin is a mill owner—a small flour mill—but he is not the hard man Hartley is. In the primary, Martin beats two candidates to his left.

To challenge Wesley Jones, 69, the dry, high-tariff Republican who has represented Washington in the Senate since 1909, the Democrats nominate Homer T. Bone, the attorney for the Port of Tacoma. Bone is a progressive. In 1912 he ran for Pierce County prosecutor as a Socialist. In 1922 he ran for state representative on the Farmer-Labor Party ticket, and was elected. Now 49, Bone is a champion of public power and taxing the rich.

Times publisher Clarance Blethen, who is rich—he has a penthouse and a yacht—is aghast that the Democrats would give their Senate nomination to a radical who "never by any stretch of the imagination could be considered a Democrat." Bone denies he is a radical. In a letter to Blethen, Bone says he opposes communism, property confiscation, free love, racketeering, and doles—"especially doles to business."

To run against Seattle's Republican congressman, Ralph Horr, the Democrats pick Marion Zioncheck, the former ASUW president who denounced Darwin Meisnest for turning the UW's student organization into a business. Zioncheck, 31, has since served as the attorney for the Unemployed Citizens League. The *Times* brands Zioncheck a radical—and Zioncheck proudly admits he is.

For the election of November 8, 1932:

The *Times* endorses Roosevelt;
The *Post-Intelligencer* endorses Roosevelt and Bone;
The *Star* endorses Roosevelt, Martin, Bone, and Zioncheck.

And all of them win. The election is a flood tide of Democrats. Franklin Roosevelt gets 57 percent of the vote in Washington. In Olympia, the

Democrats go from 9 percent of House seats to 71 percent, giving Democrats control of the lower chamber for the first time since statehood. They also take the Senate. Voters throw out a raft of Republicans, including J. Grant Hinkle, the secretary of state who approved Adolph Linden's stock offering for the American Broadcasting Company.

A notable winner is the man who will later serve as U.S. senator from World War II to the beginning of the Reagan era: Warren G. Magnuson. In 1932, "Maggie" is 28, an attorney in private practice, and an ally of Homer Bone. He is elected to the House of Representatives in Olympia. There he will be one of the authors of the McDonald Act, by which the state takes responsibility for the unemployed.

Franklin Delano Roosevelt. *The* Seattle Star, *8-19-1932, p. 1.*

Also notable is Vic Meyers, the mustachioed jazz band conductor who wields the baton in Seattle's Trianon Ballroom. Earlier in 1932, *Times* reporter Doug Welch talked Meyers into running for mayor of Seattle as a joke candidate. Meyers was the candidate of "sax appeal." When asked about civic problems, Meyers said, "The saxophone will solve them all!" At the meeting of the Shrine Club in the Olympic Hotel, Meyers paraded himself as Mohandas Gandhi, dragging a live goat and wearing nothing but trunks, a sheet, and a silk hat.

When Meyers lost his race for mayor, he told the public he was done. "I'm glad the campaign is over," he wrote in a page-one article in the *Times*. "It's about time I went home and washed the dog." But he's not done. In the fall elections he files for lieutenant governor. The press ignores him; the laughs are over. But he wins the primary, and in November, the Democratic tide pulls him in. Washington's new lieutenant governor will never be a hard-edged pol, but he is a skillful showman.

———

In early 1933, bank failures reach a national crisis. In Washington, banks fail in Palouse, Port Angeles, Sequim, Centralia, Walla Walla, Colfax, and

Blaine. On March 1, legislators in Olympia rush through a bill allowing Governor Martin to close all the banks in the state. In the hours before it goes into effect, crowds throng Seattle's banking district along Second Avenue. Worried depositors double-park their cars as they rush in to get cash.

The utility companies and department stores have cash to pay employees, but except at City Light and the Water Department, city workers are paid in warrants. Boeing has no cash for its 1,600 employees but lines up credit at gas stations and grocery stores.

On Saturday, March 4, Franklin Roosevelt takes the oath of office. In his inaugural address, he declares in biblical language that the crisis has been caused by "practices of the unscrupulous money changers." He says, "The money changers have fled from their high seats in the temple of our civilization. We may now restore that temple to the ancient truths."

Shortly after, the new president invokes the Trading with the Enemy Act, a law passed to give Woodrow Wilson emergency powers during World War I. Roosevelt declares a national emergency and orders all banks closed for a week. The New York Stock Exchange shuts down.

On Sunday, March 12, the president addresses the nation by radio. His rhetoric softens. "We had a bad banking situation," he says. "Some of our bankers had shown themselves either incompetent or dishonest in their handling of the people's funds. They had used the money entrusted to them in speculations and unwise loans. This was of course not true of the vast majority of our banks, but it was true in enough of them to put the people in a frame of mind where they did not differentiate." The president assures the people that their banks will reopen when proven sound.

No president has used radio like this. Roosevelt's "fireside chat" is a masterful performance. "The American people are gratified by the president's method and tone," says the *Seattle Times*. "He is letting them know precisely what they may expect of him."

Of Washington's 150 state-chartered banks, 100 will reopen at the end of the bank holiday and 33 more by December. Only four state banks will fail during the rest of 1933, which will be the last year without deposit insurance.

Seattle's bankers are eager to show how strong their banks are. They offer to reopen early, using $15 million in scrip they have printed: $1, $5, $10, and $20 bills. During the Panic of 1907, they used scrip for four months. This time, the U.S. Treasury says no. In 1935 the bankers will take the unused scrip to the Seattle Gas Company plant—now Gasworks Park—and burn it.

Banks reopen in Seattle on Monday, March 14, 1933, the same as in other cities. The Federal Reserve supplies them with new currency, but mostly they don't need it. On the first day, depositors bring back $20 million, some of it in gold coin. One depositor brings in $50,000 in gold. Another brings in $11,000.

By reopening only the strong banks, the government has restored depositors' confidence. On March 15, the New York Stock Exchange reopens. The Dow Jones Industrials jump 15.34 percent, the largest one-day gain in the 20th century.

To prevent another banking crisis, Congress creates the Federal Deposit Insurance Corporation. Deposit insurance is not a new idea. Earlier in the century, it was tried in eight states and failed in all of them. Washington was one. Its insurance plan, created in 1917, was voluntary—for the bank, not the depositor—and only high-risk banks signed up for it. In 1922, the largest bank in the pool failed and wiped out the entire insurance fund.

This time the insurer is the federal government, and all national banks are required to join. State banks don't have to join, but in Washington most do. On January 1, 1934, the FDIC will begin insuring deposits up to $2,500. The system will not fail.

The *Seattle Times* says Congress has given Franklin Roosevelt "greater powers than any president ever has enjoyed in time of peace"—powers that are "almost dictatorial." But that's all right, the *Times* says. "Conditions such as those confronting him had to be met immediately."

Without accusing the president of anything bad, Hearst's *Post-Intelligencer* makes allusions to the dictatorships. Arthur Brisbane, whose column runs on page one, writes, "The will of one man, Stalin, rules 150,000,000 in Russia. Another man's will rules Turkey, another Italy, and now Hitler, imitation of Mussolini, rules with absolute power in Germany. Even in this country the dictator idea becomes fashionable. Millions believe that Congress, supposed to make laws, should step aside and let one man, President Roosevelt, do everything."

The *Star* bridles at the *P-I*'s comparison of America's new president to Benito Mussolini. "He seized his power; we gave ours freely and fully," the

106 *Seattle in the Great Depression*

In Safe Hands!

Hearst will change his mind about this. *Cartoon by Walter J. Enright.* Seattle Post-Intelligencer, *3-13-1933.* © Hearst Communications Inc.

Star says. "And we can take it back just as easily. We will take it back just as soon as the emergency is over."

On April 5, 1933, President Roosevelt issues Executive Order 6102. It orders Americans to turn in all gold bullion and coins in excess of $100, except collector coins, by May 1. Once again, he invokes the Trading with the Enemy Act.

The *Seattle Times* applauds. It compares the president to a mechanic fixing a car: "Temporarily at least, the American people have made their decision," the editors write. "They have put a master mechanic on the job and told him to go ahead; he has been given blanket orders to use his own judgment; not to pay any attention to what has been done, but to get the car going and do so quickly. All the helpers have received orders to do as the new man says and not ask any questions."

The state of Washington also pushes for authority. The legislature has voted to issue $10 million in unemployment-relief bonds without a vote of the people. The state constitution allows this much borrowing without a vote only in cases of invasion or insurrection. The legislature says there is an *incipient insurrection*. State Rep. Warren Magnuson and two other officials defend this position in Thurston County Superior Court.

E. F. Blaine, a member of the Yakima County Democratic Committee, objects. "There has not been the semblance of an insurrection or rebellion in this state," he writes. "There has not even been much violence." He is right about that, but it is a losing argument. In June 1933 the Washington Supreme Court votes 5–3 to allow the state to sell the bonds. Finding buyers for them all will be difficult, and will take months. King County's relief bonds, approved by voters a year earlier, have no public market, though in December 1933 the state buys a few of them. The county continues paying its bills in warrants, which trade at a 15- to 20-percent discount.

———

Since 1929, commodity prices have fallen, making it harder for producers to earn the dollars to pay debts. Canada, Britain, Germany, and Japan have cut their currencies from gold, so their products have fallen in price even further. Washington exporters have lost business in pulp, paper, lumber, wheat, flour, and fruit. Most of the 15 pulp mills in the state have closed.

On April 18, 1933, President Roosevelt takes America off the gold standard. The dollar drops 15 percent against foreign currencies. Americans brace themselves for a shock, and none comes. Instead, investors rush to buy stocks, and speculators bid up the dollar prices of wheat, corn, rye, oats, cotton, rubber, hides, wool, silk, tin, zinc, lead, sugar, and lard. Their rise, says Hearst columnist B. C. Forbes, is "hectic, spectacular, booming, historic."

Devaluation risks inflation, but by April 1933, prices have fallen so low that inflation seems a distant danger. Seattle banker George Greenwood tells the *Post-Intelligencer* he reckons it's better to let a man pay his debt in 50-cent dollars than to write it off as a loss. The *Seattle Times* argues that devaluing the dollar will help exports and "enable our own industries to put large numbers of men to work."

In May 1933, Congress authorizes the president to create $3 billion ($72 billion in 2024 dollars) in new money. On the news alone, consumers rush to buy. Stores restock shelves. From March through July 1933, factory payrolls increase by one-third. Industrial output jumps 69 percent. Going

Not any more. *Author's scan of old $10 bill.*

off gold does more to turn the tide than anything Roosevelt will do in the next eight years.

In mid-June, more than a dozen ships at anchor in Lake Union file out through the Ballard Locks and return to service. By August, Seattle's foreign trade more than doubles from its level in the last months of the gold standard.

Another milestone is passed in 1933: Prohibition ends. The Democrats promised to bring back alcoholic drinks, and they do.

The people are ready. For more than 15 years, they have been drinking illegal moonshine and home brew, or paying top dollar for branded liquor smuggled from British Columbia. All this now changes. For Washington state, the first step comes in November 1932 with the passage of Initiative 61, which repeals all state laws against alcoholic drinks except the ban on its sale to minors.

At the federal level, the 18th Amendment won't be repealed until November 1933, but legal brew returns in April. It's only 3.2 percent compared with an average 3.7 percent in the old days, but it's *beer*. In Seattle the party begins just past midnight on April 7 at Rippe's Cafe at 1423 Fourth Avenue. (Its owner, Frank Rippe, is one of the men who posted bail for Ahira Pierce.) Hemrich Brewing, which had been making "near beer" during Prohibition, has already geared up with the real stuff. At cheap taprooms, a six-ounce glass is a nickel; at better places, a ten-ounce glass is a dime. The beer goes fast, and there follows a day of drought. Then six boxcars of Rainier arrive from San Francisco, and the party resumes.

With beer comes money for bartenders and barmaids, barrels, glasses, taps, and trucks. In the first month, the city books $104,850 in license fees. It hires two tavern inspectors. The Rainier Brewing Company promises to reopen its Seattle brewery. The Olympia Brewing Company has a stock offering to finance a new brewery at Tumwater.

Years later, the owner of the Mayflower Park Hotel, built in 1927, will complain that its kitchen was built too small because Prohibition reduced the profitability of restaurants. That now changes. Hotels, restaurants, and clubs are invigorated by legal alcohol.

Late in 1933, Governor Clarence Martin calls a special session of the legislature to make the new rules for intoxicating drinks. Since Prohibition ended, liquor, wine, and beer have been in a free market. Historian Norman Clark describes the result: "There was beer available across the street from public schools. Free lunches appeared on the polished mahogany, as did 'whiskey-flavored tonics' with an alcoholic content in excess of 40 per cent. There were taxi dancers, service to minors, and shootings."

In January 1934, the legislature creates the Washington State Liquor Control Board. The law, complains the *Seattle Times*, "is loaded down with prohibitions, as well as with rank discriminations and absurd penalties." It gives the state a monopoly on the sale of liquor by the bottle. It allows taverns to sell beer by the drink, but none stronger than 4 percent. It forbids the offer of two beers for the price of one. It forbids taverns from offering a free lunch for buying a glass of beer, which they did before Prohibition. It forbids women from sitting at the bar.

Clarence Martin. *The* Seattle Star, *8-19-1932, p. 4.*

The law allows the sale of wine by the drink only with restaurant meals. It permits hard liquor by the drink only in private clubs. The rules are onerous, and people figure out ways around them. In 1939, the *Argus* will write, "Some of the 'clubs'... are identical to the speakeasies of prohibition days and open to anybody who has a clean shirt and the price of a few drinks."

The ban on liquor by the drink will not be lifted until the hotel men push through Initiative 171 in 1948. The hotel men's law will not allow women to sit at the bar in cocktail lounges, a ban that will not be lifted until 1969. The state will keep its liquor monopoly until 2012. The people will end the state liquor stores the same way they end statewide prohibition in 1932—by a statewide initiative put on the ballot by a petition of registered voters.

The most colorful politician elected in Washington state in 1932 is Marion Zioncheck. He is also the most tragic.

Born in Poland and brought to America as a child, Zioncheck has a hard upbringing. He works his way through school and university. Backed by the students outside of fraternities and sororities—the *hoi polloi*—he is elected president of the Associated Students of the University of Washington. In January 1928, when the university's new Athletic Pavilion comes in at one-fifth over budget, Zioncheck blames the ASUW's business-oriented athletic director, Darwin Meisnest, and slams him for "dollar-chasing."

The athletes take Zioncheck's words as an attack on them. On February 2, 1928, nine hooded upperclassmen, six of them from the Husky football team, grab him, gag him, handcuff him, and drive him to the UW's Shell House on Union Bay. There they harangue him, shave his head, strip him naked, tie a rope around his waist, and cast him into the lake. They haul him out, cast him in again, and leave him naked on the dock. All of them are caught; seven are suspended, and two are expelled. For Zioncheck, it's a toughening-up. "They washed away my youthful pattern when they threw me in the duck pond," he will tell a friend years later.

Zioncheck becomes a lawyer who defends the downtrodden. He represents the Unemployed Citizens League. He organizes a recall of Seattle's mayor, Frank Edwards. In 1932 Zioncheck wins Seattle's seat in Congress, where he declares on the House floor that he does *not* represent all the people. "You cannot represent the oppressed and the oppressors, the robbed and the robbers, the poor and the rich, at the same time," he says.

In his 1934 reelection pamphlet, he calls for "economic planning of consumption" and a guaranteed income for every person willing to work. In 1935 he votes for the Social Security Act but complains that 65 is five to ten years too old for retirement, and that the benefits, $20 to $30 a month, are "miserly and inadequate."

Inspired by City Light's success in cutting the cost of electricity, Zioncheck would nationalize the banks in order to cut the cost of loans. To take the profit out of war, he would nationalize the munitions industry. He is no socialist; his secretary, Hulet Wells, who is one, writes that Zioncheck is "willing to go in as far in the direction of public ownership" as is politically useful, and no more. In 1935, five radical congressmen led by Vito Marcantonio of East Harlem invite Zioncheck to join them in forming a new left-wing party or "a movement to take over existing party machinery." Zioncheck declines. For him, that's going too far.

In Wells's estimation, Zioncheck is also "the most eligible bachelor in the House." He loves to drink, drive fast, and chase women. Early in the morning of New Year's Day, 1936, his appetites bring him to grief. He is arrested in Washington, DC, for drunk and disorderly conduct.

"I went to a cocktail party," he tells the *Seattle Times*. "I had seven or eight drinks. Enough to feel them, but I wasn't drunk. I wasn't drunk when I went to see a lady at 2:30 o'clock in Connecticut Avenue. She didn't answer the doorbell. The janitor wasn't at the switchboard."

Zioncheck takes over the switchboard and rings all the residents in the building to wish them Happy New Year. He is arrested. Lacking $15 for bail, he is locked in a cell, where he continues "raising merry hell," as he recounts, by lighting scraps of paper, tossing them through the bars and yelling, "Fire!"

After it's over, Zioncheck proclaims his innocence. Senator Homer Bone and other senior Democrats upbraid the young congressman for his wild antics in an election year. Zioncheck is unrepentant. He asks his colleagues on the House floor to allow him to read a transcript of the police interview into the record. They refuse. "As far as I can remember, we have never put police-court records in the *Congressional Record*," grumbles Minority Leader Bertrand Snell, Republican of New York.

Marion Zioncheck is undergoing what an associate will call "an amazing change." He is descending into derangement.

On the floor of the House, Zioncheck calls Postmaster General James Farley "dumb" and "incompetent." He calls FBI director J. Edgar Hoover a "dictator," and Representative Thomas Blanton "a son of a bitch Texan." The Texas Democrat jumps up and almost clocks him.

On April 22, 1936, Zioncheck does a strange thing. On the House floor he reads a letter from Hans Omenitsch of Jackson Heights, New York. The man claims to have discovered "a criminal system of codes operated daily in the press by the real masters of the country." These codes, Omenitsch says, are hidden in the dialog of syndicated cartoons such as *Smitty* and *Dick Tracy*. He is writing Zioncheck about this because one of his codes produced the congressman's surname:

4/21/36 Dick Tracy: N.Y. Daily News: Key T: 4-17-18-6 x 7 backwards downwards. AT-IRA-ON-AM-EAR-Tek-COPS-GUN-REAL-TAP-RAT-AT-BAR. Add: see letter Z in Smitthy: (Zing) see word ZION in face of ATHNEL. See checkered shadow right beneath the face on coat of Tracy ZION -CHECK ered.

After inserting this gibberish into the public record, Zioncheck says, "Mr. Speaker, I do not care whether they shoot me or not, at least I will take it standing up any time they want to come up and get started." No member comments on the record about this amazing statement, and the newspapers do not pick it up. They treat Zioncheck as a playboy or a clown.

On April 28, Zioncheck, 35, makes news by eloping with Rubye Louise Nix, a 21-year-old stenographer who cold-called him a week before. After a quick wedding, he and Rubye fly to San Juan, Puerto Rico, where Zioncheck borrows a car from a banker, rams it through a gate, and crashes it into a truck. Seeing a protest of Puerto Rican nationalists, he wires President Roosevelt, asking for the authority to take over the Puerto Rican government.

Zioncheck and his bride fly to the Virgin Islands, where Zioncheck is thrown out of a restaurant for drinking soup off his plate. Later he runs a car into the ditch by grabbing the wheel from his driver. When the couple returns to New York, Zioncheck makes news by wading in the fountain at Rockefeller Plaza.

Back in Washington, DC, Zioncheck's landlady has discovered that he has rolled the bedspread under the dinner table and tossed the chinaware

Congressman Marion Zioncheck and his new bride Rubye, circa 1935. Seattle Post-Intelligencer *Collection, 1986.5.45309, Museum of History & Industry, Seattle. Used with permission.*

out the window. When Zioncheck returns, he fights her for possession of the flat. He attacks her with a broom, saying, "I'm a witch and my broom won't behave."

By this time, Rubye has had enough. She leaves her new husband, and he goes berserk. He roars down the streets in his roadster, careening onto the sidewalk to avoid a traffic jam. He pulls up to the White House and offers the guards a gift for President Roosevelt: four beer bottles and a box of ping-pong balls. Eventually the police catch him and take him to the public hospital.

When District of Columbia authorities threaten to commit him to an asylum, Zioncheck moves to the private Sheppard Pratt Hospital in Towson, Maryland. From there he escapes by scaling a seven-foot fence and running into the woods. He makes it all the way to his office in Washington, DC, where he is arrested and sent by train to Seattle.

Back home, Zioncheck puts on a calm face. "Show's over," he tells the press. A few days later, a crowd of 1,000 gathers to hear Zioncheck to address the question, "Who's Crazy?" The congressman assures the people that he is not.

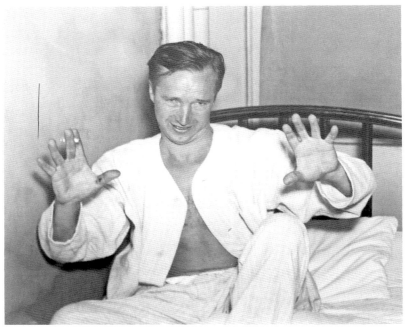

Zioncheck at his hospital press conference, 1936. *ACME Newspictures image in author's collection.*

In fact, Marion Zioncheck is manic-depressive. When he is told he has to go into a mental hospital again, it tips him over the edge. On August 7, 1936, he scrawls a garbled note: "My only hope in life was to improve the condition of an unfair economic system that held no promise to those that all the wealth of even a decent chance to survive let alone live." Then he dives head-first through the window of his fifth-floor campaign office in the Arctic Building, arms and legs flailing, and plunges to his death on the sidewalk in front of his wife.

At Eagles Auditorium, 2,000 people hear the eulogy for Zioncheck by the Reverend Fred Shorter, who calls Seattle's late congressman "a shell-shocked comrade who died at the barricades." A cannon at Fort Lawton fires 17 times, and a hearse bears the casket to the Evergreen Washelli cemetery.

In *The Nation*, Oregon journalist and future senator Richard L. Neuberger writes of Zioncheck, "He was arrogant and egotistical. He needlessly antagonized people by discourtesy or downright rudeness. Frequently he was vulgar. Against these shortcomings, he had an attractive personality when he chose to be amiable... Until his mental collapse in January he was a brilliant young liberal who might have been the dominant political figure in the Pacific Northwest."

Instead of Zioncheck, that figure will be Warren G. Magnuson. At Zioncheck's death, King County's 31-year-old prosecutor immediately files for his seat in Congress. Magnuson will win the seat and move to the Senate in 1944. He will serve in the nation's upper house for 37 years.

8
The Blue Eagle, 1933–1935

In June 1933 Congress passes the National Industrial Recovery Act. The law is good for two years. It aims to revive industry by taking wages, prices, and production out of competition. Columnist Walter Lippmann will write later that "for a few weeks at least, almost everyone had visions of a planned economy." The law falls well short of that. "In practice," Lippmann writes, "the experiment amounted to encouraging businessmen to organize monopolies, encouraging the American Federation of Labor to organize a monopoly, and then by trying from Washington by means of hot and tired officials to make all the soloists produce a symphony."

The law creates the National Recovery Administration (NRA), an agency modeled on the War Industries Board of World War I. To run it, President Roosevelt brings in the War Industries Board's military liaison, retired General Hugh S. Johnson. Known as "Old Ironpants," Johnson ran the draft in World War I. Since then, Johnson has been running a farm-implements company, and not too successfully. In 1933 he is given charge of the national economy.

The way America recovered from depressions in the past began with investors. Enticed by the fallen prices of land, labor, and capital, investors would dig into their savings or borrow money to start new ventures. Bonds and stocks would move up. Commerce would follow, profits later. Prices of land and capital would move up. When employers took up the slack in the labor market, wages would move up.

The NRA puts wages first. To increase consumer spending, the NRA orders industry to push up wages. To support the

A U.S. government poster for the National Recovery Administration (NRA).

new wages, industry is to set higher prices. To support higher prices, it is to restrict production.

In a radio address, President Roosevelt says, "If all employers in each competitive group agree to pay their workers the same wages—reasonable wages—and require the same hours—reasonable hours—then higher wages and shorter hours will hurt no employer. Moreover, such action is better for the employer than unemployment and low wages, because it makes more buyers for his product. That is the single idea which is the very heart of the Industrial Recovery Act."

The *Seattle Times* writes, "Every industry, now, it seems, is to have its 'czar;' all units in a given line of endeavor are to be induced or coerced into subscribing to uniform rules; cooperation is to take the place of competition, particularly of the destructive variety; output control is to be sought insistently; price stabilization is a major objective."

You can hear the editors' skepticism—*pay people more to produce less?*—yet the *Times* goes along. "The government is just as truly at war as if it had embarked on hostilities with a foreign government," the editors say. And in war, people pull together. "A good soldier," writes the *Times*, "does not shoot his commander in the back in the heat of a critical engagement."

A year later, the editors will look back on this as a time of "stultifying acquiescence." "In the first flush of enthusiasm for the 'new deal,'" they write, "it almost was treason to dissent from even the most extreme features of the brain-trust inspired reforms, dumped upon Congress and the country."

Critics compare the NRA to the Fascist system in Italy. In July 1933, when the Blue Eagle is freshly hatched, the *Seattle Post-Intelligencer* runs an opinion piece by Benito Mussolini. The Italian dictator—a former journalist—still has a good press in America, based on the idea that he "made the trains run on time."

"Many in America and Europe have been asking how much 'Fascism' there is in the doctrine and practice of the American President," Mussolini writes. His answer: not much. Under Fascism, control over Italy's economy is direct. The New Deal's control is indirect. The similarity, Mussolini writes, is in the "atmosphere," the call to individuals to think and act for the whole nation.

In 1933, the NRA is rolled out with a massive propaganda effort and government-sponsored demonstrations. The largest is a day-long parade down New York's Fifth Avenue that brings out 250,000 persons. Seattle is a smaller city, but on September 1, 1933, some 300 cars, trucks, and floats parade down Second Avenue and up Fourth Avenue to the cheers of 20,000 spectators. *Post-Intelligencer* reporter Doug Welch calls it "the greatest patriotic demonstration of its kind in the city's history." Its success, he writes, shows "the tumultuous acceptance by the city's commercial and industrial life of the New Deal."

A postage stamp featuring the NRA.

In Seattle, the NRA is promoted by a campaign modeled on the war-bond drives of World War I. An "army" of 1,000 men sets out to collect the promise of every business owner in the city to support the NRA code. A parallel force of 4,000 women sets out to visit every home. On each doorstep, they ask the homemaker to shop only at stores with the sign of the Blue Eagle, which says, "NRA. We Do Our Part."

People are proud to do their part. In Seattle, lumberman Andrew Roberts and his wife do their part by naming their baby daughter Nira in honor of the National Industrial Recovery Act.

Across America, one man makes news for refusing to go along: Henry Ford. America's most famous automaker says he's already paying more than NRA wages. He's willing to cut back the hours of work, but he will not cede authority over the Ford Motor Company to outsiders. "I always thought that to manage a business, you should know something about it," he says. Among big industrialists, Ford stands alone. It costs him business, including the government's business, but he doesn't care. He never signs the NRA codes.

In Seattle, the "general" of the NRA's "army" is William O. McKay, Seattle's biggest Ford dealer. McKay was a captain in the 91st ("Wild West") Division in World War I, a war Henry Ford opposed. McKay is a patriot. After Ford arch-rival Chevrolet runs newspaper ads loudly embracing the Blue Eagle (without naming Ford), McKay announces in full-page newspaper ads (without naming Ford) that he has become a Chevrolet dealer.

120 *Seattle in the Great Depression*

William O. McKay goes back to Ford, August 1934. *The Seattle Public Library, Seattle Room scrapbook.*

McKay will return to Ford a year later and never leave again, but in support of the Blue Eagle he does his part.

The Seattle School Board also does its part. Once a year, the board buys half-pint bottles of milk for school lunches. The district has 59,000 pupils, and in a school year they buy 1.5 million bottles. In three years of the Depression, the district's cost of milk has fallen from 3 cents a half-pint to 2 cents.

King County dairies respond to the drop in prices by setting up the Seattle Milk Shippers Association. In August 1933 they offer to supply the Seattle schools at 2½ cents a bottle. Carnation Farms says the increase reflects wage increases and other costs imposed by the NRA.

Qualitee Milk Products, a company supplied by dairies on the Olympic Peninsula, bids 1.95 cents. The school board accepts this bid in a 3–2 vote. Board member Dietrich Schmitz, who votes no, says the board should accept the 2½-cent bid from the Seattle-area dairies "in keeping with the spirit of the NRA."

Qualitee's bid is subject to the posting of a $5,000 bond by a noon deadline. Qualitee's people miss the deadline by 13½ minutes because of a late ferry, and the board awards the contract to the Seattle-area dairies, who agree to supply it at 2.125 cents.

The School Board rejects the 1.95-cent bid one day after the NRA parade through downtown Seattle. It has done its part.

The Blue Eagle does not produce a recovery. The mini-boom occasioned by the end of the gold standard quickly tails off. A year later, when it is obvious that restricting production is a bad idea, the editors of the *Seattle Star* will sneer at "the childish prattle that if everybody produces less, then everybody will have more." But in 1933 the Seattle newspapers go along with it.

The numbers that confirm the NRA's failure come later. At first are only effects and signs.

Beginning September 1, 1933, the NRA orders lumber mills on the West Coast to raise their 25-cent hourly wage for common labor to at least 42.5 cents. The NRA limits operations to 120 hours a month, the equivalent of 15 eight-hour days. In the first month under the NRA code, the payroll cost at lumber mills is up 5.4 percent and output down 27.4 percent. "West Coast lumber is accomplishing precisely what the Roosevelt recovery program contemplates," writes the *Seattle Times*, "better pay, more jobs, and shorter hours despite a smaller cut."

Not everyone is happy with this. The Willamette Valley Lumber Company of Dallas, Oregon, is under contract to produce electricity for a power company by burning sawdust and bark. All through the Depression it has been running two shifts and producing more lumber than NRA codes now allow. The company sues, arguing that the NRA code unfairly penalizes double-shift mills.

The *Times* is not sympathetic. "The essence of the lumber code, as of all others, is control of production," Seattle's Republican daily argues. "If any one unit can operate of its own sweet will, the whole system of regulation collapses." The West Coast Lumbermen's Association agrees, arguing against the Oregon mill.

The dispute ends up in the courtroom of federal judge John Hugh McNary, brother of Oregon senator Charles McNary. The judge sides with the government. "It is obvious that some means was necessary to limit production," he writes. Early in 1934 he rules for the NRA, declaring that some mills "must make greater sacrifices in productive capacity than others." Willamette Valley Lumber will have to comply.

"Since last March the nation has traveled far along the road toward a new social and economic order," writes the *Seattle Times'* Washington, DC, reporter, W. W. Jermane. The thought arises that the NRA may become permanent.

Business leaders are carried along in the tide of yes. Seattle investment banker Ben Ehrlichman returns from a White House dinner in November 1933 bubbling with enthusiasm for the new order. "It is inconceivable," he declares, "that the NRA should give way to the old condition of destructive competition."

The New Dealers are triumphant. Interior secretary Harold Ickes says, "Rugged individualism has become a museum piece. We have set out on a social, economic and political adventure of the first magnitude." Assistant secretary of agriculture Rexford Tugwell, a former University of Washington instructor who has become a spokesman for the New Deal left, declares, "Those people who would have us crawl back to the old ideas, like wounded animals to an abandoned den, misread the temper of the people as well as the intelligence of the present government."

In 1934, business continues to chafe under the Blue Eagle's authority to set prices. In New Jersey, tailor Jacob Maged, who dares to press a man's suit for a nickel less than the Blue Eagle price, is slapped with a $100 fine and sentenced to 30 days in jail. After three days, the judge lets him out. Maged thanks the judge for his mercy and promises to follow the NRA code. The story is printed nationwide, and it is not good press for the New Deal.

Maged's equivalent in Seattle is Elmer Crane, owner of Crane's Cash and Carry Laundry. For years Crane has been the subject of threats and sabotage from a Teamster-backed cartel that has set prices among cleaners. In 1934 the Blue Eagle is setting the prices. Crane is hauled into court and charged with cleaning and pressing a man's suit for 60 cents instead of the Blue Eagle price of 75 cents. He is made to pay $36.05 in fines and court costs.

After this ruling, Seattle cleaners post the Blue Eagle prices, but many of them "chisel" by charging lower prices to regular customers and issuing false receipts.

The Blue Eagle's equivalent in the food industry is the Agricultural Adjustment Act, which aims to help farmers by increasing the price of food that crosses state lines. In Olympia, the legislature creates a "little AAA" to do the same inside the state. Its boss is Walter J. Robinson, director of agriculture. He is an Eastern Washington wheat farmer married to Grace Ickes, second cousin of Interior Secretary Harold Ickes. The new law makes Robinson a powerful man. The *Seattle Star* calls him the state's dictator of food prices.

Robinson immediately faces opposition. In the spring of 1934, he sets the price of a one-pound loaf of bread at 9 cents. In the Pike Place Market, Lewis Argenbright sells loaves for 8 cents. Robinson orders his arrest. He also orders the arrest of L. C. Linton, owner of Green Lake Ice Cream, for selling ice cream for 25 cents a quart, a dime under the code price. King County's Republican prosecutor, Robert Burgunder, declines to prosecute either of them, declaring that the state has no authority over the price of food.

The fight is now joined by the Seattle School Board. The code price for bread bought by nonprofit institutions is 7 cents a loaf. The Seattle School Board signs a contract with the Meridian Electric Bakery at 5 cents. Robinson threatens to shut down the bakery if it delivers a single loaf at that price. The law also threatens the buyer with a penalty of six months in jail. In reply, School Board member Frank S. Bayley—a downtown Seattle lawyer—dares Robinson to send him to jail for receiving a 5-cent loaf of bread for Seattle's schoolchildren. Prosecutor Burgunder sides with Bayley and sues the state. Robinson backs down. He allows bakeries to supply bread to schools, charitable hospitals, and federal camps at 5 cents. But he warns that he will back down no more.

The fight shifts to milk. The Seattle schools need another year's worth of half-pint bottles for the 1934–1935 school year. The AAA code price is 2.75 cents a bottle, which is up 29 percent from the price reached a year earlier. All the dairies bid the code price except for the Franklin Dairy, which underbids it by a quarter-cent. Director Robinson now makes a tactical error. He starts a separate fight with the dairies over the price of milk in grocery stores. The dairies sue him, and a judge blocks the state from enforcing *any* controls on milk prices in King County. During the few days his temporary restraining order is in effect, the school board signs a one-year contract with the Franklin Dairy at 2½ cents a bottle. Still, the price to schoolchildren rises from 12 cents to 15 cents for a weekly milk ticket.

Arguing that the state has no authority over the price of milk, Kirkland dairyman Austin E. Griffiths Jr.—son of a Seattle city councilman—sues

Secretary Robinson in superior court. Farmers in Spokane file a similar lawsuit regarding tomatoes and melons. Both cases will reach the Washington Supreme Court in 1935.

———

In September 1934, state agriculture director Robinson orders the price of a one-quart bottle of milk in grocery stores raised from 9 cents to 10 cents. Seattle dairymen support him, but by December, they are sorry they did. Sales of milk have fallen 10 to 20 percent. The dairymen ask Robinson to roll back the price. He refuses. In April 1935, they defy him and roll it back to 9 cents.

Robinson is outraged. Declaring that price cuts will "destroy and demoralize" the market for milk, he serves court orders on all 28 King County dairies. Milk goes back to a dime.

In April 1935, the Washington Supreme Court strikes down the 1933 state Agricultural Adjustment Act as a "nebulous, indefinite grant of power" to Director Robinson. He ignores the ruling; he's operating under the 1935 law, he says, not the 1933 law. August Kristoferson, president of the Seattle Milk Distributors Association, sues Robinson in an attempt to kill the 1935 law, too. The judge suspends the price codes, and the King County dairies drop milk back to 9 cents a quart.

The Seattle School Board, which has learned to move quickly, sees its chance. One day after the court suspends the price codes, the School Board signs a contract to buy Carnation milk for the 1935–36 school year at 21 percent below the AAA price.

A similar push-back comes against the state version of the National Recovery Administration. When the City of Seattle hires the Mayflower Press to provide printing at below the state NRA price, the state takes the printer to court. In May 1935, Judge Roscoe E. Smith of King County Superior Court rules that the state NRA is an unconstitutional delegation of legislative power.

By 1935, all three of Seattle's daily newspapers have turned thumbs-down on the federal NRA. The *Times* calls it "a national menace." The *Post-Intelligencer* pronounces the Blue Eagle "a dead bird." The *Star* strips the symbol from its masthead. It compares the NRA to Mussolini's Fascism. The *Star* particularly hates the Blue Eagle's control of the business side of newspapers, which it says "amounts to licensing of the press."

Labor and business in the arms of Uncle Sam. *Clifford Berryman, 1933; used with permission from Granger®.*

On May 27, 1935, the U.S. Supreme Court kills the Blue Eagle. The National Recovery Administration, it says, is an unconstitutional delegation of power. *Star* national columnist Walter Lippmann writes that NRA "collapsed of its own contradictions and its irreconcilability with the American economy."

The federal Agricultural Adjustment Act will be struck down a half-year later. But Washington state's AAA dies on July 23, 1935. The Washington Supreme Court declares that the 1935 act "is a more complete abdication of legislative power than the 1933 act," and throws it on the pile of dead laws.

The price of milk in Seattle comes to rest at 8 cents a quart, 20 percent below the AAA code price.

―――

In the Blue Eagle period, the U.S. economy hardly moves. In 1933, 1934, and 1935, the national unemployment rate remains at a nose-bleeding

25.2 percent, 21.7 percent, and 20.1 percent, respectively. Conditions are not worse; the "unreasoning fear" that Franklin Roosevelt spoke of at his inaugural is gone, thanks to the relief programs and the beginning of bank deposit insurance. Of the Depression, writes the *Seattle Times*, "We have grown accustomed to it, and are perhaps a lot less intolerant of conditions which we now recognize as largely beyond our control." Still, these are very hard times.

In Seattle, unemployment is not measured, but other indicators are. By December 1933 the number of active telephone lines is down 22 percent in two years. In January 1934, one-third of the rentable space in Seattle office buildings is vacant. In 1934, building permits total 7 percent of the 1930 figure, about the same as in 1933. More old houses are being torn down than new ones built.

In 1932 only two-thirds of Seattle's apartments were occupied. Couples put off getting married or moved in with their parents. By 1935, couples are getting married again. Rents have come down, and Seattle apartments are 96 percent full. The new rents, however, are so low that in 1933 and 1934, not one apartment house is built in Seattle. A small one is built in 1935.

Landlords have adjusted to the lowered rents by carving up houses and large flats into housekeeping rooms with shared bathrooms. People who can't afford one of the shrunken spaces can buy a shack at one of the squatter camps, as Donald Francis Roy did, or build one of their own. Together, the city's Hoovervilles have about 1,100 shacks.

The office market remains weak. With no demand for new buildings, owners of old ones cannot finance tear-downs. Some abandon their properties. Even the best buildings are affected by the collapse in values. In early 1935, the Exchange Building, opened in 1930, files for bankruptcy. Leases have run out, and tenants negotiate sharply lower rents. The damage is to the investors. The building's 6-percent bonds are replaced by 3-percents, the preferred stock is swapped for common, and the old common stock is mostly wiped out.

With the end of the Blue Eagle in mid-1935, a recovery begins. There is nothing spectacular about it. Nobody is building skyscrapers. In the summer of 1935 the seven-story, 30-year-old Plaza Hotel at Seattle's Westlake triangle—today's Westlake Plaza—comes down and is replaced by Bartell Drugs' two-story "triangle store." Replacing a seven-story building with a two-story building is a sign of a severely deflated market.

Seattle's Plaza Hotel in 1935, prior to being replaced by two-story Bartell Drugs. *Pemco Webster & Stevens Collection, 1983.10.4534, Museum of History & Industry, Seattle. Used with permission.*

A modest revival begins in homebuilding. Much of the credit goes to the adoption of the fixed-rate mortgage, which has replaced the older method of shorter-term loans with balloon payments. The Federal Housing Administration backs up the new mortgages with insurance. Also, beginning in 1933, the New Deal's Home Owners' Loan Corporation (HOLC) makes more than 20,000 loans in the state of Washington. By accepting high-risk borrowers, many of them behind on existing mortgages, the HOLC stabilizes the market. Borrowers will eventually make good on most of these loans, but by 1939 the agency will foreclose on nearly 10 percent of them—a level of loan losses higher than private lenders can stand.

In the fall of 1935, the Seattle Chamber of Commerce begins a campaign to promote home ownership. The *Seattle Times* and *Post-Intelligencer* appoint editors to cover real estate news. The Frederick & Nelson department store offers prizes to the designers of four model homes. The winning design for a $4,500 house in the upscale Laurelhurst district is by an unemployed

23-year-old graduate of the University of Washington, Victor Steinbrueck. Later in the 1930s, Steinbrueck will help design Yesler Terrace, the city's first public housing project.

There are other signs of recovery. In the summer and fall of 1935, the stock market moves up. The Seattle Stock Exchange, closed since 1932, reopens in the Exchange Building. It will stay in business until the war. Ben Ehrlichman's United National Corporation pays a dividend on its stock for the first time since 1930. United National shares, which fell all the way from $50.75 to 50 cents, advance during 1935 from $2.25 to $7. The defaulted bonds of Seattle hotel and office towers also rise, but it will be years before investors put up any more tall buildings.

No one is putting up new downtown theaters, either. But by late 1935, Seattle's six first-run picture houses—the 5th Avenue, Coliseum, Paramount, Orpheum, Music Box, and Blue Mouse—are full of paying customers. On Christmas Day, 1935, the theaters begin offering double features with no vaudeville. Several theaters post an evening ticket price of 25 cents—half of what they were charging in 1929.

From 1935 to 1936, U.S. unemployment drops from 20.1 percent to 16.9 percent. Consumer business revives, but long-term investment does not. There is something the matter with it. Almost no stock is being sold in new ventures. "A silent strike of enterprising men retards recovery," writes Hearst business columnist Merryle S. Rukeyser. He blames the New Deal. "A series of laws, penalizing acts hitherto considered proper, has put many in a mood to stand by, rather than stick out their necks in new activities."

"There must be some reason why youthful, progressive, enterprising America has dragged behind [Britain] during the last two-three years," writes Hearst columnist B. C. Forbes. The reason, he says, is that in America, "politicians have ceaselessly harassed business and industry" with acts of law and rhetoric of "class hatred."

An example of the latter is Franklin Roosevelt's State of the Union address on January 3, 1936. Roosevelt speaks in different tones at different times; in his 1936 State of the Union he returns to the populist voice of his first inaugural. "We have earned the hatred of entrenched greed," the president intones. "Our resplendent economic autocracy does not want to return to that individualism of which they prate, even though the advantages under that system went to the ruthless and the strong. They realize that in 34 months we have built up new instruments of public power. In the hands of a people's government this power is wholesome and proper."

For business, this is not the voice of a friend. The Blue Eagle encumbered business with rules and restraint, but with the aim of helping owners and workers alike. With the Blue Eagle dead, the president begins a second New Deal by tilting strongly toward labor.

Businessmen are careful about what they say about this. In January 1936, Joshua Green, president of Seattle's Peoples Bank & Trust, tells the *Post-Intelligencer*, "I'd like to see Congress adjourn for two years. It keeps passing new laws which befuddle and mystify the business community."

President Roosevelt proposes one such law early in 1936: a tax on undistributed profits—corporate savings. Instead of taxing the money a company earns in one year, the Treasury will reach back and tax all the wealth it has managed to squirrel away over many years. If companies will not stick their necks out and invest, the government will tax their savings and spend the money itself. The president asks for a top rate of 74 percent.

Business hates the idea. The only way for companies to avoid the tax is to pay out retained earnings to stockholders, and they don't want the government forcing them to do that. Speaking to the Seattle Chamber of Commerce, General Motors Chairman Alfred P. Sloan argues that a company's decision to pay out dividends "must be done by somebody who knows something about the business."

Reacting to nationwide criticism, the Democratic Congress cuts the top rate of the proposed tax from 74 percent to 27 percent. In 1938 it will cut the rate again, and in 1939 it will abolish the tax entirely. But in 1936 it passes the bill into law.

9

The Left Rises, 1932–1935

All through the Depression, a part of America admires the Soviet Union from afar. In January 1932, the *Post-Intelligencer*'s theater and film critic, Everhardt Armstrong, gushes over *The Five-Year Plan*, a Soviet film playing downtown at the Pantages Theater. Armstrong, who has come to Seattle from New York, is educated, wears fine clothes, and is an admirer of Stalin's Russia.

"You can read all the books—those hymning Sovietism and those predicting its early collapse—and still miss the vivid impression of what is actually going on in Russia that the pictorial tour gives," he writes. "For here one encounters no wordy exposition, no hot argument for or against, but instead first-hand close-ups of Russians at work and play—the building of vast dams and power plants, harnessing the great rivers of Muscovy; scenes in steel mills and factories, interesting 'shots' of collective agriculture supplanting the slow and obsolete methods of peasant farmers, sidelights on Soviet education, the planning commission in sessions, and even what the communist-led millions are doing in the way of theatrical art and sports.... One feels the release of immense energies and a boundless enthusiasm in watching this film. The workers pictured all have the aspect of happy folk."

Everhardt Armstrong, 1931. *University of Washington Libraries, Special Collections, JWS32321.*

That same month, Seattle merchant Isadore D. Rosen closes his Pike Street apparel shop, Nifty Clothing. He announces that he is moving to Russia and donating his inventory to the Soviet state. That he is taking his wife's nine-year-old daughter by a previous marriage infuriates her. Rachel Rosen divorces him.

From Grays Harbor, immigrant Finns have been moving to Russian Karelia to work in Stalin's logging camps. In January 1933 the *Seattle Star* reports that Fabian Wesa, a Finnish logger at a camp near Mount Rainier, is planning to move to Russia and take his American daughter with him. Eleanor Wesa, 14, is a student at Issaquah High School. She speaks no Russian. She pleads to stay, but her father has made a promise to his dying wife to take care of the girl. A few weeks later, word comes from Russia that conditions are terrible, and her father gives up his plan.

In November 1933, the United States recognizes Stalin's government. The last three consulates of Russia's pre-Communist regime, in New York, San Francisco, and Seattle, now close.

On January 7, 1934, the ship *Soyuzpushnina* arrives in Seattle from Vladivostok. As the first Soviet vessel to call in Puget Sound, it kindles hope for exports but also worry about imports. The Hoover administration banned Russian lumber in 1931 on the grounds that it was cut with forced labor. Now the ban is lifted.

The *Seattle Times* is not happy about that. "Russia, or any other nation, is at liberty to employ forced labor whenever or wherever it may desire," it declares. Its worry is that local workers won't be able to compete "with such alien labor in the American market."

A few days later, American disinterest in the rights of Russians is put to a test. In a desperate attempt to flee the Communist state, two Russian academics, George Nolde and Ivan Boronzoff, cross the Bering Strait in a boat and crash on the beach of Little Diomede Island. Arriving in Seattle, they are granted asylum.

"If my associate, Prof. Ivan Boronzoff, and I were to return to Soviet Russia, we should be shot within 24 hours," writes Nolde in the *Post-Intelligencer*. In the Soviet state, he writes, "Death is the eventual penalty for all political conviction."

In late 1932 comes Technocracy, an ideology as radical as communism but with an American face. As envisioned by a New York engineer named Howard Scott, there would be no markets, bankers, businessmen, investors, or speculators. While communism calls for a dictatorship of the workers, Technocracy would hand control of the economy to the engineers—white-collar, college-educated professionals to run things without waste or disaster.

George Nolde and Ivan Boronzoff in Seattle, January 1934. *International Newsphoto in author's collection.*

Prices would be based on units of energy. "The currency under such a system would be more like a railroad ticket," says Seattle's most prominent supporter, Richard G. Tyler, dean of engineering at the University of Washington. "There would be no use in hoarding railroad tickets, when one could take you where you wanted to go."

In a series on the new idea, the *Seattle Star* says Technocracy promises "a job for everybody between the ages of 25 and 45—and after that you go fishing on an income paid by the state. A 16-hour working week—four hours a day for four days—and the rest of the time for leisure. A standard of living 10 times higher than our present average" and "the abolition of debt."

To a society with millions out of work, these are fetching ideas. In January 1933, Seattle has one Technocracy Club. By June 1934 it has 20. It also has a weekly paper, the *Western States Technocrat*. In early 1934 the paper has four pages. By early 1935 it has 16 pages, most of them imagining America's grand future of electrification, irrigation, and plenty.

Whether a planned economy could do all that, or be compatible with liberty and democracy, is questionable. Liberty allows private choices; democracy allows political change. Both are messy. Technocracy is pure to the point of unreality. For its believers, that will be a problem.

Technocracy's creator, Howard Scott. *Technocracyinc.com.*

Fred Shorter, circa 1930s. *From self-published volume* A Frontier of the Spirit, *by Mary E. Hopper, printed by North Seattle Printing Co. circa 1960s. The Seattle Public Library, Seattle Room.*

In 1935, Tyler's public zeal for Technocracy costs him his position as dean. The university demotes him to a professor of sanitary engineering and cuts his pay. This does not shut him up; Tyler will zealously promote a planned economy all through the 1930s.

Fred Shorter is a Christian minister. For seven years, Shorter has been pastor of the Pilgrim Congregational Church (now the All Pilgrims Christian) on Seattle's Capitol Hill. He's also on the executive committee of Seattle's first Technocracy Club. Shorter believes in a social gospel, and in 1933 he joins the Socialist Party.

Early in 1934, the *Socialist News* mentions Shorter as "a preacher who isn't afraid to carry a red card." H. A. Chadwick, editor of the *Argus*, Seattle's conservative weekly, has been hearing about Shorter from his wife, who is a member of Shorter's congregation. Chadwick suggests in his column that it is time the congregants "roust out the communists."

The *Seattle Times* soon reports that Shorter is under fire from the congregation over three political murals drawn on the walls of the church's Bible room. One is sarcastically labeled "Saint Swastika" and shows Adolf Hitler driving out the Jews. Another, labeled "Black Justice," shows the limp body of a half-naked dark-skinned man under a hangman's noose. The third shows an American farmer, his crops being plowed under, and a different farmer, described in one account as Russian, farming scientifically.

"These bludgeon home the exact theme of my sermons: Capitalism is doomed," Shorter tells the *Star*. "What is needed today is a planned social economy—call it technocracy, socialism or what you will. The church should lead the way."

On Army Day, veterans of World War I hold a patriotic show at the Eagles Auditorium. Several young radicals go in and toss antiwar leaflets off the balcony. The veterans rough them up and throw them onto the sidewalk, where police arrest them for riot. Shorter makes the news again when he leads a group of pastors to bail them out.

All this is too much for Shorter's flock. They hold a stormy meeting and vote to fire him. Shorter and 60 followers split off and form the Church of the People. The new church, Shorter says, is based on "a new conception of God as expressed in the people ... That we must produce for use and not for profit, and that the needs of men must take priority over all other considerations."

In 1937, the peak year of Stalin's Great Terror, Shorter leaves on a three-month pilgrimage to Russia, paid for by the Friends of the Soviet Union. Shorter writes that his goal is to find the truth about the world's only Communist state. Though he is on a guided tour, he sees things that disturb him. "I was shocked by the housing conditions in Moscow," he writes in his private notes. He describes Russia as a land of "dirt, rags, inefficiency, laziness, beggars ... hardship and poverty." He sees images of Lenin and Stalin "EVERYWHERE," venerated to the point of idolatry. And he excuses all of it. He tells himself he is witnessing "the greatest phenomenon of the century ... the mighty movement of millions of men and women toward a spiritual goal, the goal of human justice and human comradeship."

Shorter returns to Seattle with his faith intact. "The Soviet regime is based entirely on the will of the people," he tells a friendly journalist. Asked about Stalin's show trials and summary executions of supposed Trotskyist spies, he replies, "When spies are caught, drastic action must be taken."

In 1934 Upton Sinclair runs for governor of California. Sinclair, 55, is a socialist. Back in 1906, he wrote *The Jungle*, a novel about immigrant workers in Chicago's meatpacking plants. In one of the book's scenes, a worker falls into a vat of hot grease and is rendered into lard. Sinclair hoped his novel would promote socialism; its effect is to prompt Congress to pass the Pure Food and Drug Act. ("I aimed at the public's heart, and by accident I hit it in the stomach," he said.) Sinclair has twice run for governor of

California on the Socialist ticket and lost. In 1934 he runs in the primary as a Democrat, promoting the leftmost aspects of the New Deal.

Sinclair calls his program "End Poverty in California" (EPIC). He would create a California Authority for Money (CAM), a California Authority for Land (CAL), and a California Authority for Production (CAP). Under these alphabet agencies, he would have the state borrow money and buy out the factories and farms that owed back taxes. The state would employ the jobless in a parallel economy of cooperative industries and farms. The newspapers do not use the term "collective farms."

In Washington state, Sinclair's effort inspires a parallel group, the Commonwealth Builders. It describes its program as building "a system of state-owned farms and industries." In it, "thousands of the unemployed will produce all the flour, meat, clothing, building materials and other manufactured goods for the entire relief population." The workers would be paid in scrip to be honored in "a state-wide chain of stores" that "sell the products of this self-contained industrial system." It declares, "All the unemployed can be put to work under this plan." The essence of the plan is "production for use and not for profit."

Commonwealth Builders includes a mix of Edward Bellamy socialists, Technocracy believers, and self-helpers from the Unemployed Citizens Leagues. The organizers try to keep the Communists out. In 1934, the Reds are still carrying the banner of Marxist purity and are nasty to everyone else on the left.

For executive director, the Commonwealthers choose Howard G. Costigan, who grew up in Centralia, a town of political notoriety. He was 15 during the Armistice Day riot of 1919, in which four Legionnaires and a deputy sheriff were shot dead and a Wobbly was lynched. Costigan is intense and ideological. At Centralia High, he was class president and on the debate team three years in a row. In the yearbook, his motto was, "What shall I do to be known forever?"

At age 30, Costigan is a barber in Seattle. One of his customers is the Reverend Fred Shorter. Costigan clicks politically with Shorter. He is articulate and eager. He helps draw the murals at Shorter's church, and when the chance comes, he volunteers to set up the Commonwealth Builders. Costigan is a talker. In August 1934, he begins a regular 15-minute spiel on KIRO Radio.

Meanwhile, in the California race for governor, Upton Sinclair becomes the Democratic nominee. In a campaign that the left will complain about for decades, the Republicans smear Sinclair as radical, un-Christian, and pro-Soviet. Their campaign is nasty, but essentially accurate. Sinclair *is* radical, un-Christian, and pro-Soviet. And in a big Democratic year, Sinclair loses to Republican Frank Merriam, the safe and boring incumbent.

The state of Washington has no race for governor in 1934, but the Commonwealthers elect 27 Democrats to the 99-member state House and eight to the 48-member Senate. Notable among the winners in the Senate is Mary Farquharson, 32, the wife of University of Washington engineering professor Burt Farquharson, a founder of the Commonwealth Builders. In order to be accepted as a Democrat, she has dropped her membership in the Socialist Party. In most times that would be politically fatal, but in 1934 it is not. Another new Commonwealth-backed senator is Albert D. Rosellini, 29. Twenty-two years later, he will be elected governor.

U.S. Senator C. C. Dill, a Democrat, is retiring. To succeed him, the Commonwealthers endorse Seattle attorney Lewis B. Schwellenbach, one of the authors of their state-ownership program. He is an attorney and a regent of the University of Washington. And he wins. Over the next six years, Schwellenbach will be one of the U.S. Senate's 100-percent New Dealers.

Nationally, in 1934 Democrats gain nine seats in each house of Congress. This is the only time in the 20th century that a new president's party gains seats in both houses two years into his term. The elections are a huge win for the New Deal.

———

The *Seattle Star* will call Washington state's 1935 legislature "the weirdest . . . in many, many years."

The "many years" is a reference to the legislature of 1897, which was a mix of William Jennings Bryan Democrats, Silver Republicans, and members of the People's Party. In contrast, the legislature of 1935 is almost all Democrat. They hold 80 percent of the seats in the Senate and 88 percent in the House. The "weird" part is the left wing. The remaining Republicans vote with the mainline Democrats to deny the left control of either chamber.

The left-wingers have a big agenda. They push bills for state cold-storage plants, a state road pavement plant, a state telephone company, a state wholesale gasoline company, a state bank, and a bill to allow local government to distribute milk. They also push for the repeal of the criminal syndicalism law of 1919, which outlaws speech in support of political violence or property destruction.

All these bills are defeated. The left doesn't have the votes. In addition, the electorate has taken away legislators' money by voting down a graduated income tax and tightening the limit on the property tax.

The left's great hope in 1935 is the Economic Security Act, which would set up a state agency to spend $15 million on idle factories, mills, and ships to be operated by the unemployed. Commonwealth Builders calls the proposal "a complete and all-embracing production-for-use system" along the lines of Upton Sinclair's plan for California. Really it is a move toward a socialist Washington. It comes close in the House, but fails 48–44.

The mainline Democrats pass their bills. Governor Clarence Martin asks legislators to extend for two years the state NRA and AAA laws, and they do. Following the governor, the 1935 legislature replaces the Washington Emergency Relief Administration with the Department of Public Welfare, which becomes today's Department of Social and Health Services. For resident citizens over 65, legislators also create an old-age pension. The beneficiaries have paid nothing for it, and the money is from the general fund. The state fixes how much to pay each claimant based on need, but no more than $30 a month. For pensioners with real estate, the state will put a lien on the property to recover the money after they die. This is not the universal program the left wants, and it will not last, but it does help some people right away. The Social Security program being debated in Congress will pay no old-age benefits until 1940.

Governor Martin insists that the state pay for social spending with current revenue. No more bonds. But in the Depression, the assessed value of property has fallen back to the level of 1911, and tax levies have fallen by nearly half. At Martin's urging, legislators approve a sweeping tax bill. It includes a tax on business income, which will be struck down. It also includes the state's first sales tax, 2 percent, and its first cigarette tax, 1 cent on a 15-cent pack. Legislators pass a constitutional amendment for a graduated personal income tax, but in November 1936 voters reject it by more than three to one.

The laws that survive set the tax structure of Washington into the 21st century: levies on real estate, business revenue, retail sales, cigarettes, and liquor.

In the spring of 1935 comes a chain-letter fad. All over America, the *Seattle Star* writes, "The gullible population has gone hog wild." People are receiving letters with four names and addresses. They're asked to send a silver dime—or a dollar—to the name on top of the list, scratch out that name, add theirs to the bottom, and send eight new letters to people they know. The pull is irresistible. If everyone pays, they stand to get their money back 4,096 times.

By May 1935, Seattle's downtown post office has hired 50 additional clerks to sell stamps and handle some 150,000 letters a day, many of them laden with dimes. Chain-letter "mills" spring up, offering people spots on sure-to-win letters at double the usual cost.

Newspapers pour cold water on the people's frenzy, and letter-writers reply. "When the dimes begin circulating, doesn't that stimulate trade?" writes a woman to the *Seattle Times*. "I know if I should ever be so fortunate as to head one of the lists and receive the benefit of it as others have, I'd turn right around and spend it for a good cause, namely to get my eyes and teeth attended to. They've been sadly neglected for the simple reason that I've been out of work for over three years."

The *Times*' editors concede that chain letters are "expressing, in a way, a common desire of the American people to get things going again for the good of all." In that sense, they say, the fad "partakes somewhat of Senator Long's share-the-wealth proposals."

The reference is to Huey Long of Louisiana. Long is America's demagogue of the decade. A brilliant and forceful man, Long taps into the suspicion that the hard times were brought on by the greed of the rich. In 1934–1935 Long's followers organize Share the Wealth Clubs, including one in Seattle. In January 1935, KJR Radio broadcasts Long's speech, "Sharing the Wealth So That Every Man May Be a King."

Long attacks the New Deal from the left. To him, Franklin Roosevelt has been too easy on the One Percent. Long makes no secret of his ambition to take the presidency for himself. If elected, he says, he would bring every American "a home, an automobile, a radio and the ordinary conveniences." He would limit their work to 30 hours a week and 11 months a year. He

"Right smart feller, that Adolf." *Cartoon by Hugh M. Hutton*, Seattle Sunday Times, 9-2-1934.

would provide college for all and pensions for everyone over 60 except for the well-off. He would tax away the wealth of millionaires. He would declare a moratorium on all debts above eight dollars.

In Louisiana, Long is king, and the state legislature is his poodle. Among public officials he allows no dissent; if a board or commission opposes him, he replaces it with a new one. When leading newspapers oppose him, he slams them with a newspaper tax. When the student paper at Louisiana State University prints a letter opposing him, he orders the state police to destroy the entire press run. "That's *my* university," he says. "I built it, and I'm not going to stand for any students criticizing Huey Long."

In Baton Rouge, Long builds the nation's tallest state capitol. In September 1935, while walking its marble halls, he is gunned down by a man with a grievance. Long's movement dies with him, but the feeling behind it lives on.

Another prophet of the mid-1930s is Dr. Francis E. Townsend, a retired health officer from Long Beach, California. Townsend, 68, stirs the hopes of the elderly with his plan to give every American over 60 an income of $200 a month ($4,530 in 2024 dollars). The money would come with two conditions: that it be spent in 30 days and that the person stop working. "We will establish security in the country," Townsend says, "and there will be no need to hoard or save for the future."

Townsend's support is strongest in the West. A poll shows that in the state of Washington, 13 percent of voters support it. And Townsend's followers are motivated. They organize clubs. They sign petitions. They flood newspaper editors with letters that picture the wonderful effects of people spending $200 a month.

James T. Fullerton, a former mayor of Port Townsend, writes, "New homes will be built, starting lumber mills, cement and brick works, paper for bags to hold the lime and cement, plumbers will be kept busy with the modern bathrooms and installing oil tanks for fuel. The sale of furnaces, Frigidaires, washing machines . . . and the whole land will be a hive of industry with panic forgotten."

Carl Siegel of Seattle writes, "Four million persons over 60 now working will step out of jobs at once, and immediately this number of unemployed would get their jobs. Within six months there would be such an increase in business that an additional 4,000,000 or 5,000,000 would be reemployed, thus almost entirely eliminating unemployment."

In Canada, these ideas score. In August 1935, the province of Alberta elects radio preacher William Aberhart, whose Social Credit Party promises a kind of Townsend Plan. Aberhart's plan doesn't work; as a result, Alberta will become the first Canadian province to default on its bonds. The ideas, however, have political effect. The same month Aberhart is elected, the U.S. Congress passes the Social Security Act. Social Security offers a much smaller benefit than the Townsend plan and to a smaller share of the people than in Alberta. But it works, and it will endure.

Lowell Wakefield, circa 1930s. Voice of Action.

Lowell Wakefield is the son of a wealthy Seattle fish processor. A graduate of Broadway High School, he majors in sociology at the University of Washington (UW). In 1928, while on the UW debate team, he argues against military intervention in Nicaragua. He also opposes compulsory military training on the UW campus. He moves on to Columbia University in New York, where he earns a degree in anthropology and joins the Communist Party.

In 1931, the Party's national newspaper, the *Daily Worker*, sends Wakefield to Scottsboro, Alabama, to write about the case of nine black teenagers accused of raping two white women. Wakefield, 21, perceives that the "Scottsboro Boys" are being railroaded. His writing helps to bring their case to national attention. After they are convicted, the Communists' legal arm, International Labor Defense, takes up their defense, appealing the case to the Alabama Supreme Court and staging protests and parades to raise money. Eventually the defendants sense that they are being used and choose the National Association for the Advancement of Colored People to represent them, but the Communists have played a big part.

In the fall of 1932, Wakefield is involved with a case back home: the looting of a Skaggs Safeway store at Anacortes by jobless men and women. Their leader, Iver Moe, 24, was a wrestling champ at Anacortes High and has since joined the Communist Party. The cop who witnesses the looting doesn't stop it, but he recognizes Moe and five others, who are charged with riot and grand larceny. To manage their defense, the Party sends Lowell Wakefield.

Having seen the protests at Scottsboro, Wakefield brings in comrades from Whatcom and Snohomish counties to picket the Skagit County Superior Court and parade through Mount Vernon behind a red flag. But he hires no attorney, and the defendants lose. Eugene Dennett, then a Communist organizer in Bellingham, reproaches him. Wakefield is too provocative. Speaking for the Party, Dennett writes, "The class struggle is more than a drama."

Moe and two others are sent to prison. Just before Moe is to go in, he renounces the Communist Party and condemns it for "violence and class hatred." They, in turn, denounce him as a class traitor.

Three years after the Anacortes looting, in 1935, George Weyerhaeuser is kidnapped. Everyone remembers the death of the Lindbergh baby in 1932, and the newspapers are full of worry for young George. Seattle's three dailies make no connection between the kidnapping of the Weyerhaeuser heir and the ongoing strike in the lumber industry, which includes the company run by George's father. To the mainstream press, the story is about a nine-year-old boy held for ransom.

Not for Lowell Wakefield. By this time, he is editor of the *Voice of Action*, Seattle's Communist weekly. To the *Voice of Action*, the story is the workers. "The capitalist press," the paper writes, "centers public sympathy on one boy in order to keep thousands of other boys hungry and uncared-for, in order to divert public sympathy away from the lumber strikers and their families, in order to break the strike and preserve the profits of the lumber companies."

To mainstream Seattle, this is an alien voice. The Communists are allowed a line on the ballot, an office on First Avenue, and a weekly newspaper. But they are not allowed to distribute their paper near the public school, to speak on the university campus, or to rent a city-owned hall. When they open a "social science school" in the Burke Building (where the Federal Building is now), police arrest Party organizer Morris Raport and four others for violating the state anti-syndicalism law, which forbids the advocacy of violence. It's a toothless law, and the Reds will be released without charge. After the police leave, men from the Veterans of Foreign Wars bust up the session with their fists. Four of the vigilantes are put on trial for unlawful assembly, but the jury lets them off.

―――

In the spring of 1935, the *Voice of Action* has a contest to sell subscriptions. Its grand prize is a trip to Moscow to see the May Day celebrations in Red Square.

The winner is a University of Washington drama student named Frances Farmer. She is no stranger to notoriety. In 1931, as a senior at West Seattle High, she won a $100 prize from *Scholastic* magazine for her essay "God Dies." The essay is not an argument for atheism, though Frances, a four-year member of the school debate team, could have written it that way. Her focus is inward. It is about her feelings. But the title, "God Dies," causes a reaction. Frances becomes known as the "Bad Girl of West Seattle High."

At the university, Frances organizes a campaign of parties, dinners, and benefit shows to win the trip to Russia. Her mother, Lillian Farmer, is horrified. She tells the *Post-Intelligencer* that her daughter has been swayed by

Frances Farmer, n.d. *Author's collection.*

Red professors, and may return from Russia swayed even more. Lillian Farmer appeals to King County prosecutor Warren Magnuson to stop the trip. But Frances is 21, legally an adult. Magnuson says she has the right to go.

Replying to her mother in the *Seattle Times*, Frances says she's not a Communist and that her interest is Russia's theater.

She goes. In the years ahead, Frances Farmer will be involved in Communist-led groups to support the Loyalists in Spain. Many Hollywood figures do this. Challenged about it, she replies, "Communism has never been an issue. Fascism is."

Her priority, though, is her career. Upon her return, she signs with Paramount Studios. She makes her Hollywood debut by playing both mother and daughter in Howard Hawks's *Come and Get It* (1936). Farmer will play in several other big-budget films. Still the "bad girl," she loses her contract with Paramount in 1942 over her drinking and is later arrested for drunk driving with headlights on in a wartime black-out zone. She mocks the cop; later she is charged with assaulting a hairdresser, and in 1943 her mother has her committed to Western State Hospital in Steilacoom. For seven years Frances Farmer is in and out of mental institutions, and it will be falsely rumored that she has had a lobotomy. Released, she makes a comeback of sorts in the 1950s, but succumbs again to alcoholism. Her life is a sad story, but mostly not a political story. As with many Americans, her involvement with the left in the 1930s is one phase of a lifetime.

10
The Labor Push, 1934–1937

The National Industrial Recovery Act declares that labor has the right to bargain collectively. How this is to happen is not too clear, and companies and unions argue over it. But it is pro-labor, and the bolder labor leaders take it and run with it.

On May 9, 1934, Pacific Coast longshoremen go out on strike. They demand that employers recognize the East Coast–based International Longshoremen's Association as their bargaining agent.

Seattle has 1,500 longshoremen. About half are hired by the job. They report to an employer office by 7 a.m. and wait. Straight-time wages at the beginning of 1934 are 85 cents an hour—good pay for full-time work, but the work is not full-time. The *Labor News* writes, "Workers are hired for one or two hours three or four times a day." They are paid only for hours worked. And it is beast-of burden work; this is the era before 40-foot containers are lifted by cranes. Many longshoremen suffer hernias, varicose veins, and enlarged hearts.

The longshoremen are in a company union that does little for them. When the employer refuses to pay the extra wage for handling hazardous fertilizer, the union does nothing. In the strike, the men demand their own union, a closed shop, an increase from 85 cents to a dollar an hour, and control of the hiring hall. The employers say they are willing to talk about everything except control of the hiring hall. They insist on the right to choose who works.

On May 12, several thousand union men swarm the Seattle docks. They demand that scabs come out. As police stand aside, the union men make the nonunion men run a gauntlet of catcalls and fists. At one pier, strikers toss foreman Phil R. Gruger into Elliott Bay. At the end of "Gauntlet Day," the union announces that Seattle's waterfront has been "100 per cent cleared" of scabs. This sets the tone for the strike. It will not be gentle.

The union shuts down the port. In June 1934, ocean shipments of flour, wheat, and lumber from Seattle fall to zero. On Harbor Island, the Fisher

Longshoremen ejecting a scab, May 1934. *Courtesy of the International Longshore and Warehouse Union (ILWU), Local 23.*

flour mill shuts down. Sawmills that produce lumber for export start shutting down, putting 20,000 to 25,000 men out of work. In Alaska, grocers begin to run out of meat and green vegetables. They begin rationing milk and eggs. President Roosevelt insists that Alaska be supplied, and the union allows a few ships to go north. Other than that, Seattle's docks are quiet.

Some employers try to get around it. In the first week of June, a nonunion crew reaches the tanker *Brandywine* in Elliott Bay by riding a tug. Upon the tug's return, union men beat its three crewmen senseless. When three other strikebreakers start toward the *Brandywine* in a rowboat, union men pursue them in other rowboats, shunt them back to the dock, and beat them.

On June 7, the *Brandywine* steams out to sea, as does the tanker *Lio*. Six days later, a crew of strikebreakers armed with clubs forces its way through pickets at the Union Oil dock (now Waterfront Park) and boards another tanker.

On June 14, a driver pushes his truck through a union picket line on Harbor Island and injures a picketer, who is rushed to the hospital. Strikers drag the driver from his cab and beat him.

On June 15, police confiscate baseball bats, pieces of pipe, and rubber hoses from strikers at the Todd Dry Docks. The chief of police appeals to merchants to sell bats only to baseball players.

In San Francisco, top-level negotiations go on for weeks. Under the urging of a federal mediator, the two sides reach a compromise. The employers agree to recognize the International Longshore Association. Union negotiators agree to accept an open shop and a jointly controlled hiring hall.

Union President Joseph P. Ryan and Seattle Teamster boss Dave Beck, who controls the trucks, fly from San Francisco to sell the deal to the rank and file on Puget Sound. The men don't buy it. The negotiators try again and come back with a deal not much different.

Again, Ryan and Beck urge the men to vote yes. "This compromise is absolutely the best that could be secured for both sides," Beck says. "I don't see why the longshoremen can't have confidence in their president. He is no baby in the labor movement and he got absolutely the best that he could and exhausted every effort to do it."

Harry Bridges, 1936. *ACME Newspictures image in author's collection.*

The men are not moved. They are following a different leader, Harry Bridges. Based in San Francisco, Bridges, an immigrant, is a political radical who in years ahead will become Dave Beck's enemy in the labor movement. The *Seattle Star* runs a story describing Bridges as "a dynamic, alert, lean, tanned Australian with a prominent nose and sharp eyes." He says he's for "a closed shop and no compromise."

The *Post-Intelligencer* runs Bridges's photo. It calls him "Iron Man."

On June 10, 1934, the *Seattle Times* runs an editorial in large type that covers most of the front page. The editorial declares that a closed shop of longshoremen will kill Seattle's commerce. It ends with the demand: "OPEN THE PORT."

Seattle's new mayor, Charles L. Smith, intends to do so. Part of his plan is to hire temporary police to patrol the city so he can use real police to protect strikebreakers on the docks. When the union-friendly City Council refuses to accept this, Smith deputizes 200 men. The Seattle Citizens' Emergency Committee, a group headed by Alfred Lundin, president of the Seattle Chamber of Commerce and former King County prosecutor, agrees to pay the deputies and provide the real police with tear-gas equipment.

Smith has a force of 300 regular police and sheriff's deputies. On June 20, he deploys them at two long finger piers, today called Terminals 90 and 91, at Smith Cove.

The staging ground inland of the piers (which has been enlarged by landfill since then) becomes a place of positional warfare. The union men have their picket line, and they beat anyone who crosses it. Police won't break the line, but they provide sanctuary to strikebreakers inside it. When a truck driver tries to cross the line with food, a shout goes up, "*Food for scabs!*" Union men pull the driver from the truck and beat him.

Using a tugboat at night, the employers bring more strikebreakers, including members of the University of Washington football team. The scabs live in the ships and are paid a high wage. Cargo slowly begins to move. On June 23, the first ocean freighter to leave Seattle during the strike, the *Moldavia*, departs for Britain with a cargo of canned salmon. The next day at 4 a.m., a train is rushed past the pickets with food for strikebreakers and police.

Strikers hear of a downtown job office for scabs. They throw cordons around the Smith Tower and the Alaska Building. They catch Frank Smith, 48, who lives in Hooverville, and knock out most of his front teeth. Meanwhile, strikebreakers at Smith Cove are unloading the freighters *Hakushita* and *Tacoma*.

An employers' man breaks the informal rules of engagement—no killing—on June 30. North of Seattle at Point Wells, Standard Oil of California has a tank farm. During a demonstration at the front gate, striker Shelvy S. Daffron, 47, is shot dead. A coroner's inquest finds that he was shot in the back by someone on Standard Oil's property. The shooter is never identified. In Seattle, union men have a huge funeral for Daffron, strengthening their resolve.

In California, Governor Frank Merriam—the Republican who a few months later will take on Upton Sinclair—calls out the National Guard.

He orders them to reopen the port of San Francisco. Union men resist, and 34 persons are shot. Two are killed. In Washington, Dave Beck urges Democratic governor Clarence Martin not to call out the Guard, and Martin does not.

Still, violence flares. On July 9, strikers follow a car of sheriff's deputies from Smith Cove into downtown Seattle. At Third and Seneca, strikers swarm the car and roll it over. They hold the deputies against a wall except for Steve S. Watson, 49, who is armed with a .32-caliber pistol. Watson is later found dead, shot with his own gun. No one is ever identified as the killer.

———

To ramp up the pressure, Seattle longshoremen call for a general strike. Dave Beck disagrees. His Teamsters have been respecting the longshoremen's picket lines, but he declares that his men "will have nothing whatever to do with a general strike anywhere on the Pacific Coast." Beck remembers the General Strike of 1919. It attempted to shut down Seattle for five days and brought a political reaction that crippled organized labor for years. William Green, president of the American Federation of Labor, agrees with Beck. Green argues that by breaking labor contracts, such a strike would have workers risk the "possibility of losing all economic gains they have secured through years of sacrifice and effort." Harry Bridges briefly attempts a general strike in San Francisco, but in Seattle, a general strike never happens.

The thought of it, though, alarms business. The Seattle Citizens' Emergency Committee runs newspaper ads depicting a thuggish giant labeled "Communism," and the caption, "Shall He Rule Seattle?" The city does have a Communist weekly, the *Voice of Action*, which is gung ho for a general strike. The mayor, whom the paper calls "Fascist Mayor Smith," wants to shut that voice down. On July 19 and 20, police raid the offices of the Communist Party, the *Voice of Action*, and the Workers' Bookstore and arrest more than two dozen persons. All but four are quickly let go. The catch-and-release is for intimidation only.

The real action is on the front line at Smith Cove, where 200 police and sheriff's deputies face a line of union pickets. Police control a staging area by holding the line at the Magnolia Bridge north of the piers and the Great Northern Railway tracks to the east. On the morning of July 18, some

150 *Seattle in the Great Depression*

"Shall He Rule Seattle?" Striking longshoreman as pictured by the Chamber of Commerce's Seattle Citizens Emergency Committee. *From advertisement in the* Seattle Times, *7-11-1934, p. 8.*

1,200 to 1,500 strikers push back the police and take the staging area. By shortening the line, the strikers tighten their seal on the docks.

Mayor Smith and his chief of police, George F. Howard, have been on the job for a month. Smith wants a victory. He was a lieutenant in World War I, and he plans a military assault to retake the lost ground. Chief Howard was a longshoreman during the war, and he refuses to lead an attack on union men. Smith busts him back to lieutenant and takes command of the police himself.

On July 20 at 6 a.m., 250 Seattle police take their stations. At the north end of the staging area, up on the Magnolia Bridge, police are armed with tear-gas launchers. With them is the mayor's wife. Under the bridge, gas-masked police are mounted on horses. At the southern end of the staging area, at the piers, Mayor Smith stands with the main group of police facing 600 to 700 picketers. Some strikers are wearing makeshift gas masks with wet handkerchiefs or sponges. A megaphone voice warns them to disperse. "We're ready for your perfume," one striker shouts.

"All right. Let 'em have it, then!" a cop calls out, and the pincer attack begins. The union line breaks. The mounted police sweep the staging area and wheel to the east through clouds of gas. The strikers scatter.

Tear gas and billy clubs at the Magnolia Bridge, July 23, 1934. *Author's collection.*

After the battle, three patrolmen and six strikers are sent to the hospital, the strikers with scalp wounds. Striker Ole Helland, hit with a tear-gas canister, will die of his wounds. A coroner's jury will find that the canister hit him in the back and that his fatal head wound was caused by a fall.

The *Post-Intelligencer* sums up the aftermath: "For the first time since Seattle's waterfront was paralyzed by the waterfront strike more than two months ago, the police had the situation completely in hand yesterday, and goods were moving to and from the docks on an almost normal basis."

On July 31, 1934, the 83-day strike ends when union members in San Francisco vote to accept arbitrators appointed by President Roosevelt. The vote is a defeat for Harry Bridges, who urges members to vote no. The *Voice of Action* calls it a betrayal, and the Seattle Chamber of Commerce calls it a victory. Part of the settlement is left to the arbitrators, who impose key elements of the employers' final offer: union recognition, a joint union-management hiring hall, and an open shop. The arbitrators give the union a crucial concession: the exclusive right to appoint the dispatcher at the hiring hall. Two years later the longshoremen will go on strike again. After three months, they will win full control of the hiring hall.

For Seattle, the longshore strike of 1934 is the biggest and bloodiest of the Depression. In hindsight, it is step one of an historic union victory, but it comes at a long-term cost. The steamship lines between Puget Sound and California get back only part of the passenger and cargo trade they lost. Trucks, trains, and airplanes are all faster than ships, and they keep much of the business. From 1934 to the end of 1936, coastwise shipping drops by two-thirds.

The wave of strikes continues into 1935.

For Seattle, the big strike of the year is over union recognition at Fisher Flouring Mills. Fisher is the largest flour miller in the Pacific Northwest. Begun in 1910, the flour mill is the first industrial use of Harbor Island, a site that allows flour to be loaded onto ships for coastwise and Asian markets. By 1935 the Fisher mill has 300 employees and is run by O. D. Fisher, the founder's son. His brother O. W. Fisher, second in command at the mill, is president of KOMO Radio.

In 1934, under the Blue Eagle, a representation election is held among Fisher's Harbor Island employees. The Flour and Cereal Workers, an American Federation of Labor union, wins that election, but management recognizes a company union instead. In July 1935 Fisher's warehouse employees organize a unit of the Weighers and Warehousemen, an AFL union affiliated with the Longshoremen. The Warehousemen vote to strike. The Cereal Workers hold back for a month, but when management grants a 5 percent pay increase that the men consider an insult, both unions go out. Their strike begins October 2, 1935.

The fight is fundamental to both sides. For the workers, it is about a union that represents them. For the Fishers, it is about control of a family enterprise. The Fishers have just gone through a long and bitter strike in their lumber operations and are dead set against an "outside" union controlling "their" labor on the Seattle waterfront.

The Fisher brothers have an ally: the employer group that bought the tear gas for the police during the longshore strike of 1934. The group, which has renamed itself the Industrial Council of Washington, says it is opposed to "the enforced unionization of all industry and business"—labor's goal of making Seattle a 100-percent union town. It argues that this would mean that "no new local or outside money could be invested here, and the future development of Seattle would be throttled."

Apart from chamber president Alfred Lundin, the Industrial Council's membership is secret. Fisher Mills boss O. D. Fisher, who is vice chairman of the Chamber's committee on labor relations, is said to be one of the founders.

The Industrial Council's first public act in the Fisher strike is to set up a convoy to pick up strikebreakers at the Civic Auditorium and drive them through the picket line. The *Voice of Action* interviews a man on the picket line. He says, "It was just a phony publicity stunt . . . First, they took the few scabs they have in the mill, plus the watchmen, guards and office force, and loaded them into cars and drove them all up to the auditorium. There they were redistributed, about one to each car. The cars were filled up with businessmen and other members of the Industrial Council of Washington who acted as extras to make an impressive show for the public."

The Communist paper is the only one that bothers to interview the strikers. The *Times*, *Post-Intelligencer*, and *Star* report the company line, which is that the strike is an effort of outsiders, and that many workers have crossed the picket line to go back to work.

To keep the company in business, the Industrial Council hires men to use Fisher's trucks to move flour through the picket lines to wholesalers. The Seattle Central Labor Council asks the Teamsters not to move the flour from wholesalers to grocers. The wholesalers threaten to have the Industrial Council move the flour, and Teamster leader Dave Beck caves in and allows his men to move it. Outmaneuvered, strike leaders call for a consumer boycott of Fisher flour.

Early in November 1935, the Industrial Council sends a letter asking for donations to a $200,000 fund for "paid space in newspapers, under-cover operatives, contact men, guards and the operation of an independent trucking corporation." The unions print a copy of the letter in the *Washington State Labor News*, highlighting the "under-cover operatives."

Labor also rallies its friends. Fred Shorter, pastor at the Church of the People, holds a forum called "Labor's Side of the Fisher Strike." The Seattle dailies don't report what Shorter or the union men say, but they do report that O. W. Fisher stands up in the crowd and says to Sam Ming, president of the Flour and Cereal Workers, "Sam, your union is being run by

Communists." The *Voice of Action* mocks O. W. Fisher, reporting that he was "somewhat stewed."

The Communists are not running the Fisher strike. In 1934 they are still in their militant phase; if they were running the strike, it would declare itself as an anti-capitalist struggle for all Seattle labor. The *Washington State Labor News* would denounce its leaders as a bunch of Reds. Probably the strike would be violent. In October 1935, the *Voice of Action* urges Fisher workers "to employ every method of struggle known to labor"—an open invitation to bust heads. And none of this happens. The Fisher workers are organized by the American Federation of Labor, and they don't act that way.

Taking his cue from management, Seattle Mayor Charles L. Smith cracks down on the Reds. He orders two Communist organizers arrested for planning to use the Fisher struggle to foment a general strike. They may well have had such a plan. The *Voice of Action* tried to turn the longshore strike of 1934 into a general strike. But imagining and doing are not the same things.

In December 1935 the new National Labor Relations Board holds a hearing in Seattle. Fisher's attorneys argue that the company's labor relations are not interstate commerce and therefore none of the federal government's business. It is a losing argument, and the company knows it. In a deal brokered by the Rev. John Magee of Seattle's First Methodist Episcopal Church, Fisher recognizes the two AFL unions and agrees to a closed shop.

The Longshoremen and other industrial unions will emerge from the Depression much stronger. One union that will not is the Workers' Alliance, an organization of Works Progress Administration (WPA) workers.

The WPA, created in 1935, is President Roosevelt's program to replace leaf-raking and public charity with real work. "We have tried to put every kind of person to work," says national WPA boss Harry Hopkins. "Relief is not a matter of charity but a matter of duty. It is a matter of right and it is being administered in 3,300 counties in the United States."

In Ballard the WPA pays women to sew. At Boeing Field it pays men to extend the runway. At Union Bay it pays men to clear ground for the Arboretum. In West Seattle it pays men to build a golf course. At Green Lake it operates two dredges as part of a plan to build a lighted fountain in the lake's center. One of the dredges catches fire, and the plan runs over budget and is abandoned.

Americans respect work and the workers who do it. But is WPA work real work? In March 1936 the *Seattle Times* reports that 44 WPA men have been fired for drinking and loafing on the Arboretum job but have been taken back after promising not to do it again.

In July 1936, WPA workers have a picnic in Seward Park. The picnic offers free beer. The picnickers behave themselves, but Seattle's women's clubs complain. *Alcohol* in a public park! The *Times* puts the story of the beer, and the outrage, on page one. The story implies that public officials have fallen down on the job. The state Liquor Control Board quickly declares that beer will no longer be allowed in any public park in Washington.

Had the picnickers been Boeing workers, the *Times* would have played it differently. But WPA men have a reputation—and they know it. And that's a problem for the officials who run the program. "When a job isn't as desirable as it might be, it's manifestly difficult to make sure that everybody gives an honest day's work," says state WPA director Don G. Abel in a speech to the Professional and Business Men's Club. "People of the community should adopt a more helpful attitude toward the WPA workers. You can't hope to make better citizens of them by making fun of them."

People who do real work can organize real unions. The picnic at Seward Park is sponsored by the Project Workers' Union, which later renames itself the Workers' Alliance. The Seattle unit is part of the national Workers' Alliance headed by David Lasser, the former editor of *Technocracy Review*, and by Herbert Benjamin, a member of the Communist Party. Its leader in the state of Washington is Harold P. Brockway, the Communist nominee for governor in 1936.

In his run for public office, Brockway fizzles out. As the organizer of a union—a very political union—he is more successful.

In January 1937 Brockway calls a strike of all WPA workers in King County. There is no strike vote. He simply orders his members out, and most of them go out. Brockway demands union wages, paid sick days, paid bad-weather days, and pay for days on strike—and also that his union, the Workers' Alliance, be recognized as the exclusive bargaining agent for all WPA workers.

The question might be asked: What is the bargaining position of men given work as a favor? In mid-1937, when 40 WPA workers making shoes in Seattle go on strike, a WPA official says, "They can strike as long as they want to." And he shuts down the shop permanently. When Brockway takes thousands of workers out, WPA officials make the same threat, but they don't follow through.

Not all the WPA men honor the strike. At the West Seattle Golf Course, 200 of them attempt to return to work and are attacked by Workers' Alliance pickets. Forty-two Workers' Alliance men are arrested and charged with disorderly conduct. The Seattle Central Labor Council supports them. The Chamber of Commerce says nothing; it doesn't represent the WPA. The judge lets the men off.

Workers Alliance button.

Local WPA officials agree to pay union wages. Because the monthly pay is set in Washington, DC, they raise the wage rate by cutting the hours of work. They also recognize the Workers' Alliance as the representative of all WPA workers in King County.

The organizers of the Workers' Alliance have bigger ideas. They believe capitalism is doomed and that they will be a force for social change. They are mistaken. The WPA's employment peaks in 1938. The Workers' Alliance will never achieve statewide recognition. It will also never stage another big strike around Seattle. Nationwide, the Workers' Alliance will fold up in 1941, and the WPA will do likewise some months later. In 1948, Howard Costigan will testify at the Canwell hearings that as a political effort, the union of WPA workers was "pretty much a lost cause."

The Works Progress Administration will do real work building roads and public buildings across Washington and will go down in history as a Depression-era success. But the program will never be revived. The private-sector unions don't want to compete with it, and the social-work industry doesn't believe in it. The politicians will remember the headaches the program brought and will be happy to consign the WPA to the trophy shelf of history.

One other labor struggle around Seattle stands out as extraordinary: the fight of the Cannery Workers' and Farm Laborers' Union, the AFL's first union founded and led by Filipinos.

The Labor Push, 1934–1937 157

Anti-WPA cartoon in the *Seattle Times*, 6-3-1936. *Harold Carlisle*, Des Moines Register.

On December 1, 1936, Virgil Duyungan and Aurelio Simon are gunned down at the Gyokko Ken Café in Seattle's Japantown. Duyungan is the union's founder and president. Simon is its secretary. The shooter is Placido Patron, the nephew of a labor contractor that the union is trying to put out of business.

The union has a reason to do that. The *Alaskeros*—the Filipinos who work in the Alaska canneries—are tired of having to pay contractors each year for the privilege of having the same jobs of heading, gutting, scaling, and canning salmon. That most of the contractors are also Filipino does not make it better. "There is no reason why we should allow the cannery contractors to subjugate, enslave and harangue us," Virgil Duyungan tells his men.

158   Seattle in the Great Depression

WPA men lay culvert at West Seattle Golf Course. *Courtesy of the Seattle Municipal Archives, 30630.*

The murder of their founder and president does not stop the union men. In the spring of 1937, they begin negotiating a contract with the canneries. At this time, Seattle attorney Clarence T. Arai, president of the Japanese American Citizens' League, forms a rival union. The original union has been allowing all races to join, but the Filipinos are in control. Arai's union is controlled by Japanese, the group that was formerly the majority of the cannery workers. Many of Arai's members are second-generation *Nisei* on vacation from school or university.

By this time, the Filipino-led union has affiliated with the Congress of Industrial Organizations (CIO). The Japanese-led union is AFL.

The National Labor Relations Act sets up a way for fights between unions to be settled by a vote. But the law is new, and the AFL and the CIO are fighting the old way. In April 1937, the Japanese union throws a picket line on the Alaska Steamship Company dock to prevent the Filipinos from going north to the canneries. The Filipinos arrive with sticks, ready to fight their way onto the ship, but police are there to escort them on board.

Teamster men, who are AFL, refuse to cross the Japanese union's line, leaving passengers to carry their own luggage. The ship's crew are in CIO-affiliated unions and ignore the picket line. The *Post-Intelligencer*

Virgil Duyungan, one of the founding leaders of the Cannery Workers and Farm Laborers Union in 1933. *Filipino American Historical Society.*

writes: "Yesterday's picketing of the docks presented a strange spectacle, with longshoremen, seamen and marine firemen shoving their way through the pickets to go to work. It was the first time in waterfront history that the maritime workers defied an AFL picket line."

The Filipinos win the battle for the 1937 season. Their contract sets the terms: a union shop, higher pay, and an eight-hour day. The Filipino and Japanese unions remain, vying for supremacy. In 1938 comes a showdown vote under the new labor law. The Filipinos' Cannery Workers' and Farm Laborers' Union, CIO, gets 54 percent of the vote and is recognized as the bargaining agent for all the workers.

After World War II, it affiliates with the Longshoremen.

11
Dave Beck, 1931–1938

In November 1938, the *Saturday Evening Post* sends Garet Garrett to interview America's most successful Teamster. "Seattle," Garrett writes, "is the perfect closed-shop town. The power is in the hands of one man. His name is Beck." Garrett is a conservative, and he is wary of what Beck has done in Seattle. But he respects Beck as a man who has established a kind of industrial order.

Garrett describes the Teamster building in Seattle as a hive of activity. Beck is on the second floor. "He sits in the corner with his back to the windows," Garrett writes. "He is short and thick, with hard edges, very tight in his skin, redheaded complexion, blue eyes and blond eyelashes. One of the human-terrier breed, daring but cautious, quick to take and to give offense, friendly otherwise, very fond of combat, but not a killer. His thoughts are the very shape of himself and have fist in them."

Dave Beck, 1936. *Author's collection.*

Garrett explains Beck's regime in the *Post*. "He is for business; he is for the profit system . . . Business must make a profit or else nobody will have a job. Only, of course, it must be a reasonable profit . . . What Beck says to business is, in effect this: 'Let us collaborate. We fix wages. You fix the prices that are necessary to pay the wage and leave you a fair profit, and let us both be reasonable. We will police your prices to see that no chiseler breaks them down. That is more than you can do for yourselves.'"

Beck is wielding a kind of governmental power. It is not a revolutionary power. "If you want to talk about Russia or settle anything in Spain, get out," Beck tells Garrett. "This is unionism."

Dave Beck is the son of a carpet layer and a laundress. Growing up poor in the Belltown neighborhood near downtown Seattle, he goes to work young. At 12, he delivers the *Post-Intelligencer*. He sells Christmas trees. He catches and sells fish. He kills rats for the Health Department, which pays a $5 bounty for rats infested with plague. In high school, he drops out to work in a laundry. In World War I he serves in the Army. After the war he returns to Seattle and drives a laundry truck.

Beck has a sharp mind. While driving his truck, he envisions all the trucks going to all the businesses and imagines what might be done if all were under the control of one man.

In 1924 Beck becomes secretary-treasurer for the Laundry and Dye Workers. In 1926, he wins union recognition and pay increases at Seattle's industrial laundries, which are big operations in the era before home washers and dryers. In 1929 Beck begins organizing the smaller cleaners that send their dry cleaning to the big laundries.

The classic goal of unions is to take labor out of competition. To do that, Beck's strategy is to take the employers out first. In 1930 the laundries form an association to fix prices. They set the price to clean, press, and deliver a man's suit at $1.50, double the nonmember price. Laundries that refuse to join are hit with stink bombs, rocks through windows, and the despoiling of customers' clothes with indelible ink. One laundry is dynamited at night. The business owners finger Beck as the culprit. He says it's not him. He says the laundries are bombing themselves for the insurance money.

The campaign fails. By then, the Depression has begun, and high-priced cleaners are losing business. Several of them break ranks, and the price-fixing agreement collapses.

In February 1932 Beck tries again. "None of the plants is operating profitably," he tells the *Post-Intelligencer*. What's needed, he says, is to "bring order out of chaos, make the earnings of men and women employed in the plants more secure and ensure the proprietors a fair return on their investment."

The laundries' association hires an attorney that the newspapers dub Seattle's "cleaning-and-dyeing czar." The attorney has the power to set prices, ban competitive practices, judge disputes, collect fines, and replace managers.

King County prosecutor Robert Burgunder calls a press conference. Price-fixing is illegal in Washington, he says, on account of a 1909 Washington Supreme Court case over the price of milk. He will not tolerate price-fixing. A few days later, he backs off. Cleaning is a service. Maybe the 1909 ruling about milk would apply to a service, and maybe it wouldn't. If someone wants to bring that case to court, the prosecutor says, it's fine by him. His concern is that there be no forceful intimidation.

A few days later, in the early morning of March 4, 1932, a stick of dynamite explodes at the Cleanwell Dye Works at 3300 Rainier Ave. S. Cleanwell Dye's owner is an immigrant Pole with the improbable name of Solomon Stalin. He tells police that a cartel has been demanding that he join and raise his prices. To squeeze him, they have been sending in clothing with hidden packets of dye and acid. And now a bomb. Solomon Stalin will hold out for years, and in 1937 his shop will be bombed again. But in April 1932 most of the other shops join the cartel. Dave Beck and the Teamsters win.

In the years ahead, Beck will use the same formula: organize the employers, by intimidation if necessary, to make Seattle a closed-shop town.

―――――

In 1933, when Prohibition ends, the workers at the Northwest Brewing Company in Tacoma are organized by the Brewery Workers. The Teamsters claim the truck drivers. In September 1934, at the end of the first Teamster contract, company president Peter Marinoff decides to deal exclusively with the Brewery Workers. Marinoff, an immigrant from Russia, dismisses eight Teamster drivers. Dave Beck responds with a Teamster picket line at Marinoff's Tacoma brewery and its Seattle distribution center.

This is not only a jurisdictional fight. The Teamsters are the enforcement arm of a price cartel that Marinoff is refusing to join. A few days later he says the Teamsters will end the strike if he raises the price of a two-quart bottle of Marinoff Beer a nickel, to 55 cents. Instead, he cuts his price for a 31-gallon barrel from $18 to $16.

The Teamsters hit back. At Marinoff's Seattle depot, Teamster men force three trucks to stop. They drag the Brewery Workers' men out of the cabs and beat them with lead pipes. Two are hospitalized with scalp wounds. Marinoff appeals to King County Superior Court, and Judge James T. Ronald issues an injunction forbidding the Teamsters from interfering with the company's business.

Marinoff's attorney is former Seattle mayor John Dore. He says to the press, "In the last few years, starting in Chicago, union leaders have been entering into agreements with producers to control markets, and if you don't stand with them and establish a racket, they call a strike on you." He says the Teamsters are trying to force "a beer monopoly in Seattle."

Stymied at the warehouse, the Teamsters follow the trucks and attempt to block deliveries. At the Little Red Hen by Woodland Park and the Ben & Norman Tavern in Ballard, Teamsters heave bricks through the windows.

Marinoff sends telegrams to Washington, DC, complaining that labor racketeers are ruining his business. The Labor Department sends a mediator, but it is the former president of the Seattle Central Labor Council, which is Teamster-controlled. Seeing that the cards are stacked against him, Marinoff gives in. He hires Teamster drivers and promises to promote Teamster membership to his other employees. The Teamsters, in turn, promise Marinoff they will not dictate the price of beer.

In 1935 Marinoff breaks his promises by refusing to pay overtime rates. The Teamsters go out on strike and declare a statewide boycott of Marinoff beer. Marinoff turns back to the Brewery Workers and borrows $150,000, giving them a mortgage on the company's assets.

Again, Teamsters follow Marinoff's trucks and attempt to block deliveries. Again, Marinoff hires armed guards to protect the deliveries. In Tacoma, a picket car of Teamsters follows a car of Marinoff guards. At Pacific Avenue and South 26th Street, strike supporters throw stones at the guards' car. A Marinoff guard reaches through the broken rear window and shoots a .38 revolver at the picket car 80 feet behind. His shot hits the driver, William Usatalo, in the forehead. Usatalo is instantly killed.

Because he hired the guard and bought the gun, Marinoff is convicted of accessory to manslaughter and sentenced to 20 years in prison. He appeals, his conviction is overturned, and he leaves the state. The Brewery Workers, their loan unpaid, take over his brewery in Walla Walla—the only non-Teamster brewery in the state. Beck's Teamsters will fight that brewery for years.

In April 1936, the Industrial Council of Washington describes the regime under Dave Beck. "All industries are to be organized in prices, output and employment ... [an] administrator or dictator appointed. The employer is to be forced to give to the dictator each month a certified copy of all business he has done, his price schedule, and he will then be assessed a percentage of his gross income." The group lists as already "organized or closed" Seattle's dairies, butchers, cleaners, dyers, and brewers.

Beck defends this regime as a way of "guaranteeing to the employer a fair return on invested capital" while paying Teamster-level wages. He downplays his union's notoriety for violence. And clearly the violence is controlled. Teamsters don't carry guns. They may beat a scab senseless, but they won't kill him. An ordinary nonunion driver will generally get a warning; only if he defies them will they tip over his truck.

Still, a Teamster campaign is terrifying, and only a few businesses hold out against it. The Golden Rule Bakery and Dairy is one of them. It holds out for 11 years. Its drivers are followed and harassed, and its building vandalized. In May 1936, Teamster men roll over a Golden Rule milk truck at the Alaska Steamship pier and threaten the wrecking crew called to right it. And that is the final push. The next day, Golden Rule's tough old owner, Irish-born William H. Pemberton, dies of natural causes. His heirs quickly sign a Teamster contract.

In May 1936, the Auto Mechanics Union goes on strike against the car dealers, demanding recognition. When Teamster pickets begin beating employees who cross the line and police do nothing, the dealers complain to the city council. Dave Beck defends his men. "If there are incidents of violence, let the courts handle it," he says. "You can't show me one instance of a labor man carrying a gun or anything that would kill a man, but a Teamsters man was killed in a labor fight last year." The council does nothing.

In a speech to the Young Men's Democratic Club, Beck says, "Perhaps there has been violence, but it was not fostered by duly elected labor leaders. Whatever violence there has been is the work of irresponsible people under strong emotions." In so many words, this is Beck's declaration that he will not restrain his men. And violence works: the car dealers settle. They agree to pay the union five dollars on every car sold.

―――

The *Seattle Post-Intelligencer* strike of 1936 is the first time a union of journalists shuts down a daily newspaper anywhere in the United States.

The *P-I*, the *Times*, and the *Star* all employ union typographers, stereographers, and mailers. Newspapers accept unions in the back shop, but not in the newsroom. "The prestige and success of the paper depends not on how

Attorney George Vanderveer (left) and Dave Beck, 1936. *International Newsphoto image in author's collection.*

much copy is produced but on how good that copy is," Hearst's *New York Evening Journal* says. "The effort of the individual is not and cannot be collectivist. It is, on the contrary, almost exclusively individualistic." The industry believes that writers and photographers do not belong in unions.

That belief is challenged by Heywood Broun, a columnist at the *New York World-Telegram*. Broun founds the American Newspaper Guild on the idea that journalists need a union for the same reasons other workers do. He is also a man of the left; in 1937 he will say publicly that he agrees with much of the Communist Party's program. At the *Seattle Post-Intelligencer*, some journalists lean that way and many more resent their paper's right-wing crusades against communism and its mockery of the New Deal.

In 1936, employees at the *P-I* begin organizing a unit of the Guild. Under the National Labor Relations Act, the company can't fire an employee for supporting a union, but it can fire one for other reasons. In July 1936, the *P-I* fires the manager of the photo department, Frank Lynch, ostensibly for leaving the photo shop in a mess. Another manager tells theater and movie critic Everhardt Armstrong to go on vacation immediately. Armstrong demands to know if he is being discharged and is fired for "gross insubordination." The union claims that Lynch and Armstrong are fired because of their support of the Guild, and probably they are.

Guild activists are hot for a strike, but the union has signed up only 35 members—less than half the editorial staff and only 5 percent of the *P-I*'s total employment of 650. Thirty-five guildsmen have no ability to shut down the paper, and the backshop men are under contract to work. The man who makes the strike possible is Dave Beck, who dominates the Seattle Central Labor Council. With his support, the Newspaper Guild goes out on August 13, 1936. Joining the reporters and photographers in its picket line are timber workers, longshoremen, and Beck's Teamsters.

Word goes out that the *Post-Intelligencer* has hired Harold E. Hiatt, Peter Marinoff's guard who drove the car for the man who shot Teamster picket William Usatalo. The Washington Supreme Court has just set aside Hiatt's conviction for manslaughter. The Teamsters lay for him, and when Hiatt crosses the picket line, they stomp him, inflicting severe head injuries. Pickets also beat four *P-I* men who try to cross the picket line, leaving one with a broken jaw.

The violence lasts only one day, but it is enough. The paper shuts down. After that, all that's needed is a push. When someone tries to cross the line, he is stopped, asked where he is going, and pushed back until he gives up.

The *Times* denounces Dave Beck as a labor dictator, enforcing his rule through "his brawny crew of teamsters, loggers and longshoremen." It prints a statement by the *Post-Intelligencer* accusing Beck of a "reign of terrorism." Beck sues them both for libel.

The Industrial Council of Washington tells the *New York Times* that Seattle businesses fear a closed-shop town "in contrast with open-shop Los Angeles" and that they "are solidly behind William Randolph Hearst."

For their part, Seattle unions put on their first Labor Day parade in 17 years. Led by the drill team and band of the Seattle Police Department, 15,000 participants move through the central business district past 50,000 spectators. A year hence, the Teamsters and Longshoremen will be rivals, one for the AFL and the other for the CIO. On September 7, 1936, they are united.

The *Seattle Times* calls the parade "one of the greatest demonstrations organized labor ever held here." It is followed on November 3 by the reelection of Franklin Roosevelt, which is one of the greatest victories of the Democratic Party in the 20th century.

The *Post-Intelligencer* has nothing to say about any of it. The city's anti-New-Deal morning newspaper is closed during the 1936 campaign, from mid-August to the end of November.

———

In November 1936, William Randolph Hearst writes to the Newspaper Guild that Roosevelt's landslide reelection "is absolutely stunning to those who opposed him." Hearst gives up on the strike and tells the *Post-Intelligencer* to recognize the union.

The *P-I* takes back all the strikers except Frank Lynch and Everhardt Armstrong. In January 1937 the National Labor Relations Board orders the company to reinstate them with back pay, though by the time the *P-I* accepts this, Armstrong has died of a heart attack in a Seattle hotel room. The *Post-Intelligencer* returns to the newsstands on November 29, 1936.

Hearst also caves in editorially. As publisher he appoints former *Chicago Tribune* manager John Boettiger, 36, who is married to Anna Roosevelt, the president's daughter. Under the wing of "the New Deal's royal family," the *P-I* moderates its voice. It carries no more of Hearst's right-wing attacks on the New Deal, though it does not become an organ of the New Deal, either.

The big winner of the *Post-Intelligencer* strike is the man who insured its success: Dave Beck. The *P-I* and *Times* settle Beck's libel suit, paying him $25,000. They also stop their attacks on Beck and the Teamsters. On page one of the *P-I*, John Boettiger refers sweetly to the Seattle union boss as "the omnipotent Dave Beck." The *Seattle Times*, write historians William

John and Anna Roosevelt Boettiger, 1936. *Wide World Photo image in author's collection.*

Ames and Roger Simpson, runs "no locally written criticism [of Beck], either editorial or letters to the editor," for the next 20 years.

The Guild will survive at the *P-I* until it closes in 2009.

The *P-I* strike is Seattle's crucial labor battle of the 1930s. In January 1937, the Chamber of Commerce's new president, George K. Comstock, announces that the fight against the closed shop is over. Finally defeated by labor, the Industrial Council of Washington is disbanded. In its place, the Chamber announces a group of negotiators. Much of organized labor is skeptical of the employers' switch from fighting to talking, but Dave Beck, the man the Industrial Council damned as Seattle's "dictator," welcomes it.

Labor has split into two factions. The American Federation of Labor has historically been made up of craft unions—carpenters, plumbers, machinists. Inside the AFL, the Committee for Industrial Organization is organizing unions that span entire industries. To do this, the CIO has a new tactic, the sit-down strike. Union men occupy the workplace so that the company can't bring in scabs. The sit-down strike is illegal. It is trespassing, plain and simple. It will not be much used in Seattle, but business fears it.

Later in 1937, the CIO will leave the AFL and rename itself the Congress of Industrial Organizations. But already the AFL and CIO are enemies. The Teamsters are AFL and the Longshoremen are CIO—and that pits Dave Beck against the Longshoremen's Pacific Coast leader, Harry Bridges.

Bridges is a radical. In 1939, the federal government will try to deport him to Australia as a member of the Communist Party. The effort will fail, but the red-baiting of Bridges is not entirely wrong. In a speech at the University of Washington in May 1937, Bridges says, "We take the stand that we as workers have nothing in common with the employers. We are in a class struggle and we subscribe to the belief that if the employer is not in business his products still will be necessary and we still will be providing them when there is no employing class. We frankly believe that day is coming."

Statements like that are meat for Dave Beck. He tells business that Bridges is their enemy. The Teamsters are business unionists. They don't like to strike, and they don't use the sit-down. Speaking to the Seattle Real Estate Board, Beck says, "The mass seizure of private property is a form of revolution." At the Seattle Junior Chamber of Commerce, he says, "I am for the capitalistic system."

Beck also emphasizes that *he* will be fighting the CIO. "When we fight them, we will be battling in *your* plants and in *your* factories," he says. Better to join forces, set prices that can support union-scale pay, and run the nonunion shops out of business.

In December 1937, the CIO sends Eugene Dennett of the Inlandboatmen to answer Beck. Dennett has been a secret member of the Communist Party since 1931. But at the Young Men's Business Club of Seattle, Dennett speaks in moderate words. "Unlike our chief adversary," he says, "we are not trying to organize the employers, or police the employees." Under Dave Beck and his "goon squads," Dennett says, "We have all the elements in the Pacific Northwest of a budding American fascism."

It is too late. Seattle business leaders have made up their minds. They will accept Dave Beck. Harry Bridges can have the waterfront, but Beck will have the rest.

The reason for labor's triumph is not the National Labor Relations Act. The new law opens up a way for workers to create unions by vote, but unions are winning battles the old-fashioned way. In the *Post-Intelligencer* strike of 1936, the Newspaper Guild wins recognition at the *P-I* not with a democratic vote—there is none—but because the Teamsters shut down the paper.

Labor makes no apologies for bare-knuckle tactics. To labor, a scab is a thief of an honest man's job. Even when there is no strike, the union man believes the unorganized man is a threat.

In 1937, labor is demanding that *all* workers be in unions. One example: In February, a picket line is thrown around a roadhouse on Lake City Way called the Coon Chicken Inn. The complaint is not its racist name— African Americans have already objected to that and been ignored—but that the business employs nonunion cooks, servers, and musicians. The picketers carry signs saying "unfair." On a Saturday night, two men attack the restaurant with stink bombs. The manager chases them and corners them with a gun. They are not his employees. After a few weeks of harassment, the manager signs with the unions.

In March 1937, Building Trades men block the roads to Magnolia Bluff and turn back trucks carrying supplies to 30 nonunion building sites. They say they are protecting union men at 20 other work sites. The nonunion builders give in. Within a few days, all the Seattle homebuilders accept union wages. They also accept a six-hour day, a concession they will regret.

In June 1937, Building Service workers shut down the elevators at the 13-story Northwestern Mutual Building, the former Shopping Tower. They demand a union contract. After two hours of the tenants having to use the stairs, management gives in.

All these are side stories. The big labor story of 1937 is the unionization of whole industries: Seattle's principal hotels and department stores; 350 grocery stores; 600 restaurants; 400 dealers in coal, wood, and fuel oil; and 900 Seattle apartment houses. The agreements are done without strikes or worker elections by dealing with organized groups of owners. In the case of the hotels, the owners watch from a distance as unions shut down all the principal hotels in San Francisco. Fearing the same, they approach Beck and offer to accept the Teamsters.

Typically, these agreements come with large wage increases. In November 1937, the Retail Clerks sign a contract with Seattle department stores that increase wages by more than 20 percent.

For business owners, writes historian Roger Sale, "Once the deals were struck, they need fear nothing from Beck's unions. Beck always kept his word and his contracts."

Beck's aim is to keep Seattle an island of union wages, hours, and rules in a competitive sea. "Gifted with a passion for research and a good business head, he would decide how many filling stations there should be in Seattle, or how many clerks a department store needed, or if there were enough restaurants in a given area," Sale writes. "He would then make his deal for just that many gas stations or clerks or restaurants. If someone tried to move in, or to undersell the others, or to lay off clerks, Beck would simply refuse to let trucks go there, and, as a result, the industry was what Beck called, 'stabilized.' No labor leader before Beck had thought of such things, or got them done if he did."

Seattle people call the regime "Dave's little NRA." As with the National Recovery Administration, Beck aims to raise wages by shielding employers from competition. This immediately benefits people who keep their jobs. So did the NRA; but by raising costs and controlling output, the NRA made it harder to create new jobs.

This bothers Garet Garrett, the man sent by the *Saturday Evening Post*. Garrett puts it to Beck that he is sacrificing the future for the present.

"Suppose then it works," Garrett says to Beck in his 1938 interview. "Wages are right, prices are right, everybody makes 'reasonable' profits. Therefore, peace and stability. But are you sure that under such happy conditions Seattle would not decay at the roots? What incentive would there be for a man to improve his methods, to risk his capital in new machinery?"

Long-term investment again.

Beck replies, "I have thought of all that. I don't know the answer. It hasn't happened yet. If it does, we'll have to think of a way to deal with it."

He never does. Beck's regime doesn't last long enough to require that. Still, it lasts quite a while.

Early in 1942, just after America has officially entered the war, English journalist Alastair Cooke, 33, takes a road trip around the United States. Years later, Cooke will be known to Americans as the genial man who introduces PBS-TV's Masterpiece Theatre. In 1942 he arrives in Seattle and asks about the famous Dave Beck.

"In Seattle, it is like making a secret Masonic sign," Cooke writes. "One man will declare that all law and order is due to the Teamsters' benign influence. Another will act as if you were digging for material on the Ku Klux Klan . . . [Dave Beck] is symbolically the sheriff of Seattle. He is simultaneously respected, feared, hated, worshiped."

A decade later, in 1951, popular historian Murray Morgan writes in *Skid Road* of an interview with Beck, "the large, bald, blue-eyed man" who sits at a big desk and issues commands. Morgan writes, "It was the Depression that made the Teamster boss the ruler of Seattle."

In 1952, Dave Beck is elected international president of the Brotherhood of Teamsters. In 1957, he is called to a U.S. Senate committee to testify on labor racketeering. Interrogated by committee counsel Robert F. Kennedy, Beck invokes the Fifth Amendment 117 times. In 1959 Beck is convicted in state court of embezzlement and in federal court of income-tax evasion. From 1962 to 1965, he is imprisoned in the McNeil Island Penitentiary in Puget Sound. Upon his release, Beck lives a private life. Until his death in 1993, he uses money from his Teamster pension to invest in parking lots.

12
John Dore, 1932–1938

John Dore is the emblematic Seattle politician of the 1930s. Born in Boston in 1881, Dore came to Seattle with his parents, went through the public schools, and then went back to Boston for a time at Harvard. At 19, he returned to Seattle and joined the *Post-Intelligencer* as a reporter. He moved to the *Times*, where he covered courts. "He met and knew all the lawyers in town," writes Howard MacGowan of the *Star*. "He got a key to the county's law library and after the day's work was done, after the courts had closed, John would go up and spend many silent hours in the old courthouse building poring over the county's calf-bound volumes." Without going to law school, Dore passed the bar and opened an office as a trial attorney.

Dore describes his courtroom strategy: "Take a simple point and drive it home. The fewer details, the better. Have no evidence except your one big outstanding fact. Drive it home to your jury and they'll be with you." Push straight ahead and concede nothing.

A *Times* feature on Dore calls him "the leading trial lawyer in the Pacific Northwest, a sort of local Clarence Darrow." It says, "Dore has developed contempt to a subtle degree. It leaves superior court judges white-faced and gasping. It has caused him to be fined innumerable times. He always pulls the cash out of his pocket and hands it to the bailiff with a grand flourish. He doesn't say it, but his manner suggests that the money was well spent."

Dore campaigns hard for mayor in 1932. He avoids candidates' forums where rivals sit politely and take turns defending their views. He stages his own events and infuses them with passion. He never defends. He attacks.

John Dore, 1932. *ACME Newspictures image in author's collection.*

174 Seattle in the Great Depression

Franklin Roosevelt, Mayor John Dore, and Senator C. C. Dill in campaign car, 1932. Dore, nominally a Republican, has endorsed Roosevelt. Behind Dore is Vic Meyers, and at Dill's elbow is Warren Magnuson. *ACME Newspictures image in author's collection.*

Twice he packs the Eagles Auditorium with folks eager for a show, and he gives it to them. He mocks his opponents. He blasts "the gang of crooks at the city hall."

"John Dore thinks and acts in pictures," says the *Times* man. "The most graphic utterance of the late campaign, for instance, was his promise to move the 'Hollywood furniture' out of the $18,000 mayor's office ... That was something his hearers could see, a tangible, colorful something they could get their mental teeth into."

In March 1932, a sore and gloomy month, Seattle's voters elect John Dore in a landslide.

In the campaign, Dore promised the people he would solve the city's financial crisis by cutting big salaries of city executives, including his own. But when it comes to it, cutting only the big salaries won't do the job. Once elected, Dore asks to cut the pay of all city employees, with the highest percentage at the top.

The unions ask to cut the workweek instead, from 44 hours to 35. The cut in hours would cut the paychecks of those at the bottom by the same percentage as the top. The unions know that, but they want to preserve the hourly rates. They also want the shorter week. The city council compromises. It cuts the workweek from 44 hours to 40—a 9 percent across-the-board cut—and wage rates by 9 to 20 percent, depending on income. For the average city worker, the pay cut is 16 percent.

Labor is furious. James A. Duncan, president of the Washington State Federation of Labor, calls it "the biggest double-cross the city ever administered to organized labor." City Attorney Anton C. Van Soelen warns Dore that employees will challenge the cuts in court. They will, and the city will lose some challenges, but that's a problem for later. Dore makes the cuts.

Dore wants to win back labor's support. In August 1932, he gets his chance when the big Seattle laundries announce a 15 percent pay cut and demand an open shop. Eight hundred women at 11 laundries go out on strike. They demand to keep their pay and their closed shop. The employers bring in strikebreakers. At the Quality Laundry, women pickets beat a scab—and the laundries ask Mayor Dore to protect the scabs from union violence.

Dore refuses. "I have ordered that all police protection be removed from laundries employing strikebreakers," he declares. "If there is any ensuing trouble it will be just too bad." The strike ends with the employers accepting the closed shop and the union accepting the pay cut. (Later, Dave Beck will cite this pay cut as proof that he is sensitive to the needs of business.)

Dore then goes after the city's largest taxpayer, the Pacific Telephone & Telegraph Company. Before Dore was elected, I. F. Dix, the company's manager, headed the city-county task force to create relief work. Dix's volunteer work earns no favor from Dore, who attacks the phone company for not having a city franchise since 1925. Several years earlier the city issued a franchise to Pacific Telephone, but it was referred to the voters, and they said no. Now Dore tells Dix that if Pacific Telephone does not sign a franchise agreement by September 1, "I, as mayor, will remove your poles and wires from the streets of Seattle." He also sends Pacific Telephone a bill for $2 million for use of public rights-of-way since 1925.

Dore's threat is all bluff. He is not going to rip down the telephone lines. And City Attorney Van Soelen advises Dore that he can't force the company to pay the $2 million, a number that Dore has pulled out of his head.

The long-term problem facing John Dore is the streetcars. In 1918 an earlier mayor, Ole Hanson, agrees to buy the streetcar lines from the Puget Sound Traction, Light and Power Company—today's Puget Sound Energy. It is a war measure. Streetcars move workers to the shipyards, and in the wartime inflation, the 5-cent fare can't cover the cost. State law doesn't allow a private utility to charge more than a nickel, but the law does not apply to a municipality (which soon raises the fare to 10 cents or three rides for a quarter). Under pressure from federal officials, the city agrees to pay Puget $15 million in 5-percent, 20-year revenue bonds for the whole system. Promised that the bonds will be paid entirely from the fare box, the citizens vote 3 to 1 to approve the deal.

In the 1920s, about half the debt is paid off. But with the Depression, the remaining debt becomes unpayable. Critics blame the streetcar problem on "political management," but the larger problem is that people are buying private cars. In the 1920s, street railway ridership falls by one-third. Other indicators show the trend. In 1928, the year the state opens the Pacific Highway between Seattle and Tacoma, the Puget Sound Power & Light

Seattle streetcar at First and Marion, 1937. *Author's collection*.

Seattle Streetcar map, 1933. *Courtesy of Seattle Municipal Archives.*

Company (no more "Traction") shuts down the Seattle-Tacoma rail line. Called the Interurban, it has lost money for years. And in November 1930, the Puget Sound Navigation Company ends the steamer service to Tacoma that has existed since the 1880s.

The streetcars from Puget are old. The *Star* complains of "the hard, wooden seats, the noise, the vibration, the window that won't open—or close—the hideous color, the glaring lights." In 1929, the farebox revenue fails to cover the principal payments on the streetcar bonds. From then on, the city will pay Puget interest only.

The Depression makes even that difficult. To pay Puget the interest due March 1, 1932, the Street Railway pays its employees in warrants. Unlike the warrants for police and fire employees, which are backed by the city's credit, Street Railway warrants are backed by the farebox revenue only. That makes them less secure, and the banks are quicker to reject them. They do this in January 1932. The 1,474 streetcar workers will have to hold their pay warrants until the system has the cash or sell them at a discount.

In desperation, the city council turns to Walter M. Brown. He is president of the Seattle & Rainier Valley Railway, the city's last private streetcar line, which runs from downtown to Renton. The council hires Brown for three months to save the city's system.

Brown talks the car men out of their vacations, but when he asks for pay cuts, the men threaten to strike—and the city does not allow him to use strikebreakers. He does other things. The streetcars stop an average 17 times per mile, slowing progress to 8½ miles an hour. Brown speeds the service by cutting the number of stops. He reduces off-hour service. He replaces the Madison and Yesler cable runs with buses, leaving only the James Street run, which is steep. But he can do nothing about the city's prewar equipment and what the *Argus* describes as its "miles and miles of rusty rails and rotten ties, sunken at the joints."

Brown says the Street Railway's fundamental problem is that it is "using 1903 streetcars to compete with 1930 automobiles."

Brown's service cuts are not popular. In the city elections of March 8, 1932, Seattle voters throw out the mayor who hired him, Robert Harlin, and elect John Dore. In his campaign, Dore promises to fix the streetcar mess. He says the cars should charge children only 2½ cents, and that the cars should have smoking sections. Even before he takes office, Dore sues to block Walter Brown's service cuts, and Brown backs down on some of them. Dore promises to fire Brown, and Brown quits. Dore also says he will deal with the problem of the debt to Puget by defaulting on the bonds.

Dore will do that, but not in 1932. In his first street railway crisis, he accepts most of Brown's cuts and the system keeps going.

———

In 1934, the Washington Supreme Court tells Seattle that it must restore the cuts it imposed on police and fire employees in 1932. The court's ruling pastes an antilabor label on John Dore, who is running for another two-year term as mayor. In March 1934, Dore loses the election to attorney Charles L. Smith, the man who will lead the police against the longshoremen that summer.

Smith has no happy answer for the city's financial crisis. At year-end 1934, he lays off 21 policemen and two policewomen. The Fire Department retires 23 men on disability. Other city departments go on four-day weeks. In March 1935, a court orders the city to issue back pay to police and fire employees. The city pays in warrants. At the end of 1935, Smith lays off more cops.

Out of office, Dore resumes his law practice, representing brewery owner Peter Marinoff against the Teamsters. But Dore can read a crowd, or a city— and he changes his stripes. In 1936, he runs again for mayor, this time as the Teamsters' friend. Dave Beck is keenly interested in local politics; the union tells its men how to vote and it makes sure they voted. With Beck's support, Dore is elected again. After his victory, Dore tells the Washington State Federation of Labor that he owes "Dave Beck a debt and I am going to pay it back in the next two years . . . This will be a labor union administration as long as I am in office."

Dore is soon tested. Truck farmers in the Green River Valley, many of them Japanese, have been bringing vegetables to an outdoor exchange. Teamster men arrive and demand that the farmers join the union or have their trucks wrecked. When the story appears in the *Seattle Times*, Mayor Dore rejects it as fake news. Most of Seattle's industrial labor is working in a closed shop, he says, "and everybody is satisfied."

With his usual flair, Dore offers $100 to anyone who has been victimized while "bringing his own produce to the city of Seattle." A few days later, orchardists arrive from east of the mountains to claim the $100. Accompanied by the mayor of Cashmere, they say that when they drive their apples to Seattle, they are forced to hire Teamster men they don't need. Clyde L. Trapp of Orondo says he delivers his apples in the middle of the night in order to avoid paying off Teamster thugs.

Dore refuses to meet the group or to pay the $100.

During the 1936 strike against the *Post-Intelligencer*, when pickets beat Harold E. Hiatt senseless, police arrest two Teamster men. Dore lets them go. Challenged by the *P-I*'s publisher to enforce the law, Dore says, "I don't care now whether the *P-I* ever publishes again. Maybe it would be a good thing for the town if it didn't." As for the labor violence, Dore allows that "there were a few fights," but adds, "Why, I used to have more fun at a picnic when I was a boy."

Dore has made good on his promise to Dave Beck.

The unions have divided into two teams, the AFL and the CIO. John Dore is forced to choose, and he chooses the AFL, the Teamsters, and Dave Beck. In the 1937 strike against the *Seattle Star*, this makes Dore an enemy of the workers on strike.

Nineteen circulation managers at the *Star* have signed with the Newspaper Guild. Because they use their cars to move bundles of papers, the Teamsters say they are drivers. The Teamsters insist that no newspapers will move until those jobs are held by Teamster men. The *Star* gives in and replaces the Guild men with Teamsters. The Guild calls a strike, and for a few days the *Star* is closed.

This is not the *Post-Intelligencer* strike. Then the Teamsters, the Seattle Central Labor Council, John Dore, and the strikers were on the same side. But the Newspaper Guild is now CIO, and the Teamsters and the Labor Council are AFL. Because the Labor Council does not support the strike, Mayor Dore announces that the Guild can have no more than two pickets. "You can't let every Tom, Dick and Harry take up picketing and shut down plants," he says. Dore's police chase away the pickets. The *Star* reopens.

The Guild sends the pickets back, and Teamster men beat them up. Paul O'Neil, a *Times* reporter covering the fracas, is left on the ground with a concussion. Dore is furious—not at the Teamsters but at the Guild. "As long as you behave, you can have your two pickets at the *Star*," he says. "But if you try to mass-picket the *Star*, there'll be trouble and the police will disperse you. Anyone who resists will go to jail. Anyone who resists too much will go to the hospital or the morgue."

Once again, Dore pays back his debt to Dave Beck.

The Teamsters win on the street but lose at the National Labor Relations Board. The Board orders the *Star* to give the Guild men their jobs back.

The *Star* survives, but it is already the weakest of Seattle's three dailies. It has just ten years to live.

———

On January 1, 1937, Walter Brown's Seattle & Rainier Valley Railway Company goes out of business. It has been without a city franchise since the beginning of 1935. It has not paid its property taxes, it has defaulted on its bonds, and it has failed to pave around its tracks, which run in a dirt strip down the middle of Rainier Avenue. Back in 1928, the city agreed to buy the company for $1.2 million, but the voters said no. In the last weeks of 1936, the city buys it for 6 cents on the dollar of the 1928 offer. It lacks the cash and pays Brown in warrants. The city rips up the rails, sells the cars to a junk dealer and begins serving the public with buses.

The city's streetcars are in no better condition than Walter Brown's. Some of them date from the turn of the century. Their steel wheels have become "squared" from millions of stops. The ride is bumpy, noisy, slow, and dangerous. Every year streetcars jump the tracks and smash into light poles. Every year streetcars in the middle of the street are hit by automobiles when they turn across traffic. Every year, people are killed.

The city official in charge, Albert Pierce, wants to junk the whole system. Working with a New York transit consultant and Wall Street bankers, Pierce offers a plan to replace all the streetcars with rubber-tired trolleys and buses.

Seattle people are wary. They like their streetcars; they just want new ones. But the new, heavier streetcars require concrete roadbeds. The city has 231 miles of tracks, many of them on brick, cobblestones, or rotting wooden ties. New roadbeds would cost millions. The bond men say it's rubber-tired transit or nothing.

The problem is the debt from 1919, of which $8.3 million remains. Under the Wall Street plan, the city would issue $12 million in new revenue bonds. It would pay the Puget Sound Power & Light Company $4.7 million to erase the $8.3 million debt. Another $1.5 million would pay off the outstanding Street Railway warrants in full. The remaining $5.8 million in new money would pay for rubber-tired trolleys and buses.

Put on the ballot, the plan faces a political problem. The consultant that helped devise this plan, John Beeler, was hired by Puget, and his plan gives Puget 56 cents on the dollar of an uncollectable debt. Mayor Dore tells voters the plan is a "steal," a "wicked swindle," and "so crooked it smells to high heaven." He accuses the councilmen who support it of being "enemies of the people" who are "owned body and soul by the Puget Sound Power & Light Company." He insinuates that the newspapers that support the plan are in Puget Power's pocket.

Wary of being cheated by the "Power Trust" again, Seattle voters kill the plan, voting 58 percent no. They also give Dore and organized labor a majority on the city council for the first time. The election of March 1937 is the high point of John Dore's political life.

Dore now says *he* will fix the streetcar problem. He boasts that he can make Puget Power erase the $8.3 million debt by paying only $1 million— 12 cents on the dollar. To negotiate this deal, he picks Dave Beck's attorney, George Vanderveer. The city council offers Vanderveer 7½ percent of any further concessions he can squeeze out of Puget. Back in 1932 Dore threatened to default on the streetcar bonds and pay employees instead. Now he does it, aiming to give Vanderveer more leverage over the power company.

Vanderveer gets nowhere. However, stiffing Puget Power does keep the show going in John Dore's grandest political year.

―――

On May 1, 1937, the Washington Commonwealth Federation, the Communist Party, the Longshoremen, the Cannery Workers, and other left-wing unions have a May Day parade through downtown Seattle. The parade is ten blocks long, led by marchers flying the flags of the United States and the Soviet Union.

The Seattle Central Labor Council and the Teamsters want nothing to do with May Day. They have their parade on Labor Day, with the CIO not invited. The Stars and Stripes is the only flag they allow. Their parade is five *miles* long—and at the head of it is Mayor John Dore and his chief of police.

John Dore knows what side he's on. "Russia has nothing we want," he tells the regional Teamster convention.

In October 1937, President Roosevelt comes to Seattle. Mayor Dore greets him at the King Street railroad station along with the state's two senators, six congressmen, and Governor Clarence Martin. Lieutenant Governor Vic Meyers and other left-wingers are not invited. The Washington Commonwealth Federation pickets the event with signs urging U.S. sanctions against Japan for invading China. Police confiscate the signs.

A few days later, Dore shuts out the left again. The Communist Party has put money down to rent the Civic Auditorium to celebrate the 20th anniversary of the Russian Revolution. Dore cancels the contract. "The Communist Party and all its allied organizations have no place in Seattle," he says. When the Communists threaten to protest in front of the building, Dore declares, "There'll be no demonstration inside or outside of the building, nor within a quarter of a mile of the place."

The Communists sue Dore in King County Superior Court, claiming that the city has broken its contract and violated their freedom of assembly. Dore argues that he canceled the contract in order to prevent a riot, even though it was the American Legion, not the Communists, threatening to riot. The judge sides with Dore, and the Communists lose the hall.

In 1938, the city faces a financial crisis. Real estate values have fallen, and property-tax revenue is less than one-third the level of 1931. By January 1938, the city is almost a year behind in redeeming employee pay warrants. As in 1932, the banks refuse to take any more of them.

Dore refuses to cut the city's spending. "Balancing the budget is a lot of nonsense," he says in mid-1937. "Persons advocating a balanced budget for Seattle are living off special privileges. Seattle is a corporation. No corporation ever has a balanced budget."

Dore also refuses to tap a new source of revenue: parking meters. In April 1936, before Dore takes office, the City Council votes to install 700 nickel-an-hour meters, but lame-duck mayor Charles Smith vetoes it. Though Portland and other Northwest cities install meters, Dore blocks them. Seattle will not install parking meters until 1942.

Seattle also might have followed Tacoma, Spokane, and Portland and begun charging residents for picking up the garbage. It doesn't. Instead, Dore asks the legislature for a larger share of state revenues. The answer is no. The city asks the state treasurer to buy city warrants, which he has done before. The answer is no. In the new depression of 1937–1938, state revenues are down. To prop up Seattle's warrants in the resale market, the city treasurer raises the interest rate on new warrants from 3 percent to 5 percent.

Early in 1938 the city council approves a tax on business gross revenue and a tax on water. Mayor Dore vetoes both.

He offers no solution to the crisis.

In the spring of 1938, John Dore faces a reelection fight against two high-profile opponents. To his right is Councilman Arthur Langlie, who attacks Dore for wrecking the Street Railway deal and bringing on the warrant crisis. To Dore's left is jazz-band leader and lieutenant governor Vic Meyers, who attacks Dore for siding with the AFL against the CIO and with the Teamsters in their price-fixing rackets. Both are right. The Municipal League brands Seattle's two-term mayor as "unqualified for reelection on his official record."

John Dore, loved or hated. *Courtesy of Seattle Municipal Archives.*

Dore fights dirty. When the *Daily Worker*, the Communist Party's New York paper, runs a flattering article about Vic Meyers—all in the spirit of the Popular Front—Dore smears Meyers as a stooge of the Reds. "Let us keep this an *American* city!" he urges. Writing in *The Nation*, Selden Menefee says Dore is running "a vicious, red-baiting campaign." It *is* vicious, because Meyers is not a Communist. Dore's final speech is so nasty to Meyers that KJR Radio, which is broadcasting it live, cuts him off the air.

Dore has deeper problem. He has heart disease. The newspapers report that he has been in and out of hospitals since November 1937, but they omit his underlying condition. They report his optimistic statements, but also that he has lost weight and that he makes his final campaign speech sitting down. Their deference is expected; President Roosevelt is never shown in a wheelchair or struggling with leg braces (see the cartoons on pages 103, 106, and 266). But Roosevelt is up to the job; John Dore is not. Voters sense this, else they are sick of him. In the February 1938 primary, they give Dore just

18 percent of the vote. The contest narrows to Vic Meyers versus Arthur Langlie.

To the conservatives, Meyers is the candidate of the Commonwealthers, the CIO, and Harry Bridges. If elected, warns the *Argus*, Meyers would put Seattle government in the hands of "fantastic theorists, reckless experimenters and radical adventurers." Langlie represents stability and safety. And in the election of March 1938, Langlie beats Meyers in a landslide.

A month later, John Dore dies of pneumonia. He is 56.

In the *Post-Intelligencer*'s obituary, political reporter Lester M. Hunt honors Dore without praise. "He was spectacular in everything he did," Hunt writes. "He counted both his friends and his enemies by the thousands. There never was any half-way feeling toward him among those who were thrown in contact with him. People loved him or they hated him."

With Dore gone, Seattle's financial picture immediately brightens. Mayor Langlie's cut in the 1939 budget is only 5 percent, and he does not touch employee pay. But his attitude is different, and with the bankers that makes all the difference. They resume cashing the city's general-obligation warrants. Early in 1939, Seattle floats a bond issue that pays off most of its warrant debt.

Langlie also breaks the logjam on transit. In September 1938, the Reconstruction Finance Corporation agrees to lend the city $10.2 million. It's a revenue-bond deal, much the same as the one rejected by voters a year before. This time, the council does not ask the voters. The deal is done. Puget Power accepts 36 cents on the dollar for the defaulted Street Railway bonds, and the old debt is wiped out. The rest of the money goes to buses and electric trolleys and to pay off warrants. More than 200 miles of streetcar tracks will be sold as scrap, some of them to be loaded onto ships for Japan.

The *Argus* suggests that the city save the James Street cable car, "America's last cable car outside of San Francisco," arguing that it "would lend a romantic color to the city." But the transit deal has no provision for romantic color. All the cable cars go, and the last streetcar stops running in 1941.

13
J. D. Ross, 1930–1939

In the 1930s, all Seattle knows the head of City Light. J. D. Ross has been the administrator for two decades. He is *Mister* City Light. He signs the newspaper ads for "*Your* City Light." Writes the *Argus*, "Mayors may come and go, but Superintendent Ross stays on."

Except in 1931.

The problem is a skyscraper. Announced in the palmy days of September 1929, the building is a project of a Seattle man named Lorenzo A. DeCou. For years his company has worked hand in hand with City Light to market electric ranges. Making the most of this connection, DeCou teams up with architect Earl W. Morrison, the designer of the Textile Tower, and proposes a 26-story City Light Tower. Morrison's artwork shows it topped with a proud electric sign: "CITY LIGHT."

The site is in the center of town at Third and Madison. The city has already bought the land for a substation, so it won't be subject to property tax. Rival developers are unhappy about this; they complain that it gives DeCou an advantage. He offers to square the deal by leasing the land for 50 years, after which the city would own the building. He offers the space below ground rent-free for the substation. City Light would take a 20-year lease of floors 1, 2, 3, and 26. The plan is unusual, and to cover itself, the city council puts it to the voters. In March 1930, they approve it.

To finance the project, DeCou arranges a multistate deal. The Mortgage Investment Company of Portland owns a stable of Oregon savings-and-loans. It will borrow their money to buy stock in DeCou's City Light Building Company at $80 a share. DeCou will use that money to pay his contractor. Meanwhile, Mortgage Investment will sell the $80 stock to investors at $100, repay its savings-and-loans, and book the rest as profit. Once all the shares are sold, lenders in St. Louis will take a mortgage on the building.

Deals of this sort are much in vogue in the late 1920s. The failure of Puget Sound Savings in February 1931 changes the weather. Suddenly depositors are demanding their money at savings-and-loans across the Pacific Northwest. The Oregon S&Ls run out of cash to fund their parent company's purchases of stock in DeCou's building. DeCou, in turn, runs out of cash to pay his contractor. Work on the City Light Tower stops.

Because the contractor has quit, officials in Olympia revoke the Portland company's permit to sell stock in Washington. Oregon shuts down the Mortgage Investment Company. Its president, Jay S. Moltzner, is convicted of violating banking laws and sentenced to two years in the Oregon State Penitentiary.

DeCou is finished. He offers to sell the city the work that's done, the basement and sub-basement, and use the money to pay his architect, his contractor and his 400 stockholders. Several councilmen object: under DeCou's contract with Seattle, the city gets the basement and sub-basement for free. The city never agreed to pay the architect or the contractor, and certainly not the stockholders. But many public investors thought the City Light Building Company was a municipal project, on account of the name. The state has accused the stock salesmen of saying so. Reluctantly the city council agrees to buy the abandoned project. It hasn't the cash, so it pays DeCou in City Light warrants.

The tower will never be built. In 1935 City Light will build out the project into a two-story headquarters with the substation below. In the 1950s the building will be expanded to seven stories. In 1995 City Light will finally move to a skyscraper: the 57-floor Seattle Municipal Tower, which it shares with other city departments.

―――――

Mayor Frank Edwards, Ross's superior, has his office in Seattle's low-rise city hall. To him, Mister City Light is getting too big for his britches. To Edwards, the thought of J. D. Ross looking down on him from the 26th floor of a City Light Tower is too much. In March 1931, when the project to build the City Light Tower is falling apart, Edwards makes his move. He says Ross has been "inefficient and disloyal to the city's best interests, extravagant and wasteful in the matter of public funds." He accuses Ross of furnishing a list of City Light customers and vendors to the peddlers of the building-company stock. Ross is fired.

Ross denies the accusations. Later he writes the attorney of the Federal Trade Commission that he has "pretty good evidence" that Edwards was paid off, with the bribe deposited in a British Columbia bank. It is never proven that Edwards is in the pay of the "Power Trust," but people believe it.

Edwards announces Ross's ouster to the newspapers on the eve of the March 1931 city elections. His aim is to sink Charter Amendment 2, which would give City Light its own engineering department. Ross has big plans to build dams, power plants, power lines, and substations, and he wants his own staff of engineers. His enemies call this a power grab. The *Seattle Times* accuses City Light of becoming "a separate and distinct institution in its operating methods, its business practices, its accounting system and its political propaganda." The *Times* has never liked municipal ownership, either of the lighting department or the streetcars. In a page-one editorial, publisher Clarance Blethen declares that the purpose of Amendment 2 is "to perpetuate Mr. Ross in office and to make him and his heirs and assigns forever kings of Seattle."

Ross *has* perpetuated himself in office and engaged in public rhetoric. There is no arguing that. But his dream is not to build a tower befitting a king. Ross has subscribed to $1,100 of stock—11 shares—in the City Light Building Company. He has paid $250 and received one share. For City Light's top man, this is a token investment. Ross is moved by other things. In 1935, he writes to the head of the employee union, "I have been for 32 years with one thought in mind, and that is to give the people of Seattle and King County the lowest possible light and power rates in the United States."

He has done that, and City Light customers know it. On election day, the voters support "Mr. City Light" by approving his engineering department. They also elect three of his supporters to the city council, and unelect the council's president, who supports the mayor. The *Post-Intelligencer*, which is friendlier to Ross than the *Times*, shouts the next morning: "City Light Ticket Is Victorious!"

Ross's supporters quickly mount a campaign to recall the mayor. Co-organizer of the petition drive is Marion Zioncheck, the radical who a year and a half later will be elected to Congress. The signatures are collected, and in July 1931, the people of Seattle toss out Frank Edwards in

CITY LIGHT BUILDING
To be erected 1930-31, on west side of Third Avenue, between Madison and Marion Streets

City Light Tower: The vision, left, and the reality, above. *Courtesy of Seattle Municipal Archives.*

a 62-to-38 percent landslide. Seattle politicians will remember this for a long time. This is what happens when you attack J. D. Ross and Seattle City Light.

The city council chooses one of its own, Robert Harlin, as interim mayor. He quickly rehires Ross, who returns triumphant. In a letter, Ross writes, "Our victory here was a wonderful one and has changed the entire complexion of everything for the better."

It is one of the high points of his life.

Born in 1872 in Chatham, Ontario, a town between Detroit and Toronto, James Delmage Ross finishes the equivalent of high school and becomes a schoolteacher.

He teaches for only a few years. Told by the family doctor that he should "get outdoors," he signs up in 1898 for a pack train going north from Alberta to the gold fields of the Yukon. Two years later, he arrives in Seattle by boat, strong, healthy, and needing to work. He begins an electrical business. In 1903 he goes to work for the city's Water Department, building a small dam to generate power for street lights. He builds the dam and stays on with the city.

192 *Seattle in the Great Depression*

Caricatures of Frank Edwards (left) and Robert Harlin. *Sam Groff,* Seattle Star, *12-30-1931/12-31-1931.*

In 1910, Seattle voters approve the creation of City Light, and after a few months, Ross, 38, is put at the head of it. In an era of progressives and socialists, Ross is no radical; in the General Strike of 1919, when the head of the linemen's union vows to plunge Seattle into the dark, Ross insists that City Light workers stay on the job—and they do. He becomes the power industry's most influential champion of public ownership. Seattle has a private utility, the Puget Sound Traction, Light & Power Company, which is owned by a company back East. City Light, as Ross never tires of saying, is owned by the people it serves.

J. D. Ross in 1911. *Courtesy of Seattle Municipal Archives, 112348.*

City Light starts small. Except for the street lights, Puget Sound Traction has the market for electricity, which is growing explosively. For most of the next three decades, City Light will push, first to gain a foothold, then parity, and, ultimately, supremacy. In that fight, Puget will have the financial and legal backing of its corporate parent, Stone & Webster of Boston, and later, the Engineers Public Service Company of New York. As a Seattle company, it will also have the support of business leaders and of the *Seattle Times*. City Light will have the support of the public-power movement, a spreading number of customers and the leadership of J. D. Ross.

In his first decade, Ross's goal is to find sites for dams. In 1913, the federal government grants City Light's private competitor a permit to dam the lower Skagit, the most powerful river flowing into Puget Sound. Puget Power builds no dam, but as long as it holds the permit, no other utility can have it. In 1915 Puget is allowed to extend its permit for two more years. In 1917, Ross goes to Washington, DC, and convinces Secretary of Agriculture David Houston not to extend it again. Without waiting to consult Seattle Mayor Hiram Gill, Ross stakes City Light's claim to all of the Skagit. World War I is on, and City Light can't build right away, but it goes out to bid as soon as it can. It finishes the Gorge Dam, the smallest of three it will build on the Skagit, in 1924.

City Light and Puget Power each grow in the decade after the war. From 1920 to 1931, Puget absorbs 30 small power companies, creating an empire from Centralia to Canada. City Light expands in Seattle's residential districts. By aggressively marketing electric appliances, it doubles its load every five and a half years. By 1930, it boasts that Seattle has more electric kitchen ranges than any city in the United States.

During these years, City Light and Puget Power each build a coal-burning steam plant, Puget's at Renton and City Light's on Lake Union. (The Lake Union plant is now the Fred Hutchinson Cancer Center). City Light begins the Diablo Dam on the Skagit, and Puget builds the Rock Island Dam on the Columbia. Each ends the 1920s with about 2,000 miles of power lines within the Seattle city limits.

By the 1930s, Ross writes, Seattle City Light is the only big municipal utility in America "in direct and bitter competition with a private company for every customer in its territory."

One of them, he believes, will eventually drive the other out.

In the Depression, the progressives, who have been pushing for public power, switch their attention to unemployment. The fight between City Light and Puget Power cools. Both are struggling to stay alive.

Diablo Dam. *From Seattle City Light ad in* Seattle Times, *3-14-1933, p. 7.*

At City Light, Ross works to finish Diablo Dam. The dam is built but the power house and transmission line are not. City Light has taken delivery of two big turbines and miles of aluminum cable, but it has paid the suppliers in warrants. To redeem the warrants and finish the project, it needs to sell bonds.

Under state law, public agencies cannot pay more than 6 percent for bond money. After the bond-market crash of 1931, bond buyers demand more than that. The result: in December 1931, Ross writes, "Today, no city can sell bonds." City Light, he writes, "has ceased all construction work that is not absolutely necessary."

In 1932, Ross goes to Washington, DC, with a group of Seattle politicians. Their aim is to get a 4-percent loan from Herbert Hoover's Reconstruction Finance Corporation. Officially, the RFC refuses because its loans are reserved for new work only, and City Light wants to use some of the money to pay off old warrants. Unofficially, RFC board member Jesse Jones tells Seattle Councilman Ralph Nichols, "It is not our policy to insure competitive conditions" among power companies. The way Ross hears it from an RFC engineer is that there is no way the government will finance a competitor to the Puget Sound Power & Light Company.

Work on Diablo is stopped for two and a half years. From 1930 to 1933, City Light's revenue falls 11 percent. In the same period, Puget's revenue falls 26 percent. Puget serves downtown Seattle's Metropolitan Tract and department stores and much of its industry, as well as rural areas outside the city. In the Depression, its customers cut back more than City Light's. Puget's dam at Rock Island is finished; it is the first big dam on the Columbia, and will be the only one built by a private utility. It's a fine asset, but building it has cost the company a load of debt.

To pay down the debt, Puget stops paying dividends to its stockholders. In 1931, Puget suspends the common-stock dividend to its corporate parent in New York "to preserve the stability of the company." In December 1932 it suspends dividends on its publicly traded junior and senior preferred stock, which is widely held in the Pacific Northwest. Puget will restore the dividend on the senior preferred for one year, 1936, but in 1937 the city will default on the streetcar debt to Puget, and Puget will go back to paying nothing.

City Light doesn't need to pay dividends. Still, in order to finish his dam, J. D. Ross needs to sell bonds. Even if the law allowed it, in early 1933 he would have to pay 10 percent for money.

In 1933 the Democrats come to power, and Ross goes to the nation's capital, hat in hand. Franklin Roosevelt is a friend of public power, as are Washington's Democratic senators, C. C. Dill and Homer Bone. Ross comes with a big ask: a loan of

Harold Ickes, "the modern caliph." *National Portrait Gallery* (detail), Smithsonian Institution, gift of Estrellita Karsh in memory of Yousuf Karsh. © Yousuf Karsh.

$26.5 million—the equivalent of $633 million in 2024 dollars. That much money would finish Diablo and finance City Light's third dam on the Skagit, a bigger one six miles up the river.

In July 1933, President Roosevelt approves initial work on the Grand Coulee and Bonneville dams on the Columbia. They are funded by the Public Works Administration. The *Seattle Times* calls the PWA's boss, Interior Secretary Harold Ickes, "the modern caliph . . . the heaviest of all dispensers of federal cash." Ickes famously insists that PWA money go to useful projects, not the "leaf-raking" of the Civil Works Administration.

The line at Ickes's door is long. Ross waits for seven months, living out of a Washington, DC, hotel room. He repeatedly tells reporters that the loan to City Light is coming right up. In October, the *Seattle Star* reports that its favorite senator, Homer Bone, is on the verge of getting the money after making "a red-hot fight." But Ickes turns thumbs-down on City Light. Even the New Deal's treasury is limited, and he says the Evergreen State has already received its share of money for dams.

Ross steps off the bus in Seattle two days before Christmas 1933. He has had a long ride from Washington, DC. He's tired and empty-handed. City Light's projects on the Skagit River, he grouses, have been "sacrificed to the Coulee Dam."

In 1934 the bond market improves. Working with Ross, Seattle investment banker Ben Ehrlichman puts together a group of bond houses in New York, Chicago, and San Francisco to provide $5 million at 5.77 percent. Mayor John Dore, by then a lame duck, vetoes the no-bid deal, but the council overrides him and the bonds are sold. In the future, City Light will borrow millions more at better terms with Ehrlichman's help. The bond sale of 1934 is its first since 1931 and is a happy event.

Interior Secretary Harold Ickes is impressed that "the soft-spoken six-footer from the West," as one journalist describes Ross, is able to squeeze $5 million out of Wall Street bankers. Ickes puts in a word with the president, and in 1936, Franklin Roosevelt appoints Ross to the new Securities and Exchange Commission. Ross is a borrower, not a banker, and is from a place far from Wall Street—just the sort of person Roosevelt wants on the board. For two years Ross will take a leave from City Light and live with his wife, Alice, out of a hotel in Washington, DC. It's not the life either of them wants, but it's what the president wants of him. In 1937, Roosevelt names Ross to head the Bonneville Power Administration, which allows Ross and Alice to return to Seattle.

The money raised from City Light's 1934 bond sale is enough to bring Diablo on line in September 1936. It also pays off the warrants issued three years earlier to the disgruntled stockholders of the City Light Building Company, and for City Light to make something of the abandoned building site. Its new headquarters will be two stories only—the *Argus* snidely calls it an "earthscraper"—but that's OK with Ross. He cares about building dams. That the region has no immediate need for the power doesn't stop him. "The time is going to come when the country will use it," he says.

Ross's last effort at City Light is to build the biggest dam on the Skagit. Approved in 1937 while he is in Washington, DC, the dam is financed 45 percent by a grant from Harold Ickes' Public Works Administration and 55 percent from City Light bonds. It will be finished after Ross's death and bear his name: Ross Dam.

———

As the Depression eases, the political push for public power revives. In 1930, state voters passed a ballot measure, sponsored by the Grange, to allow counties to create public utility districts (PUDs). The PUDs have the authority to condemn power-company property, borrow money, and go into the power business. Nothing much happens in the first few years, but in 1936, the people of Whatcom and Snohomish counties vote to create PUDs. In 1937, Congress passes the Bonneville Power Act, which gives public utilities first call on the cheap power from the new federal dams. The Act gives ratepayers a strong reason to vote for public power.

For years there has been talk that either City Light or Puget Power would buy out the other. By the mid-1930s, Puget's ambition has faded, but J. D. Ross's has not. In October 1934, after he raises the $5 million through Ben Ehrlichman, he suggests publicly that if the city council would let him raise another $95 million, City Light could buy out all of Puget Power, including the Rock Island Dam. In the late 1920s, Ross proposed buying out Puget's lines and substations in the city only. His idea then was to condemn the property, which would have required payment in cash. But by 1934, Puget is paying no dividends and the stock has been hammered down. Ross suggests that Puget's directors might accept payment in revenue bonds.

J. D. Ross in 1937. *Courtesy of Seattle Municipal Archives, 15832.*

Ross makes an engineer's argument. "The revenue of each is about $5,000,000 a year; each sells about 275,000,000 kilowatt-hours; each has a peak load of about 85,000 kilowatts; each has a power plant capacity of about 175,000 kilowatts; and it costs each about $1,750,000 a year to maintain and operate its respective system," he writes. Why have two electric utilities in the same city? "Why do we not have two water systems, two sewer systems, two city halls, two mayors and two city councils?"

Combining the two systems, Ross figures, would save $3 million a year. Part of the savings would come from ending the under-the-table discounts that both utilities have been offering business customers. In a report to the city council, Ross argues that one of the two systems will eventually beat the other, and that the winner will inevitably be City Light. "The trend of the times is now toward public ownership," he writes. If Puget Power continues fighting a losing battle, he writes, its stockholders and bondholders "might be crushed to earth." Better for them to sell out now.

Politically, Ross's argument falls flat. In a blast of rhetorical excess, former Mayor Dore denounces the proposal as "madness." Puget Power, he argues, has already been beaten in Seattle. Why waste money buying the company?

Even the *Seattle Star*, which has long been a cheerleader for Ross and City Light, balks at the proposal. "Let's see," the *Star*'s editors write. "A few years ago, the City of Seattle bought a dilapidated, money-losing streetcar system from Stone & Webster [Puget's corporate parent at the time] for twice its true value. We are still wondering how we can pay for it. Maybe the Puget Sound Power & Light Company is worth $95,000,000. But is it worth that much to us? Do we need all of it? Is this the time to take on this mammoth new load?"

In fact, electric power is a far better investment than streetcars. But the opponents win the argument.

Ross shrinks his proposal to Seattle only, plus Puget's Shuffleton steam plant in Renton and its hydro stations at White River and Snoqualmie Falls. Still, the proposal recalls the irritating history of the streetcars. A poll finds the people of Seattle voting no 4 to 1. And that kills it.

On March 14, 1939, J. D. Ross dies of a heart attack. At 66, he has worked himself to death.

Mourners at Ross's memorial service fill Seattle's First Presbyterian Church. Hundreds stand outside. Governor Martin is there, and Mayor Langlie. Representing President Roosevelt is his daughter, Anna Boettiger, and her husband, *Post-Intelligencer* publisher John Boettiger. The newspapers print a statement from the president eulogizing Ross as "an outstanding mathematician and equally great engineer ... with the practical ability to make things work in the sphere of public opinion and successful business." At the service, the Rev. E. Raymond Attebery remarks that Ross did it all without attending college or technical school. For an industrialist not to have a degree was common in the previous century but is less so by the 1930s.

At his death, Ross leaves behind the second-largest municipal electric utility in the United States. It carries 40 percent of the city's commercial load, 53 percent of the industrial load, and 75 percent of the residential load—60 percent in all. It operates with fewer than 1,000 employees. It has turned a profit for 32 consecutive years and never defaulted on its debt. In 1938 its power rates are just 56 percent of the U.S. average. In Seattle, public power is more than a success; it has become a civic religion. Politicians might object to City Light buying the Puget Sound Power & Light Company, but they would never side with Puget *against* City Light.

Puget Power ends the 1930s politically and financially damaged. The company's bylaws require it to make up all the skipped dividends on the senior preferred stock before it can pay on the junior, and all the dividends on the junior before it can pay on the common. After nine years of falling behind, Puget's directors give up. In 1940 they cancel all the unpaid dividends. They convert the junior preferred to common and erase 95 percent of the old common in a 1-for-20 reverse split. This cuts Puget loose from its East Coast owners and allows the utility to have a board of directors entirely from Western Washington.

Like the Rainier Valley streetcar line, Puget Power's permission to operate in Seattle is time-limited. Puget has a 50-year franchise, granted in 1902. As 1952 approaches, the city notifies Puget that its franchise will not be renewed. In 1951, City Light buys out Puget's properties within the city for $26 million—$310 million in 2024 dollars.

Holders of Puget's senior preferred stock, which sold as low as $11 in 1938 when it was paying no dividend, are cashed out in May 1950 at $110 a share.

By mid-century, public utility districts are taking big bites out of Puget's territory. The company sells the Rock Island Dam to the Chelan County Public Utility District. But the postwar world is different from the 1930s; the push for public power fades out, and the company survives. Now based in Bellevue, the state's fifth-largest city, it is called Puget Sound Energy. It is owned by Canadian and Dutch pension funds and is the largest private utility in Washington. Through merger, Puget has become the distributor of natural gas in Seattle, but as a retail supplier of electricity, the company has been out of the Seattle market for more than 70 years.

City Light has Seattle to itself, as J. D. Ross wanted.

14
The Popular Front, 1936–1938

Writing in *The Nation* in 1936 about politics in the Evergreen State, Seattle-born journalist Mary McCarthy quotes James Farley, the chairman of the Democratic National Committee: "There are 47 states of the union and the Soviet of Washington." Farley will later deny he said this, but it does sound like him. McCarthy goes on: "The State of Washington is in ferment; it is wild, comic, theatrical, dishonest, disorganized and hopeful, but it is not revolutionary ... A hundred Democratic barkers are peddling their own specially bottled political patent medicines."

At the center of this ferment is the Washington Commonwealth Federation (WCF), an alliance of the Commonwealth Builders, the labor unions, and the Washington State Grange. The Federation's platform calls for "a planned economy, based upon production and distribution for use rather than for profit."

The Communists also believe in a planned economy, but at the beginning they are not welcome. They are nasty and condemn others on the left as "social fascists." The Commonwealth Federation's first convention, in Tacoma in 1935, refuses to seat 15 Reds. Later that year, the Communist International in Moscow changes strategy. The directive goes out: Party members are to set aside Marxist purity and to cozy up to progressives in a "popular front against fascism."

In March 1936, Lowell Wakefield, editor of the *Voice of Action*, runs as a Communist for the Seattle City Council. The Commonwealthers don't endorse him, but the *Voice of Action* endorses the Commonwealth candidates for school board. One is University of Washington Professor Burt Farquharson, Mary Farquharson's husband. He is a socialist, a Technocracy man, and a member of Fred Shorter's church. The other is the Rev. Wilfred Withington of Green Lake Congregational Church. He's a believer in Technocracy.

All three lose—and the Commonwealth Federation's president, Cyrus Woodward, wants no more Red endorsements. "The Washington

Commonwealth Federation has NOTHING IN COMMON WITH THE COMMUNIST PARTY," he writes in the group's newspaper. This is not exactly true, but Woodward—who years before was labor editor of the only labor-owned daily in America, the *Seattle Union Record*—wants to keep the unions in the tent. For that, he needs to keep the Communists out.

To get in, the Communists form front groups. The second Commonwealth convention, at Everett in April 1936, admits some of these groups. It also admits the Workers' Alliance, the WPA union.

The Communists are in.

Years later, the Commonwealth Federation's executive director, Howard Costigan, will recall the change in the Communist line. One day, he was no longer a "social fascist." "Those who had been my enemies," he writes, "suddenly began to act as my friends." By late 1936, 56 of the 72 members of the Federation's executive board are Party members—and they are the hardest workers and most zealous advocates of the Federation's program.

In December 1936, Costigan joins the Communist Party.

In May 1936, the Democrats hold their state convention in Aberdeen. The 3,000 delegates are divided by color: yellow armbands for the regular Democrats and orange for the Townsendites and the WCF. At 3 a.m., after the old-liners have gone to bed, the orange forces elect King County Prosecutor Warren Magnuson as convention chairman. He is not a communist, but at the convention he sides with the left. Under Magnuson, the delegates adopt a platform calling for production-for-use, public ownership of national banks, the creation of money, the Townsend old-age pension plan and putting Supreme Court decisions up to a public vote. Writes J. H. Brown of the *Argus*, "Not one of the Democratic elective state officers from Governor Martin down endorses the adopted platform."

The convention names U.S. Senator Lewis Schwellenbach to the platform committee at the national convention in Philadelphia. It instructs him to push production-for-use,

Warren Magnuson, circa 1944. *U.S. Senate Historical Office.*

which in 1934 was one of his ideas. But the senator has become a Roosevelt loyalist. And in 1936, Franklin Roosevelt is not running as a radical. At the national convention, Schwellenbach refuses to push production-for-use.

Hearing this, Howard Costigan fires off a sarcastic telegram. "Is it true that you are ducking production for use? You ran on it in 1932; you were elected by it in 1934. Your EPIC baby carried to Philadelphia by the Washington delegation is looking for its papa. Will you admit paternity?"

No, he won't.

To knock out Governor Clarence Martin in the 1936 Democratic primary, the WCF backs John C. Stevenson. He is the dominant member of the three-man King County Commission and a dispenser of patronage to Commonwealthers. He also has an illegal source of campaign funds: kickbacks from suppliers on county road projects.

Stevenson is a man of uncertain identity. In Buffalo, New York, he called himself John P. Stockman. In 1922 he was indicted there for cheating clients of his stock and bond company. He flees to Seattle, changes his name, goes on the radio, and is elected to public office. When *Post-Intelligencer* reporter Lester Hunt breaks the story about his past, Stevenson says his brother was the crook. When Governor Herbert Lehman of New York orders Stevenson extradited, Governor Martin of Washington refuses to send him. Now Stevenson is after Martin's job.

Because another man named Stevenson once ran against him, John Stevenson has changed his name to Radio Speaker Stevenson. Like Howard Costigan, he has a radio show. But Costigan's voice is harsh. Stevenson, writes Mary McCarthy of *The Nation*, has "a radio voice that sets old ladies a-weepin."

Stevenson is also a left-winger; Costigan's third wife, Barbara, will remark years later that Stevenson "tried to out-radicalize Howard." McCarthy describes Stevenson as "a Robin Hood who robs the rich to give to the poor, takes his own cut, and makes no bones about it."

Governor Martin denounces Stevenson as one of the "strange and arrogant leaders"

Radio Speaker Stevenson circa 1935. *Author's collection*.

backed by the Commonwealth Federation. "As governor," he says, "I could not serve their program and serve the rest of the people." The Commonwealth leaders are not quite sure of Stevenson, either. They demand that he sign their agenda before they endorse him. He signs it.

Stevenson has two problems in running against Martin. The first is that State Treasurer Otto Case is also running in the Democratic primary. As a supporter of the Townsend plan, Case splits the votes of the left. Stevenson's second problem is the state's new election law, which was put on the ballot by the Grange and passed by the voters. Called the blanket primary, it allows voters of one party to cross over and vote for the other party's candidates. For that reason, the U.S. Supreme Court will rule it unconstitutional 64 years later. In the election of September 8, 1936, it allows Republicans, who have no contest in their party, to cross over and vote for the centrist, Clarence Martin, who wins the Democratic nomination. Stevenson takes only King, Snohomish, and Kitsap counties—Seattle, Everett, and Bremerton. His political career is over.

The Commonwealth Federation will not oppose Martin in the general election. The Federation's president, Cyrus Woodward, now finds himself more radical than the Reds. He resigns in protest. He goes off to run the gubernatorial campaign of William Bouck, a radical Skagit County farmer he knew during World War I, when the Wilson administration charged Bouck with disloyalty. Bouck, the former master of the state Grange, is a no-hope candidate on the Farmer-Labor-Commonwealth ticket.

The Communists, who now dominate the WCF, are happy to see Woodward go. They don't like idealists and are not interested in no-hope candidates of dinky political parties. They are interested in the Democratic Party.

In November 1936 comes the Commonwealth Federation's last effort of the Woodward era: Initiative 119. This is the production-for-use measure the legislature failed to pass—a state takeover of unused farms and factories. The conservative press denounces it as radical. The Communists are in their Popular Front phase, and it is too radical for them. To the *Western States Technocrat*, it's not radical enough. "Just what could they produce?" the paper asks. In the final vote, Initiative 119 goes down hard: 79 percent no, the strongest rejection of any Washington initiative to the people in the

20th century. The failure of Initiative 119 marks the end of leftist utopianism at the Washington Commonwealth Federation.

On the same ballot, a property owners' measure to continue the 40-mill cap on tax rates passes with 78 percent yes. In 1936, Washington's voters reject the radical left's ideas decisively.

They also vote for Democrats decisively. Franklin Roosevelt is hugely popular. Three months before the election a writer at the *Star* describes a scene in a Seattle cinema. When the President appears in a newsreel there comes a "sudden and prolonged burst of applause." And on November 3, 1936, Roosevelt takes 66 percent of Washington's vote. Nationally he beats the Republican nominee, Alfred Landon, in every state but Maine and Vermont. Democrats take nearly four-fifths of the seats in each chamber of Congress.

Democrats take all six U.S. House seats in Washington state and Warren Magnuson, 31, wins the U.S. Senate seat he will keep for 44 years. Clarence Martin is reelected governor in a Democratic sweep of all statewide offices. In Olympia, Democrats win 41 of 46 seats in the Senate and 93 out of 99 in the House.

Never in the history of the Evergreen State have Democrats had power like this. Governor Martin asks legislators to be careful with it. The voters, he reminds them, "rejected proposals for new forms of taxes and turned down a number of radical and experimental projects and propositions." Legislators, he says, should offer business and industry "freedom—or, at least, a moratorium from further new taxes, impositions and annoyances" and focus instead on "consolidating our social gains."

Legislators pass a bill for the state to join the employment insurance system created by the Social Security Act. Martin signs it. They also pass a six-hour-day, 30-hour-week bill for state employees and contractors. Highway Director Lacey Murrow says the bill is "entirely incompatible" with the job of clearing highways of landslides, and Martin vetoes it.

Clarence Martin, circa 1933. *Washington State Archives.*

In total, legislators give Martin one-third more social spending than he asks for. To pay for it, they vote to extend the 2-percent sales tax to fresh vegetables, milk, butter, bread, and cheese, but the governor vetoes that. Already there are warnings that legislators are spending more money than the state will have.

The left-wingers—14 of the 48 members in the Senate and 39 of the 99 in the House—offer a long list of bills that *Argus* correspondent J. H. Brown calls "freakish, almost revolutionary." They don't have the votes, but they are able to stop a few things. They block a ban on mixed-race marriages. Senator Earl Maxwell of Maple Valley, the Democratic majority leader, offers the bill in response to a public furor over a 14-year-old white girl's marriage to a 38-year-old Black man. The bill ignores the age difference and instead targets the racial difference. In the 1930s, left-wingers push for racial equality when no one else does, and in defeating the Maxwell bill, they preserve Washington's status as the only Western state that allows non-whites to marry whites. They fail, however, to block a Grange-sponsored bill to ban Filipinos from owning or leasing land unless they are green-card holders or citizens. Senator Mary Farquharson compares the bill to Germany's persecution of the Jews, but it passes and Governor Martin signs it.

Mary Farquharson. Drawing by Sam Groff, 1-25-1937, p. 4. © The Seattle Times.

Farquharson, a Seattle Democrat, is responsible for the left's notable achievement of the session: repeal of the criminal syndicalism law of 1919. Passed over the governor's veto a month before the Seattle General Strike, the law makes it a felony to advocate any unlawful method to promote social, political, or industrial change. Radicals hate the law because it gives police a free hand to harass them, as in the Seattle Police's catch-and-release of Communists during the longshore strike. Prosecutors say the law is too vague to use in court. A similar law in Oregon has already been struck down by the U.S. Supreme Court, and the Washington law is ripe for plucking. Farquharson convinces enough moderates and conservatives to put the repeal bill on Governor Martin's desk, and he signs it.

A final political note: In March 1937, voters elect a new Seattle councilman, Hugh DeLacy. At Queen Anne High School, DeLacy was valedictorian. He graduated from the University of Washington in 1932, and for three years has been a UW English instructor. When he announces his campaign, the University fires him for running for office, which is against UW policy. The firing gets his name in the papers. He runs as a progressive, organized labor backs him, and he wins. He is 27 years old, and he is secretly a member of the Communist Party.

Hugh DeLacy, circa 1937. *Courtesy of Seattle Municipal Archives.*

One of the first popular-front projects in which Communists take an interest is to start a left-wing daily newspaper in Seattle. For a decade, the city had the *Union Record*, which was labor-left but not overtly socialist, but it died in 1928. In 1936 organizers set up the Northwest People's Publishing Company. At the head is Richard G. Tyler, professor of engineering at the University of Washington and a founder of Commonwealth Builders. The executive committee includes Sydney Strong, whose daughter, Anna Louise Strong, wrote the *Union Record*'s famous editorial cheering on the General Strike. While visiting Seattle, she is offered the job of editor, but she wants to return to the Soviet Union, where she edits the *Moscow News*. Instead, the new company hires journalist Harvey O'Connor, who was charged with criminal syndicalism after the General Strike, though he was never brought to trial.

The "people's daily" is announced just before the *Post-Intelligencer* strike of August 1936. The shutdown of the Hearst paper opens a window to jump into the market, but Tyler's group is not ready. It has the reporters and editors, but not the money.

When the plan is set aside, the *Voice of Action* shuts down. It's short of money, too, but editor Lowell Wakefield, who goes back to writing for the Communist Party's *Daily Worker*, portrays the closure as an act of solidarity. He says the purpose of shutting down the *Voice of Action* is "to head up all progressive political action in one center"—the Washington Commonwealth Federation.

The Commonwealthers have been expanding their weekly paper in an effort to jump-start the new daily. In August they begin a homemakers' page under Howard Costigan's new wife, Isabel, an advertising writer at Frederick & Nelson. In November they hire one of the celebrities of the *Post-Intelligencer* strike, photographer Frank Lynch, as sports editor. The weekly also changes its name from the *Washington Commonwealth* to the *Commonwealth News*. In November 1936 it adopts the unpolitical name *Sunday News*.

A year later, Howard Costigan is still holding out hope that the *Sunday News* will become a real newspaper. In October 1937, he writes that the public needs "a people's press as opposed to the present kept press," and that the Federation "stands ready to throw its entire resources behind the building of such a newspaper." The weekly paper has 15,000 paid subscribers, but its revenue covers only half its costs, and there is never enough money to go daily. In 1938 the paper renames itself the *Washington New Dealer*, a sign that it resigned to being a niche-market weekly.

Anna Louise Strong in Moscow, 1937. *From the* New York World and Sun Newspaper Photograph Collection, Library of Congress, 98501299.

Meanwhile, Richard Tyler, who was going to produce the new daily, makes his peace with the Stalinists. Tyler was an early backer of Technocracy; in 1935, he criticized Stalin for turning against Russia's scientists and engineers. But in 1937, Tyler goes on a pilgrimage to the Soviet Union and meets with Anna Louise Strong. Upon his return, he tells the Commonwealth weekly that 99 percent of the people support Stalin's purges and show trials. "They have suffered too much in building up socialism to stand by and see it endangered by enemies in their midst," he declares.

By the spring of 1938, the political winds in America have shifted. Voters are uneasy about the sit-down strikes and the president's plan to pack the Supreme Court. The "Depression within the Depression" of 1937–1938 has weakened support for the New Deal. Franklin Roosevelt is still popular, but less than before.

In Seattle, the people have elected Arthur Langlie as mayor. After the fervent populism of John Dore, Langlie is a calm and moderate conservative. Governor Martin likes him, even though Langlie is a Republican. "It is a pleasure to work with that young man," he says. In a much-quoted statement, Martin tells a Seattle crowd, "Please don't send any more no-good Democrats down to Olympia and expect us to do anything for them. If you must send worthless men to Olympia, send no-good Republicans because they are not quite so bad as no-good Democrats."

To Martin, the number-one no-good Democrat is his lieutenant governor, Vic Meyers. The jazz-band-leader-turned-politician is backing the left's demand for a special session of the legislature to raise money for relief. But only the governor can call a special session, and Martin wants no more spending. In April 1938 comes Meyers's chance to call a session himself.

Evelyn and Arthur Langlie, Seattle's new first couple, 1938. *ACME Newspictures image in author's collection.*

Under the state constitution, when the governor leaves the state, the lieutenant governor takes over. For six years, Clarence Martin has made a point not to leave the state. But after losing the race for mayor of Seattle, Vic Meyers has gone on a fishing trip out of San Diego. Martin wants to testify against a bill in Congress. He sees his chance and takes a flight to Washington, DC.

Vic Meyers's allies see *their* chance. Unable to reach him on the fishing boat, they put out a news release to radio stations that he is urgently needed at home. Meyers hears the call. In Washington, DC, Clarence Martin is warned that Meyers is about to usurp him. He boards a flight for Chicago.

Meyers travels by train but gets back first. At 8:45 a.m. on April 19, 1938, he crosses the Columbia River and becomes acting governor of Washington. He orders the State Patrol to drive him to Olympia. To call up the legislature, he needs to file papers with the secretary of state, but he has not decided to do it. He passes through Olympia and continues on to Seattle. Late in the day he makes up his mind, rushes to Boeing Field, and charters a plane for Olympia. He does not phone ahead for the secretary of state's office to stay open. He arrives at 5:10 p.m., and it is closed. He gives up, returns to Seattle, and makes a speech on the radio.

Vic Meyers: not serious enough, 1935. *ACME Newspictures* image in author's collection.

Back in his hotel room, Meyers meets with three officials of the Washington Commonwealth Federation: Howard Costigan, Hugh DeLacy, and Eugene Dennett. All three are Communists, though probably Meyers doesn't know that. They go to work on him, and in the wee hours, Meyers signs a proclamation calling up the legislature. The next morning, April 20, he is at the secretary of state's office in Olympia promptly at 8 a.m. Clarence Martin, however, has crossed into Washington airspace at 7:52 a.m. on a chartered Lockheed Sky Zephyr. Vic Meyers is no longer acting governor, and the legislature is not called up.

Three months later, Meyers admits that when Martin returned, "I was just as much relieved as 95 percent of the people of this state." Meyers is weak. He will be elected lieutenant governor three more times, but he will never have the top job.

Meyers's push for a special session is not without reason. In the renewed Depression, the state is overwhelmed by the demand for relief. By October 1937, one of every eight persons in Washington—12.7 percent—is on some form of public support.

Governor Martin has had enough. In April 1938, he says the renewed Depression "is teaching America it cannot go on forever getting something for nothing, but must work."

Martin is a conservative Democrat, a small-town mill owner from Eastern Washington. And after years of paying out relief, he is sounding more and more like his tight-fisted Republican predecessor, Roland Hartley. So is Martin's director of relief, Charles F. Ernst. "Many people have been on relief so long they don't want to do anything else," Ernst says. "The problem now is to force them off relief and to work."

On April 1, 1938, Ernst ends state relief for the unemployed. He closes the Blue Ox Lodge, the homeless shelter and cafeteria near Seattle's Pioneer Square. The state will spend its remaining welfare money on dependent children and for the aged, crippled, and blind. King County, which administers state relief, cuts food aid by almost three-quarters, to $11 a week in 2024 dollars.

The Workers' Alliance is outraged. On April 1, the day of the relief cutoff, 300 of its men occupy the seventh floor of the County City Building in downtown Seattle. Many stay all night. On April 11 they occupy the offices again. "We are hungry," complains one of the men. "We want to eat *now*. We want to know what the county commissioners are going to do about it *today*."

To conservatives, this is a voice that grates. The man is not asking for charity. He is demanding his share.

King County commissioners Louis Nash and Tom E. Smith agree with the protesters. They order the Blue Ox Lodge reopened and the aid cuts rescinded. They order the jobless men paid with vouchers, and they dare the state to refuse payment. The state responds by cutting off all relief funds to King County. If the unemployed want money, they will have to find work.

212   *Seattle in the Great Depression*

Many of them sign up with the Works Progress Administration. The agency's peak employment is in 1938.

In July, protesters resume their campout in the hallway of the County City Building, demanding that the state restore the cash benefit. The protest goes on for weeks. Officials do not budge on the cash benefit, but when they agree to distribute surplus federal food, the protesters give in. The monthly ration for a family of three is 24½ pounds of flour, 6 pounds of rice, 3 pounds of dried beans, 3 pounds of raisins, 6 pounds of powdered milk, 6 pounds of butter and 25 pounds of oranges.

The fight over relief will resume in 1939. The cash benefit will come back, but it will be small.

In July 1938, the Democrats have their state convention in Tacoma. As in 1936, the left aims to control it. Their leader is Howard Costigan, executive director of the Commonwealth Federation. Costigan, who has been a secret Communist since 1936, is the King County Democrats' delegate to the state platform committee.

The left's strength is in the big counties. Its plan is to use the unit rule to bind the big-county delegates to vote as a bloc. Martin's men are ready for this. On the convention's first day, state party chairman D. Elwood Caples moves to throw out the unit rule.

Fifty left-wing delegates, mostly from Whatcom County, swarm the platform, yelling. Hanging on to the microphone with one hand and his gavel with the other, Caples screams that the convention is adjourned and storms out. It's not adjourned. Senator Lewis Schwellenbach takes over and keeps it going.

The convention supports President Roosevelt's "quarantine of aggressor nations." It endorses larger old-age pensions and the "redistribution of national wealth," government ownership of natural monopolies, and control of credit. It calls for a graduated state income tax, a state minimum wage, and the dismissal of Charles Ernst as state director of welfare. The Whatcom delegation offers a resolution condemning Clarence Martin, but the governor's men adjourn the convention first. Left-wingers try to turn a picture of Martin to the wall, and when stopped, they rip it down.

Disgusted by the raucous tactics, Vic Meyers releases a statement denouncing the Washington Commonwealth Federation as undemocratic and "a breeding ground for Communism." Martin publicly welcomes his lieutenant governor back into the fold. The next day Meyers says he was misled and takes it all back.

After the convention is over, the conservatives call for the Communists to be cast out. They have an ally in the *Seattle Star*, which runs a page-one editorial, "A Job for Democrats: Clean Out the Communists!" The *Star* has an affidavit from former Communist Party member Ralph Howard naming eight members of the Commonwealth Federation's executive committee as Reds. Three of the eight—William J. Pennock, University of Washington Professor Harold Eby, and State Senator Harry C. Armstrong—threaten to file libel suits against the *Star*. It's a false move; all three are, in fact, Communists, which they will admit years later.

The *Star* challenges Howard Costigan to say whether he's in sympathy with Communism and whether the Commonwealth Federation welcomes Reds as members. Costigan says he's not, and that the Federation welcomes anyone who supports the New Deal.

A few months later, Senate majority leader Earl Maxwell of Renton proposes a committee to investigate Communists in Washington. He wants to start with five members of the House and two of the Senate. He gets no support. Maxwell is a decade early. After the war, the legislature will set up the Canwell Committee.

———

The elections of November 1938 begin the political retreat of the New Deal. The Republicans gain 81 U.S. House seats, the largest midterm gain by either party in the 20th century. Still very much in the minority, they have increased their share of House seats from 20 percent to 39 percent. The state of Washington is an outlier. It returns to office the largest all-Democratic delegation outside the South. In that region, all-Democrat does not mean all-New Deal; in the Evergreen State, it does.

In the 99-seat House of Representatives in Olympia, the Republicans take 26 seats, up from six in their disaster year, 1936. Of the Democrats, the left elects 30 members and the centrists 37. After the election, a conference of the Washington Commonwealth Federation in Seattle passes resolutions supporting public housing, free medical care, free state college, free legal aid, and increased pensions. The legislature will pass a law to qualify the state for federal public-housing money. It will fund legal-aid clinics in Seattle, Tacoma, and Spokane. It will have no money for the other things.

In the November 1938 elections, voters are offered an initiative that would let state officials delay a strike against a private employer for 30 days. The AFL and CIO unions are united in opposing this, and it fails. Voters also reject a state income tax by two to one and reenact the 40-mill lid on property taxes—in both cases, for the third time.

15
The Front Shatters, 1937–1939

In the late 1930s there is a German American Bund, which promotes the National Socialist regime in Berlin. In 2016 the Seattle internet site Crosscut will have a six-part series on them. The headline on the first installment is, "When Nazis Walked the Streets of Seattle." Under the headline is a black-and-white photo of a Bund parade, with swastika flags flying side by side with the Stars and Stripes. The parade, however, is in New York.

In Seattle, the Bund never amounts to much. Its high point is in November 1937, when West Coast leader Hermann Schwinn comes up from Los Angeles to speak at the German Club at Ninth and James. In a hall draped by swastika flags, Schwinn addresses an audience of 75—in German. Afterward, Seattle city councilmen Hugh DeLacy and David Levine threaten to pull the business license of the club for disturbing the public peace. The club's president swears he didn't know he was renting the hall to Nazis and promises never to do it again. The rest of the city council is satisfied, and nothing more is done.

The club president keeps his word. In April 1938, Seattle's Bundists are reduced to celebrating Adolf Hitler's birthday at an Italian restaurant.

In 1939, the *Post-Intelligencer* runs a 16-part series on "Fascism in Seattle." The writer, Richard T. Forbes, is a University of Washington student. He joins the Bund as a mole, then writes of meetings in private homes of middle-aged men who are afraid to give their real names. The men read and discuss Nazi propaganda, speaking in German. The women serve coffee cake. One of the Nazis has guns scattered through his house. Apparently, the guns stay there. In Forbes's account, the Bundists talk a lot, but their most overt act is to paste anti-Jewish stickers on the windshields of parked cars.

Seattle's Nazis have no office and no bookstore. They control no newspaper. They include a few small businessmen, but no union leaders, legislators, city councilmen, or university professors. They have no influence over a major political organization, and they have no political party of their own with a place on the ballot.

Seattle's Communists have all of these things. In May 1938, 350 delegates of the Communist Party of Washington hold a two-day convention in a Seattle hotel. They are quite open about it. They conduct their business in English and use their real names. At the end of their convention, they send copies of their resolutions to the White House and every member of Congress.

In Seattle, the Communists are the ones to watch.

The great cause of the Communists in the late 1930s is the Spanish Republic. In 1936, after a left-wing coalition is elected in Spain, General Francisco Franco leads a revolt of the right. The result is the Spanish Civil War, which becomes a rehearsal for World War II. The United States, Britain, and France are neutral. Franco is backed by Nazi Germany and Fascist Italy, and the Republic is backed by the Soviet Union. The Communists make a worldwide crusade of it, recruiting volunteers from Europe and America to fight in the International battalions.

One man in Seattle who takes up the challenge is Thane Summers, 24. Summers is remembered for his letters, which are preserved at the University of Washington. None are to his parents. He regards his father, Lane Summers, as a hopeless reactionary. The elder Summers, a maritime attorney and a member of the downtown Rainier Club, has no use for his son's Marxism.

Thane Summers writes most of his letters to his friends Sophie and Arthur Krause. As the letters begin in the fall of 1935, Summers is studying philosophy at the University of Washington. His interest in social ethics—the rights and wrongs of societies—has pulled him to the left. His letters are mostly about what his political beliefs imply for his personal life.

In November 1935 he writes, "If I marry a rich girl and become a reactionary just for the money, it will be a big tragedy." Later he writes of his girlfriend, Naomi: "I would have to be sure of her attitude toward social questions before I would marry her. It would be impossible for me to have a philosophy and not act on it."

He does act on it. In May 1936 he skips his exams and drops out of the university. He decides to become a revolutionary—an ethically consistent one. He believes there are "certain values of bourgeois culture which should be retained." Still, he joins the Communist Party. "I felt that since I agreed with them on most issues, I could try to influence them on the issues of difference," he writes, "and if they still disagreed, I would be willing to subject myself to the democratic disagreement of the group will."

Thane decides that it's wrong to accept his father's support. He moves in with his psychology professor, Ralph Gundlach. Later, Gundlach will deny that he persuaded Summers to fight in Spain, but Gundlach is a vocal supporter of the Republic and one of several of Thane's professors with Communist sympathies. In 1949 the university will fire Gundlach for refusing to say whether he was ever a member of the Communist Party.

Summers leaves for Spain on April 27, 1937. He arrives in June. He writes to his friends, "I am in the International Brigade with workers from all over the world fighting for Spanish democracy and against world fascism." Joining up, he writes, is "a logical result of my views as a communist."

In another letter, he writes, "I am having one of the best, most interesting times of my life." By submerging his personal will, he becomes part of something bigger than himself. "How I feel & how you feel is nothing compared to the tremendously important problems mankind is facing," he writes. "Happiness is the sort of thing that one searches for & loses—one forgets & finds."

Thane Summers, off to Spain in April 1937. *The* Seattle Times, 6-21-1938, p. 5.

In July 1937, Summers becomes his section's political officer. To his sister, he writes (in care of a friend, so his father won't see it), "The political organization of our army is necessary because of the democratic character of a people's army, which makes it necessary to have some means for expressing the will of the men & explaining to them the directives of the officers."

That's the party line. The political officer's job is mostly about keeping the men on the path of correct thought and feeling.

Summers's unit leaves for the front in September 1937. He fights well and is sent to officers' training. In November, he interrogates captured Italians. "I have smelled fascism," he writes.

That letter is one of his last. In March 1938, a year before the Republic loses the war, Thane Summers is killed. The details of his death are not recorded: there is a great battle as Franco's forces push through to the sea, and Summers is no more. When the news of his death reaches Seattle, the comrades put up black-bordered posters of him to promote a memorial service that a thousand people attend. His father is furious at the Communists making hay of his son's death. "More Moscow," he fumes.

The father never understands his son. And in his 120 pages of letters, the son never has a thought of what the Communists are doing in Russia—the famine, the purges, the show trials, the labor camps—and what that means for the world he dreams of.

There are peaceful ways to resist fascism. For several years, Japanese companies have been buying scrap metal at West Coast ports. In Seattle, this has included old sawmill machinery, junk automobiles, and the Rainier Valley streetcars and rails. The American steel companies are still in the Depression and don't want much scrap, but Japan needs steel for its war with China. And that makes the export of scrap a political issue.

In the spring of 1938, about 200 demonstrators, many from the Washington Commonwealth Federation, set up a picket line in Seattle to protest the loading of scrap onto the Danish ship *Malayan*, which is bound for Japan. They make a tactical mistake: they picket the exporter's offices instead of the dock. The ship steams out.

In the winter of 1938–1939, Chinese Americans in San Francisco and Portland picket ships at the dock, where the longshoremen are. Harry Bridges's men will not cross the picket line, even when under contract to work. Loading stops for a while, but when the employers threaten to shut down the whole port, the pickets, not the longshoremen, back down.

In March 1939, the fight comes to Seattle. At Pier 91, about 75 pickets stop the loading of five railcars of scrap onto the freighter *India Maru*. The longshoremen honor the line, and the next day a thousand picketers join

Chinese Americans in Seattle protest the sale of scrap to Japan, 1939. *Courtesy of the Wing Luke Museum.*

in. "Pickets include many Chinese, as well as members of Seattle peace, labor and political organizations," says the *Seattle Times*. "A large number of the pickets in the past three days have been women."

As at San Francisco and Portland, the employers threaten to shut down the port if the longshoremen won't honor their contracts. Mayor Arthur Langlie pleads with picketers to stop before Seattle's commerce is wrecked. He tells them they have made their point. And the picketers back down. The American Chinese, writes the *Argus*, "are not the kind of people"—unlike the longshoremen—"who demonstrate with brickbats and clubs."

But war is coming, and more Americans are thinking of trade in terms other than commerce. If the country should find itself in a war, the *Post-Intelligencer* argues, scrap sold to Japan "might come back to this country in the form of shrapnel." Senators Homer Bone and Lewis Schwellenbach, as well as Representative Warren Magnuson, introduce bills to shut off the trade. Congress is beginning to ramp up military spending, but it is not ready to impose an embargo. The export of scrap to Japan will continue for almost two years, and will include rails from Seattle's municipal streetcar lines. Congress will shut down the trade at the end of 1940, a year before Japan's attack on Pearl Harbor.

In January 1937, a town east of the Cascades makes page one of the *New York Times*. Chelan, population 1,400, is conducting what the New York paper calls "the first practical experiment of the Townsend pension plan."

The plan, devised by Dr. Francis Townsend, promises a much more generous benefit than Social Security, which won't pay its first pension until 1940. Townsend would have everyone over 60 retire and receive $200 a month. They would have to spend all the money within the month. The cost would be paid by a 2 percent national sales tax.

Critics say the numbers don't work. Isom Lamb, who is from a Townsend club in Southern California, aims to prove the doubters wrong. He's financing the test. He says he will pay one person in Chelan $200 a month (in 2024 dollars, $4,300) for six months. The cash is tagged. Merchants who receive marked bills agree to pay a 2 percent tax. "I believe this test each month will produce enough revenue to add at least one new pensioner every month," says Lamb. "Before the guaranteed test of six months is over, we will see all eligible under the Townsend plan provisions in Chelan receiving the maximum $200 a month."

The first person chosen is Curtis C. Fleming, 63, an unemployed orchard worker. He's ecstatic. "Mother, we're rich!" he tells his wife, Elizabeth, 56. He buys an overcoat for himself and a box of cigars for his friends. He gets a haircut. She gets a permanent wave, her first in years. She buys a five-dollar hat. They buy a bed, mattress, box spring, and blanket. For their 16-member extended family she cooks up a feast of pork, chicken, and dumplings. At church they leave a dollar in the collection plate, a sum the *Seattle Times* notes is more than some folks leave in a year.

Two hundred dollars goes a long way in 1937, but in less than two weeks, the Flemings burn through it. A second recipient, a widow, is given $200. She spends hers in nine days.

The "tax," which is voluntary, brings in only $67.50. Much of the reason is that souvenir hunters buy up the marked bills. Isom Lamb leaves town, disgusted that tourists have spoiled his test. He takes his money with him, breaking his promise to keep paying for six months.

If the Townsend experiment at Chelan falls somewhat short of scientific fairness, it is *their* experiment. They set it up and predicted it would work. The newspapers respond with an editorial smirk. A critic writes in the *Seattle Star* that the Townsend test has left Chelan "just as poor as before in things to eat and wear." Declares the *Yakima Republic*: "It isn't a business getter."

In Olympia, the House of Representatives doesn't wait for the results. It passes a resolution urging Congress to adopt the Townsend plan.

Another utopian experiment: in 1938, several thousand people are growing food on 200 acres of cooperative gardens around Seattle and Bremerton. They call themselves "Workaneaters."

This is "production for use rather than profit," the idea once pushed by the Washington Commonwealth Federation. The head Workaneater, Cyrus E. Woodward, was the Federation's president back in 1936. Interviewing Woodward in 1938, *Post-Intelligencer* reporter Doug Welch describes him as "a quiet-spoken but intense individual, completely

Workaneaters prepare a canned-food "lighthouse" to celebrate the harvest. Seattle Times, *10-20-1938, p. 11.* © *The* Seattle Times.

absorbed in the Workaneat movement almost to the point of mildly religious fervor."

"People sometimes think we are socialists," Woodward says. "But we're not." In fact, his program *is* a kind of socialism, and many of its members are from the Technocracy clubs. But Woodward uses safer words. "We believe the only cure for unemployment is work," he tells the Republican *Seattle Times*.

The Workaneat program was designed for the unemployed, but it attracts a wider following. Most members have jobs. They are obligated to work only 15 hours a season, mostly in the fields or in a state cannery in Kirkland. At harvest time each worker is paid an equal share of food, calculated Technocracy-style in weight and labor-hours rather than dollars.

The food is plentiful and good. But this is a business paying all its output as dividends. Under production-for-use, nothing is sold. Members are proud of this, but it is a problem. The program's source of money, dues of 50 cents a month, leaves it cash-poor. The program needs cash to pay for trucking—especially drivers, because in Seattle all truck drivers must be Teamsters.

The Unemployed Citizens Leagues solved the problem of money by accepting government help. Perhaps recalling how that brought political control, Woodward declares, "We want the government to leave us alone."

The program is, however, using land at Boeing Field provided rent-free by the King County government. Probably this is patronage from Commissioner Tom E. Smith, who is a member of the Commonwealth Federation. At the Federation, Woodward backed Smith's political career, and after Woodward left the Federation in 1936, Smith got him a job as an investigator in the King County welfare department.

Woodward says he wants Workaneaters to own the land it tills. But his friends cannot give him that. In the late 1930s, good farmland costs $1,000 an acre, and his program doesn't have that kind of money.

When *P-I* reporter Welch suggests that the Workaneat program is like the collective self-help of the old Unemployed Citizens Leagues, Woodward shakes his head. "Those were belly movements," he replies. "We are not only trying to improve our immediate physical condition out of work but our future salvation as well." In the future, he says, "We will take on other functions, even building our own houses."

It is not to be. In 1939 the program folds. It was a belly movement after all.

In February 1939, State Senator Mary Farquharson, the legislator who knocked out the criminal syndicalism law, asks the Works Progress Administration to investigate Communist influence in the Federal Writers Project. She's not against giving writers' jobs to Communists. She's a former member of the Socialist Party herself. But she says the Communists are pushing everyone else out of the Seattle office and trying to take over. She says that Howard Costigan, head of the Washington Commonwealth Federation, said the Federation would have full control of the office within 30 days.

Mary Farquharson, 1941. *Washington State Archives.*

Costigan denies saying this, and state WPA head Don G. Abel denies that the Writers' Project is influenced by Reds.

Farquharson's source is Ray Young, 31, an editor who worked at the Writers' Project to produce a state travel guide. Shortly after Farquharson goes public, Young confronts his former colleagues. "The battle was on when I called some of them Communists to their faces," Young says. He claims that he was attacked "by six or seven of the Communist writers while one held his arms from behind . . . One of them hit me on the head with a bottle." He is sent to the hospital.

Farquharson has had her fill of Reds. The Commonwealth Federation supported her in 1934, but in the 1938 Democratic primary, they ran a Communist, Dorothy Butterworth, against her. The Communists, Farquharson tells an interviewer years later, "refused to endorse me because of certain things I didn't agree to. They were very much put out with me . . . And there is no one the CP hates worse than a liberal or a radical who doesn't follow the line."

Farquharson wins the Democratic primary and keeps her seat in November, but she does not forgive the Reds.

In Seattle, City Councilman Hugh DeLacy, himself a secret Communist, declares that Farquharson's "attempt to smear red over the Writers' Project coincides with the efforts of open anti-New Deal forces to discredit and eliminate the WPA." In a reference to the House Committee on Un-American Activities, he says, "The Democratic Party is growing tired of pseudo-radicals joining the chorus of Martin Dies and his big-business pro-Nazi admirers." DeLacy is brown-baiting—a tactic he uses against the red-baiters.

Farquharson is alarmed by such talk in her own party. She writes to U.S. Senator Homer Bone that she is "convinced that if the Democratic Party is to continue in power in the state with any possibility of furthering a liberal program, it will be necessary to do some house cleaning and do it soon."

One such chance comes in January 1941. In Olympia, the Senate is about to seat Lenus Westman, 31, a victor in the November 1940 elections. Westman is an immigrant from Sweden and a Snohomish County farmer. He admits he was a member of the Communist Party in 1938 and 1939. Actually, he was a member as far back as 1934. He does not disavow his beliefs, but says he ran as a Democrat so that voters wouldn't be prejudiced against him.

After questioning Westman and others, including witnesses from the Communist Party, the Senate votes 27–17 not to seat him. This is the only time in the 20th century that the Washington State Senate denies a seat to the winner of an election.

Among those voting against him is Mary Farquharson. That Communist witnesses testified for Westman proves to her that he is still one of them. And she is not mistaken. Lenus Westman will keep the Marxist faith for the rest of his life.

Years later, Farquharson will say, "I felt it was not right for people who were members of the Communist Party to run on the Democratic ticket." She adds, "I had a great many arguments with liberal friends."

―――――

In early 1939, Howard Costigan is invited to the White House for a 15-minute meeting with President Roosevelt. Political reporters assume that *Post-Intelligencer* publisher John Boettiger, Roosevelt's son-in-law, made it happen. He and Anna Boettiger, the president's daughter, are confidants of Costigan.

Costigan wants the Washington Commonwealth Federation to lead the effort in the Pacific Northwest to back Roosevelt for a third term in 1940. The president is all for it. In Washington, DC, syndicated columnists Drew Pearson and Robert S. Allen report that the president "was so impressed that he invited the colorful young radical to dinner so that they could talk more leisurely." They add, "Roosevelt heartily approved Costigan's realistic views and assured him of full cooperation."

Five years earlier, Howard Costigan was drawing murals on the walls of Fred Shorter's church. In January 1939 he meets with Eleanor Roosevelt and cabinet members James Farley, Harold Ickes, Harry Hopkins, Henry Wallace, and Frank Murphy, as well as White House advisers Tom Corcoran and Ben Cohen and CIO leader John L. Lewis. Costigan is at the very center of power.

Howard Costigan, circa 1938. *Washington New Dealer.*

Seven months later, in August 1939, comes the event that shatters the world of Costigan and his fellow American Communists: the Hitler-Stalin pact. In September, Germany and the Soviet Union carve up Poland. This begins World War II in Europe.

For years, the Communists have been loudly anti-Nazi. How to explain a pact with Hitler? The Commonwealth Federation's paper runs an article by Melvin Rader, a professor of philosophy at the University of Washington. Rader writes, "The Russian leadership must have decided it was better to snatch while they could the White Russian and Ukrainian minorities in Poland which formerly had been under Russian sovereignty . . . than to allow these people to fall under Nazi domination." Thirty years later, Rader will write *False Witness*, a book in which he says that in 1948 he was falsely accused at the Canwell hearings of having been a Communist in the late 1930s. In 1939, he may not be a Party member, but he is an apologist for Stalin.

Commonwealth Federation President Hugh DeLacy also takes the Party line. He writes in the organization's paper that the responsibility for the attack on Poland "must be divided equally between the fascist aggressors, the British and French appeasers and the American Tories." No mention of Stalin.

In November 1939, Stalin orders an invasion of Finland. The Commonwealth Federation's paper says little about the Winter War until it is over. In March 1940, it blames British Prime Minister Neville Chamberlain for using Finland "as the field from which to launch an attack" *on Russia*, which has responded by "understandable efforts at national defense." The paper calls the territory taken from the Finns "a bit of ground which they do not own."

The gymnastics of the Party line are putting a strain on Howard Costigan's mind. In November 1939, *Post-Intelligencer* publisher John Boettiger asks Costigan to explain why the Commonwealth Federation is parroting the Communist line. "We could get nothing out of Howard," writes Anna Boettiger to a friend, "except a reiteration that he stands firmly for peace."

She adds, "John is persuaded that he is a Communist. I hate to believe this, because I feel that the man has definite ability and certainly a definite rank-and-file following." Later she writes that the main thing she has against Costigan that he talks so much that he dominates conversations.

Costigan, Hugh DeLacy, and Eugene Dennett—the leaders of the Washington Commonwealth Federation—have been occasional dinner guests of the Boettigers, talking politics into the evening. In the spring of 1940, John Boettiger finally asks them flat out if they are Communists. They admit that they are. Dennett recalls that after that, "the dinner invitations to us stopped."

In May 1940, Costigan goes on a religious retreat. This is his break with the Communist Party. "We thought we were anti-Nazi idealists," he writes, "and while most of us thought *Das Kapital* boring and Leninist tomes unappetizing, we naively accepted the tenets of Soviet doctrine." No more.

———

Costigan is also out of the Washington Commonwealth Federation. "Those who could not accept the Stalinist view of things," writes historian Albert Acena, "were no longer home" there.

Early in 1940, Commonwealth-backed Washington state senators Paul Thomas and James T. Sullivan, and representatives Ed Henry, Jurie B. Smith, Michael B. Smith, Harry Armstrong, H. D. Hall, Ellsworth Wills, and M. T. Neal sign an open letter condemning Stalin's invasion of

Finland. The Communists are outraged at this betrayal. They take Armstrong to a house in Seattle's Magnolia district for a struggle session. "I sat there for five long hours, from one o'clock in the afternoon to six o'clock at night, and I took the most tremendous verbal beating I ever took in my life," Armstrong recalls a decade later. "Each and every one of them had their little say. [Communist district organizer Morris] Raport became actually almost insane there toward the end of the meeting when he couldn't get me to recant." Armstrong never goes to a Communist meeting again.

Richard Tyler, the UW professor who tried to organize a left-wing Seattle newspaper and who went on a tour of Russia, leaves the Washington Commonwealth Federation in May 1940. In his letter of resignation, he cites "the ever-narrowing dogmatism of the expressed official views of the Federation."

Hugh DeLacy stays true to the faith. He takes over from Howard Costigan as executive director of the Washington Commonwealth Federation. In the Seattle elections of March 1940, DeLacy is red-baited—justifiably so—and loses his seat on the city council. The *Argus* notes that he has been a lone vote on the council for the hard left. It says, "He hasn't harmed a soul in the three years he has been in office, because he hasn't done a single thing."

In July 1940, DeLacy is on the minority side of one more vote. At the Democratic national convention in Chicago, he is the only delegate from the Pacific Northwest not to support Franklin Roosevelt for a third term. He abstains, saying, "I can see no candidate the people can rely on to keep the nation out of war."

In 1941, Hitler breaks his pact with Stalin and invades the Soviet Union. The Communist line changes again, and Hugh DeLacy changes with it. In August 1942, at a rally in front of Seattle City Hall, DeLacy

DeLacy protests Japan's sinking of a U.S. Navy gunboat in China, 1-3-1938. *ACME Newspictures* image in author's collection.

demands an immediate Second Front in Europe and a declaration of war against Finland.

———

Finally, a story of what the left of the 1930s is not: a defender of women.

The equality of women has been one of the left's trademark ideas, and will be in the future. But in the hard, early years of the Depression, when the cry arises to fire the married women, the labor movement sides with the men. The left goes along. In 1938, this happens again.

Otto Messelheiser, 57, a surveyor at the Civilian Conservation Corps camp near North Bend, writes in January 1938 of the lost hope in the faces of the men. "The girls take the men's jobs," he says in a letter to the *Post-Intelligencer*. "Then they won't marry the men when they are out of work. Men don't build homes if they don't have wives." Hire the men instead, he writes, and "they'd marry the girls in the offices. And the whole plan would create a home-construction boom."

Messelheiser is just one man, yet his letter becomes a news story on page 3 of the *P-I*. Somebody wants the public to read it.

The push to dismiss married women is not just talk. In 1937, the legislature considers, but does not pass, a bill dismissing women from state jobs if their husbands are able to work. Three days before Christmas, Governor Clarence Martin issues an executive order to do it anyway. Several dozen women are let go. In February 1938 King County dismisses 20 women under a similar order.

Since January 1936, the University of Washington has had a quiet policy not to employ husband and wife in full-time academic work. The policy is so quiet that an instructor in fine arts, Lea Puymbroeck, doesn't know about it. In August 1937, while studying in Europe, she marries Robert C. Miller, a UW professor of zoology. She learns of the policy when she returns to Seattle as a married woman. The university allows her to work fall quarter while it finds a replacement. In January 1938 she is dismissed.

The newspapers play up the story. They interview her replacement, a man from New York (so much for local employment). His wife tells the papers *she* expects to work, and that she thinks the UW's policy is a waste of human talent. Seattle attorney Willie Forbus, a leader of the women who blocked the "working wives" bill in the 1937 legislature, speaks out against the university. She says Lea Miller's dismissal violates women's "economic rights as free individuals." State Senator Mary Farquharson, the wife of UW Professor Burt Farquharson, complains to Governor Martin, the man who appoints the UW Regents. Several clubs representing professional women support Miller.

And none of it matters. The support for Lea Miller is too weak. The Seattle City Council's leftist, Hugh DeLacy, who was fired from his teaching position at the UW because he ran for office, is quoted nowhere. The Washington Commonwealth Federation runs one letter supporting Miller in its *Sunday News*, but is more interested in Lieutenant Governor Vic Meyers, who is running for mayor of Seattle—and Meyers makes no issue of it. The Seattle Central Labor Council agrees with the university; it says it will support any public agency "which dismisses any married woman whose husband is eligible to work." The Chamber of Commerce says nothing. The *Seattle Times* seems eager to quote anyone who supports Miller, and it supports her in an editorial, but it uses words that are weak. The *Post-Intelligencer* runs the opinions of Otto Messelheiser.

Lea P. Miller, 1938. *Author's collection.*

At King County, commissioners Louis Nash, Jack Taylor, and Tom E. Smith sense the drift of public sentiment and vote to dismiss married women from the county welfare department. When professional women circulate a petition in protest, Seattle City Councilwoman Mildred Powell publicly refuses to sign it. Powell is the only woman on the council and is up for reelection. A few days later, she is reelected with a resounding majority.

The Millers accept the UW's decision. They move to California, where she becomes an associate professor of decorative arts at the University of California, Berkeley.

As written, the University of Washington's policy is gender-neutral. On its face it is about nepotism, but because the tenured staff is mostly men, it works against women. It will remain in force for more than 30 years, ending in 1971.

16
The Great Builder, 1930–1939

During most of the 1930s, the great builder is the government, though some of the more fanciful ideas don't get built. One is a deep road-and-rail tunnel under Stevens Pass, 29 miles long. Years earlier, Hiram Chittenden, the builder of the Ballard locks, proposed it, and in 1925 the legislature set up a three-member commission that recommended it. One of the commissioners was Clarence Martin, then mayor of Cheney in eastern Washington. In 1933 Martin becomes governor. But by then, the highway over Snoqualmie Pass is being kept open all year—and at Stevens Pass, the Great Northern has its own tunnel. There is no need for a new one.

Another idea is a series of canals to link Puget Sound to the Columbia River. The longest, 48 miles, would be from Olympia to Grays Harbor, rising in a series of locks to Black Lake, 90 feet above sea level. Two sea-level canals would connect to Willapa Bay and the Columbia. In 1933 the Legislature commissions an engineering report on it. Building the canals, says the report, "will be the largest make-work project in the state of Washington." To the Corps of Engineers, that's not a good reason to build it—and state highways director Lacey V. Murrow worries that it would soak up too much road money. In 1936 the state rejects the plan.

In Seattle, the more modest project of the early Depression is rebuilding the sea wall on Elliott Bay and the street behind it, which is made of thick planks on wood pilings. By the 1930s, the fill under the pilings is gone, the wood is rotting, and truck wheels are breaking through. The street is called Railroad Avenue, because it has railroad tracks so that trains can reach the finger piers. But the tracks will not be replaced. The street needs a new name.

In 1932 the Seattle Maritime Association has a contest for the best name. It chooses—no surprise—"Maritime Avenue." Its runners-up are "Puget Portal" and two Indian names, "Klatawa Avenue" and "Hiak Avenue," meaning "waterfront" and "lively." But the city council doesn't like those names. The *Seattle Times* suggests "Marine Way." Early in 1934, construction begins with the help of a grant from the state. But there is no name.

In 1935 the council almost chooses a name proposed by George D. Root, a shipping-industry man: "Cosmos Quay." Root says the name will become famous, like "The Embarcadero" in San Francisco and "The Bund" in Shanghai. Root's idea appeals to Councilman Austin E. Griffiths, who a decade earlier had been a big backer of the Cascade tunnel. But "Cosmos Quay" is a strange name, and people laugh at it. *Times* publisher Clarance Blethen calls it a "lexiographical monstrosity." Reader R.C.A. DeVries writes that "Cosmos Quay" would be a fine name if Seattle were a place for "interplanetary ships arriving from other worlds."

The *Seattle Star* offers "Alaska Way," but by then the City Council has moved on.

By May 1936, the work is done. No longer a wooden deck on pilings, the street has become a broad avenue behind a sea wall. The *Post-Intelligencer* calls it "Seattle's most spectacular public improvement in years"—but it still has no name. "Forget the funny ones," plead the editors of the *Times*. "Let's get a real one." Mayor John Dore offers a $50 prize and appoints a committee to choose a name. From 9,000 names submitted by the public, the committee narrows it down to "The Ramshorn," "The Seawall," "The Seaway," and "The Pierway," finally choosing the latter. The *Argus* does a thumbs-down. "The Pierway," it declares, is "as nutty as 'The Doreway,'" a jibe at Mayor Dore. Councilman Griffiths complains that "The Pierway" is not specific to Seattle, nor is "Pacific Way."

The *Star* pumps again for "Alaska Way," a name it says is "dignified, rugged, easy to say and has the tang of the sea." A delegation of Alaskan sourdoughs lobbies the council, and the *Star*'s suggestion prevails. The council adds an "n" to make the name about the people rather than the place, and Seattle's waterfront street becomes Alaskan Way.

For Seattle, the big construction works of the 1930s are bridges.

Plans begin in 1929 to build a high-level bridge across the Lake Washington Ship Canal for U.S. 99. To keep the ship canal open for the Navy, the War Department insists on a clearance of 152 feet—18 feet higher than the city wants—which raises the cost. Mayor Frank Edwards asks that the state add a streetcar deck under the roadway, which would raise the cost even more. The War Department gets its way; Mayor Edwards does not. This is in the Hoover years, and the federal government pays nothing. The city, county, and state each pay one-third, with Seattle voters giving their approval for a bond issue in March 1930. The ironworkers on the project will earn $1.25 an hour—good pay in 1930.

The city also rebuilds two bridges over the ship canal, the University Bridge, originally opened in 1919, and the Ballard Bridge, opened in 1917. Both have central drawbridges of concrete and steel, and both have approaches on timber piers that need to be replaced. Also, in both projects, the City of Seattle is unable to finance the work by selling bonds to private investors. Unlike the toll bridge planned earlier in the decade between Mercer Island and Seward Park, this roadblock doesn't stop the projects. They are public, not private, and the city is taken care of.

The University Bridge goes out for financing after the 1931 collapse in the bond market. The state rescues the city by buying the bonds, and the bridge is finished in April 1933.

Financing the Ballard Bridge would push the city over its debt limit, which is based on the value of assessed property, which has gone down. The city argues in court that replacing the bridge's rotting piers is an urgent matter of public safety. The Washington Supreme Court already allowed the city to ignore the debt limit to feed the unemployed, but for the Ballard Bridge the superior court says no. In 1938, Governor Clarence Martin comes to Seattle's rescue with gas-tax money. That, plus a grant from the Public Works Administration, and the new bridge is opened in 1940.

Finally comes the bridge across Lake Washington. Unlike the private project abandoned in 1931, this will be a public project funded in part by tolls and in part by money from the New Deal.

At first the plan is to build from the Seward Park peninsula, as in 1931. But in August 1937 comes a new plan for a bridge three miles to the north that would float on concrete pontoons. No such bridge exists anywhere in the world.

The idea of concrete pontoons is from an engineer named Homer Hadley. During World War I, Hadley worked in Philadelphia building barges for the war effort. Because steel was reserved for ships, he used concrete. In 1921 he presented a plan to the American Society of Civil Engineers for a Lake Washington bridge supported on concrete pontoons.

Supported by wood: The Ballard Bridge, 1938. *Courtesy of Seattle Municipal Archives.*

His plan went nowhere. In 1989 the second Mercer Island bridge will be named for him, but in August 1937, when the plan for the original bridge is unveiled, Hadley gets no credit. The bridge is named for Lacey V. Murrow.

The *Post-Intelligencer* likes the plan. "Despite the fact that the bridge at this new location will be three times as long," the *P-I* says, "it can be constructed for less than half the cost of any of the bridges so far suggested for the south end of the island. In addition, it will be wider and will serve the city better."

The *Times* is not impressed. Its first headline is "Pontoon Span Called Costly and Dangerous." It writes that "the proposed 8,000-foot concrete fence across Lake Washington" would be "a gross and wholly unnecessary obstruction . . . an architectural monstrosity, hideous at all times, wobbly and wet in stormy weather, and subject to such strains as must incur continuing and heavy costs to hold it together and in place." The *Times* says the new

Building Homer Hadley's dream bridge, December 1939. *Photograph by Alfred G. Simmer. L. R. Durkee Collection on the Lacey V. Murrow Bridge Construction Project, 2003.30.174, Museum of History & Industry, Seattle. Used with permission.*

design is "unspeakably worse" than the "mud-filled causeway" proposed years earlier and "should be abandoned at once."

Back in 1930, the *Times* opposed the extension of Aurora Avenue through Woodland Park. It lost that fight, and it loses this one, too. In December 1938, the city council approves the floating bridge by a 5–4 vote. Work begins in January 1939. Of the cost, 45 percent is from a federal grant and 55 percent from 30-year state bonds backed by tolls. The skeptics say the tolls—25 cents for car and driver, 5 cents for each passenger—will never pay off the bonds. They are wrong. The bonds will be paid off in nine years.

A final note: As government is building and rebuilding three bridges across the ship canal, the private Seattle-Everett Interurban rail line, which also crosses the canal, closes in February 1939. Doug Welch of the *Post-Intelligencer* recalls the early years of the century, when the railcars ran through stretches of old-growth forest. "They carried 'standing loads' in those days, 150 or more in two cars; they operated on half-hourly schedules, with limiteds and locals, and for a brief spell they offered parlor car accommodations with observation platforms," he writes. The ride took an hour and fifteen minutes.

By 1939 the public is using the roads.

17

Up, Down, and Up Again, 1936–1939

For Seattle, a normal level of building, real estate men say, would be half of the boom level of 1930. In 1933, 1934, and 1935, Seattle building permits come in at rock bottom: 6 percent, 7 percent, and 12 percent of the 1930 figure. In 1936, with the Blue Eagle dead, the figure creeps up to a more promising 20 percent.

Most of the work is repairs. The *Argus* writes, "In almost every community, dwellings are being repainted, repaired and even sold to an extent that for several years has been infeasible." A few new houses are being built, but in September 1936 the *Star* reports that no apartments are being built anywhere in the city.

During 1936, the city's office buildings are still more than one-quarter empty. Hawthorne K. Dent discovers a buyer's market when he sets out to provide a home for the General Insurance Company of America, which he founded in 1923. Dent plans to build a five-story building on First Hill, east of downtown. When the news gets out, he is offered the eight-story Brooklyn Building in the University District. When built in 1928, it was the tallest building north of the ship canal. By 1936, it has defaulted on its 6½-percent bonds and has been seized by its bondholders. Dent buys it, and his company moves in. Atop the building it will erect the largest illuminated sign in the Pacific Northwest, 75 feet high. Four decades later the company, renamed Safeco, will replace the Brooklyn Building with the 22-story Safeco Tower (now the University of Washington Tower, still the tallest building north of the ship canal).

Seattle's hotels have a hard time in the Depression. Many of them make it through by renting rooms to "permanent guests" at deep discounts. By 1936, they have more travelers, but the improvement is not enough for the U District's Edmond Meany Hotel, which files for bankruptcy in 1937. Nobody is building new hotels.

In August 1937, the stock market panics. The economy tanks, and two years of gains are lost.

The economy's fall is not gentle. The fall is not as far as in 1929–1932, but it hurts. Factories close. Workers are laid off. In Seattle, from 1937 to 1938, the number of marriages drops by 10 percent. Suicides increase by 15 percent.

The panic takes business by surprise. The economy is not overheated. Back in 1929, national unemployment was pushed down to 3.2 percent. In 1937, the jobless rate is at an ultra-loose 14.3 percent. Of the three great economic factors—land, labor, and capital—all are in surplus. *Gross* surplus. In mid-1937 the economy is halfway out of the Depression at best. There are no foreign-debt crises, no demands for gold and no runs on the banks. The public is not in the stock market. Trading volume is low.

Stock prices have come up, but not like 1929. At Ben Ehrlichman's United National Corporation, the stock peaked above $50 in 1929 and fell in 1932 to 50 cents. At the peak in the market in the spring of 1937, United National is bid at $12.50. When the market starts down in August it is bid at $10. Over the next six months it drops to $3.

The deep Depression is back. But why? The panic has come in the stock market—that is, from investors. Consider the world of 1937 from their eyes. In March, a week before the stock market's peak for the year, B. C. Forbes lists three big worries for investors: "Washington. Labor. Europe."

"Labor" is shorthand for the fastest spread of unions in the 20th century, aided by violence and the sit-down strike. Unions are cutting into company profits, in some cases taking all of them.

"Europe" is shorthand for war. World War II has begun in China, and in Europe, fighting rages in Spain. War will eventually end the Depression, but war brings conscription, taxes, and controls. It is not the kind of recovery investors want.

"Washington" is shorthand for the New Deal, which has become hostile to corporate America. The Blue Eagle was an experiment that didn't work, but it was meant to help owners and workers alike. The Second New Deal is not for owners.

The last friend of business among the three branches of government has been the courts. In the spring of 1937, the Supreme Court stops resisting the New Deal—and the stock market turns down. The market recovers for a while, but in August, President Roosevelt nominates Alabama senator Hugo Black, a staunch New Dealer, for an open seat on the Court. Two days after Black is nominated, the market begins a steep decline.

"Washington-Labor-Europe" might be called the investors' theory of the 1937 panic. There are others. Robert H. Jackson, assistant U.S. attorney general and future Supreme Court justice, argues that the nation's capitalists are on strike, with the aim of wrecking the New Deal. Apparently, this is what President Roosevelt thinks. Economists will argue later that the plunge is caused by a slowdown in federal spending. Their theory is accepted by many historians. Note, though, that it implies an economy too weak to grow without constant injections of federal money, which is not the kind of economy America has had.

Each group—politicians, economists, investors—explains the new depression in terms of what it knows. To the economists, it's about monetary aggregates and budgets. To the politicians, it's about politics. To investors it's about uncertainty: Washington, Labor, Europe.

The stock market falls for seven months, until April 1938. Then Congress, which has Democratic supermajorities in both chambers, defies President Roosevelt on two bills. The House votes down the government-reorganization bill, a grant of executive power. The stock market notches up. The next day, the Senate passes a bill to repeal a tax on undistributed company profits—a tax that the president wants to keep and business hates. Stocks rise again. The last bear market of the 1930s is over.

As usual, the economy lags the market. In 1938, national unemployment hits 19 percent, up almost five points over 1937. This is the first big jump since 1932. The pain is not as great as then, but it comes on suddenly and feels undeserved.

Industry is hit hard. By May 1938, only 8 percent of the men in Western Washington's lumber industry, the region's largest, are working full-time. This is only partly the new Depression. It's also Britain's response to the Smoot-Hawley tariff: Britain has been buying its lumber from Canada.

Overall, construction is affected less. In Seattle, the value of all building permits in 1936, 1937, and 1938 is stuck at 20 percent of the 1930 level. The market is strangely split. Fifteen percent of commercial space is still vacant, and little is being built. In housing, vacancy has shrunk all the way to 1½ percent, a rate that should be fueling a boom. The building of single-family houses perks up, but there is no boom.

Tenants are saving money by doubling up. In May 1938, a city report finds young couples living with parents. "A goodly number of old-style apartments containing from four to six-room suites have also been subdivided," the report says. "Old hotels and even buildings constructed for office use have been provided with facilities for cooking, so that single persons and even families have turned to this type of housing. We have found as many as a dozen housekeeping units in a building that was constructed as a single-family residence . . . The living conditions of many of these places are such that it is doubtful if we can any longer say that Seattle is a city without slums."

From 1932 to 1937 the construction of apartments in Seattle virtually stops. In mid-1938, this changes with the Edgewater, a project worth more than all the apartment buildings built in Seattle in the previous six years.

Big names are behind it. The developer is Manson Backus II, grandson of the late chairman of the National Bank of Commerce. The architect is the John Graham firm. The land, at the northern tip of Madison Park, is from the estate of Judge Thomas Burke, whose namesakes are the Burke Museum and the Burke-Gilman Trail. The land sale is handled by Seattle's top real estate man, Henry Broderick. The financing is a 5-percent loan guaranteed by the Federal Housing Administration, an agency of the New Deal.

If this were the 1920s, the Edgewater's 304 units would be stacked skyward in Art Deco towers. But the *zeitgeist* of the 1930s is leveling. The units will be built close to the ground, in 18 two-story buildings shorn of ornament and set out in rows like public housing. But the Edgewater "is not to be confused with any of the federal low-cost housing projects," its managers tell the press. This is private housing for the middle class.

The real-estate people love it. After Seattle's "long, lean years in apartment construction," says Bert G. Owen, president of the Seattle Real Estate Board, "the ball has started rolling."

There is a problem with labor. At the bottom of the Depression in 1932, union contractors agreed to a six-hour day in order to spread the work. Later the whole industry agreed to it. But by 1938, contractors complain that work is taking too long to get done. The eight-hour day was more efficient, and they want it back.

The Edgewater, Seattle's great apartment project of the 1930s. *Pemco Webster & Stevens Collection, 1983.10.13945.1, Museum of History & Industry, Seattle. Used with permission.*

The building trades resist. The Depression is still on. The eight-hour day, says one union man, would "put every fourth member out of work." There is a deeper reason. For the past half-century, the workday in America has been reduced from twelve hours to eight—and in the Seattle building trades, to six. Never has it gone back. "If, after five years and nine months of the six-hour day, we should return to the old standard, we would be the laughingstock of labor throughout the whole United States," says Harry Ames of the Seattle Building Trades Council. "We never will consider it. We are all washed up with the eight-hour day."

The contractors promise a flood of work if the unions will accept an eight-hour day. The workers put it to a vote and say no. The unions agree, however, that if the contractors can't fill six-hour shifts with acceptable workers, they may stretch the shift to eight hours. That satisfies the contractors. The six-hour day will last until September 1940, when the war ends it.

The developers of the Edgewater also make a demand on the city. Seattle's building code calls for walls of lath and plaster. The contractors want to use the new product: plasterboard. The cost saving is huge. The Plasterers' Union objects. "Our men are out of work," says Charles Johnson, their business agent. Labor loses this fight. The city council, eager for the project to go forward, okays plasterboard. In June 1938, construction begins.

In January 1939, the new Edgewater units are offered at $40 to $62.50 a month. These are just about the only new apartments in the city. In March, a developer announces plans for a 20-story apartment hotel, but he can't swing it.

The dearth of apartment construction in the 1930s will lead to a shortage by 1941, when war workers flood into the city.

In 1939 the value of building permits in Seattle reaches 39 percent of the 1930 figure. Most new construction is houses. The price of land has come down, mortgage rates have come down from 7 percent in 1929 to 5 percent, and the new 12- to 15-year amortizing loans require lower payments than the old five-year balloon-payment loans. By mid-1939, new houses, at an average value of $4,000, are going up in Seattle at the rate of 100 a month.

Suburban development revives. In 1939 comes the debt restructuring of Normandy Park, a 1,200-acre development south of Seattle on Puget Sound.

Normandy Park is the creation of Alvo von Alvensleben, a high-flying German whose business career crashes three times. Born in 1879, he is the younger son of a Prussian count. As a lieutenant in the German army, he embarrasses his father with his gambling debts. In 1904 he quits the army and sails off to El Salvador, where his brother has a coffee plantation, then to the Pacific Northwest. After a stint in Seattle as a common laborer, he moves to Vancouver, where he begins attracting money from the old country to invest in mining, timber, and urban real estate. With his personality and family connections, he attracts funds from high German officials, including Kaiser Wilhelm himself.

By 1908, von Alvensleben is a prominent figure in Vancouver business. He has a British wife, three children, and a fine home. Real estate booms, and that year he helps finance the 17-story Dominion Building, the tallest in Canada.

In 1913 von Alvensleben's empire collapses. In 1914, the British Empire goes to war with Germany, and Canada seizes his remaining assets. His wife and children flee British Columbia and meet him in Seattle. For several years, he continues to work with a remaining German asset, the Issaquah

& Superior Coal Mine on Squak Mountain, but it fails, too, and is seized by its bank.

In April 1917, the United States enters the war. Based on the word of the British government that he is a German spy, von Alvensleben is interned as an enemy alien at Fort Douglas, Utah. He is no spy, but he is a troublemaker. He becomes the spokesman for the 335 German internees and writes a letter of protest to the Swiss Embassy. As punishment, he is put in solitary confinement. Though he is never charged with a crime, he is kept at Fort Douglas 16 months after the war's end.

Reunited with his family, von Alvensleben begins his third push for fortune. In 1926 he entices German bankers in Chicago to buy 2½ miles of wooded waterfront between Seattle and Tacoma for $450,000 ($7.9 million in 2024 dollars). The sellers are the heirs of the Schwabachers, a family of German Jewish immigrants who became Seattle's foremost hardware wholesalers.

Alvo von Alvensleben in younger days. *Vancouver (British Columbia) City Archives.*

With businessman Russell H. Phinney, von Alvensleben forms the Seattle-Tacoma Land Company. To finance their project, they offer 7-percent bonds of a special kind. Each $1,000 bond is worth $1,250 for buying a building lot. In that way, the debt can be paid off not in dollars, but in dirt.

At first, they name their project Olympic Park, due to its views of the Olympic Mountains. But when they imagine a community of Norman-style homes, they rename it Normandy Park. They open the development in May 1929. A clubhouse and two houses are begun. The first house is a four-bedroom, red-brick, waterfront home for a manager at Frederick & Nelson. (In 2021, that house will be offered for $3.39 million, four times the median price of a house in King County.) A similar house is built for a young man soon to be president of the Northern Radio & Telegraph Company.

Two years later, in 1931, the Depression is on. The Northern Radio man, Leon Fobes, 31, is losing his home. Unable to cope, he holes up at the Benjamin Franklin Hotel in downtown Seattle and commits suicide, leaving behind his wife, Dorothea, and their two children. She sells the house to a Chevrolet dealer. In that same year, the bondholders foreclose and take back Normandy Park. They sell the clubhouse to a downtown Seattle jeweler, who makes it his home.

Years pass. In December 1938, a court approves the formation of the Normandy Park Company, with each $100 in the dead company's bonds exchangeable for one share of the new company's stock. In January 1939 the new company offers building lots for sale at much reduced prices, with half the price payable in stock.

"Informed persons in the financial district," writes *Post-Intelligencer* business columnist Fred Niendorff, "have been 'going to town' snapping up choice tracts that once were priced to sell for $1,000 to $10,000 for a few hundred dollars and in many cases less than that." Normandy Park revives as a middle-class suburb of wooden houses rather than Norman-style brick homes with double doors and leaded glass.

In March 1939, as Hitler pushes toward war, von Alvensleben faces the risk of being interned again as an enemy alien. He renounces his allegiance to Germany. As a U.S. citizen, he will not be interned. But he is 60, and his days as a major land developer are over.

In 1938 comes a private investment in a baseball park.

For almost 20 years, the Pacific Coast League's Seattle club, the Indians, play at the wooden 10,000-seat Dugdale Park in the Rainier Valley. In the boom year 1929, the team owners announce plans for a 15,000-seat stadium near downtown at the site of the future Seattle Center, but they give up after the crash. In 1932, serial arsonist Robert Driscoll, who tells police he hates "the bosses and capitalists," burns Dugdale Park to the ground.

For six Depression years, the Indians play in the Civic Stadium. It is a poor venue, suitable for a poor team. By 1937 the owners are unable to pay the rent, and they put the team up for sale.

Emil J. Sick, a Canadian who has moved to Seattle since the end of Prohibition, restarts the Rainier Brewery on Airport Way and proudly erects a big "R" on top. Unlike brewer Peter Marinoff, Sick becomes a pal of Dave Beck. The Teamster leader advises Sick that a new baseball park would be a fine place to sell beer.

Sick buys the Indians and renames the team for his beer: the Seattle Rainiers. At the site of the old Dugdale Park, he builds a stadium with 15,000 seats, the same number as was planned in 1929. The main section is made of concrete and steel. Sick raises the money, $7.7 million in 2024 dollars, without public subsidy.

Emil Sick, stadium builder, 1930s. *David Eskenazi collection.*

Opening day, June 15, 1938, is a civic event. In a flash of inspiration, the *Seattle Times* sends society columnist Virginia Boren to cover the event. "I met the same people that one meets at Symphony concerts, the theatres, teas and charity events," she writes, except that at Sick's Stadium they "ate peanuts, chewed gum (the moving jaw was much in evidence), drank pop and beer, ate hot dogs, applauded the players and admired this new ball park."

A church is an enterprise. It has no stockholders to pay, but it needs to bring in enough funds to sustain itself. In Seattle, St. Mark's Episcopal Cathedral is unable to do that in the Great Depression.

The plan for the cathedral begins in the 1920s. "It will be a stately example of ecclesiastical architecture, Gothic in style, and patterned after Old World cathedrals in design of nave, transepts and chancel," the *Post-Intelligencer* writes in 1926. "Above it will tower a stately spire 120 feet in height, and occupying one of the highest points in the city." As the project moves ahead, the imagined spire triples in height, to 390 feet.

Money for the project is raised by Seattle businessmen, and as the Depression begins, they come up short. In 1930, the church dean, John McLauchlan, argues for a smaller project. He's not trying to impress anybody. The businessmen are, and they have their way. The building goes ahead,

The St. Mark's cathedral plan, with Gothic spire, circa 1927. *University of Washington Libraries, Special Collections, SEA2773.*

with the spire saved for later. The church takes out a $200,000 mortgage from a bank in St. Louis.

The cathedral opens in 1931. It is too big for the congregation to support, and they fall behind on the mortgage payments. This goes on for years. By 1939 the debt has swollen to $250,000. The St. Louis bankers are desperate. They don't want to own a cathedral; they want their money. They tell the church they'll be happy if it will just pay the original amount: $200,000. Forget the rest. The church says it will have a fund drive, but no fund drive comes. Dean McLauchlan provides weddings, memorials, and Sunday services, but leaves the finances in the hands of God.

The reality, 1931: a "holy box." *From St. Mark's Episcopal Cathedral webpage, https://saintmarks.org/.*

In May 1941, one week after the cathedral's tenth birthday, the St. Louis bank seizes the property. The mortgage banker they send to take the keys from Dean McLauchlan is Walter Williams, president of the Seattle Chamber of Commerce.

The foreclosure makes national news. "Bankers took over the biggest Episcopal church in the Pacific Northwest last week—Seattle's massive, unfinished St. Mark's Cathedral," writes *Time*.

In desperation, an appeal is made to the original money men who bankrolled the building. Moritz Thomsen, the donor for the chapel, has died, and his son has lost his father's company, Centennial Mills, in the Depression. But John W. Eddy is still around. Eddy made his fortune in lumber and, during World War I, in the Skinner & Eddy shipyard. Dean McLauchlan's wife, Adelaide, goes to see him.

"We did not want this big cathedral," she tells him. Eddy and the other money men, she says, "took our little church away from us and insisted on building a great structure."

Her appeal to guilt doesn't work. "I do want to see a big cathedral, not just a cold, cellar-like pile of concrete like you have now," Eddy says. "But you will never be able to get it until you get another dean. It takes money to run a big church, and its affairs have to be handled by the vestry, the parishioners. But the dean wants to keep all the reins in his own hands." And then sit on them. Eddy sums up: "Nobody can work with him. Get a younger man."

Eddy's words, printed in the newspapers, are the final no. When war comes, the St. Louis bank rents the cathedral to the U.S. Army for use as a training center for anti-aircraft gunners. During the time the Army has the cathedral, the parishioners get a younger dean, Richard Watson. After the war, he undertakes the promised fund drive, which includes a banquet hosted by brewer Emil Sick and Teamster boss Dave Beck. The church pays off the St. Louis bank and reclaims its cathedral.

It never does build the spire.

18
Enterprise, 1933–1939

Risk-takers in industry make key investments in the Depression, some at very low prices.

Alexander Peabody is the young president of the Puget Sound Navigation Company, which owns the dominant Black Ball ferries on Puget Sound. By the 1930s, the need is for car ferries, but the company is not earning enough to buy new ones.

In 1933, Peabody buys the hull of a ferry in Oakland that has been burned to the water line. A shipyard on Lake Washington builds a new topside in radically streamlined form. Named the *Kalakala*, the boat goes into service in 1935. It becomes a Seattle icon; people call it the Silver Slug. But Peabody needs more boats. In 1937, the new Bay Bridge to San Francisco puts the ferries there out of business, and Peabody buys 17 of them at bargain prices.

The Black Ball line has a hard time in the 1930s. The deckhands' union shuts it down four times, twice for more than 20 days, and the state keeps a lid on rates. In 1951 Peabody will sell most of the company's assets to the state. This is the beginning of the Washington State Ferries. The only Black Ball service left will be the run between Port Angeles and Victoria, BC.

Another investment comes in February 1934, when Seattle taxi magnate Paul Pigott buys control of the Pacific Car & Foundry Company. A maker of railcars, it was established by his father, William Pigott, in 1905 but was sold out of family hands. Its plant in Renton has fallen into disrepair; its workforce, which was 800 in mid-1930, has shrunk to 125, most of them part-time. Pigott pays the rock-bottom price of $50,000 ($1.16 million in 2024 dollars). By 1936 the plant will have 500 employees building refrigerator cars. A decade later it will be busy assembling Sherman tanks. His company will survive into the 21st century as PACCAR, the producer of Kenworth and Peterbilt diesel trucks.

Some companies find new markets. In the summer of 1929, lumber and veneer men form Aircraft Plywood. They start with an offering of

250 *Seattle in the Great Depression*

The *Kalakala*, the "Silver Slug" of the Black Ball Line. *Postcard in author's collection.*

6½-percent bonds and nine acres at the south end of the Ballard Bridge. Their aim is to build the largest veneer and plywood plant in the Pacific Northwest.

Plywood is a new industry. The company's business plan targets the most glamorous part of it: airplanes. At the end of the 1920s, airplane wings are being made of straight-grain Sitka spruce, which has a high strength-to-weight ratio. Spruce is difficult to work with; the veneer has to be sliced rather than peeled. The founders expect that at first spruce will be only one-quarter of their output. But aircraft plywood is to be their signature product, and they name their company for it.

The plywood men are right about aviation. It has a big future, but on wings of steel. Aircraft Plywood will never win a single contract to produce plywood for airplane wings.

There are other uses. By the spring of 1930, the company is running two eight-hour shifts, manufacturing Douglas fir panels for automobile floors and running boards. The buyer is Fisher Body, which has plants across the United States, including one in Seattle to supply the Ford assembly line.

The Depression comes, Ford closes its Seattle plant, and Fisher Body cancels its contract. Aircraft Plywood closes its doors. It defaults on the bonds it sold in 1929, and the bonds drop to 15 cents on the dollar. The company's stock suspends trading. At its lowest point, its plant in Ballard, which cost $1 million, goes dark.

At the bottom of the Depression, plant manager William C. Bailey travels east to hunt for investors. He finds three plywood distributors willing to put money into the Seattle plant. With their money, Aircraft Plywood starts up in 1932, producing fir panels for doors, cabinets, running boards, radio sets—any use that pays.

The company survives the Blue Eagle years, when its output is limited to 7.91 percent of the U.S. market. By late 1935, with the Blue Eagle dead, the plant is running flat-out with three shifts and accounting for 12 percent of the fir plywood capacity on the West Coast. By 1937 it is a union shop paying the highest wages in the industry. That year, its largest investor, U.S. Plywood Corporation, buys out the Seattle investors. Holders of the defaulted bonds of 1929 get their principal back. The stockholders get 30 cents on the dollar of the original offering price.

The plant will produce plywood for World War II and the boom that follows. For many years the plant built to produce plywood for airplanes will

Handling veneer at Aircraft Plywood, a company that survived. *Courtesy of APA—The Engineered Wood Association.*

be the nation's largest producer of plywood for boats. Long after the plant is closed, the name "U.S. Plywood" will be visible from the Ballard Bridge.

And then there is Boeing.

At the peak of the 1920s boom, William Boeing is at the head of a nationwide holding company, the United Aircraft & Transport Corporation. Based in Hartford, Connecticut, it includes the Seattle aircraft builder he founded plus several parts and engine companies and some tiny airlines that will soon blend together into United Air Lines. United Aircraft has bought these companies by swapping its shares for theirs. In April 1929, its shares go public on the New York Stock Exchange at $80.

At the peak of the bull market, William Boeing sells some of his shares at $157. Then comes the Depression and the political urge to scourge the rich. In February 1934, Senator Hugo Black, Alabama Democrat and future Supreme Court justice, calls Boeing to testify at a kind of American show trial.

By then, United Aircraft shares have fallen back to around $30. But Black wants to know about the founder's sales at $157. "Well, it's no fault of mine" that the stock went so high, Boeing says in the Senate hearing. "Aviation has been my life's work. I went through all the hazards and through periods in which everyone thought I was a fool. I risked a good part of my personal fortune. Maybe these profits are a reward for my life's work."

William Boeing at the Black hearings, 1934. *International Newsphoto* image in author's collection.

Senator Black also goes after Walter F. Brown, who was Herbert Hoover's postmaster general. Black's focus is on a meeting in which Brown insisted that some of the carriers merge before bidding on airmail routes. Brown makes no apologies; at the time, the airlines were small, and he wanted carriers that would stay in business. But critics dub this the "spoils conference," and in February 1934, President Roosevelt cancels all airmail contracts. He orders Army pilots to fly the mail. It's a bad decision;

they aren't equipped to fly cross-country in winter storms, and they begin falling out of the sky. By the end of March, twelve Army pilots are dead.

Black pushes through the Air Mail Act of 1934, which returns the work to private carriers. The law allows no airline represented at the "spoils conference" to bid on a route and no person who was at the conference to work for an airline holding a contract. President Roosevelt signs the bill.

Postmaster General James Farley, who opposed the bill, tells the carriers they can avoid it by reincorporating. Boeing Airplane becomes Boeing Aircraft; United Air Lines becomes United Air Lines Transport, and so on. The holding company cannot get around the law and is broken into three parts. In Seattle, the original Boeing company reclaims its independence.

Decades later, Washington's senators will be known as "senators from Boeing." Not in 1934. At the height of the flap, Senator Homer Bone offers an amendment to an appropriations bill to allow the government to nationalize production of Navy aircraft. Bone says he is trying to "take the profit out of war." The measure fails, but it shows a startling lack of support for the largest industrial company in his home state.

William Boeing quietly retires. He is 52, and has said he wanted to retire early. Seattle's newspapers run no stories about this, which suggests that they are keeping quiet as a favor to him. He dies in 1956 of a heart attack while on his yacht, the *Taconite*.

The Boeing company takes huge risks during the Depression. The man behind the decisions is Clairmont ("Claire") Egtvedt, whom William Boeing hired out of the University of Washington in 1917. When the founder retires, Egtvedt takes over. In the 1930s he bets the company on a new generation of big, all-metal, four-engine monoplanes of a kind that a decade before did not exist.

Already the company has partly embraced these ideas. As the decade begins, its engineers are at work on designs to replace the old wooden-wing biplanes. In

Claire Egtvedt, 1942. *Author's collection.*

Boeing's B-9 "Flying Panatella" with pursuit plane, 1931. © *The Boeing Company.*

May 1930, they test a prototype all-metal single-engine monoplane with retractable landing gear, though still with an open cockpit. They call it the Monomail. A year later, the company rolls out a prototype bomber it calls the B-9 and the *Post-Intelligencer* calls the "Flying Panatella." It has two engines, with the pilot and copilot in separate open cockpits. The War Department likes the B-9's size, range, and speed—158 miles per hour. Design work continues.

On the civilian side, Boeing develops its first modern airliner, the 247. The company brags that the new plane will cut the flight time from Seattle to New York from 27 hours to only 21, with 7 stops instead of 14. But at the insistence of United Air Lines, its first customer, it makes the plane too small: ten seats. Two years later, Douglas Aircraft comes out with the DC-3, which has 25 seats—and it sweeps the market.

The year 1934 begins a rough period for the Boeing company. Employment in Seattle drops to less than 700. This is when Claire Egtvedt bets it all. The U.S. Army has a competition to design a multi-engine bomber that can deliver one ton of bombs 2,000 miles at 200 miles per hour. Unlike his rivals, Egtvedt interprets "multi-engine" to mean *four* engines. The plane becomes the B-17 "Flying Fortress" of World War II.

But not without trouble. On October 30, 1935, at the Army testing ground in Dayton, Ohio, a prototype of the B-17 falters 200 feet off the ground and crashes. One man is killed. The Army's first reaction is to end all interest in the plane, but it finds that the crash was the pilot's fault. He left the tail elevators locked, forcing the plane into a stall. The Army orders 13 more B-17s. In Seattle, where the Boeing plant has poked along during 1935 with little to do, Egtvedt is ecstatic. The Army's order, he says, is "the finest kind of Christmas message we could have wished."

In the spring of 1936, Boeing breaks ground on Plant 2, its assembly building between Boeing Field and the Duwamish River. To accommodate the big bomber, WPA workers begin lengthening the airfield's earthen runways.

In 1937, at a time when few companies are selling stock, Boeing does. It pays stockholders their first dividend. These are moves of confidence, but are premature. In 1938 the company loses money, partly because of a pay increase for union workers, but mainly because of all the money it is spending on the development of four-engine airplanes.

———

In June 1938, Boeing rolls out—*floats* out—a completely different airplane: the Clipper, a huge flying boat.

When the first Clipper is towed down the Duwamish and into Elliott Bay, thousands gather along the West Seattle shore to gawk at the winged whale, with its four propellers, 14 feet in diameter.

On the plane's third day in salt water, the pilot revs up the engines and begins taxiing down the bay. At Smith Cove, the site of the police's battle with longshore strikers four years before, the Clipper turns. The wind catches its left wing, pushes it upward and dunks ten feet of the right wing into Puget Sound—so far that the blades of the outboard propeller hit the water. At the next turn, test pilot Edmund T. Allen has three crewmen stand near the tip of the leading wing to weigh it down. The next day workers add fuel and weights for ballast.

Finally, Allen guns the engines. When the behemoth reaches 80 miles per hour it lifts off, rises a few feet, splashes down on its belly, and lifts off a second time, rising gradually into the sky.

The flight is a success, but it does reveal problems. The tail rudder is too small for good control. Allen has had to throttle down the engines on the leading wing in order to bank for a turn. Engineers quickly give the plane a bigger rudder and a third tail. They also give it new stub-wing sponsons on the plane's belly, so that it won't tip over in the water.

The Clipper is not the largest flying boat ever built: Claude Dornier's Do-X, built in 1929, was slightly larger. But Dornier's biplane design with

Boeing Clipper with third tail and new sponsons. Note the Northern Life Tower, Harborview Hospital, and the Smith Tower in the background. © *The Boeing Company*.

12 engines wasn't practical. He built only two of them, and in 1938 the last one is sitting in a German museum, which will be destroyed during the war. In 1947, Howard Hughes will build the Spruce Goose, which is also bigger than the Clipper. But the Goose will fly only once, just a few feet off the water, and will end up in a museum at McMinnville, Oregon. Boeing's Clipper, which has a wingspan about that of a future Boeing 767, is the largest flying boat to be put into commercial service.

A luxury service: for a flight across the Pacific, Pan American Airways will charge the equivalent of $17,000 in 2024 dollars. On the Pacific flights, the Clipper carries 30 passengers in seats that convert into beds. It has two decks for passengers, joined by a spiral staircase. It has waiters that serve meals on real china with real silverware. The Clipper is the first commercial airliner in the world with flushing toilets—separate for women and men. It even has a bridal suite.

Back in 1929, founder William Boeing wrote, "The thing aviation has to sell is *speed*." The Clipper is fast compared with an ocean liner, but not with its competitors in the air. In commercial use, it cruises at 155 miles an hour. To travel by Clipper across the Pacific means hopping from Oakland to Hawaii to Midway to Wake to Guam to Manila to Hong Kong. The trip takes six days.

In 1938, Boeing engineers show Pan American executives plans for a flying boat to be bigger and faster: a 100-passenger behemoth with a wingspan of 300 feet, six engines, and a speed of 300 miles per hour. It would have a dining room, a cocktail lounge, and passenger staterooms.

But it will never be built, because it cannot overcome the fundamental problems of flying boats. They are heavy, they are slow, and they land in the ocean.

Oceans are not good places to land. Twice Clippers that are forced down due to engine trouble sink after colliding with rescue ships. One, afloat near Baltimore, sinks in a storm. A hard runway is safer—and during World War II, U.S. Navy Seabees will build runways on islands all over the Pacific.

Boeing's last Clipper will leave commercial service in 1946, only eight years after the first one lifts off from Puget Sound. None has survived.

Boeing's other four-engine civilian transport of the late 1930s, the Stratoliner, is the right technology. It lands on hard runways. It is the world's first commercial airliner with a pressurized cabin. To equalize pressures, the engineers have given it a dirigible-shaped fuselage. To check for air leaks, they swab all the seals with Ivory soap and look for bubbles. Fully pressurized, the plane is designed to fly above the weather at 26,000 feet.

But on March 18, 1939, disaster strikes. On the plane's 19th test flight, near Mount Rainier, test pilot Julius Barr turns off the engines on one wing and slows the speed. He's testing the plane's stability, and the plane fails the test. It stalls and tips into a spin, plunging downward. When the pilot pulls it out, the pressure on the wings, which are designed to withstand 4½ gravities, is more than double that, and they shear off. The plane crashes, killing everyone aboard. The *Seattle Times* calls it the "worst airplane disaster in the history of the Pacific Northwest."

Boeing engineers fix the control problem with a new tail, new ailerons, and a dorsal fin, but the crash has soured the market. Five Stratoliners, already ordered, go into commercial service with Trans World Airlines. It flies them at only 14,000 feet, but they are mostly above the weather and provide a smoother ride than the unpressurized DC-3s. They are also faster. For the 18 months they operate, the Stratoliners are popular with passengers. But in 1939, Hitler is threatening war in Europe, and Japan begins its third year of its war in Asia. War is pushing the civilian market aside.

In May 1939, Boeing moves the assembly of the last Stratoliners out of Plant 2 to build a mass-production line for the B-17s. In the last half of the year, Boeing's employment will swell by 50 percent, to 6,000. At its wartime peak in 1944, the company will have 50,000 employees.

Boeing 307 Stratoliner, its right two engines feathered, minutes before the fatal crash.
© *The Boeing Company*.

Thanks to the military market, Egtvedt has won his bet on four-engine airplanes. Of its three four-engine designs in the late 1930s, Boeing will build 12 Clippers, ten Stratoliners and 6,942 Flying Fortresses. The company will reenter civilian transport 15 years later, with the jet-propelled 707.

During World War I, Seattle entrepreneurs opened shipyards to build merchant ships on cost-plus contracts for the government. In two years, the industry grew from 1,000 employees to 35,000. City leaders hoped shipbuilding would continue, but it was not cost-competitive. After the General Strike, the government canceled its contracts and the shipyards died.

At the end of the 1930s, war is again in the air. A hope rises that Seattle could become a shipbuilding city again, and this time get it right.

In June 1938, the federally subsidized American Mail Line folds. Seattle still has service to Asia under foreign flags, but the Chamber of Commerce declares the lack of U.S.-flag service a civic crisis. The state's Democratic senators lobby the U.S. Maritime Commission for ships, and

Enterprise, 1933–1939 259

Celebrating the five thousandth B-17 at Boeing's Seattle Plant 2, 1944. © *The Boeing Company*.

the commission promises to build four new ones. A cry rises in the newspapers: build them here!

Horace P. Chapman, president of the Port of Seattle Commission, and chamber president Walter Williams—the man who took the keys to St. Mark's Cathedral—set out to buy and re-equip an old shipyard on the Duwamish Waterway. The Chamber calls a meeting of 300 business leaders. It challenges them to raise $750,000 in capital ($16.5 million in 2024 dollars) to create the Puget Sound Shipyard Company.

The question is not whether investors have the money. "Of course, there are half a dozen men who could do the whole job," writes *Seattle Times* publisher Clarance Blethen in a page-one editorial. But to impress the federal government, he writes, Seattle needs a community effort: "Just about every businessman in Seattle will have to do his part."

The Chamber's meeting raises a quarter of the sum in pledges. Teams set out to raise the rest. The word they stress is *investment*. "Donations are not wanted and will not be accepted," says team leader Thornton Magee. "We want business men and others who are able and willing to invest.

We do not want 'widows and orphans' money. The minimum subscription we will take is $500."

The drive comes up short. The sales pitch is not working. The Chamber group changes its theme to civic duty, and that doesn't work, either. Seattle's wages are 15 percent higher than in the East, which is probably the reason why Seattle builds no ships. Early in 1939 Chamber President Williams admits that investors are chary of the city's reputation as a high-cost, closed-shop town.

The *Star* enters the fray with a page-one editorial. "For nearly a decade the city has been in the economic doldrums," it says. "This is no time for a sit-down strike by capital," it says. But investors remain idle. The capital is not raised, and the shipyard is not equipped. The government builds the ships in Pennsylvania.

Late in 1939, after war has begun in Europe, Todd Dry Dock & Construction Company announces a plan to build hulls in Tacoma and fit them out in Seattle. To do this, the unions accept a 9 percent cut in pay.

During World War II, Todd's Harbor Island yard will build several dozen destroyers for the U.S. Navy. The yard survives today as Vigor Shipyards, but mainly as a place for ship repair.

In April 1938, Adolph Linden returns from Walla Walla after serving five years in the state penitentiary for wrecking Puget Sound Savings. A reporter from the *Star* asks Linden what strikes him as different. The automobiles, he says. They are streamlined. They have fatter tires and more powerful engines. "I drove over here from Walla Walla in a car which hit 70 miles an hour as easily as we used to hit 40 and 50 before I went away," Linden says. "It was startling to me how much they have changed."

All through the decade, the government has been building good, all-weather roads. Investors have followed with gas stations, hot-dog stands, and motels. Road travel improves so much that in 1936 the *Star* laments that "the tang of adventure has gone out of it."

Automobiles have brought changes in land development. In 1931, early in the Depression, John E. Burkheimer—the developer of the Edmond Meany Hotel—opens the Cove Mid-City Market just south of the Magnolia Bridge. It's a small thing, but the idea behind it is new. It has a Piggly Wiggly grocery, a Bartell Drugs, a Van de Kamp's bakery, and 250 free parking places. "The new market," writes the *Post-Intelligencer*, "is patterned after the drive-in markets which originated in the traffic-congested cities of Southern California." The strip mall allows the housewife to go shopping, the *P-I* says, without having to change her dress to go downtown.

The 1930s brings other innovations. In 1936, the Frederick & Nelson department store offers its first charge card, a wallet-sized metal plate that eliminates the paperwork for a credit sale. In 1936, Eba's supermarket at 23rd and Union introduces the grocery cart. "A person merely wheels the carriage around the store, filling the baskets with purchases, thus eliminating the labor of carrying a basket of heavy groceries," the *P-I* explains. In 1938, Gold Star Creameries opens a plant in Everett to package milk in paper cartons, which its ads call "milk bottles from Washington trees." In 1940, Carnation introduces homogenized milk, with "the cream mixed with every drop of milk."

By the end of 1938, the number of telephone lines in Washington has almost reached the all-time high set in 1930. The cheapest service has always been the party line, in which you share your line with your neighbors. You can hear them talk, and they can hear you talk. In November 1938, Pacific Telephone announces that all four-party lines in Seattle will be replaced by two-party lines.

Seattle had its first scheduled air-passenger service in 1926. Capacity was four seats a day. By 1937, the airlines are offering 244 seats a day. During that time, planes have changed from single-engine, open-cockpit biplanes flying close to the ground to streamlined, twin-engine, sealed-cabin airplanes flying at 10,000 feet. In 1938, Boeing Field begins its first radio flight control, effective within 14 miles. Air travel is still a luxury product little used by the middle class, but it is expanding quickly.

With all this progress, the Depression is still on. In 1939, national unemployment averages 17.2 percent. By that measure, the country is only one-third out of the hole it fell into in 1932–1933. No depression in America has ever lasted this long. Banks are still loaded to the gunwales with money, and loans are available at rock-bottom rates. To a frustrating extent, there is still a "sit-down strike of capital" all the way up to the beginning of the war.

19
Forward from Hard Times

For Seattle, the messenger that the 1940s will be much different from the 1930s is Jim Marshall. In February 1938 he arrives in town from China. Nobody yet calls the war in China "World War II," but it's the beginning.

Seattle knows Jim Marshall as a former columnist for the *Star*. In the mid-1930s, a writer from *Collier's* magazine recruits Marshall over a bottle of Scotch. By December 1937, Marshall is the *Collier's* man in Nanjing, China's capital, covering the invasion by Japan. The United States is not a belligerent, but the U.S. Navy does have a gunboat on the Yangtze River called the *Panay*. U.S. officials have told the Japanese about that boat, and it has a big U.S. flag painted on it, but on December 12, 1937, Japanese aircraft dive-bomb it and sink it. Marshall is on board, along with other Westerners being evacuated from Nanjing. Marshall makes it to shore but is wounded by shrapnel.

When he arrives in Victoria, BC, two months later, Marshall has lost 22 pounds and his left arm is hanging limp in a sling. Speaking to reporters, he describes the first scenes of what will become known as the Rape of Nanjing. "The Japanese soldiers roped captive Chinese soldiers together and used them for saber practice. Japanese officers slashed off their heads." Of the Chinese, he says, "They have no medical service whatever. If a soldier is wounded, he just dies." Neither side takes prisoners.

Marshall was a flier in Europe in World War I. That was dignified compared with this. The war in China, he says, is "an insensate, cold-blooded slaughter."

Jim Marshall in a hospital in Shanghai. *ACME Newspictures image in author's collection.*

His message to his fellow Americans is to stay out. He says, "If we ever get into a war, God help us."

The United States won't be officially in the war for another four years, but in the year that Marshall returns to Seattle, America begins getting ready. The war will end the Depression. It does not bring prosperity, but it gives everyone something to do.

As the war approaches its end, many fear that the Depression will return. In 1944, investment banker Ben Ehrlichman tells the Seattle Chamber of Commerce that 22 percent of Seattle-area industrial employees—not counting Boeing and the shipyards—are employed at companies that have never done peacetime work. In Seattle's five largest office buildings, 36 percent of the space has been leased to the government. The Exchange Building, which Ehrlichman financed back in 1929, is occupied by the Navy.

At war's end, the Navy moves out. Boeing's employment falls by more than half. Nationally, federal spending plunges. Wage and price controls end. Consumer prices jump, and millions of workers go out on strike. In a two-year period, one-third of the American workforce is released from government work—and the Depression does not come back. Private investment revives. The private economy takes up the slack. "That event," writes economic historian Robert Higgs, "is unique in U.S. economic history."

Several reasons may be offered why the economy does better after the Second World War than the First. The Western allies do not squeeze Germany for reparations but aid it with the Marshall Plan. In place of beggar-thy-neighbor trade policies, they create the General Agreement on Tariffs and Trade—now the World Trade Organization—to remove barriers to commerce. They also create a new monetary system, with gold limited to central banks. In the United States, the Federal Reserve keeps interest rates low to carry the government's war debt. Most of the private debt from the 1920s boom has been paid down, written off or inflated away.

By 1946, Harry Truman is president. The New Dealers are mostly gone. Business and government have had to cooperate during the war and have a better relationship. The public's yearning is for normal life, not social reform.

The adventurers who wrecked their companies no longer have charge of other people's money. In Seattle, Hi Pierce and W. D. Comer are dead.

Adolph Linden is reduced to making recordings of local night-club bands. His former sidekick, Edmund Campbell, works as a small-time credit manager. The postwar business world is more regulated than the 1920s and the atmosphere more cautious.

Finally, it is time to invest. In 1948, Ben Ehrlichman goes back to his life's work of funneling investors' money into long-term ventures. On 60 acres north of downtown Seattle rises one of the country's first regional shopping centers. Ehrlichman's wife, Genevieve, names it Northgate. The seed money for Northgate is not raised by sale of stock or bonds to the public, which still remembers the Depression. The money is from private investors and from Allied Stores, the East Coast company that owns the Bon Marché.

Northgate has deep connections to downtown Seattle. The original Bon Marché is there, in a block-sized building opened in the pre-Depression year 1929. The downtown Bon was designed by Seattle architect John Graham; the Northgate Bon is designed by his son, John Graham Jr. The downtown store, however, was designed with the assumption that customers would come by streetcar. Northgate is designed for people with cars. Seattle's new shopping center offers 3,500 parking places, all of them free.

As medicine for economic revival, much of the New Deal is doubtful, but as social reform, it endures. In the Depression, the people clamor for government to help them, and Franklin Roosevelt provides it. When the war comes, he leads them against foreign enemies. The people elect him four times, making him president for life. When he dies, Congress puts his head on the dime.

The failure of Herbert Hoover hurts the Republicans for decades. Before the Depression, Washington was a Republican state. From 1900 to 1930, Democrats averaged hardly more than 10 percent of the seats in the House of Representatives in Olympia. In 1932, Democrats sweep more than 70 percent of the seats. After 1936, they hold 94 percent of the seats. After that, the tide recedes. Still, from 1932 to 1962, Democrats in Olympia control the lower house three-quarters of the time. At the time of this writing, Washington has not elected a Republican governor in 44 years.

In the private economy, the winners of the Great Depression are the unions. In the 1930s, the National Labor Relations Act tilts the law toward

266 Seattle in the Great Depression

This political cartoon features Roosevelt as a farmer with wedges and a team of horses labeled "NRA" and "PWA" to pull the economy out of the mud, November 1935. *Cartoon by "Ding" Darling, Des Moines Register, published in the* Seattle Times, *11-10-1935, p. 6.* © *"Ding" Darling Wildlife Society.*

the unions, but the change is more than that. Enforcement is pro-union. People's beliefs are pro-union. The spirit of the times is pro-union.

During the reign of John Dore, the Teamsters under Dave Beck make Seattle into a closed-shop town. That lasts for years, but competition, both economic and political, eventually wears it down.

The companies that rise in the last quarter of the 20th century—Microsoft, Starbucks, Costco, Amazon, and the other technology houses—mostly keep the unions out. In the 1930s, unions organize the city's barbers, waiters, newsboys, and elevator operators. By the 21st century, the barbers and waiters are nonunion, and the newsboys and elevator operators are gone. The percentage of Washington's workers in unions has fallen by more than half in 60 years, to 16 percent in 2024. Still, that figure compares with 9.9 percent for the country as a whole. The relative strength and political influence of unions in Washington, particularly in the central Puget Sound area, is a direct legacy of Dave Beck, Harry Bridges, and the gains they make during the Great Depression.

In politics, the 1930s is the 20th century's decade of radicalism. In Seattle, Communists take a leading role in the Washington Commonwealth Federation, which promotes a left-wing faction in the state Democratic Party. In Olympia, the left becomes the principal opposition to the mainline Democrats, replacing the Republicans. But the left never has the votes to push through a radical agenda. It does help launch several Democrats into big careers, notably Warren Magnuson, who is elected to the U.S. Senate in 1944. But "Maggie" legislates as a liberal. His old allies complain that he has gone "soft on capitalism," but he is in the Senate and they are not.

In 1944, the Commonwealth Federation's president, Hugh DeLacy, runs for Magnuson's House seat. Among seven rivals in the Democratic primary, DeLacy's chief opponent is the now-reformed Howard Costigan, who denounces him for following the Communist line. DeLacy beats Costigan with 27 percent of the vote. In the general election, the Republican nominee, former city councilman Robert Harlin, reminds voters that in 1940, DeLacy refused to back Roosevelt, declaring him a warmonger. But in 1944 DeLacy supports Roosevelt, and at a speech in Seattle, the President's running mate, Harry Truman, endorses him. The war is on, it's a Democratic year, and in the general election DeLacy wins with 53 percent of the vote.

On foreign policy, DeLacy promotes friendship with the Soviet Union. In March 1945, he goes to the Soviet Embassy in Washington, DC, with his fellow Communist, Jess Fletcher, president of the Seattle Building Service Employees, to lobby Ambassador Andrei Gromyko to open a Soviet consulate in Seattle. (Their effort fails.) In 1946, when Winston Churchill denounces the "Iron Curtain," DeLacy accuses him of promoting an "anti-Soviet war."

In the election of 1946, DeLacy's opponent denounces him as a Communist, and this time it sticks. It's a Republican year, and Homer R. Jones wins, leaving DeLacy with only 36 percent of the vote.

Hugh DeLacy in Washington, DC, 1945. *ACME Newspictures image in author's collection.*

After losing his seat, DeLacy has a hard time finding a job. For about a year, he edits the monthly magazine of the International Association of Machinists, the union of Boeing assembly workers. In 1948, he goes to work for the third-party presidential campaign of Henry Wallace, which takes him to Ohio. When Wallace's Progressive Party disbands, DeLacy becomes a contractor, a type of work in which his Marxism doesn't matter. In 1954, he is called by the House Un-American Activities Committee (HUAC) and takes the Fifth Amendment when asked about his Communist affiliations. 1975, DeLacy and his wife tour China for three weeks at the invitation of the Communist government.

Howard Costigan is also called by HUAC, and by the Canwell Committee in Washington, to testify about the Communist Party in the 1930s. He names names—including DeLacy's. Costigan moves to Southern California, where he works for the Labor League of Hollywood Voters, a group led by Ronald Reagan. Later he becomes a public-relations man in Hollywood.

Cyrus Woodward, the "production for use" man, also moves to California, where he edits the *California Grange News*.

Mary Farquharson steps down from the state senate in 1942 after taking too many unpopular positions. She has opposed the draft, and she opposes the internment of Japanese Americans. In 1945, before the atom bomb is dropped, she signs a petition opposing the demand for Japan's unconditional surrender. In 1950, she tries to win back her state senate seat but loses in the primary. She never runs for public office again.

Richard Tyler's resignation from the Washington Commonwealth Federation in 1940 ends his campaigning for a planned economy. The postwar Red hunters leave him alone; he never joined the Party, and he is a professor of sanitary engineering, not social philosophy. Tyler retires from the University of Washington in 1954. At his death in 1967, the *Seattle Times* says of his time as a promoter of Technocracy, "Mr. Tyler was active in community affairs in the 1930s."

In the following decades, a handful of believers hang on. Up to the late 1970s, Seattle Communists maintain a tiny bookshop, Co-op Books, at 710 Stewart Street, where the federal courthouse is now. The dusty, museum-like shop offers the collected works of Marx, Engels, Khrushchev, and Mao. Another group of 1930s radicals, the followers of Technocracy, keep the faith for the rest of their lives. In the hope that the theories of Howard Scott will rise again, they maintain an office on Phinney Ridge into the 1990s.

In September 1949, two months after the first trial of Soviet spy Alger Hiss, a former Communist tells the U.S. Senate that he knows of a Red fishing-boat skipper in Alaska. The Bering Sea, the accuser says, is just the place where a spy "could contact Russian ships and submarines."

He is referring to Lowell Wakefield, the former editor of the *Voice of Action*. After Seattle's Communist weekly folds, Wakefield goes back to the Party's national paper, the *Daily Worker*. In 1938, he covers the trial of German spies, which the Party press makes into a book, *Hitler's Spy Plot in the U.S.A.* But Wakefield and his wife, Jessie, are too independent-minded to swallow the Hitler-Stalin pact. In 1939 they leave the Communist Party. They return to Seattle to work for the Wakefield family's Pacific herring company, which becomes Wakefield Seafoods.

In 1941, Lowell Wakefield sees an unusual sight on Kodiak Island, Alaska: a "haystack" of king crabs, piled on each other at low tide. At the time, U.S. companies have tried selling canned king crab from Japan and Russia with little success. Wakefield discovers how much better it tastes fresh. At the end of the war, he builds the 140-foot trawler *Deep Sea*. To finance it, he uses his and his wife's money, a private sale of stock to business associates and a loan from the Reconstruction Finance Corporation.

The venture almost fails. It loses money the first two years and defaults on its RFC loan. It stays in business because of Wakefield's personal ties at the agency and because the *Deep Sea*—the collateral—is too specialized for easy sale. In 1949 the crab catch is bigger, and the company is saved.

Wakefield's Seattle boat makes history. It is the first American vessel designed to catch, cook, and freeze Alaska king crab at sea. It pioneers the use of water and compressed air to de-shell the crab meat. In the mid-1950s, it begins using wire cages instead of trawl nets in order to reduce damage to the crab. The *Deep Sea* is also the first boat in the industry to work the Bering Sea in winter.

And Wakefield does deal with the Russians. In 1959 he sends a boat into the Bering Sea to document how Soviet boats are wrecking the crab habitat with trawl nets. After Wakefield's death in 1977, Stanton Patty of the *Seattle Times* writes, "It was Wakefield who turned the spotlight on the Russian invasion of Alaska's fishing grounds when the State Department could have cared less."

After two decades in king crab, Wakefield sells his company to Hunt-Wesson Foods. He is regarded today as the founder of Alaska's king crab industry.

In Seattle's Green Lake is a little island, a blob of spongy turf topped by a tuft of trees. Millions of people have driven by the lake on old U.S. 99 and seen that island. Maybe they thought it was a leftover piece of nature; as a child, that's what I thought it was. Actually, it was the Works Progress Administration's project after giving up the plan to build a fountain in the middle of the lake. The revised project was supposed to build a home for two swans donated by Victoria, B.C., but the swans didn't take to it. The ducks did, and the WPA project became Duck Island.

A WPA legacy: Duck Island, surrounded by winter ice. Seattle Post-Intelligencer, *n.d.* © *Hearst Communications Inc.*

Public money builds other things in Seattle during the Depression. The Arboretum and the West Seattle Golf Course are WPA projects. The Aurora bridge is built with state and local money, and the Lake Washington floating bridge is built with New Deal money and tolls. Public money built Alaskan Way and the seawall. But in the private sector, commercial projects stop in 1931 after the completion of the Edmond Meany Hotel (now the Graduate Seattle). In the fall of 1931, jobless men begin their own construction project on the Seattle waterfront: Hooverville.

The shacks of Hooverville are long gone. To see the Depression's mark on Seattle, you have to imagine the things not there—the City Light Tower and the Seattle Trust Tower that were never built, or the gothic spire that was never put atop the St. Mark's Episcopal Cathedral on Capitol Hill.

A number of Seattle's pre-Depression buildings—the Olympic Hotel, the Edmond Meany Hotel, the Exchange Building, and the Dexter Horton Building—go through bankruptcy in the 1930s. Most of the old buildings are still there, though some of the uses are different. The Camlin Hotel is a timeshare. The Shopping Tower is condominiums. The Mehlhorn Building, from which August Mehlhorn vanished in 1935, houses the E3 Company Restaurant Group, which owns the Metropolitan Grill. The Ford Motor Company plant on the Duwamish was used to assemble missiles for the Boeing Company during the 1960s, and as offices of the Army Corps of Engineers during the 1990s and 2000s. Now it is used by the U.S. Military Entrance Processing Command to screen volunteers for

The Seafirst Building, 1969, with the Seattle Tower, 1929, at right. Seattle Post-Intelligencer *Collection, 1986.5.50411.1, Museum of History & Industry, Seattle. Used with permission.*

the Army. The Olympic is still a luxury hotel, and the Washington Athletic Club is still the Washington Athletic Club.

At the beginning of this book is artwork of a young giant looming over an imaginary Seattle skyline. It was printed as a section front in the *Seattle Post-Intelligencer* on October 6, 1929, less than three weeks before the crash. The image is a vision of what Seattle might become. The Depression postpones that vision by several decades, but Seattle does become something like that. The change doesn't happen quickly. The city's first post-Depression office tower, the Norton Building, does not open until 1959—and at 17 stories, it adds little to the skyline. The Space Needle, a private project built for the World's Fair in 1962, changes the skyline, but it is more of a showpiece than a commercial venture. The real beginning of Seattle's second skyscraper age comes in 1969 with the construction of the Seafirst Building (now Safeco Plaza).

The Seattle-First National Bank was formed in the city's biggest bank merger of the 1920s. In the summer of 1929, two months before the crash on Wall Street, the Dexter Horton National Bank merges with nine other Seattle banks, creating the largest commercial bank in Seattle. During the Depression, Seattle-First begins buying up banks around the state, setting up its network of branches. Its corporate home, the Dexter Horton Building, is a different story. Financed with 6-percent bonds in the 1920s, the building falls into bankruptcy in the 1930s. Its bondholders struggle for years, and ultimately have their interest payments cut in half. Bad investments are not easily forgotten, and not until 1969 does Seattle-First move into its 50-story tower.

The new Seafirst Building is a great black monolith, unlike anything else in the city. People dub it "the box the Space Needle came in," and it does look like that. It is also a statement of confidence in Seattle. It sticks up all by itself, but will be alone for only a short time.

Appendix
Seattle Dailies and Their Biases

In the research for this book, I discovered an article in the *Journal of Mass Media Ethics* from 1991: "Choosing Silence: A Case of Reverse Agenda Setting in Depression News Coverage," by Sandra Haarsager of the University of Idaho. For her study, Haarsager, a former newspaper reporter and editor, read through the *Seattle Times* and *Seattle Post-Intelligencer* of November 1930 through November 1932. She argues that in those years, the *Times* and *P-I* replaced bad economic and social news with boosterism to such an extent that "the average Seattle reader might not know from reading his or her daily newspaper a Depression was occurring in those years and certainly not its local economic and social ramifications."

Haarsager argues that the newspaper publishers were worried that honest reporting of unemployment would promote leftist radicalism. Using the terms of sociologist Todd Gitlin, she concludes that "the prevailing hegemony, the safeguarding of existing power structures from above and within, operated to construct reality."

She labels this "strategic silence."

The *Times* and *Post-Intelligencer* were the principal sources for this book. When she made her argument against them, Haarsager was questioning their value for daily readers, not historians. Still, it implies that they are bad sources. And I don't think they are.

As commercial enterprises, their economic motive was to survive and grow. They did this by attracting readers with a package of news, features, comics, stock tables, ads, and so on. The writers' and editors' motives were professional. They were not interested in suppressing news in order to favor the rich. To say that in 1930–32 newspapers were intentionally keeping their readers in the dark by "constructing reality" in order to "safeguard existing power structures" is offering a high-level theory to explain ordinary facts.

It's true that the *Times* and *Post-Intelligencer* were too upbeat from November 1930 to November 1932. They were even more upbeat in the Depression's first 12 months. On Christmas Eve, 1929, the *Times*' business columnist, Paul Lovering, wrote that some readers had accused the papers of making "propaganda in support of prosperity." He admitted that they were, but wrote that it should "not be open to harsh criticism" because the motive was good.

Lovering's full-throated bullishness is embarrassing. Everyone he quoted was an optimist. In the 1980s and 1990s, I worked at the *Post-Intelligencer*, holding the same position as Lovering had at the *Times*. I found that interviewing optimists was easy. It took an effort to find pessimists willing to go on the record. Still, it was doable. At least Lovering should have muted his cheerleading. His counterpart at the *P-I*, L. E. Hill, did. But that doesn't mean that the *Seattle Times* was "constructing reality" in order to "safeguard existing power structures."

It's an exaggeration to say that "the average Seattle reader might not know from reading his or her daily newspaper a Depression was occurring in [1931–32] and certainly not its local economic and social ramifications." Of course, they knew. It was not all happy talk. There was bad news and worry about the future.

From a journalist's point of view, the largest failure of Seattle's newspapers was their reluctance to write of the *experience* of unemployment. The *Post-Intelligencer* broke this pattern in January 1932, when it published ten articles by Lidablanche Robe about the life of an unemployed woman pounding the streets for work. Sandra Haarsager mentions Robe's work in a footnote, but doesn't credit it as a counterexample to her thesis.

The *Seattle Times* and *Post-Intelligencer* had a reason to avoid coverage of that sort. Newspapers made their money by selling ads. Advertisers aimed at readers with money. If newspapers were reluctant to dive into the world of the desperate and poor, their obvious motive was economic, not political.

And once in a while they did enter that world. In May 1934 the *Times* and *P-I* reported the story of Angelina D'Ambrose, age 4, who died of hemlock poisoning from eating weeds in her backyard. The *Times* ran the story under the headline, "Weeds Kill Starving Child." The *Times* reported that the father, Angelo D'Ambrose, was an immigrant shoemaker, long unemployed, and had no food in the house. "Asked why he had not asked for public relief, the father said he had not known how to go about it," the *Times* said.

The *Post-Intelligencer* came back the next morning with the story that the father *had* received relief and *did* have food in the house but no green vegetables. In its follow-on story, the *Times* quoted state welfare director Charles Ernst that the father "had waited until near-desperation before asking for public relief" and had not bought any greens. "It is possible that had our home visitor been better acquainted with the family than she could become on a single visit, the child's dietary lack would have been seen," Ernst said. "People on relief lists resent 'interference' by our home visitors, but we are always ready to suggest diet changes when such suggestions seem to be required."

Seattle newspapers were not about to ignore a dead child. Their coverage brought the attention of the highest welfare official in the state. Whether Ernst's explanation was accurate, or, in modern parlance, blaming the victim, may be argued. The *Times* and *P-I* soon dropped the story. But they had covered it for three days, all on page one.

In 1933 the *Seattle Times* wrote of the Spaulding family, who were living in a shack in Bellevue. The *Times* told the story as a celebration of endurance. The Spauldings were poor but self-reliant, and they were going to make it. In 1939, the *Seattle Star* published a much different story about the Currier family. Leon Currier, 42, his wife, Bertha, and their five sons—Bobby, Arthur, Leon, Carl, and Douglas, all of them under 12—had been evicted from their home in south Seattle and were camped on a vacant lot. The Curriers needed help. The father was no bum; he had found a job, but it wouldn't start for another ten days, and his family had run out of food.

Neighbors responded to the story by bringing the Curriers canned food and bread. An owner offered to let them use a two-room shack. It had no electricity or plumbing, and when health officials read about it in the *Star*, they sent out an inspector to declare it unfit for human habitation. The family stayed in the shack.

The Census report taken a year later showed the Curriers living in a house on the same street. The oldest son, Douglas, 12, had gone, and a sixth child, Ronney, had arrived. Leon Currier had a WPA job as a painter. They, too, had made it through the Depression.

The papers under-covered the human-suffering side of the Depression, but they did cover the political side. They printed columns about the Depression, editorials about it, speeches about it, and cartoons about it.

Seattle had three daily newspapers, the *Times*, the *Post-Intelligencer*, and the *Star*. Each of these papers had its biases. An example is their thoughts early in the Depression on what to do about the unemployed. The sharpest argument was over the idea of cash relief, which critics called "the dole."

The *Times* was against it. Its editors said: "Every man in this country is an independent contractor." In September 1931 the *Times* argued, "Every American worker of mature years has been through 'hard times'; most of them have suffered experiences that enable them to smile grimly when younger persons complain of present conditions ... They know, moreover, that the country will take care of its people; not by conscription under penalty of imprisonment or death, as in Russia; not by the indiscriminate dole that encourages unthrift and idleness and brings on bankruptcy as in England."

On page one of the *Post-Intelligencer*, William Randolph Hearst called for the federal government to borrow and spend enough money to put Americans to work. This was not a dole. He wrote, "Nothing that approaches the European dole should ever be inaugurated in this free country."

The *Star* was willing to accept cash relief, arguing that "the government exists for the people." What the *Star* opposed was the reliance on *charity*, which "waits until misfortune happens and then attempts to palliate the results." Argued the *Star*, "The only real solution of the nation's problems will be in reorganizing our economics so that the worker can afford to cover himself with insurance against illness or accident and built up a surplus for possible unemployment. Then there will be real independence."

It's true that the Seattle dailies opposed the radicals, especially the Communists. But that fight came up after the period Sandra Haarsager wrote about. And in that fight, the newspapers did not try to put their readers to sleep. They tried to wake them up.

In May 1936, the *Post-Intelligencer* raised an alarm when the School Board voted to allow the Second Northwest Congress Against War and Fascism to use the Broadway High School auditorium on the weekend. The

P-I called the group a Communist front, and the School Board quickly pulled back its offer.

Whether use of school property should be denied for such a reason may be debated, but the Congress Against War and Fascism was, in fact, a Communist front. The *P-I* was wrong when it reported that the Communists were behind the Fisher Flour Mills strike. That was a falsehood propagated by Fisher management. But the *P-I*'s hostility to the Communists served it well on one of the most important international stories of the decade. At the direction of William Randolph Hearst, the paper ran British journalist Gareth Jones's stories exposing Stalin's famine in the Ukraine. Jones famously contradicted Walter Duranty's stories in the *New York Times*, which accepted the Soviet lies. (The story of Gareth Jones is told in Agnieszka Holland's 2019 film, *Mr. Jones*.)

The *Seattle Times* was also against the radicals. In 1936, it denounced the Washington Commonwealth's Federation's production-for-use initiative as "the very essence of Communism." But the tone of the *Times*' coverage was less strident than the *P-I*'s. Before the *P-I* strike, the *Argus*, Seattle's conservative weekly, joked that the *Post-Intelligencer* had become "screamingly conservative since William Randolph Hearst came down with the Red Horrors."

Seattle's third daily, the *Star*, began the decade defending the rights of Reds to speak and assemble. In 1930, when Communists organized a parade of the unemployed, and police broke it up, the *Star* defended the protesters. "A hundred or more jobless men and women, incited to action by a few agitators, reputed to be communists, gathered together some banners and started for the city hall to tell the mayor how they were hungry and needed work," the *Star* said. "For every 'communist agitator' in America there are a thousand sane and sensible working men whose only desires are to work."

In 1932, the *Star* jeered at the *Seattle Times* for raising an alarm over Communists at the food banks. In 1933 it jeered at University of Washington President Hugo Winkenwerder for banning a talk on campus by Jessie London Wakefield, the wife of Communist newspaperman Lowell Wakefield. The *Star* said the state university was trying to ban "anything with which the upper crust might disapprove."

By 1937, the peak year of Stalin's show trials, the *Star* had stopped defending the Reds. When Mayor John Dore banned the Communist Party from renting the city-owned Civic Auditorium, the *Star* was OK with it. In 1938, the *Star* demanded that the state Democratic Party clean out the Communists in their ranks. The *Star* was correct in its accusation, and the party did eventually clean them out.

The *Times*, the *Post-Intelligencer*, and the *Star* were not the same. Each had its biases, hobby horses, and sins of omission. The Blethen family's *Times* was Republican. It broke with that tradition in 1932 to endorse Franklin Roosevelt, and in 1933 it cheered the Blue Eagle. But it soon returned to its Republican roots. The *Post-Intelligencer* was conservative Democrat. Channeling the mind of William Randolph Hearst, it turned hard against the New Deal until the 1936 strike, whereupon it moved to the center. The *Star* began the decade as a liberal paper, and over the decade moved rightward, partly over the New Deal's economic ideas and partly over the court-packing issue.

Finally, there were the weeklies. The Washington State Labor Council had a union weekly. The Washington Commonwealth Federation had its weekly. The Technocracy people had a paper. Also, early in the decade, the hard left had the *Vanguard*, and, later on, the *Voice of Action*. Seattle almost always had at least one weekly, and often more than one, representing the left with no pretense of neutrality. There was also the *Argus*, which was conservative in a nonideological, pipe-and-slippers way.

Together, the Seattle newspapers are a mine of news, thought, and feeling about Seattle in the 1930s.

Endnotes

Key: ST = *Seattle Times*; P-I = *Seattle Post-Intelligencer*; NYT = *New York Times*; CR = *Congressional Record*; Labor News = *Washington State Labor News*

Introduction
Recalling the Depression: Ramsey, "50 Years Later: The Memories and Lessons"; Baker, "Even the Lucky Ones Paid Attention," *P-I*, 10-7-79, p. B8.

Miner Baker: "9 U. Students Suspended after Wakefield Talk," *ST*, 5-27-33, p. 1; "U Students Lunch Club Is Ordered Dissolved," *ST*, 5-28-33, p. 1.

Bonds: "City Light Is Paying Debts, Economizing," *P-I*, 12-9-31, p. 15.

Unemployed: Robe, "7 Ways to Help Jobless Revealed by 'Mary Reeves,'" *P-I*, 1-24-32, p. 9.

1. Top of the World, 1929
Russian colony: McIlroy, "Russians Hark Back to Golden Days," *P-I*, 1-30-39, p. 11.

Glaser: "Russian Flyers Here 3 Days," *ST*, 10-14-29, pp. 1, 8; "Deportation of Glaser Is Asked by U.S.," *P-I*, 6-24-31, p. 1; Dennett, *Agitprop*, p. 25.

Consulate: "Japan Buys $6,000,000 Old Russian War Supplies Stored Here," *P-I*, 10-21-33, p. 2; "Late Czar's Consul Lives in Hope Here," *P-I*, 10-22-33, p. 3.

Aviators: "Soviet Airplane Now Has Wheels for Flight East," *ST*, 10-15-29, p. 11; "White Russians Demand Part in Program of Red Aviators," *ST*, 10-16-29, p. 1; "Soviet Trade Will Follow Airmen Here," *P-I*, 10-16-29, p. 19; "Russian World Aviators Cheered at Detroit," *NYT*, 10-29-29, p. 31; "Soviet Flyers Here, Get Wild Greeting," *NYT*, 11-2-1929, p. 1.

Ford: "American to Build Soviet Auto Plants," *NYT*, 5-7-29, p. 14.

Bread: Davidson Baking ad, *ST*, 9-9-29, p. 2.

Labor: "State Prosperity High, Olympia Reports Reveal," *Star*, 8-22-29, p. 2; Jermane, "Beneficiaries of 5-Day Week Grow in Number," *ST*, 6-13-29, p. 1; Forbes, "Vacation-with-Pay Proposal Creates Widespread Interest," *P-I*, 5-29-29, p. 25.

Air mail: ad, "Now Adding Wings to Seattle's Financial Progress," *ST*, 9-15-29, p. 14; "Seattle Air Mail Route East Started," *P-I*, 9-16-29, p. 1; "County Seeks Better Field as Direct Air Mail Starts," *ST*, 9-16-29, p. 1.

Art of giant: *P-I*, 10-6-29, p. C1.

Theaters: McGrath, "Stage-Screen-Music," *Argus*, 3-18-33, p. 7; Flom and Caldbick, "5th Avenue Theatre" and "Paramount Theatre," *historylink.org*.

Hotels: Shannon, *Seattle's Historic Hotels*, Arcadia, 2010; "The Olympic Hotel," *Argus*, 12-24-32, p. 3; "West's Most Noted Hotel [Rainier Grand] Under Hammer Wednesday," *Star*, 5-21-30, p. 20; "Court Says Quiet Order for Butler Will Stand," *ST*, 5-7-29, p. 1; "Butler Hotel Now in Hands of Receiver," *P-I*, 5-16-29, p. 3.

Bon: "Bon Marche Changes to Credit Plan," *P-I*, 5-30-29, p. 13; ad, *P-I*, 6-13-29, p. 6; "Bon Marché's Fine New Home Opens to Public Tomorrow," *P-I*, 8-24-29, p. 9.

Office towers: Dotty, "Northern Life/Seattle Tower," *historylink.org*; Seattle Dept. Neighborhoods web page; Fisher Flour ad, *ST*, 4-10-29, p. 8.

"New capital": "The Banking Business," *Argus*, 9-28-29, p. 1.

Ehrlichman: "Local Capitalists Form New Bank," *ST*, 5-30-15, p. 19; "Meet Mr. Ben B. Ehrlichman," *P-I*, 3-25-29, p. 17; Tate, "Ehrlichman, Ben Bernard," *Historylink.org*; Porteous, *Taking Stock*, pp. 52–53; U.S. Census 1900–1940.

United National: tombstone, *ST*, 3-1-29, p. 35; "Millions Placed in Firm Here" and "United Stock Climbs Price Ladder Fast," *ST*, 6-5-29, pp. 1, 28, 31; "Capital Increased by United National," *ST*, 8-9-29, p. 27; tombstone, *ST*, 9-4-29, p. 25.

Warnings: Hill, "Bond Experts Diagnose Ills of Securities," *P-I*, 3-26-29, p. 19; "Warning Given by Ehrlichman," *P-I*, 6-1-29, p. 21; "Ehrlichman Sounds Note of Caution to Margin Investors," *ST*, 9-18-29, p. 21; Ad by Drumheller, Ehrlichman & White, *ST*, 9-19-29, p. 34; "Gas Company Development Being Planned," *P-I*, 10-14-29, pp. 17, 20.

Shopping Tower: "Shopping Tower Will Be Thrown Open to Public on Saturday," *P-I*, 10-31-29, p. 7; "Long Lease Signed for Occupancy of Shopping Tower," *P-I*, 12-3-32, p. 1; "Gene Hanner Not 'Evicted,' Court Decides," *ST*, 6-6-35, p. 3; Margeson, "3rd & Pine Corner Transferred in $500,000 Deal," *ST*, 2-9-36, p. 22.

Exchange Building: tombstone, *P-I*, 8-9-29, p. 32.

Background: Hanford, *Seattle and Environs, 1852–1924*, pp. 430–433; "W.D. Comer to Put Up $50,000 Home," *P-I*, 8-21-27, p. 41; "Mrs. W.D. Comer Dies after Long Illness," *ST*, 12-3-29, p. 10; "W.H. Parsons Buys Home of W.D. Comer," *ST*, 6-5-31, p. 1.

Business model: *State v. Comer, 28 P.2d 1027 (Wash. 1934)*.

Ad copy: *ST*, 1-7-29, p. 24.

Expenses: 1923 income statement, Box 14, File 432, Dept. of Licensing files, State Archives, Olympia.

Deals: Tombstones: Marcus Whitman, *ST*, 1-30-28, p. 22; Benjamin Franklin, *ST*, 6-25-28, p. 23.

Bridge: Hill, "$5,800,000 Financing Ends Comer's Fight," *P-I*, 10-31-28, p. 27; "Right Now!" *ST*, 10-31-28, p. 1; tombstone, *ST*, 11-2-28, p. 36; "State's Homage to Longview," *P-I*, 3-1-30, p. 28; Margeson, "Longview Bridge Stockholders to Receive Cash and Securities," *ST*, 10-29-36, p. 31; "Losses Follow Predicted Profit from Columbia Span," *ST*, 6-22-38, p. 1.

WAC: "2,000 Assured Athletic Club," *P-I*, 7-22-28, p. 33.

"A belly full": "Text of Nicely Letter Reveals How He Worried," *P-I*, 10-16-31, p. 15.

Suicide: "Death Leap from Leary Bldg.," *ST*, 9-5-29, p. 1; "Shadow of Death Hovers Close to Comer Loan Case," *ST*, 11-1-31, p. 5.

Foreign bonds: Jorgensen and Sachs, "Default and Renegotiation of Latin American Foreign Bonds in the Interwar Period," p. 7; tombstones: *P-I*, 2-22-29, p. 20; 6-28-29, p. 32; 8-22-29, p. 26; *ST*, 2-14-29, pp. 22, 24; 9-16-29, p. 22.

Sedro-Woolley: "Plan to Sell Bank's Assets," *Star*, 12-5-33, p. 3.

Defaults: Ferrero, "Germany Facing Greatest Crisis in All Europe," *P-I*, 9-8-29, p. M1; "Foreign Defaults on Bonds Here Exceed $815,000,000," *NYT*, 1-2-32, p. 1; "Says Debt in Brazil Ran up

Unchecked," *NYT*, 1-22-33, p. N7; *The Pecora Investigation: Stock Exchange Practices and the Causes of the 1929 Wall Street Crash*, Senate Committee on Banking & Currency, 1934, pp. 132–133.

Tariff: Jermane, "Hoover Faces Job of Curbing Tariff Zealots," *ST*, 1-9-29, p. 1; "Pending Tariff Bill Means Much for Washington," *ST*, 7-5-29, p. 4; "The Assault on the Tariff," *ST*, 7-11-29, p. 6.

Backus: Hill, "M.F. Backus Reviews Speculation's Effects," *P-I*, 3-16-29, p. 22; Knight, *Gold Horizon*, pp. 140–141.

Dimond: Wood, "Huge Stock Scheme Here Probed," *Star*, 10-4-29, p. 1; Wood, "Dimond Witnesses before Grand Jury," *Star*, 10-15-29, p. 1; "Dimond Reported Missing," *ST*, 1-3-30, p. 1; "John E. Dimond, Fugitive Broker, Adjudged Bankrupt," *P-I*, 6-10-30, p. 3; "Creditors Say Dimond Owes $2 Million," *Star*, 7-16-30, p. 1; "John Dimond Sued by Wife," *P-I*, 5-6-32, p. 4; "Divorce Granted," *P-I*, 7-12-32, p 16; "Dimond 'Chose' His Investors, Witness Says," *P-I*, 12-13-32, p. 11.

Stocks: Hill, "Along Finance Row," *P-I*, 10-4-29, p. 21; "Bankers Stem Crash of Stocks," *P-I*, 10-25-29, p. 1; "Leading Stocks Tumble to New Lows," *P-I*, 10-29-29, p. 1.

United National prices: *Seattle Stock Exchange Annual Report 1930*, p. 15.

Bastheim: "2nd Ave. Finance Man Ends Life at Office," *Star*, 10-26-29, p. 1; "Seattle Broker Found Dead," *ST*, 10-26-29, p. 1; "Seattle Financier in Ill Health Takes Own Life," *P-I*, 10-27-29, p. 11; "Seattle Broker Ends His Life in Downtown Office," *ST*, 10-27-29, p. 2; "$30,000 Fund Deficit Bared after Suicide," *P-I*, 1-18-30, p. 1; "Insurance Deal Centers around Broderick Firm," *ST*, 8-29-30, p. 29.

On the Crash: "Partisan and Petty Criticism," *ST*, 2-25-30, p. 6; "State Banks in Fine Shape, Says Johnson," *P-I*, 11-5-29, p. 19; Lovering, "Trend of the Times," *ST*, 11-17-29, p. 32; "Not Back to 'Business as Usual,'" *Star*, 11-4-29, p. 4.

Ford: Brisbane, "Today," *P-I*, 11-22-29, p. 1.

Textiles: "Nation Spends Huge Sums with Seattle Firms," *ST*, 5-11-30, p. 30.

Commercial: "Record Building This Year Predicted for Seattle," *ST*, 12-8-29, p. 14; "Building in Seattle Due for Big Gain," *ST*, 12-29-29, p. 12; "Seattle Leads in Building," *Star*, 3-27-30, p. 16; "Anhalt Program This Year Will Set High Mark," *ST*, 3-30-30, p. 20.

Government: "U.S. Will Spend Millions Here in '30 on Buildings," *ST*, 12-29-29, p. 13; "Aurora Avenue Bridge over Lake Union," *Journal of Commerce*, 1-30-30, p. 4; "New Bridge to Open Friday," *Star*, 7-28-30, p. 1.

Projects that die: "Seattle Men Will Develop Mexican Land," *ST*, 9-12-29, p. 1; Ad, German-Mexican Co., *ST*, 10-6-29, p. 41; "State Revokes 2 Permits for Sale of Stocks," *ST*, 2-27-30, p. 27; "Mexican Company Files $2,000,000 Suit in Seattle," *ST*, 6-21-30, p. 3; "New Gowman Will Be 30 Stories," *ST*, 5-12-29, p. 1; Lovering, "Finance and Bank Chiefs in Insurance Corporation." *ST*, 7-12-29, p. 1; "Chain Will Acquire 200 New Stores," *ST*, 8-7-29, p. 1; "Insurance Co. Plans to Quit, Repay Million," *P-I*, 11-17-29, p. 1; "$1,100,000 Addition to Building Is Announced," *ST*, 10-24-1929, p. 1.

Stadium: "New Seattle Baseball Park Planned for 1930 Season," *P-I*, 3-2-29, p. 16; "Architect's Sketch of Proposed Seattle Baseball Park," *ST*, 4-14-29, p. 27.

Transit: "$15,000,000 Rapid-Transit Plan Is Drafted by Business Leaders" and "Taxpayers and Riders Would Share in Cost," *ST*, 1-6-29, pp. 1, 10; "Rapid Transit Plan Is Opposed by Realty Board," *ST*, 1-31-29, p. 1; "Transit Program Waits on Mayor's Finance Mission," *ST*, 6-14-29, p. 2.

284 Notes for pages 22–29

Bridge: "Million Dollar Bridge across Lake Is Planned," *ST*, 1-7-26, p. 1; "Rivals for Lake Bridge Get Hearing," *P-I*, 1-9-29, p. 25; "Franchise Awarded for $3,000,000 Mercer Toll Bridge," *P-I*, 2-12-30, p. 3; "Mercer Island Bridge Campaign Dates Back Many Years," *Star*, 7-6-38, pp. 1, 7.

2. Denial, 1930

Times: "Work Begins on Times' New Home," *ST*, 9-26-29, p. 1; house ad, *ST*, 11-3-29, p. 58.

Ridders, Blethens: Blethen, "Announcement," and "Junior Partners Join Col. Blethen in Times," *ST*, 1-5-30, p. 1; "Banks to Offer $2,000,000 Bond Issue on Times," *ST*, 1-7-30, p. 20; tombstones: Seattle Times Co., *ST*, 1-8-30, p. 24; Blethen Corp., *ST*, 6-9-30, p. 27; L. M. Arnold to C. H. Bowen, 1-6-30, Box 49, File 1578, Seattle Times file, Dept. of Licensing, State Archives, Olympia.

Sale price, 1930 salary: *Ridder Bros. v. Blethen*, 142 F2d 395 (9th Cir. 1944).

Penthouse: "Two Palatial Homes to Be Built Here," *P-I*, 3-1-30, p. 1; Hughes, *Pressing On: Two Family-Owned Newspapers in the 21st Century*, pp. 29–30; "Roundabout," *P-I*, 9-12-41, p. 17.

Buyout, pay cut: SEC Form A-2, Amendment No. 1, Box 67, File 2329, Seattle Times file, Dept. of Licensing, State Archives, Olympia.

Keaton: "Mrs. Keaton's Up in Air! Police Halt Buster's Hop," *P-I*, 4-5-32, p. 3; "Blethen's Yacht Is Sold to Frozen-Faced Comedian," *Star*, 6-22-32, p. 2; "Keaton's Fight: It All Began on New Yacht," *Star*, 7-15-32, p. 1; "Wife Sold Boat, So Buster Would Buy One Like It," *P-I*, 8-23-32, p 10.

Note: The Seattle-First National Bank was called the First Seattle Dexter Horton National Bank. It changed its name shortly afterward.

Communists: "Seattle Police Battle Radicals," *ST*, 2-26-30, p. 1; "Reds Stage Riots in Three Cities," *P-I*, 2-27-30, p. 1; "Reds Defy Seattle Police Order against Demonstration," *P-I*, 3-5-30, p. 3; "Police Break Up March of Communists," *Star*, 3-6-30, p. 1; "World-Wide Red Plots Fail; Parade Broken Here," *P-I*, 3-7-30, p. 1.

Unemployment: BLS, "UNEMP. RATE, Civilian Labor Force 14 Yrs. & over, Not Seasonally Adjusted," data.bls.gov; letter from Ralph E. Harbeck, *ST*, 3-14-30, p. 6; from "Citizen," *ST*, 5-19-30, p. 6; "Seasonal Unemployment," *ST*, 2-17-30, p. 6.

Optimism: Forbes, "New Year's Debut Held Quiet but Encouraging," *P-I*, 1-6-30, p. 17; "Every Reason Why It Should Be," *Star*, 12-27-29, p. 4; Lovering, "Growth of Seattle in Financial Lines Outstanding in 1929," *ST*, 1-6-30, p. 17; Lovering, "Trend of the Times," *ST*, 12-24-29, p. 16; 2-16-30, p. 28; 6-30-30, p. 24.

Exchange Building: Hill, "Along Finance Row," *P-I*, 10-12-29, p. 17; 60% leased: "City's New Skyscraper Ready for Monday Opening," *Star*, 5-2-30, p. 6; not full: "Exchange Building Earns Surplus over First Mortgage," *P-I*, 9-27-34, p. 16; bonds at 27c: Niendorff, "New Auto Sales up in This State," *P-I*, 1-30-35, p. 16; bankruptcy: Niendorff, "Exchange Bldg. Plan," *P-I*, 6-26-35, p. 18.

Yachts, mansions: "Boeing Builds Luxury Yacht," *P-I*, 5-8-30, p. 1; "Biography of William E. Boeing," Boeing.com, accessed 1-6-17; "$350,000 Home Contract Is Let," *P-I*, 2-25-30, p. 17; "Two Palatial Homes to Be Built Here," *P-I*, 3-1-30, p. 1; Patti Payne, "Storied Highlands Estate with Ties to Frederick & Nelson Founder Lists for $3.2m," *Puget Sound Business Journal*, 11-15-2019.

Panhandlers: "Begging Competition Keen, Coins Slow, So They Fight," *Star*, 4-11-30, p. 1.

Filipinos: "Filipino Immigrants," immigrationtounitedstates.org (accessed 9-13-2020); Alisago, "Defends Filipinos," *ST*, 5-4-31, p. 6; "No More Should Come," *ST*, 1-27-31, p. 6.

Persecution: "Highway Police Ready to Guard Kent Filipinos," *ST*, 5-7-30, p. 1; "Beatings Given Filipinos Cause Youths' Arrest," *ST*, 1-23-31, p. 2; "Shotguns Blaze in Outbreak against Filipino Laborers," *P-I*, 5-27-32, p. 1; "Filipinos to Go, Peace Declared," *P-I*, 5-29-32, p. 13.

Steamship lines: tombstone, City Light bonds, *ST*, 7-9-30, p. 25.

People indifferent: "Right Now!" *ST*, 6-14-30, p. 1.

Tariffs: *Historical Statistics of the United States, 1789–1945*, International Trade Commission, dataweb.usitc.gov.

Hartley: "B.C. Exports Assailed in Memorial," *P-I*, 5-13-30, p. 2; "Washington Tops States in Lumbering," *ST*, 5-26-30, p. 23.

Hearst: "Senate Should Meet Challenge by Rejecting Grundy Tariff," *P-I*, 6-13-30, p. 36; for 1935 see *P-I* cartoons of 6–28, 7–1, 7–3 and 7–5, also "Northwest Lumber," *P-I*, 11-11-35, p. 1.

Tariff fight: Jermane, "Hoover's Timidity Makes Tariff Issue," *ST*, 5-22-30, p. 1; "Senate Passes Tariff Bill by 2-Vote Margin," *P-I*, 6-14-30, p. 1; "Senator Dill Rebuked," *ST*, 6-16-30, p. 6.

Markets: "Hoover Gives His Reasons for Approving the Tariff," and "Stocks Swept to New Lows in Big Selling," *ST*, 6-16-30, pp. 5, 21; "Commodities at Lowest Levels in Past 13 Years," *ST*, 6-19-30, p. 26.

World reaction: "New Tariff Wrecking Foreign Trade," *P-I*, 8-4-30, p. 2; Jermane, "Report Shows 11 Nations Act on U.S. Tariff," *ST*, 10-14-30, p. 1; "American Tariff Causes World Retaliation," *ST*, 4-12-31, p. C11.

Canada: Jermane, "U.S. Tariff Big Issue in Coming Canada Election," *ST*, 7-24-30, p. 1; "Canadian Liberals Beaten," *ST*, 7-29-30, p. 1; "Renewed Trade with Canada and Mexico Is Asked," *ST*, 12-5-31, p. 3; O'Leary, "Hawley-Smoot Tariff Last Straw to Canada," *P-I*, 2-24-32, p. 24; Niendorff, "Empire Pact Hits Port Hard, Says S.M. Wilson," *P-I*, 5-11-38, p. 16; McDonald, "Trade Wars: Canada's Reaction to the Smoot-Hawley Tariff," *Journal of Economic History*, 12–97, p. 803.

USSR trade: "Soviet Crew Here to Resume Trade," *P-I*, 4-19-29, p. 21; Jermane, "Russia's Economic Phase Eclipses Political Side," *ST*, 8-4-30, p. 1; "Russia Advances in Importance as Customer of U.S.," *ST*, 8-11-30, p. 20.

Fishing: "Ten New Soviet Ships Will Use Seattle Design," *ST*, 1-26-30, p. 5; "Siberia Salmon Fleet Will Be Equipped Here," *ST*, 3-18-30, p. 27.

Aircraft: "Seattle Plays Host to Soviet Air Commission," *ST*, 1-24-30, p. 4.

Placer mining: "U. Graduate Wins Highest Mining Position in Russia," *ST*, 3-25-30, p. 17.

Tunnels: "Russian Official Thinks Seattle Most Beautiful," *ST*, 3-13-30, p. 1; "Western Railroader May Help Build World's Longest Tunnel for Russia," *Star*, 6-5-30, p. 5.

Work in USSR: Lovering, "Trend of the Times," *ST*, 6-25-30, p. 28; "450 Americans Imprisoned in Russ Tractor Plant," *ST*, 9-21-30, p. 21.

USSR wood: "U.S. Bars Russian Convict-Made Pulpwood," *ST*, 7-25-30, p. 27; "Convict-Made Russ Lumber, Pulp Barred," *ST*, 2-10-31, p. 1; Patch, "Soviet-American Political and Trade Relations," *CQ Researcher*, 2-24-33.

Hamilton Fish: "Reds Here Work for Revolution, Committee Told," *ST*, 10-4-30, p. 1.

WA anti-communism: "4 Men, Asserted Communists, Are Held by Police," *ST*, 2-8-31, p. 31; "Tax Relief Bills Law; Teachers to Take Oaths," *ST*, 3-21-31, p. 1; "Spencer Bans U Communism," *ST*, 5-12-31, p. 1.

Amtorg exit: "Soviet to Close Seattle Agency," *ST*, 4-15-31, p. 1.

Siwash economics: "Hemphill's Talk Raps 'Long Faces,'" *ST*, 7-11-30, pp. 1, 5; "Business Men Told: Forget Stock Crash," *P-I*, 7-12-30, p. 3; "Seattle Employers of Labor Say 'No Wage Reductions,'" *P-I*, 8-7-30, p. 22.

Forbes: "Buyers of Stocks Now Will Profit in Time," *P-I*, 6-20-30, p. 25; "Cheap Money Oxygen Will Assist Revival, *P-I*, 6-24-30, p. 18; "Forbes on Way Here, Escapes East's Gloom," *P-I*, 7-18-30, p. 1; "Lumber Is Key to NW Trade, Forbes Avers," *P-I*, 7-23-30, p. 1; "There IS Something Different about the Pacific Northwest," *P-I*, 7-28-30, p. 1.

Lumber: "Production of Lumber Cut, Sales Drop," and "Lumber Wage Cut Criticized," *P-I*, 7-12-30, p. 19.

Hartley: "Hartley Decides to Close Out His Lumber Business," *Tacoma News Tribune*, 6-26-30, p. 1; "Hartley Urges Tax Reduction," *P-I*, 10-4-33, p. 19; "Clough-Hartley Mill Is Burned," *ST*, 12-30-37, p. 7.

Western Hotels: "Seattle Hotels in $12,000,000 Merger," *ST*, 8-31-30, p. 1.

Nordstrom: "Nordstrom's Shoe Store to Open in Enlarged Quarters," *ST*, 8-18-30, p. 4.

Fraser-Paterson: "Seattle Dry Goods Co. Disposes of Business," *ST*, 1-12-13, p. 3; "Million-Dollar Store Planned, Fraser Reports," *ST*, 2-11-30, p. 1; "New Home of Fraser-Paterson, *ST*, 2-12-30, p. 4; "Fraser-Paterson Store Opens Doors to Throngs," *ST*, 10-6-30, pp. 1, 9; "Fraser-Paterson to Retire from Seattle Business," *ST*, 1-3-33, p. 5; Margeson, "Carew & Shaw Store Is Sold to New Firm," *ST*, 8-30-36, pp. 1, 14; "Nordhoff Store Is Liquidating," *ST*, 12-18-38, p. 11; "J.C. Penney Gets Nordhoff & Moore Site," *ST*, 1-15-39, p. 11; Michaelson, "Fraser-Paterson Company Department Store #2, *Pacific Coast Architecture Database*.

No bank failed: The only bank to fail in WA Oct. 1929–July 1930 is Security State Bank of Richland, 3-31-30—*Division of Banking Liquidation Record*.

Continental: "New Bank Is Opened," *ST*, 7-2-22, p. 7; "Savings Bank Moves into Tyee Building," *ST*, 1-2-26, p. 4; see notes on state bank examinations of 11-19-27, 4-27-29, 11-27-29, and 3-22-30, Washington Division of Banking, V4-E-13-1.

WaMu: *Bank Histories 1907–1937*, Box 5; "Washington Mutual Acquires Continental," *ST*, 7-24-30, p. 27; ad, *ST*, 10-1-29, p. 2; ad, *P-I*, 9-4-29, p. 7.

Auburn banks: "Auburn Bank Closes," *P-I*, 10-28-30, p. 18; "First National Bank Closed after Panic," *Auburn Globe-Republican*, 10-30-30, p. 1; "Auburn Men Jailed for Cash Shortage," *Auburn Globe-Republican*, 12-25-30, p. 1; "State Shows Stand in Trial of Bankers," *P-I*, 5-17-33, p. 13; "Depositors Tell Story of Stock Buying," *P-I*, 5-18-33, p. 7; "Aged Cripple Tells of His Lost Savings," *P-I*, 5-20-33, p. 11; "Potts Links Colvin with Run on Bank," *P-I*, 5-22-33, p. 13; "Accused Bank Officials Tell of Stock Deal," *P-I*, 5-26-33, p. 13; "Walters Says He Discounted Exact Truth," *P-I*, 5-27-33, p. 13; "Walters and Son, Auburn Bankers, Are Found Guilty," *P-I*, 5-28-33, p. 15; "Walters Dies; Pardon Futile," *P-I*, 3-16-34, p. 17; "Firm's Assets Sold for $10," *P-I*, 9-23-34, p. 5.

Bank stock: Macey, "Double Liability for Bank Shareholders," 27 *Wake Forest Law Review* 31, 1992; Marquis and Smith, "Double Liability for Bank Stock," *The American Economic Review*, 9–1937.

Other failures: *Report of the Comptroller of the Currency*, 1937, p. 387; Richardson, "Banking Panics of 1930–1931."

Mehlhorn's m.o.: *Ross v. Johnson*, 19 P.2d 101 (Wash. 1933); "1,500 Pieces of Seattle Property to Go on Block," *ST*, 1-22-31, p. 46.

Disappears: "Mehlhorn Sought," *P-I*, 9-5-30, p. 1; "Financial Row Wondering If Mehlhorn Lives," *ST*, 9-5-30, p. 1; "Mehlhorn Seen Saturday," *ST*, 9-7-30, p. 3; "Wife Says Mehlhorn Alive," *Star*, 9-8-30, p. 1; "Private Firm of Detectives Aids Mehlhorn Hunt," *ST*, 9-8-30, p. 2; "Mehlhorn Suicide Theory Advanced by Close Friends," *ST*, 9-17-30, p. 3.

Caught: "August Mehlhorn, Fugitive Seattle Real Estate Man, Jailed by Oakland Police," *P-I*, 7-17-35, p. 1; "I'm Ready to Face Clients," *P-I*, 7-18-35, p. 6; "The Week," *Argus*, 7-20-35, p. 3; "Plea of Guilty by Mehlhorn," *P-I*, 11-16-35, p. 9; "Mehlhorn Sentence Tuesday," *P-I*, 12-2-35, p. 13.

Released: "Mehlhorn, Broker, Freed from Prison," *ST*, 4-10-40, p. 1.

Mehlhorn's company: "Mehlhorn's Liabilities Mounting," *ST*, 9-6-1930, p. 1; "Receivership for Mehlhorn's Block Granted," *P-I*, 9-13-1930, p. 13; final settlement of 1.76167611c/$ from minutes of final creditors' meeting, 12-7-37, bankruptcy of Osner & Mehlhorn, Case 31248, U.S. District Court, Seattle.

Else Mehlhorn: "Mrs. Mehlhorn, in Need of Funds, to Sell House," *ST*, 4-5-31, p. 2; "Mrs. Mehlhorn Asks Divorce from Larcenist," *ST*, 11-20-36, p. 19.

"Bright ray": "The Nightmare of 1930 Is Over," *Journal of Commerce*, 2-5-31, p. 3.

Projects that continue: Harborview: "Right Now!" *ST*, 12-6-30, p. 1; "Athletic Club Bldg. to Open During Week," *P-I*, 12-14-30, p. 10; "The Roosevelt, City's Newest Hotel, Opens," *P-I*, 12-21-30, p. 12; tombstone, "University Community Hotel Corporation," *P-I*, 3-2-30, p. 6; "Work Starts at Once on $750,000 University Hotel" *P-I*, 12-5-30, p. 1; Niendorff, "Meany Hotel Plan Submitted to Court," *P-I*, 2-16-37, p. 19.

Projects that stop: "Gwinn Leading Building on Regrade" and stock ad, *Star*, 5-29-30, pp. 18, 19; "$1,500,000 Hotel for Regrade," *ST*, 8-24-30, p. 1; "New Washington Hotel Has Memory Treasure," *Star*, 5-29-30, p. 22; "Enlarging of Leary Bldg. [Insurance Bldg.] to Cost Million," *P-I*, 11-5-30, p. 1.

Optimism: "Seattle Marches Proudly On," *Star*, 11-7-30, p. 1.

3. Bankers, 1931–1932

12th largest: "Seattle Deposits Gain $947,357," *P-I*, 10-9-29, p. 23.

History: *Bank Histories 1907–1937*, V4-E-13-1. Box 5, Washington State Division of Banking, Washington State Archives; Gary Iwamoto, "Rise & Fall of an Empire Furuya: Imm 1890," *International Examiner*, 8-29-2005.

Closure: Hill, "M. Furuya's Bank Closed by Supervisor," *P-I*, 10-24-31, pp. 14–15; "Japanese American Bank Is Taken Over," *Star*, 10-23-31, p. 3; Wood, "Speaking for the Times," *ST*, 2-26-38, p. 6.

Aftermath: "Leaders Pushing Plans for Loans to Reopen Bank" and "A Rude Awakening," *Japanese American Courier*, 10-31-31, pp. 1, 3; Esse, "10,000 New Shares Issued This Week to Raise $250,000," *Japanese American Courier*, 11-14-31, p. 1; "The Coming Months," *Japanese American Courier*, 1-9-32, p. 3.

Payout: *Division of Banking Liquidation Record*, Olympia.

Early career: Pierce, *Eccentric Seattle*, pp. 221–238; "Linden Began Career Here as Messenger," *P-I*, 2-8-31, p. 2; "Chronology of Linden's Career," *P-I*, 2-17-31, p. 2.

McKay, oil: Hunt, "Million of Loan Funds Admitted Taken by Linden," *P-I*, 7-1-31, p. 1; "Intentions Hold Center of Stage at Linden Trial," *ST*, 9-21-31, p. 2; Hunt, "Linden Says He Helped Drain Home Loan to Offset Shortage," *P-I*, 9-19-31, p. 3.

Camlin: "Prosecutor Outlines to Jury How Linden Used Loan Funds," *ST*, 6-23-31, p. 7; Hunt, "Nicely Assailed for Loan Crash at Trial of Linden," *P-I*, 6-26-31, p. 1; Hunt, "Linden, On Stand, Defends Handling of Loan Affairs," *P-I*, 6-30-31, pp. 1, 5.

Post-Camlin: Hunt, "Loan Firm Paid $2,300 to State Official, Jury Told," *P-I*, 4-16-31, p. 1; Hunt, "Prosecutor Bars Thomas Testimony in Linden Trial," *P-I*, 6-27-31, pp. 1, 12; Hunt, "Million of Loan Funds Admitted Taken by Linden," *P-I*, 7-1-31, p. 1; "Mrs. Linden Final Witness; Case Going to Jury Today," *ST*, 7-1-31, pp. 1, 10, 11; "Only Clothing, Toiletries Left, Says Mrs. Linden," *ST*, 10-17-31, p. 3.

House: "Former Adolph Linden Estate Is Sold," *ST*, 6-27-37, p. 22; Aweeka, "Kirkland Man Working to Save Wurdemann Mansion," *ST*, 5-21-86, p. H4.

Bible: "Formal Opening Great Success," *ST*, 6-27-25, p. 36.

Nicely: "Grand Jury Blames Politics," *ST*, 5-3-31, pp. 1, 10; "Nicely Opposed Linden Ouster," *ST*, 6-25-31, p. 1; Hunt, "Linden 'Fixed' State, Nelson Tells Jurors," *P-I*, 6-25-31, pp. 1, 14; Hunt, "Nicely Assailed for Loan Crash at Trial of Linden," *P-I*, 6-26-31, p. 1; "Nicely to Confront Linden!" *ST*, 6-27-31, p. 1; "Loan Trial Livens State Politics," *ST*, 6-28-31, pp. 1, 12; "Linden Describes Efforts go Get Nicely State Job," *ST*, 9-22-31, p. 3; "Linden Denies 'Buying' Nicely His Job," *Star*, 9-22-31, p. 1; Hunt, "Linden Admits Engineering Nicely's Job," *P-I*, 9-23-31, p. 5; Hunt, "Nicely Testifies Against Linden; Denies He Dictated Group," *P-I*, 10-4-31, p. 3; "Nicely's Memory Fails on Stand," *ST*, 10-4-31, pp. 1, 5; "Nicely Says He Is Not Trying to Protect Anyone," *ST*, 10-6-31, p. 11; Hunt, "Linden Under Cross Fire by Own Lawyer," *P-I*, 10-11-31, pp. 13, 14; "Campbell Tells Unwillingness to Stay in Firm," *ST*, 10-19-31, p. 7.

Radio: John Schneider, "Seattle Radio History: KJR and KOMO," theradiohistorian.org (accessed 7/21/17); "Adolph Linden's Career Shows Capitalist's Dreams," *ST*, 2-17-31, p. 11; Hunt, "Linden 'Fixed' State, Nelson Tells Jurors," *P-I*, 6-25-31, pp. 1, 14.

Radio withdrawals: "Partner Details Linden Radio Loans," *ST*, 6-24-31, pp. 1, 15; Hunt, "Flow of Gold to Linden's Radio Told," *P-I*, 9-16-31, pp. 17, 26; Hunt, "Puget Sound Secret File Disappears," *P-I*, 9-17-31, p. 17; "Loan Officers Took Cash at Will, Says Ex-Teller," *P-I*, 10-2-31, p. 7; "Linden Explains Leaving Loan Job for Radio Berth," *ST*, 10-13-31, p. 7.

Shank: "Loan Attorneys in Clash," *ST*, 9-30-31, pp. 1, 11.

Overview: *State v. Linden*, 171 Wash. 92, P.2d 635 (1932).

Stock sales: J. O. Adams (as J. Grant Hinkle) to Kerr, McCord and Ivey, 1-12-29; Adams to J. G. Rake, 1-19-29; Rake (as Hinkle) to Linden, 1-19-29; Amended Articles of Incorporation, ABC, 4-14-29; minutes of board meeting, ABC, 5-13-29; Charles R. Maybury to Frank P. Hupe, 7-9-29; all in American Broadcasting Co. file 1358, Box 43, Securities Issuers Permits 1928–29, WA Dept. Licensing, WA State Archives; tombstones for ABC stock, *P-I*, 5-19-29, p. 9 and 6-3-29, p. 21.

Blue Sky: "'Blue Sky' Law Victims in Arms Against Hinkle," *ST*, 2-12-29, p. 2; "State Urged to Fight Repeal of 'Blue Sky' Law," *ST*, 2-17-29, p. 15; "Hinkle Stripped of Authority in Securities Act," *ST*, 3-12-29, p. 2; "J. Grant Hinkle Dies in Oregon," *ST*, 2-22-39, p. 12.

Politicians: "Politics, Radio, Prove Poor Mixers with Savings and Loans," *ST*, 7-9-31, p. 1; "Grand Jury Blames Politics," *ST*, 5-3-31, p. 1.

Outdoor concerts: ads, *ST*, 5-5-29, p. 11, and 6-21-29, p. 25; Armstrong, "Skies Smile on Symphony at Stadium," *P-I*, 6-13-29, p. 9.

Nicely and Linden loans: Hunt, "100 Cents' Payoff for Each Dollar Is Loan Co. Hope," *P-I*, 4-4-31, p. 1; "Campbell, Comer, Nicely, Nelson, Linden Indicted in Puget Loan Failure," *P-I*, 5-3-31, p. 1; Hunt, "Linden 'Fixed' State, Nelson Tells Jurors,'" *P-I*, 6-25-31, pp. 1, 14; Hunt, "Nicely Assailed for Loan Crash at Trial of Linden," *P-I*, 6-26-31, p. 1; Hunt, "Linden, On Stand, Defends Handling of Loan Affairs," *P-I*, 6-30-31, pp. 1, 5; "Nicely Gets 4 to 15 Years in Loan Case" and "Change in Loan Assn. Law Aim of Batchelor," *P-I*, 4-3-32, pp. 1, 7.

National plans: "KJR Is Key Station in New Radio Chain," *ST*, 4-7-29, p. 20.

Play records: "Radio," *ST*, 9-9-29, p. 12; "Fans Helping KJR in Fight to Keep Its Wave Length," *ST*, 9-24-29, p. 8; "Galli-Curci Is to Be Highlight on KOMO Tonight," *ST*, 2-6-30, p. 11.

Kiting checks: "Burgunder Says Linden Took $40,000 in One Day," *ST*, 2-19-31, p. 1.

ABC fails: "Phone Action Forces ABC Radio to Quit," *P-I*, 8-23-29, p. 1; "Linden Says He'll Repay ABC Losses," *Star*, 8-23-29, p. 1; "ABC Chain Now in Hands of Receiver," *P-I*, 8-24-19, p. 1; "ABC Assets Appear Close to Nil Mark," *P-I*, 8-25-29, p. 18; "ABC Sale Near Says Linden," *Star*, 8-26-29, p. 5.

Payouts: Northwest Radio Service Co., minutes of creditors' meetings 11-21-29, 5-2-30, and American Broadcasting Co., minutes of creditors' meeting of 6-3-30, NARA Kansas City.

Comer: "Comer Given Quizzing on Merger of Loan Firms," *P-I*, 4-15-31, p. 1; Hunt, "Puget Sound Bought, Sold, Comer Bonds," *P-I*, 10-30-31, p. 6; Hunt, "Comer's Firm Borrowed Big Sum, Jury Told," *P-I*, 10-31-31, p. 13; Hunt, "Loan Funds Borrowed on Low Security," *P-I*, 11-1-31, p.11; Hill, "U.S. May Loan 3 Million on P.S.L. Assets," *P-I*, 1-31-34, p. 1.

Dead man's note: "Shadow of Death Hovers Close to Comer Loan Case," *ST*, 11-1-31, p. 5.

False report: Statement of Condition, Puget Sound Savings, *P-I*, 12-27-30, p. 3; "Diverted Money Listed as Asset by W.D. Comer," *ST*, 11-4-31, p. 5; Hunt, "Comer Pleads Ignorance of Bookkeeping in Puget Loan Trial," *P-I*, 11-5-31, p. 3; "Comer Convicted!" *ST*, 11-6-31, pp. 1, 9; Hunt, "Hoffman Remains as Loan Receiver by Court Ruling," *P-I*, 4-3-31, p. 1.

Nicely: Brown, "Under the Capitol Dome," *Argus*, 2-28-31, p. 6.

Vault: "Savings Bank Moves Today; New Home to Open Monday," *ST*, 1-1-27, p. 3.

The run: "State Orders Puget Sound Savings, Loan Suspension," *P-I*, 2-8-31, p. 1; "Adolph Linden Is Accused of Defalcations," *ST*, 2-8-31, pp. 1, 4; "Probe Launched Over 'Leak' on Firm's Affairs," *P-I*, 2-18-31, p. 1; "Receiver Reports on Loan Funds," *ST*, 5-26-31, p. 1; "Colvin Attempts to Show Closing Was Prejudiced," *ST*, 11-2-31, p. 2; "Comer Phoned, State Acted, Jury Is Told," *P-I*, 11-3-31, p. 7.

Deposits: $15.7m at Puget Sound Savings, from Statement of Condition, *P-I*, 12-27-30, p. 3; $57.1m at Washington Mutual, from Statement of Condition, *ST*, 1-5-31, p. 18.

Deposit rates: Washington Mutual ad, *ST*, 1-2-31, p. 5; Prudential Savings ad, *ST*, 9-3-29, p. 2; Northern Savings ad, *ST*, 12-22-30, p. 21; Home Savings ad, *ST*, 2-27-31, p. 10.

"Safety", "Do not fail" ads: *ST*, 3-2-30, p. 5; *ST*, 9-24-29, p. 3.

"Sound laws" ad: *ST*, 2-2-31, p. 13.

6-month notices: "Business Men Confer with Mayor Edwards," *P-I*, 2-10-31, p. 17; Home Savings ad, *ST*, 2-27-31, p. 10.

WaMu runs: Murray Morgan, *Friend of the Family*, Washington Mutual, 1989, pp. 79–81; "Washington Mutual Bank Open Tonight," *ST*, 2-11-31, p. 1.

"Cannot promise you": "The Stroller," *Argus*, 2-21-31, p. 3.

Reopening, payout: Niendorff, "Puget Sound Savings and Loan Association Again Going Concern," *P-I*, 1-23-35, p. 16; "6,000 PSL Shareholders Neglect Books," *ST*, 4-12-35, p. 10; "S&L Assets Sold; Savers Get Dividend," *ST*, 10-17-45, p. 21.

Directors' offer: "Savings Unit Has Plan to Reorganize," *P-I*, 2-14-31, p. 1; "Here's Text in Savings Offer," *Star*, 2-16-31, p. 1; "Depositors Oppose Savings Cut," *Star*, 2-19-31, p. 1.

Blame: "Adolph Linden Is Accused of Defalcations," *ST*, 2-8-31, pp. 1, 4; Hunt, "Campbell, Comer, Nicely, Nelson, Linden Indicted in Puget Loan Failure," *P-I*, 5-3-31, p. 1; "Grand Jury Blames Politics," *ST*, 5-3-31, pp. 1, 10.

Tearoom: "Linden, Near Tears, Admits Making 'Terrible Mistake,'" *ST*, 6-30-31, p. 1; "Prosecutor Hammers Loan Chief's Ventures," *ST*, 7-1-31, p. 11.

Home Savings: "Pierce Had Full Control of Loan Firm, Says Eddy," *ST*, 5-12-32, p. 16; Hunt, "Pierce of Home Loan Arrested" and "Association President Is Astonished by Pierce's Revelations," *P-I*, 7-8-31, pp. 1, 3; Hunt, "$225,000 of Loan Funds Missing," *P-I*, 7-10-31, p. 17; "Ahira Pierce Free; $60,000 Bond is OK'd," *ST*, 9-19-31, p. 1.

"Adored son": Yerkes, "As I See It," *Argus*, 11-26-32, p. 12.

Father: funeral notice, *P-I*, 1-19-27, p. 20.

Marriage: "Lovely as Bride," *P-I*, 11-20-27, p. 61.

Suit: "Gunmen Kind to Financier," *P-I*, 7-25-31, pp. 13, 17.

Washington Loan: State v. Pierce, 175 Wash. 461, 27 P.2d 1098 (1933) and Howard MacGowan, "Widows, Orphans Lose in Pierce Firm" and other stories in *Star* series 11–27, 28, 30; 12–1, 2, 3, 4, 7, 8, 9, 10, 12, 14, 15, 16, 18, 19, 22, 1931, all p. 1.

Hinkle's neglect: MacGowan, "How State Aided Pierce," *Star*, 12-12-31, p. 1.

House: "Pierce's Home in Wife's Name," *ST*, 7-16-31, p. 2.

"Wake": MacGowan, "How Pierce's Friends Held Liquor 'Wake,'" *Star*, 12-22-31, p. 1.

Liquor: "State Men Drank Pierce's Gin Is Charge," *Star*, 9-22-31, p. 1; "Pierce's Rare Liquors Have Disappeared," *P-I*, 9-23-31, p. 17; "Home Savings Liquor Denied," *Star*, 12-12-31, p. 3; "Court Told How Pierce's Liquor Oozed," *P-I*, 12-13-31, p. 5; "Rum Raiders Nab 'Hi' Pierce," *Star*, 1-9-32, p. 1; "Hi Pierce's Home Raided," *ST*, 1-9-32, p. 1.

Brewery: MacGowan, "How 'Hi' Pierce Owned Brewery," *Star*, 12-14-31, p. 1.

Radio: "Radio Chain to Spend $300,000," *Star*, 8-22-30, p. 2; Hunt, "Jay Thomas Got Cash from Puget Sound, Linden Discloses," *P-I*, 9-20-31, p. 3.

Pierce and Linden: "Linden Describes Efforts to Get Nicely State Job," *ST*, 9-22-31, p. 3; "Politics, Radio, Prove Poor Mixers with Savings and Loans" and "Earnings Will Repay $246,500 Loan Firm Loss," *ST*, 7-9-31, p. 1.

Confession: "Courts," *Argus*, 11-5-32, p. 4.

Suicide idea: "Confession by Pierce Bared Before Court," *P-I*, 5-18-32, p. 15.

Stealing deposits: Hunt, "$225,000 of Loan Funds Missing; State to Seek Suspected Money Hoard," *P-I*, 7-10-31, p. 17.

Plea: "Pierce Refuses to Plead Guilty in Home Savings Case," *Star*, 7-14-31, p. 1.

Hiding assets: "Pierce's Assets Being Uncovered," *Star*, 7-22-31, p. 1.

Delay: "Magnuson Scores Neglect and Delay in Prosecutions," *P-I*, 10-26-34, p. 7.

Vs. Puget Sound Savings: "May Reorganize," *Argus*, 9-15-34, p. 4.

Creditors: "Minutes of Adjourned Meeting of Creditors," filed 4-2-36, Washington Loan & Securities Co. bankruptcy, case 31992, U.S. District Court, Seattle; "Home Savings' Sale Approved," *ST*, 3-31-41, p. 22; Notice of final payment, *ST*, 5-19-41, p. 8.

Trials: "Judge Dismisses Linden Jury," *P-I*, 7-4-31, pp. 1, 2; "Linden Jury Dismissed," *ST*, 9-26-31, p. 1; Hunt, "Linden and Campbell Are Declared Guilty," *P-I*, 10-25-31, p. 1; Hunt, "Nicely Found Guilty," *P-I*, 3-6-32, pp. 1, 4; "Comer Convicted!" *ST*, 11-6-31, pp. 1, 9; "Comer Guilty on 10 Counts," *P-I*, 7-25-32, p. 1; "Pierce Convicted on 19 Counts of Larceny, Forgery," *P-I*, 11-12-32, pp. 1, 5.

Intent: "Hold-Out Juror Explains Mistrial of Linden Case," *ST*, 7-4-31, p. 1; "Intentions Hold Center of Stage at Linden Trial," *ST*, 9-21-31, p. 2; "Linden Jury Dismissed," *ST*, 9-26-31, p. 1; "Judge Stresses Intent in Charge to Linden Jury," *ST*, 10-21-31, p. 14; Hunt, "Linden and Campbell Are Declared Guilty," *P-I*, 10-25-31, p. 1; "Campbell and Linden Denied New Loan Trial," *ST*, 12-10-31, p. 1.

Steinert's tirade: "Scorching Words of Judge Sear Linden and Campbell," *P-I*, 3-12-32, p. 3.

"Popular as a boil": "The Stroller: At a Boy, Judge," *Argus*, 3-19-32, p. 3.

"You big crook!": "Adolph Linden, Campbell Get Prison," *P-I*, 3-12-32, p. 1.

Linden's house: "Harry Vanderbilt Wurdemann House," *Wikipedia*; "Mrs. Linden Final Witness," *ST*, 7-1-31, pp. 1, 10, 11.

Comer's house: "Corporate Filings," *P-I*, 8-25-27, p. 21; "W.H. Parsons Buys Home of W.D. Comer," *ST*, 6-5-31, p. 1.

Campbell: Hunt, "Campbell, Comer, Nicely, Nelson, Linden Indicted in Puget Loan Failure," *P-I*, 5-3-31, p. 1; Pierce, *Eccentric Seattle*, pp. 221–238.

Sentences: "Linden, Campbell Get 5–15 Years," *Star*, 3-11-32, p. 1; "Nicely Given 4 to 15 Years," *ST*, 4-3-32, p. 1; "Comer Given 5–15 Years in Walla Walla," *P-I*, 8-25-32, p. 13.

Releases: "Nicely Parole" *ST*, 7-9-37, p. 3; Williams, "Adolph Linden Paroled," *P-I*, 3-22-38, p. 1.

Pierce: "Ahira Pierce Operated On," *Star*, 11-5-31, p. 1; "Hi Pierce Trial Underway," *ST*, 3-14-32, p. 2; Bermann, "Judge Halts Pierce Trial over Illness," *P-I*, 3-16-32, p. 13; "Pierce Seeks New Trial on Loan Charge," *P-I*, 11-13-32, p. 4; "Pierce Loses Fight against Court Ruling," *P-I*, 3-28-33, p. 9; "Here's Chronology of Legal Delays in Pierce Case," *P-I*, 2-11-34, p. 6; *State v. Pierce*, 175 Wash. 461, 27 P.2d 1098 (1933); "The Stroller: Paying the Piper," *Argus*, 11-26-32, p. 3; "Former Pierce Home Sold," *ST*, 3-12-39, p. 27; "$400 in Estate of Ahira Pierce," *ST*, 6-22-39, p. 16.

Linden: Whitehouse, "Linden Comes Back!" *Star*, 4-28-38, p. 1.

4. The Bottom, 1931–1932

Prices: "Barbershop Haircut Price to Half Dollar," *P-I*, 12-6-30, p. 13; "Depression Strikes Bootleg Fraternity," *P-I*, 12-17-30, p. 2.

Committee of 59: "Seattle Spirit Reawakened," *ST*, 11-20-30, p. 1; "Seattle Bids for Coast Leadership," *Star*, 11-20-30, p. 2; "Millions Ready for Industry Next Year," *ST*, 12-28-30, p. 1; "House Passes 'Committee of 59' Bill," *ST*, 3-3-31, p. 1; "Executive Veto Nulls 53 More of State's Bills," *ST*, 3-24-31, p. 9; Seattle ad, *Saturday Evening Post*, 3-6-31, p. 25.

Elephant: "Right Now!" *ST*, 4-7-31, p. 1.

Germany: Straumann, *1931*, pp. 32–33; "Fascist Gains Outstanding in German Voting," *ST*, 9-15-30, p. 1; "'Western Front' Starts Riot in Berlin Theatre," *ST*, 12-6-30, p. 3.

German bonds: "German Reparations Issue Oversubscribed" and tombstone, *ST*, 6-12-30, pp. 28–29; "German Issues Believed Safe," *ST*, 10-14-30, p. 24; "Debt Repudiation by Berlin Coming, Gerard Declares," *ST*, 11-10-30, p. 17; "M'Fadden Flays Floating of Weak Foreign Bonds in U.S.," *P-I*, 11-29-30, p. 13; Norton, "German Bond Owners in Seattle Anxious over Their Holdings," *P-I*, 7-8-34, p. 21.

United National: Hill, "United National Omits Its March Dividend," *P-I*, 2-10-31, p. 17; "United National Bought at $5," *P-I*, 4-28-31, p. 18.

Unemployment: "Jobless Ratio Here Is among U.S. Lowest," *P-I*, 3-29-31, p. 10.

Economy: "Year's Building Permits Decline," *Journal of Commerce*, 1-30-32, p. 5; "Unions Tell What Is Wrong with the Business Condition," *Star*, 1-12-31, p. 7; "Labor Tells of Job Ills," *Star*, 1-23-31, p. 1.

Abandoned: "Half-Burned Shacks Held Menace," *Star*, 4-15-31, p. 1.

Anhalt: "16th Anhalt Apartment Home Opens," *ST*, 2-16-30, p. 30; "$101,567 Judgment against Anhalt Properties Given," *ST*, 3-11-31, p. 5.

New stores: "J.C. Penney Company Store Makes Bow to Public," *ST*, 8-13-31, p. 11; "Littler's Premiere Will Lure Tonight," *ST*, 3-25-31, p. 13; "Anson A. 'Bob' Littler, 90, Owner of Clothing Store Chain," *ST*, 1-14-91, p. D7.

Quitting ads, in *ST*: Knettle's, 3-5-31, p. 12; Jordan's, 5-27-31, p. 4; Florence, 4-24-31, p. 11; Browning King, 4-22-31, p. 4; Blumenthal's, 3-19-31, p. 30; Coplin's, 5-26-31, p. 17; Reed's, 6-10-31, p. 8; Miller Trunk, 5-12-31, p. 20; Ray Bigelow (auction), 5-7-31, p. 16.

Falling prices: "Seattle Living Costs Decline 7.9 Pct. In Year," *ST*, 7-19-31, p. 3; Olympic Hotel ad, *P-I*, 5-26-31, p. 2.

Olympic: "Olympic Bond Sale $190,000 First Day," *P-I*, 1-24-29, p. 22; "Olympic Hotel Reorganization Plan Underway," *ST*, 8-9-31, p. 30; "Refinancing of Olympic Hotel Asked," *P-I*, 8-30-31, p. 11; Ad, First Bondholders Reorganization Committee, *P-I*, 3-25-32, p. 12; Hill, "Olympic Hotel Bondholders' Groups Hold Hope of Reorganization Success," *P-I*, 11-4-32, p. 13; Niendorff, "Olympic Hotel Bond Interest in Sight, New Plan Approved," *P-I*, 3-29-36, p. 25.

Frederick Meisnest: Branom, "Against the Hun," pp. 6–18, 38.

Darwin Meisnest: "Elected Basketball Pilot Because of Merit," *ST*, 12-16-17, p. 45; "Varsity Has New Athletics Manager," *ST*, 3-2-19, p. 64; "Record Crowd to See Washington and California Play,"

P-I, 11-23-19, p. 50; photo, *P-I*, 11-28-20, p. 39; Eskenazi and Rudman, "Genesis of Husky Stadium," SportspressNW.com, 8-27-2013.

Pavilion: MacHarrie, "U. of W. Pavilion Official Program Dedication," 12-27-27; "U Student Hits Meisnest's 'Dollar Chasing,'" *ST*, 1-29-28, p. 14; "Meisnest—Storm Center of the University Crisis," *ST*, 2-5-28, p. 1.

WAC building: Gordon, Landmarks Preservation Board report, 3-11-2008; Speidel, "The WAC's Works," Washington Athletic Club, 1956, WAC archives.

WAC crisis: "Athletic Club Is Reorganized; Has New Owners," *ST*, 3-20-31, p. 2; Harrison, "Watch Meisnest Put Heart, Pepper into New WAC," *Star*, 3-21-31, p. 8; "The Stroller: Athletic Club Reorganized," *Argus*, 3-28-31, p. 3; "Washington Athletic Club," WAC, 4–31, vol. xvi, No. 4; "A Happy Outcome," *ST*, 5-7-31, p. 6; "Athletic Club to Claim Meisnest," *P-I*, 5-7-31, p. 4; Hill, "Growth of Athletic Club Aids in Reorganization," *P-I*, 5-26-31, p. 17; "Ward of WAC Is Named Head of Bergonian," *ST*, 11-22-31, p. 2.

Dues: "'Bring in Friends' Plan Adopted for New Athletic Club," *ST*, 3-23-31, p. 1; Eskenazi and Rudman, "The Washington Athletic Club," sportspressnw.com, 10-29-2013.

Initiation fee: "Athletic Club Prepares for Rush," *ST*, 3-25-31, p. 9.

Follow-up: "Report Reveals Refinancing of W.A.C. Complete," *ST*, 1-3-32, p. 2; "Athletic Club Reorganized," *P-I*, 1-3-32, p. 4; Hill, "Washington Athletic Club Pays Interest on Its Bonds," *P-I*, 5-1-32, p. C6; "The W.A.C. 'Family Club' Idea Wins Favor," *P-I*, 9-29-32, p. 20.

Bonds: ASUW Board of Control, Minutes of 12-31-31, UW Special Collections; banker to M. Lyle Spencer, 3-9-32; M. Lyle Spencer to John H. Dunbar, 4-11-32; M. Lyle Spencer to Dietrich Schmitz, undated; Dietrich Schmitz to Lyle Spencer, 4-14-32, all in Records of UW Office of the President, UW Special Collections; UW Board of Regents, minutes, 6-9-33, UW Special Collections; "Bondholders Aid Stabilization of U of W Finances," *ST*, 8-27-33, p. 4; "Regents Announce $530,000 Building Program for UW," *P-I*, 2-6-33, pp. 1–2.

Crisis: Harrison, "Inside Story about Busted Student Body," *Star*, 4-6-32, p. 3; "Spencer Views ASUW Crisis," *P-I*, 4-26-32, p. 11; "Need for Funds Immediate, Says Earl Campbell," *ST*, 4-26-32, p. 16; "Campus Daily to Face Suspension if U. Loan Fails," *P-I*, 4-27-32, p. 11; "Husky Finances Cry for Relief," *ST*, 4-27-32, p. 11; Varnell, "Money or Not, Team to Play," *ST*, 4-28-32, p. 23; Hill, "Bankers' Cooperation Aids Associated Student Finances," *P-I*, 4-30-32, p. 13; "Banks to Lend Students Cash," *Star*, 4-30-32, p. 1; "Students Retire Bonds," *ST*, 1-18-38, p. 16.

Bookstore: Longnecker, "History of the University Book Store 1900–1955," pp. 101–110; E. Lyle Goss, "University Book Store: A Personal Overview," 1979, p. 10–13, both in UW Special Collections.

ASUW election: *Krebs v. Frankland*, King County Superior Court, case 267309, 11-9-33; Charles Frankland, Special Appearance and Motion to Quash, 11-6-33; dismissal by Judge J. T. Ronald, 12-1-33, all in ASUW Records, UW Special Collections; "Fraud Charged in Frankland Ouster Election," *P-I*, 11-7-33, p. 5; "ASUW Ballot Fraud Charged in Open Court," *ST*, 11-15-33, p. 9; "Court Kills ASUW Fight on Frankland," *P-I*, 11-18-33, p. 9.

Frankland: Lovering, "Frankland Handles Hard Job Well at University," *ST*, 4-5-36, p. 23.

Currency crisis: Aguado, "The Creditanstalt Crisis of 1931 and the Failure of the Austro-German Customs Union Project," pp. 199–221.

Canadian exchange: "Canadian Money Finds New Welcome Signs in Seattle," *ST*, 9-28-31, p. 6; Hill, "J.W. Ruggles Finds Discount Favors Canadian Business," *P-I*, 9-30-31, p. 19.

Foreign bonds: "Drastic Losses Recorded; Volume Biggest for 1931," *P-I*, 9-25-31, p. 20; "Foreign Defaults on Bonds Here Exceed $815,000,000" and "Record of Foreign Dollar Bond Issues in Default," *NYT*, 1-2-32, pp. 1, 2; Jorgensen and Sachs, "Default and Renegotiation of Latin American Foreign Bonds in the Interwar Period," pp. 16–19.

Bridge: "Lake Washington Bridge Included," *ST*, 1-4-34, p. 4.

P-I's story: Robe, "A Job at Last? Not Yet; Mary First Must Raise $2," *P-I*, 1-17-32, p. 9.

Marriages: *Report of the Department of Health and Sanitation 1932–1935*, p. 31; "Hard Times Blamed for 1931 Drop in Marriage, Divorce," *Star*, 4-29-32, p. 11; "Seattle Courts Granting Divorcees Less Alimony Now," *Star*, 12-9-32, p. 2; Masterson, "Dad Jobless, Children Now Working to Support Family," *Star*, 4-13-32, p. 3.

Suicides: *King County Coroner's Annual Report*, 1933, p. 14, and "190 Suicides Total for Year," *P-I*, 1-2-33, p. 2.

Not built: "Unfinished Business," *ST*, 10–9, 16, 23, 1930; 11–6, 13, 20, 27; 12–4 and 11, 1932, all in Sunday Brown Section, mostly on p. 8.

Permits: "Business Review of Year" and "Statistical Graphs Show Trend of Local and Northwest Business," *Journal of Commerce*, 1-3-33, p. 7.

Art museum: "A Brief History of the Seattle Art Museum," *P-I*, 5-3-2007; "$250,000 Given City for Art Museum," *ST*, 10-1-31, pp. 1, 3; "Art Museum Opens," *ST*, 6-28-33, p. 8.

Vacant: Niendorff, "Apartment House Occupancy Tempts Investors," *P-I*, 1-17-35, p. 16.

Doubling up: "Have You Aunt in Your Home?" *Star*, 4-21-32, p. 1.

Ford plant: "Big Ford Buy," *ST*, 2-28-30, p. 1; "Ford Motor Company, Assembly Plant #1, South Lake Union, Seattle, WA," *Pacific Coast Architecture Database*, #4902.

Opens: "Ford Factory Puts 600 Men to Work Here," *P-I*, 5-24-32, p. 13; "$3,000,000 for Convenience," *ST*, 7-3-32, Sunday supp., p. 6; "Seattle Site Selected for Shipping Facilities" and "Seattle Plant Turns Out Fir Block Floors," *ST*, 7-17-32, pp. 10, 11; "Huge Throng Visits New Ford Plant," *P-I*, 7-20-32, p. 3; "You Are Invited!" Ford ad, *ST*, 7-20-32, p. 3; "Courtesy Cars Ready Today," *P-I*, 7-22-32, p. 16.

Closes: Ford closures, askus.thehenryford.org; "Seattle Ford Plant Temporarily Closed," *ST*, 1-27-33, p. 12.

Sale: "Ford Plant Purchase Closed Here by U.S.," *P-I*, 9-6-41, p. 17.

Today: "Federal Center South, Bldgs. No. 1201 & 1206, Seattle, WA," General Services Administration website.

Wage cuts: "Ford Cuts Pay Dollar a Day," *P-I*, 10-30-31, p. 1; "Business & Finance," *Argus*, 3-5-32, p. 5; Jermane, "Salary, Wage Survey Shows Extent of Cuts," *ST*, 6-30-32, p. 1.

Wives: *ST* letters of 6-10-29, 10-4-29, 2-4-30, 7-2-30, 7-22-30, 7-28-30, 8-29-30, 11-29-30, 1-17-31, 6-25-31, 10-30-31, all p. 6; "Chamber Chief and Rigger Talk of Jobs," *Star*, 7-11-30, p. 1; Oakley, "Don't Be So Stupid," *ST*, 2-6-31, p. 6; Grey, "Why Not Oust Single Girls Who Do Not Have to Work, Asks Wife," *Star*, 11-21-30, p. 18; "One Per Family Enough for City," *Star*, 11-23-31,

p. 6; "Law Urged to Bar City Job If Mate Works," *P-I*, 8-27-31, p. 14; "Northern Pacific's Women Employees Must Stay Single," *ST*, 12-9-31, p. 5.

Fighting back: Cooper, "Wives Block Move to Bar Them from Holding City Jobs," *P-I*, 12-2-31, p. 1; "Women Winning," *ST*, 12-3-31, p. 6.

Foreigners: "Hire American Is Order," *P-I*, 3-9-33, p. 9; "Board Bans Aliens from Public Jobs," *P-I*, 3-21-33, p. 11.

Warrants: "Deep Budget Slash Looms, Says Nichols," *P-I*, 5-13-32, p. 17; "Banks Refuse Warrants as City Dallies," *P-I*, 5-22-32, p. 13; "Banker Tells Why No Cash for Warrants," *Star*, 5-28-32, p. 1; "Warrants Refused by Retailers," *ST*, 5-26-32, p. 1; "City Warrants Poor Bank Risks," *ST*, 5-29-32, p. 1; "Banks to Accept City's July 25 Pay Warrants," *ST*, 7-17-32, p. 1; Cooper, "Banks May Reject Warrants Unless City Cuts Budget," *P-I*, 9-4-32, p. 1; "Banks Cash Warrants after City Cuts Costs," *ST*, 9-28-32, p. 1.

Pay cuts 1932: "Dore, Council Agree on Cuts," *ST*, 7-12-32, p. 1; "Council Sustains Dore Cost Cuts in Stormy Session," *P-I*, 7-23-32, p. 1; "City Wage Slashes Effective Today as Mayor Signs Law," *P-I*, 8-6-32, p. 11.

1933 budget: Cooper, "Council Approves $1,960,000 Slash in City's Budget," *P-I*, 9-27-32, p. 1; Cooper, "Seattle Tax Levy Down 3.76 Mills for 1933," *P-I*, 10-1-32, p. 19.

Tax delinquencies: Niendorff, "Tax Collections Show Big Gains," *P-I*, 3-6-37, p. 18.

City pay cuts 1933: "Dore Orders 17.7 Pct. Cut in Salaries," *P-I*, 3-22-33, p. 1; "Dore's Order for Economy Closes Nine Fire Stations," *P-I*, 4-2-33, p. 1; "Increased Protection from City at Same Cost," *ST*, 12-8-33, p. 1; "Council Approves Full-Time Plan for Police in 1934," *P-I*, 12-27-33, p. 4.

School cuts: "Old Timers of Schools Hardest Hit by Salary Slash," *Star*, 3-15-32, p. 12; "Teachers Face Pay Cut from 17–19 Per Cent," *P-I*, 4-6-33, p. 1.

UW tuition: "25 Bills Signed and 4 Vetoed by Gov. Martin," *P-I*, 3-19-33, p. 9; "Regents Slash University Pay to $620,000," *ST*, 4-3-33, p. 1.

Geraghty: "Nominations," *Spokane Chronicle*, 11-2-1896, p. 2; "Geraghty, New Justice, Takes Oath of Office," *P-I*, 8-16-33, p. 4.

Income, B&O: Spitzer, "A Washington State Income Tax—Again?" *University of Puget Sound Law Review*, Vol. 16, 1993, pp. 515–531; "State Income Tax Held Invalid by Supreme Court," *P-I*, 9-9-33, p. 1; *Culliton v. Chase*, 174 Wash. 363, 25 P.2d 81 (1933); *State ex rel. Stiner v. Yelle*, 174 Wash. 402, 25 P.2d 91 (1933); *Denny v. Wooster*, 175 Wash. 272, 27 P.2d 326 (1933); Wash. constitution, Art. VII, Sect. 1.

Exchange: Niendorff, "Seattle Stock 'Change Opens," *P-I*, 9-29-35, p. 22.

Markets: Wall, "Stocks Slip to New Lows; Volume Light," *P-I*, 7-6-32, p. 15; Wall, "Stocks Rise; Reports from Lausanne Rosy," and Norton, "American Exchange Bank May Reopen for Business July 15," *P-I*, 7-7-32, p. 15; Whiteleather, "Next Move in Debt Revision Up to America," *ST*, 7-9-32, p. 1; Anderson, *Economics and the Public Welfare*, pp. 273–277.

5. Homeless, 1931–1941

Closures: McGrath, "Gossip of Plays and Players," *Argus*, 6-6-31, p. 4 and 7-4-31, p. 4; Flom, "Orpheum Theatre," *historylink.org*.

Notes for pages 71–76

Box-office: "Film Firms Find Going Rough," *P-I*, 8-8-35, p. 14.

Cutbacks: "Opening of Paramount to Be Abandoned," *P-I*, 9-9-32, p. 13; "Fox West Coast and Unions in Agreement," *ST*, 10-6-32, p. 15; "Theatres Here Are Put under Receivership," *P-I*, 1-3-33, p. 8; McGrath, "Stage-Screen," *Argus*, 1-7-33, p. 6, and 3-4-33, p. 7.

Oeconomacos: "Oeconomacos Will Play in Street to Live," *ST*, 5-14-31, p. 1; "Oeconomacos Plays Today on City Streets," *P-I*, 5-21-31, p. 13; "Those in Street Listen Today as Maestro Plays," *ST*, 5-21-31, p. 3; McGrath, "The Musicians' Plight," *Argus*, 6-20-31, p. 1; McGrath, "Nicolas Oeconomacos Replies," *Argus*, 6-27-31, p. 4; "Oeconomacos Is Sued by Krueger on Unpaid Note," *ST*, 2-17-33, p. 5; "Wanted—a Beer Parlor for Oeconomacos' Dulcet Notes," *ST*, 8-15-33, p. 3; "12 Symphony Players Lose Out in Shakeup," *P-I*, 10-11-33, p. 10; "Concert May Redeem Home," *P-I*, 1-20-35, p. 16; Mildred Masterson, "It Will Be Home Sweet Home No Longer—Sheriff Sold It," *Star*, 1-21-35, p. 2; "Oeconomacos, Fine Musician, Finds He's Builder as Well," *ST*, 9-27-36, p. 10S; "Oeconomacos Bought Ticket to Maine, Rail Agent Discloses," *ST*, 3-27-44, p. 11; "Deaths," *ST*, 2-21-45, p. 12.

In Seattle Archives: Woodland Park Zoo, Box 8601–01; Gus Knudson, "History of Tusko," File, 15/3; Knudson to Board of Park Commissioners, 10-11-32, and 7-29-33; J. E. Stanley to Board of Park Commissioners, 10-3-32; B. B. Lustig to Dore, 1-12-33; contract with H. C. Barber and John Dore, 3-23-33, File 15/7; Allen Erickson to Seattle City Council, 4-5-40, "Tusko the Elephant, 1932–1933."

Fleet Week: "Is Tusko a Killer?" *Star*, 9-1-32, p. 1.

After Fleet Week: "Tusko Turning into White Elephant!" *P-I*, 9-8-32, p. 10; "Tusko Worry to His Owner," *Star*, 9-8-32, p. 5; "'Tusko Committee' Studies Problem of Huge Elephant," *ST*, 9-15-32, p. 3.

Seized: "Mayor Saves Life of Tusko," *ST*, 10-7-32, p. 8; "Tusko Rides to Woodland with Parade," *ST*, 10-8-32, p. 1; "Tusko Gets Favorable Hay but Faces Court Monday," *P-I*, 10-9-32, p. 3; "Thousands Visit Tusko at New Woodland Home," *P-I*, 10-10-32, p. 7.

Close zoo? "Park Board May Drop Zoo for Economy," *P-I*, 1-27-33, p. 10; "Mayor Backs Move to Drop Woodland Zoo," *P-I*, 1-28-33, p. 3; Welch, "Tusko-lot-omy," *ST*, 1-27-33, p. 13.

Jettison Tusko? "Tusko Must Go," *P-I*, 2-3-33, p. 12.

Death: "Tusko Dead Is Real Asset; Alive, Merely a Big Liability," *ST*, 6-11-33, p. 20.

After: "Tusko's Body, Etc., but His Old Claims Go Marching On," *ST*, 7-11-33, p. 5; "No Release in Death for Tusko; Body Will Be Stuffed," *P-I*, 6-11-33, p. 3; "Tusko in Death Gets No Rest from Lawsuits," *P-I*, 7-1-33, p. 3; "Tusko's Hide Being Tanned," *P-I*, 6-14-33, p. 3; "Tusko's Heart," *ST*, 8-29-33, p. 4.

Later: "Tusko's Still a Big Problem," *P-I*, 2-23-39, p. 22; "Tusko's Ghost Discovered in Cold Storage," *P-I*, 3-8-40, p. 1; Cooper, "The Elephant in the Room," pp. 34–38.

Arson: Hunt, "Widow, 64, Jailed; Burned Own Home to Help Sick Son," and Stuart, "Here's Woman's Own Story of Firing Home," *P-I*, 12-9-32, pp. 1, 2; "Dore to Aid Widow Who Fired House to Help Her Son," *ST*, 12-9-32, p. 1; "Dore's Appeal Frees Widow in Arson Case," *P-I*, 12-10-32, p. 3; "Widow Pleads Guilty of Arson," *P-I*, 1-19-33, p. 10.

Foreclosures: Niendorff, "Foreclosures Setting Low Record in County," *P-I*, 9-1-37, p. 18; "Foreclosures Speeded by Court Rule," *P-I*, 1-7-33, p. 9; "Mortgage Moratorium Bill Vetoed by Governor," *ST*, 3-22-33, p. 1; "Mortgage Holders Must Be Lenient, Warns Gov. Martin," *P-I*, 4-16-33, p. 1.

Frandsens: "Bannick, 9 Deputies Beaten as Jobless Rioters Resist Eviction of Needy Family," *P-I*, 4-27-33, p. 1; "Judge Warns Riot Jurors to Ignore Asserted Threats," *P-I*, 6-15-33, p. 1; "Bannick Tells Graphic Story of Riot Clash," *P-I*, 6-17-33, p. 11; "Home Payments Lapse Mentioned at Riot Hearing," *ST*, 6-30-33, p. 17; "Oratory Flood Loosed as Riot Case Nears End," *P-I*, 7-6-33, p. 13; "Crowds Parade as Eviction Fighters Face Biased Court," *Voice of Action*, 6-14-33, p. 1; "11 Men Convicted in Eviction Riot," *ST*, 7-10-33, p. 1; "11 Sentenced in Riot Case," *ST*, 7-18-33, p. 1; "Negro Revolt Owned as Aim by Communist," *P-I*, 5-3-34, p. 13; "Frandsen Order Signed," *P-I*, 3-24-35, p. 5.

Duwamish: "Forbes Orders Hobos to Evacuate Seattle Jungle," *Star*, 12-30-30, p. 2; "In the City of Waiting Men," *Star*, 2-20-31, p. 3; "Order 1,000 Out of Homes on Waterway," *Star*, 5-14-31, p. 1.

Hooverville: "Squatters Driven into Rain when Police Fire Shacks," *P-I*, 10-26-31, p. 1; Wolfe, "Jungle Housing," *American Architect*, 1–33, pp. 24–25; Gravelle, *Hooverville and the Unemployed*, pp. 40–64; Elinor, "Shackletown Preparing for Winter Rains," *P-I*, 9-23-32, p. 19; "Dehorn Drunks Are in a Bad Way," *Star*, 3-31-32, p. 5; Lee, "City of 'Forgotten Men' Now Occupies Shipyard Site," *Star*, 10-7-32, p. 4; Menefee, "Studies in Rugged Individualism," *The Unemployed Citizen*, 11-25-32, p. 3, and 1-20-33, p. 3.

The destitute: Robe, "7 Ways to Help Jobless Revealed by 'Mary Reeves,'" *P-I*, 1-24-32, p. 9; Heise, "Homeowners Warned to Beware of 'Professional Bums,'" *Star*, 4-15-32, p. 5.

Hooverville: Gravelle, *Hooverville and the Unemployed*, pp. 40–64; Elinor, "Shackletown Preparing for Winter Rains," *P-I*, 9-23-32, p. 19; "Dehorn Drunks Are in a Bad Way," *Star*, 3-31-32, p. 5; Lee, "City of 'Forgotten Men' Now Occupies Shipyard Site," *Star*, 10-7-32, p. 4; Menefee, "Studies in Rugged Individualism," *The Unemployed Citizen*, 11-25-32, p. 3, and 1-20-33, p. 3.

Spaulding: "Family Poor, But Wealth Cannot Buy Their Spirit," *ST*, 7-2-33, p. 16.

Moen: "Modern Crusoe Finds Peace in Home on Floating Island," *ST*, 2-25-34, p. 7.

On relief: "Relief Outlays Are About Same as Last Year," *ST*, 9-2-34, p. 4.

Dehorns: Jamison, "Waterfront Dehorn Pit Is Sargasso Sea of Misery," *Star*, 8-9-38, p. 4.

McIlroy: "Hillyer Named UW Daily Editor," *P-I*, 5-20-36. Her first byline in the *P-I* is "Camel's-Eye View," 7-15-36, p. 5.

Shacks: "Jungle Hit as Eyesore and Menace," *P-I*, 3-10-38, p. 4; "Heated Debate Marks Hearing on Shacktown," *P-I*, 11-30-38, p. 6; "Action Taken in Council on Shacktowns" and Olson, "Plea for Shacktowns," *P-I*, 12-1-38, pp. 1, 8; McIlroy, "Should Shacktowns Be Torn Down Here?" *P-I*, 12-2-38, p. 1; McIlroy, "People of Many Types Reside in Shacktown," *P-I*, 12-3-38, pp. 9, 20; McIlroy, "Shacktown Boom Arouses Citizens," *P-I*, 12-6-38, pp. 11, 22; McIlroy, "Shacktown Linked to City Housing Shortage," *P-I*, 12-16-38, p. 32; Gravelle, *Hooverville and the Unemployed*, pp. 209–220; "WPA Planning Elimination of Shacktowns," *P-I*, 4-10-38, p. 4; "Shacktown Becomes Just Pile of Ashes," *P-I*, 5-7-41, p. 3.

Frandsen: McIlroy, "Plans Offered to Solve Shack Problem Here," *P-I*, 12-9-38, pp. 1, 3; 1940 Census, 1950 Census.

SHA: "Housing Board Asks U.S. Funds," *P-I*, 3-21-39, p. 5; "U.S. May Come to Rescue of Shacktowns," *P-I*, 4-12-39, p. 13.

Yesler: "Families Will Be Selected," *P-I*, 7-16-41, p. 11; Markel, "Rent in Yesler Terrace to Be among Lowest," *P-I*, 7-22-41, p. 12; Markel, "Yesler Terrace Families Move In," *P-I*, 11-7-41, p. 13.

298 *Notes for pages 87–90*

Displacement: Griffey, "Race, Class and Conflict," p. 50; Asaka, *Seattle from the Margins*, pp. 160–166.

6. Relief, 1931–1935

Brannin, Wells and the UCL: Gravelle, *Hooverville and the Unemployed*, pp. 25–32, 36–39; "To All Our Readers," *Vanguard*, 1–1930; "Jobless Citizens Organize," *Vanguard*, 8–1931, p. 2; Mullins, *The Depression and the Urban West Coast, 1929–1933*, pp. 81, 110; "King County's Relief Problem Dates Back to Crisis Born in '31," *P-I*, 5-2-38, pp. 1, 8.

Dix: "Dix Wanders on Skid Road, Sees Jobless," *P-I*, 11-28-31, p. 13.

Public relief: Willis, Terry R., "Unemployed Citizens of Seattle," pp. 11, 57, 107–111, 124, 151, 196–204; "Right Now!" *ST*, 8-28-31, p. 3, and 11-10-31, p. 1; "City Jobless Aid Is Urged," *P-I*, 8-27-31, p. 3.

City response: "Bond Issue for Relief Sugar Coats Land 'Joker,'" *ST*, 9-13-31, pp. 1, 12; "$50,000 Will Be Assigned at Once for Relief Jobs," *ST*, 9-14-31, p. 7; "City Providing Jobs for Many," *P-I*, 10-18-31, p. 9.

Donations: "Tons of 'Spuds' to Feed Needy," *ST*, 12-10-31, p. 21.

Food Banks: Fussell, "City-Wide Relief Force Organized in District Plan," *P-I*, 10-30-31, p. 17.

Relief pay: "Jobs, Relief Scale Hit by Case, Levine," *P-I*, 10-6-31, p. 5; "More Fireworks Due Monday on Jobs Pay Scale," *ST*, 11-15-31, p. 10; "City Relief Fund Enough for Only Four Days Work," *ST*, 11-17-31, p. 3.

Funding: "Relief Funds Nearly Gone," *P-I*, 12-22-31, p. 3.

Tenino: Hill, "Numasmatists Put Tenino Wooden Money above Par," *P-I*, 3-2-32, p. 18; Pederson, "How Wooden Money Helped Make Tenino Famous," *Lewis County Chronicle*, 2-3-2007.

Engineers: "$20,000,000 Plan of Public Works Is Before Council," *ST*, 3-8-32, p. 3; "Bonds on Relief Work May Meet Legal Barriers," *ST*, 4-13-32, p. 7.

Tokens: "Seattle May Pay Track Workers in Car Tokens," *ST*, 10-16-32, p. 4; "City Hall," *Argus*, 10-29-32, p. 4; "Furse's Plan to Pay with Tokens Killed," *P-I*, 10-28-32, p. 5.

Transfers: Hunt, "Street Car Transfer 'Racket' Exposed Here," *P-I*, 8-5-38, p. 1.

Water Dept.: "Court Ruling Costs Jobs of 500 for City," *P-I*, 12-8-32, p. 1.

Dix: Dix, "Here's Digest of Essential Points in Dix Relief Plan," *P-I*, 4-26-32, p. 12; "Dore to Fire Relief Group," *Star*, 4-28-32, p. 2; "Shemanski Will Succeed Dix as Fund President," *ST*, 7-12-32, p. 20; Niendorff, "Pacific Phone Payroll Gains Over 13 Pct.," *P-I*, 4-8-37, p. 19.

Evans quote: "County Takes White Center Commissary," *P-I*, 9-17-32, p. 4.

Johnston: "County Shuts Three More Food Depots," *P-I*, 10-6-32, p. 15.

Resentment: "Unemployed Will Not Accept 'Garbage Dump' Standard," *Vanguard*, 3–32, p. 1; "Boos Resound as Speakers Address 5,000 'Jobless'," *P-I*, 3-30-32, p. 13.

King County relief: "County Fund Drained by Relief Costs," *P-I*, 3-22-32, p. 13; "$1,500,000 County Bond Bond Issue Asked," *P-I*, 4-21-32, p. 1; "Relief Measures Upheld in Supreme Court Decision," *P-I*, 7-1-32, p. 13.

Discount: "Bond Issues Supported by Muny League," *P-I*, 11-2-32, p. 13.

Hartley: "Hartley's Record," *Star*, 1-14-33, p. 2; Right Now!" *ST*, 7-11-32, p. 1; "Session Is Not Needed—Hartley," *P-I*, 7-12-32, p. 1.

The left: "Communist Disruptors Not Wanted," *Vanguard*, 1–32, p. 2; "Dole Offers Reds' Utopia Here," *ST*, 5-6-32, pp. 1, 8; "Seattle Must Stay United," *Star*, 5-7-32, p. 1; Swain, "Communists in Seattle and the Unemployed Citizens League," *Star*, 1-19-38, p. 9; "Communists, Jobless Fight," *Star*, 7-5-32, p. 1; "Hartley Not in Office When Jobless Call," *ST*, 7-5-32, p. 5; "UCL Leader Communist, He Tells Council," *P-I*, 3-28-35, p. 2; Constitution of the Unemployed Citizens League, Seattle Public Library.

Meat: "Settlement of Jobless Food Crisis Sought," *P-I*, 9-1-32, p. 13; "Jobless Win Two Demands on Food Issue," *P-I*, 9-2-32, p. 13; "Fancy Dole Meat Cuts Strike Snag," *ST*, 9-2-32, p. 1; "Politicians Trifle with Misery of Unemployed in Attack on UCL," *Vanguard*, 9-9-32, p. 1.

The county: "Commissary Defies County Control Plan," *P-I*, 9-8-32, p. 1; "County to Get RFC Funds" and "Jobless Rift Aids County in Food Control," *P-I*, 9-11-32, pp. 3, 13; "County Rejects UCL Plan to Run Food Depots," *ST*, 9-13-32, p. 2; "County Takes White Center Commissary," *P-I*, 9-17-32, p. 4.

Paying for it: Duerr, "Two County Bond Issues Vital to Relief, Says Grant," *P-I*, 10-31-32, p. 9; "City, County Bonds Carry," *P-I*, 11-9-32, p. 3; "County Welfare Work Ends Year $471,000 Behind," *ST*, 1-1-33, p. 12; "$3,000,000 in King Bonds Beg for Bids," *P-I*, 1-18-33, p. 11; "RFC Grants $800,000 Loan to King Co.," *ST*, 1-20-33, p. 2.

McDonald Act: Fussell, "Washington House Passes Bill for Jobless Relief," *P-I*, 1-20-33, p. 1; "Dictatorship Is Possible in New Relief Program," *ST*, 1-29-33, p. 8; "Relief Board Drops 1,000 Families Here," *P-I*, 4-12-33, p. 13; "State Action on Relief Crisis Taken in '33," *P-I*, 5-3-38, p. 4.

UCL: "Courthouse Campers Spurn Slave Program" and "Dore and Stevenson Evict Demonstrators," *Unemployed Citizen*, 2-17-33, p. 1; "4,000 Now Encamped in City Hall," *P-I*, 2-16-33, p. 11; "Police Roust 4,000 at City Hall," *P-I*, 2-17-33, p. 1; "Martin Baits Jobless and Flouts Demands," *Vanguard*, 3-3-33, p. 1; "The Truth About the March to Olympia," *A New Weekly Paper*, 3-25-33, p. 3; Gilbert, "Martin Assails Stevenson and WCF Tactics," *ST*, 8-12-36, p. 1; "Demonstrators Quit Olympia; Six Put in Jail," *ST*, 3-3-33, p. 2; "'Hunger Marchers' Leave Olympia in Trucks, Cars," *Star*, 3-3-33, p. 2.

After Olympia: Mullins, *The Depression and the Urban West Coast, 1929–1933*, pp. 107, 109; Willis, Terry R., "Unemployed Citizens of Seattle, 1900–1933," p. 274; "Communists Get Jobless Here to Join," *P-I*, 4-27-34, p. 15.

Cafeteria food: Stevenson, "Meals for Unemployed," *ST*, 6-3-33, p. 6; "Stevenson and Brinton Booed over Free Food," *ST*, 11-13-33, p. 2; "Nash Demands Food Probe; Commissioner Squelches It," *Star*, 2-19-34; "County Heads Fail to Act on Report of Indigents' Food," *P-I*, 3-27-34, p. 9.

CWA: "Relief Board Asked to Pay 'Living Wage,'" *P-I*, 8-8-33, p. 12; "Jobless Grow 100 Tons Food," *P-I*, 9-7-33, p. 12; "45-Cent Basis Set on County Relief Work," *P-I*, 3-29-33, p. 2; "Relief Administrator to End 'Forced Labor' for Jobless," *P-I*, 11-15-33, p. 3; "County Prepares to Give Jobs in Federal Program," *ST*, 11-17-33, p. 36; "No Work, No Aid, Will Be Relief Policy," *P-I*, 11-2-34, p. 1; see also Mullins, *The Depression and the Urban West Coast*, pp. 120–135.

Relief: "President Roosevelt Outlines New 'New Deal' to Seventy-Fourth Congress," *P-I*, 1-5-35, p. 8; "Relief Rolls Increase," *P-I*, 3-30-35, p. 4; "Pauper Oath Relief Rule Is Strongly Protested," *Commonwealth Builder*, 6-21-35, p. 1.

Chiselers: "County Wins Decision in Relief Case," *P-I*, 4-27-35, p. 2; "Dole Woman Surrenders Hidden $3,500," *P-I*, 4-5-35, p. 1; "Magnuson Hunts 'Leeches' on Dole," *ST*, 4-5-35, p. 2; "Woman

Gets 15 Years for Relief Fraud," *P-I*, 7-14-35, p. 3; Washington State Penitentiary Commitment Record No. 16335.

Resettlement: "The Land Provides an Economic Safety Valve," *P-I*, 5-25-32, p. 20; "Land Settlement Best Relief," *ST*, 2-5-33, p. 6; Marshall, "Back to Land Success Depends on Hard Labor," *Star*, 3-30-33, p. 1; "Commonwealth Set on Olympia Fight on Security Bill," *Commonwealth Builder*, 12-22-34, p. 1.

More farms: "Gain in State Agriculture," *P-I*, 10-11-35, p. 3.

Newhaven: classified ad, *ST*, 3-31-34, p. 11; Fitchett, "4020 Acres Bought by Colonizing Group," *P-I*, 5-21-35, p. 13; "Colonists to Sue for Work Pay," *ST*, 12-5-35, p. 8; "Zwarg to Ask for New Trial," *ST*, 6-5-36, p. 2; "20-Month Term for Mail Fraud," *ST*, 6-13-36, p. 1.

Lake Forest Park: Squire, "Offer to Return WERA Families to City Meets with Resistance," *Star*, 5-17-35, p. 5.

Urban people: "Jobs Spurned; Men on Relief Will Not Work," *P-I*, 8-11-35, p. 7.

Matanuska: Calkins, "4 Ships to Carry Settlers North," *ST*, 4-1-35, p. 22; "Matanuskan Madness," *Voice of Action*, 6-28-35, p. 4; "Matanuska OK If Men Forget Gold, Says Doctor," *ST*, 8-22-35, p. 8.

7. Hope, 1932–1936

Times turns wet: "No Longer to Be Tolerated," *ST*, 6-12-32, p. 6.

Times endorses: "Roosevelt Means Prosperity!" *ST*, 7-3-32, p. 1; "State and Local Issues of Vital Importance," *ST*, 11-6-32, p. 1.

P-I endorses: Hearst, "Roosevelt Will Make Great President, Garner Splendid Aid, Says W.R. Hearst," *P-I*, 7-3-32, pp. 1, 2; "Bone's Enlightened Liberalism Needed in National Affairs," *P-I*, 10-16-32, p. 1.

Star's stand: "Shall They Rule?" *Star*, 1-2-32, p. 1; "A Land of People, Not Dollars," *Star*, 5-24-32, p. 4; "Hoover Proves Nation Needs Roosevelt," *Star*, 10-5-32, p. 1; "Elect Martin," *Star*, 11-3-32, p. 1; "Why Jones Should Be Defeated," *Star*, 11-4-32, p. 1; "Which—Miller or Zioncheck?" *Star*, 11-5-32, p. 2.

Not a radical: Jermane, "Middle of Road Is Route Selected for Roosevelt," *ST*, 8-14-32, p. 1; Forbes, "Financial Leaders Pull in Horns," *P-I*, 10-6-32, p. 16.

Dore: "Hoover Failure to End Distress Scored by Dore," *ST*, 7-16-32, p. 3.

Bone: Macgowan, "Bone—Modern Robin Hood," *Star*, 8-25-32, p. 1; "Bone Is the Man," *Star*, 9-6-32, p. 1; Blethen, "Hard on the Stomach," *ST*, 9-23-32, p. 1; "Right Now!" *ST*, 9-26-32, p. 1; "The Agile Bone," *ST*, 9-29-32, p. 1; Bone, "Man of Many Parties Does About Face," *ST*, 10-3-32, p. 1; "Bone's Enlightened Liberalism Needed in National Affairs," *P-I*, 10-16-32, p. 1.

Zioncheck: "'I'm a Radical,' Says Zioncheck during Speech," *ST*, 10-12-32, p. 8; "Which—Miller or Zioncheck?" *Star*, 11-5-32, p. 2.

Legislature: "A New Experience," *ST*, 11-16-32, p. 6; Brown, "Under the Capitol Dome," *Argus*, 1-21-33, p. 10.

Meyers: "Vic in Perfect Harmony," *ST*, 1-25-32, p. 1; Welch, "Onion Sandwiches and Ghost Writers," *ST*, 2-24-32, p. 1; Welch, "There'll Be No Gags when Vic Rules Senate," *ST*, 11-9-32, p. 1; Squire, "Vic Meyers the Best Gavel Pounder in State," *Star*, 1-11-37, p. 9; "The Stroller," *Argus*, 12-11-37, p. 2.

Bank crisis: *Comptroller's Reports*, 1933 and 1934; Division of Banking Liquidation Record, *Bank Histories 1907–1937*, V4-E-13-1, Box 5, State Archives, Olympia; "Seven Far Western States Act to Aid Depositors in Hundreds of Banks," *P-I*, 3-3-33, p. 4.

FDR: "Text of Speech by President Explaining Finance Situation," *P-I*, 3-13-33, p. 2; "Man to Man," *ST*, 3-13-33, p. 1.

Currency: "Seattle Firms Supply Cash to Their Employees," *ST*, 3-7-33, p. 5; "It's Pay Day at City Hall," *ST*, 3-10-33, p. 3.

Scrip: "A Statement to the Public," *ST*, 3-7-33, p. 2; "$15,000,000 Burns," *ST*, 4-19-35, p. 4.

Banks reopen: "Deposits Swamp Seattle Banks," *ST*, 3-14-33, p. 1; "$20,000,000 Deposited in One Day as Banks Reopen," *P-I*, 3-15-33, p. 1; "State Banks of Washington Show Gain in Deposits," *P-I*, 12-1-33, p. 16; "Full Text of Governor Martin's Talk," *ST*, 12-5-33, p. 11.

FDIC: "U Professor Hits Deposit Surety Plan," *P-I*, 1-6-34, p. 10; White, "State-Sponsored Insurance of Bank Deposits in the United States, 1907–1929," *Journal of Economic History*, Vol. XLI, No. 3, pp. 9–81; Hill, "Deposit Insurance Guaranteed 100 Per Cent to Banks in State," *P-I*, 1-5-34, p. 16.

Centralized power: "Right Now!" *ST*, 3-10-33, p. 1; Brisbane, "Today," *P-I*, 3-22-33, p. 1; "What We Gave and What We Got," *Star*, 5-4-33, p. 14; "The New Master Mechanic," *ST*, 6-4-33, p. 6.

Relief bonds: "Magnuson Named to Test Legality of Relief Measure," *P-I*, 3-16-33, p. 9; "Big Relief Bond Issue Attacked by E.F. Blaine," *ST*, 5-3-33, p. 2; "Relief Bond Issue Legal, Court Rules," *P-I*, 6-6-33, p. 13; Hill, "State Sells $1,000,000 4½ Per Cent Bonds to Local Syndicate," *P-I*, 9-19-33, p. 14; "State Buys Own Relief Bonds," *P-I*, 11-30-33, p. 26.

County bonds: "$1,000,000 Bonds Attract No Bids," *ST*, 9-6-33, p. 2; "Discounting Warrants Assailed by Nash," *P-I*, 10-14-33, p. 9; "Relief Money Transfer Hit by Burgunder," *P-I*, 12-20-33, p. 11.

Gold standard: "Depreciated Currencies," *ST*, 1-9-33, p. 1; Niendorff, "Pulp Comes Back," *P-I*, 1-29-35, p. 16; "Foreign Exports of Washington Show Increase," *ST*, 1-28-33, p. 8; Forbes, "U.S. Deflation Suddenly Ends," *P-I*, 4-25-33, p. 13; Hill, "George H. Greenwood Sees Advantage in Guarded Exercise of Inflation Plan," *P-I*, 4-23-33, p. 18.

Mini-boom: Forbes, "Wave of Buying Sweeps over Entire Country," *P-I*, 5-17-33, p. 15; Anderson, *Economics and the Public Welfare*, pp. 331–337.

Ships: "Fifteenth Ship Quits Lake to Enter Service," *P-I*, 6-6-33, p. 13; "Seattle Stages Speedy Recovery in Ocean Trade," *ST*, 1-28-34, p. 26.

Initiative 61: "State Bone Dry Repeal Rouses Bitter Fight," *P-I*, 10-3-32, p. 6; "11 Counties Vote Bone Dry," *P-I*, 12-15-32, p. 12.

Beer: Ferriss, "Brewing Beer—Within the Law," *ST*, 8-10-30, Sunday supp., p. 9; Hill, "American Brewers Favor Light Beer, Says Peter Schmidt," *P-I*, 7-9-33, p. 20; "Beer Supply Fails," *ST*, 4-7-33, p. 1; "6 Cars of Beer Arrive, But Fails to Meet Demands," *P-I*, 4-10-33, p. 1; "1,305 Cases of Eastern Beer Arrive in City," *ST*, 4-13-33, p. 4.

Rippe's bail: "Hi Pierce Is Back in Jail," *Star*, 12-8-33, p. 1.

Beer revenue: "Two A-1 Inspectors Wanted to Look After City Beer," *ST*, 4-28-33, p. 12; "Beer Licenses Help Fill Coffers of City," *ST*, 5-2-33, p. 3.

Beer investments: Hill, "Olympia Brewing Co. Preferred Stock Is Offered," *P-I*, 4-28-33, p. 13; Ramsey, "The Mayflower Lands on Shores of Uncertainty," *ST*, 5-28-2008, p. B8.

No regulation: Norman Clark, *The Dry Years*, University of Washington, 1988, p. 241.

Steele Act: "Right Now!" *ST*, 1-14-34, p. 1; "Steele Bill Highlights," *Star*, 1-13-34, p. 1; "Here Are Provisions of State Liquor Law," *P-I*, 1-24-34, pp. 1, 8.

Clubs: "The Stroller," *Argus*, 3-18-39, p. 2.

Women: "Tacoma Woman Files Suit in Bid to Win Right to Sit at Bar Stool," *ST*, 11-13-68, p. 39; Robinson, "The Last Male Refuge," *ST*, 11-22-68, p. 13.

Pavilion: "U Student Hits Meisnest's 'Dollar Chasing,'" *ST*, 1-29-28, p. 14; "Students Sift Pavilion Cost," *ST*, 1-31-28, pp. 1, 5; "Cash Spent Lavishly on Pavilion Except Roof," *ST*, 2-1-28, p. 1; "Pavilion OK Hotly Flayed," *ST*, 2-2-28, pp. 1, 2.

Dunked: "Zioncheck Is Given Ride and Dives," *P-I*, 2-3-28, p. 1; "U Student, from Sickbed, Tells of His Tortures," *ST*, 2-3-28, p. 1; Niendorff, "Student Hazers' Names Given Spencer," *P-I*, 2-4-28, p. 1; "Students Confess Attack on Zioncheck, Beg for Leniency," *ST*, 2-4-28, p. 1; "Spencer Orders Pavilion Audit, Punishes Student Night Riders," *ST*, 2-7-28, p. 1; Forder, "Friend of Zioncheck Gives Close-Up View," *Star*, 8-8-36, pp. 1, 2.

Zioncheck quotes: *CR*, 5-23-33, pp. 4040–4041.

1934 pamphlet: Box 1, Acc. #3169–001, *Zioncheck Papers*.

Social Security: *CR*, 4-17-35, p. 5910.

Banks: *CR*, 5-23-33, p. 4041.

Munitions industry: *CR*, 4-17-33, p. 1851.

"Willing to go as far": typescript, *Hulet Wells Papers*, Box 1, Folder 12, p. 354.

Marcantonio letter and program: Folder 3/9, *Zioncheck Papers*.

"Eligible bachelor": *Hulet Wells Papers*, Box 1, Folder 12, p. 356.

New Year's arrest: "450,000 Drunks, I Was Only One in Jail, Says Zioncheck," *ST*, 1-15-36, p. 1; *CR*, 1-8-36, p. 155; Hunt, "Stevenson and Zioncheck Split," *P-I*, 1-19-36, p. 3.

"Amazing change": typescript, Hulet Wells Papers, Box 1, Folder 12, p. 357.

Farley: *CR*, 2-7-36, p. 1682.

Hoover: *CR*, 2-10-36, p. 1731.

Blanton: "Congressman Swings Fist at Zioncheck," *P-I*, 4-15-36, p. 3.

Omenitsch: *CR*, 4-22-36, pp. 5890–5891.

Wedding: "Zioncheck Weds after Week's Courtship," *NYT*, 4-29-36, p. 1.

Honeymoon: "Zioncheck Is in Crash, Then Smashes Gate in a Borrowed Automobile," *NYT*, 5-13-36, p. 19; "To Clean Up Island," *NYT*, 5-14-36, p. 12; "Zioncheck Laps Soup, Finds Himself in It," *NYT*, 5-19-36, p. 25; "Zioncheck on Dare Wades in Fountain," *NYT*, 5-27-36, p. 25.

In DC: "Zioncheck Hunts for Wife in Vain," *NYT*, 6-1-36, p. 22.

Mental ward: "Zioncheck Is Held for a Sanity Test," *NYT*, 6-2-36, p. 6; "Court Orders Zioncheck to Lunacy Hearing," *NYT*, 6-20-36, p. 1; "Zioncheck Scales Fence at Hospital, Flees into Woods," *NYT*, 6-29-36, p. 1.

To Seattle: "Zioncheck Travel by Plane Is Balked," *NYT*, 7-1-36, p. 28; "Zioncheck at Home Says 'Show's Over,'" *NYT*, 7-4-36, p. 16; "Zioncheck Calls Self Exhibit No. 1," *NYT*, 7-14-36, p. 28.

Death: "Zioncheck Commits Suicide!" *P-I*, 8-8-36, pp. 1, 3; "Zioncheck's Suicide Held Due to Fear of Sanitarium," *ST*, 8-8-36, p. 1; "Colorful Rites for Zioncheck, 'Friend of Poor,'" *ST*, 8-11-36, pp. 1, 2; Neuberger, "Zioncheck: An American Tragedy," *The Nation*, 8-22-36, p. 207.

8. The Blue Eagle, 1933–1935

NRA: Lippmann, "America as I See It," *Star*, 12-8-34, p. 7; "Here Is Text of President's Appeal," *P-I*, 7-25-33, p. 1; "Guild Idea Revived," *ST*, 6-16-33, p. 6; "A Nation at War," *ST*, 8-1-33, p. 6; "Time Has Come to Muzzle Barking Obstructionists," *ST*, 8-24-33, p. 1; "Vote Must Map America," *ST*, 8-26-34, p. 6; Mussolini, "Roosevelt's Theory of Intervention by State Resembles Fascism—Il Duce," *P-I*, 7-2-33, p. 2M.

In Seattle: "'Onward to Better Days' Is Cry at NRA Rally," *ST*, 9-2-33, p. 1; Welch, "Parade, Program Launch Big Prosperity Drive," *P-I*, 9-2-33, p. 1; "Seattle's NRA Canvass Gets Started Today," *P-I*, 8-21-33, p. 2; "City Victorious in NRA Canvass," *ST*, 9-3-33, p. 1.

Nira: "Seattle Baby Named Nira when Father Gets 6-Hour Day," *Star*, 8-19-33, p. 1.

Henry Ford: Brisbane, "Today," *P-I*, 9-2-33, p. 1; Charles E. Sorensen, *My Forty Years with Ford*, Wayne State University Press, 2006, pp. 258–259.

McKay: "Former P-I Carrier Grows to be Leader," *P-I*, 9-1-35, p. 6; "William O. M'Kay Is General of Seattle's NRA," *ST*, 8-2-33, p. 5; Chevrolet ad, *Star*, 9-7-33, p. 5; McKay ad, *Star*, 9-27-33, p. 14; "William O. McKay Signs Up with Ford," *P-I*, 8-24-34, p. 12.

Milk: "Milk Prices Up a Cent in Seattle" and ad by Seattle Milk Shippers Association, *ST*, 2-16-33, pp. 1, 17; "Outside Dairy to Cut School Milk Bid If Seattle Firms Refuse," *P-I*, 8-25-33, p. 3; "School Board OK's Cut Rate Bid For Milk," *P-I*, 9-2-33, p. 3; "Qualitee Dairy Loses Schools to Kristofferson," *ST*, 9-4-33, p. 2.

NRA: "Price Fixing Must Fail," *Star*, 5-1-34, p. 6.

Lumber: "Right Now!" *ST*, 8-22-33, p. 1; "Right Now!" *ST*, 9-1-33, p. 1; "Right Now!" *ST*, 11-1-33, p. 1; "Lumber Firm Fights NRA in Federal Court," *P-I*, 12-20-33, p. 2; "Lumber Industry Aided by NRA Says Greeley," *ST*, 12-28-33, p. 5; "Right Now!" *ST*, 11-26-33, p. 1; "Judge Praises NRA Mill Quota," *P-I*, 12-21-33, p. 2; *Willamette Valley Lumber Co. v. Watzek*, 5 F. Supp. 689 (1934).

Permanent NRA? Jermane, "Permanence of New Deal to Be Issue," *ST*, 1-14-34, pp. 1, 10; "NRA Is Here to Stay, Asserts B.B. Ehrlichman," *ST*, 11-14-33, p. 7.

Maged: "Tailor, Imprisoned under Recovery Act, Released," *P-I*, 4-24-34, p. 3.

Crane: "Independents in Dyers' War Balk at Dictatorship," *ST*, 2-6-32, p. 4; "Burgunder Says Dyeing 'Czar' Illegal," *P-I*, 2-6-32, p. 1; "Seattle Clothes Cleaner Faces Code Charges," *ST*, 2-17-34, p. 3; "State Cleaning Code Fair Price Cutter Is Fined," *ST*, 3-27-34, p. 2.

Chiseling: Marshall, "Seattle a la Carte," *Star*, 5-17-34, p. 4.

Robinson: Brown, "Under the Capitol Dome," *Argus*, 1-10-34, p. 6; Voorhees, "Washington's Dictator Is Busy Regimenting All Food Supplies," *Star*, 5-11-34, p. 1; "Codes," *Argus*, 4-13-35, p. 4.

Ice cream: "City's Ice Cream Dealers Defy Price Fixing Order," *Star*, 5-30-34, p. 3; "Violation of Milk Code Laid to Man," *P-I*, 6-1-34, p. 15; "Burgunder Holds State Price-Fixing on Food Illegal," *P-I*, 6-7-34, p. 1.

Bread: "Bakers Split over Fixing of Bread Prices," *P-I*, 3-27-34, p. 1; "Court Forbids Price Cuts on Bread and Milk," *P-I*, 6-3-34, p. 1; "Schools Defy State's Ruling on Bread Price," *P-I*, 6-2-34, p. 1; "State Drops Bread Price Cutting Case," *P-I*, 6-19-34, p. 18; "Schools Buy 5-Cent Bread; State Price Code Ignored," *P-I*, 6-23-34, p. 6; "School Board Sues to Avert Price-Fixing," *ST*, 7-1-34, p. 2; "Bread Price in Schools for Relief to Be Cut," *ST*, 7-3-34, p. 1.

Milk: "Milk Groups to Unite under New State Law," *P-I*, 1-16-34, p. 15; "Code Prices on School Milk Are Again Rejected," *ST*, 7-28-34, p. 7; "Battle Opens as School Milk Bids Received," *P-I*, 8-9-34, p. 11; "Edict on Milk Price Halted by Injunction," *P-I*, 8-17-34, p. 1; "Robinson Can't Interfere with School Milk," *ST*, 8-25-34, p. 7; "State AAA Forces Up School Milk Prices," *Star*, 9-13-34, p. 1; "Seattle Milk Price Up 1 Cent," *ST*, 9-19-34, p. 1; Gilbert, "Dairymen Denounce State AAA," *ST*, 12-23-34, p. 1; "All Seattle Milk Prices Slashed," *P-I*, 4-2-35, p. 1; "Court Halts Milk Cut," *P-I*, 4-4-35, p. 2; "Milkmen Dodge Process Servers," *ST*, 4-5-35, p. 1; "Milk Now Dime," *ST*, 4-9-35, p. 3; *Griffiths v. Robinson*, 181 Wash. 438; "State 1933 AAA Act Held Invalid," *ST*, 4-11-35, p. 1; "School Milk Bid Let Despite AAA," *ST*, 4-13-35, p. 3; "Kristoferson to Test State Milk Price-Fixing Act," *P-I*, 4-30-35, p. 1; "Superior Court Holds State Industrial Recovery Act Unconstitutional," *P-I*, 5-18-35, p. 2.

Comments on NRA: "State NRA Bill," *P-I*, 3-8-35, p. 26; "The One Safe Course," *ST*, 3-12-35, p. 6; "Fascist Schemes Foster Monopoly," *Star*, 4-29-35, p. 1; "Liberty or a License," *Star*, 5-22-35, p. 4; Lippmann, "New Dealers Nearly Upset Whole Show in July 1933," *Star*, 6-3-35, p. 5.

End of AAA, NRA: *State v. Matson Co.*, 182 Wn. 507; "Milk Price Cut One Cent Retail," *ST*, 7-2-35, p. 2.

Telephones: Niendorff, "Phone Installations Mark Recovery Trend," *P-I*, 12-3-37, p. 20.

Vacancies: Niendorff, "Office Building Rentals Firming," *P-I*, 2-5-37, p. 24.

Building permits: "Year's Building Permits Decline," *Journal of Commerce*, 1-2-35, p. 1.

"Accustomed to it": "A New Year and a New Hope," *ST*, 12-30-34, p. 6.

Marriages: "4,788 Sets County Wedding Mark," *P-I*, 1-1-36, p. 1; "Marriage Rate Climb Implies Home Building," *P-I*, 5-23-35, p. 7.

Apartments: Niendorff, "Apartment House Occupancy Tempts Investors," *P-I*, 1-17-35, p. 16; Margeson, "Apartments to Boost Rentals," *ST*, 8-1-35, p. 19; Gordon, "Rental Situation Analyzed Here," *ST*, 11-8-37, p. 17; "Report of Department of Buildings 1936–1937," City of Seattle, 5-17-38.

Office: Niendorff "Real Estate Values in Seattle Reverse; Trend Now Upward," *P-I*, 1-26-35, p. 14.

Teardowns: Fitchett, "Realtors Face New Problem," *P-I*, 7-22-35, p. 6.

Exchange Building: Niendorff, "Exchange Bldg. Plan," *P-I*, 6-26-35, p. 18; Niendorff, "Exchange Building Bondholders in Agreement," *P-I*, 10-29-35, p. 18.

Bartell: Fitchett, "New Building Will Rise at 4th and Pine," *P-I*, 7-2-35, p. 5.

Housing: Painter, "Realty Boom Seen," *ST*, 11-15-36, p. 10-S; Fitchett, "Real Estate Bargains and Easy Terms Make Home Owning Attractive," *P-I*, 5-8-35, p. 15; "Judge Assails HOLC," *ST*, 1-20-38, p. 1; Niendorff "Washington Sets High Standards in HOLC Payments," *P-I*, 6-20-39, p. 19; "Local Region Wins High Score for HOLC Loan Repayments," *ST*, 7-25-39, p. 20.

Steinbrueck: "Young Seattle Architect Is Winner in Home Contest Here," *Star*, 9-16-35, p. 3.

Finance: Niendorff, "Seattle Stock 'Change Opens," *P-I*, 9-29-35, p. 22; Niendorff, "United National to Pay Dividend," *P-I*, 7-14-35, p. 21; "NW Security Prices Climb," *P-I*, 1-6-36, p. F9; Margeson, "Local Real Estate Bond Issues Shown Making Strong Gains," *ST*, 12-15-35, p. 35.

Theatres: Hays, "Two Features on Every Program," *ST*, 12-22-35, p. 1.

New Deal: Rukeyser, "Laws Restrictive, Enterprises Deterred," *P-I*, 8-8-36, p. 15; Forbes, "British Prosperity," *P-I*, 4-16-36, p. 19; "Bankers Hopeful," *P-I*, 1-6-36, p. F9.

Tax, dividends: "Sloan Assails Roosevelt View," *P-I*, 5-20-36, p. 3; Anderson, *Economics and the Public Welfare*, pp. 372–382; Niendorff, "Puget Power Will Resume Cash Dividend," *P-I*, 5-29-36, p. 1.

9. The Left Rises, 1932–1935

Armstrong: "'Five-Year Plan' Reveals Russia," *P-I*, 1-2-32, p. 7.

Rosen: "No Butter, So He Loses Wife," *P-I*, 1-18-32, p. 3; "Divorces Granted," *ST*, 8-23-32, p. 19.

Wesa: "Finns to Leave U.S. for Soviet," *P-I*, 3-5-32, p. 3; Masterson, "Father Would Force Girl to Go with Him to Russia," *Star*, 1-22-33, p. 1; Masterson, "Wesa Says He Will Fulfill Promise to His Dying Wife," *Star*, 1-27-33, p. 1; "Russia Not So Promising; Girl to Remain Here," *ST*, 2-18-33, p. 2.

Diplomacy: "Late Czar's Consul Lives in Hope Here," *P-I*, 10-22-33, p. 3; Martenson, "Czar's Agent Quits His Post," *Star*, 11-20-33, p. 1.

Trade: "Seattle Given First Glimpse of Soviet Flag," *P-I*, 1-8-34, p. 5; "U.S. Rescinds Restrictions on Russian Lumber," *ST*, 1-24-34, p. 5; "Right Now!" *ST*, 1-26-34, p. 1.

Asylees: "Russ Roiled by Scientists' 'Revolt' Here," *P-I*, 1-25-34, p. 3; Nolde, "Russ Scientist Describes Flight, Says Death Waits," *P-I*, 1-31-34, p. 11; "Russ Scientists Stay Extended," *ST*, 6-30-34, p. 4.

The idea: Harrison, "Technocracy Promises Jobs and Leisure in Nation Run by Science," *Star*, 12-23-32, p. 1, and follow-on stories 12–24, -26, -28 and -29; "Technocracy: Old Idea, New Name, Say Critics," *ST*, 12-23-32, p. 1; "Want $20,000 a Year? Try out Technocracy," *P-I*, 12-16-32, p. 12.

The movement: Acena, *The Washington Commonwealth Federation*, p. 16.

Shorter: Acena, *The Washington Commonwealth Federation*, p. 16; "The Stroller," *Argus*, 2-10-34, p. 2; "'Radical' Murals Split Seattle Church," *Star*, 4-7-34, p. 1; "Church Members Here Split on Murals in Edifice," *P-I*, 4-8-34, p. 1; "Church Loses Donations in Mural Dispute," *P-I*, 4-9-34, p. 1; "'Red' Foes Ruin 2 Unfinished Church Murals," *P-I*, 4-10-34, p. 11; Hopper and Gipson, "A Frontier of the Spirit," box 1, file 1, *Church of the People Papers*; Acena, *The Washington Commonwealth Federation*, p. 3.

Army Day: "Army Day Event Concludes with Parade Meeting," *ST*, 4-7-34, p. 1; Tjaden, "Woman Tells How Army Day Riot Was Started in Hall," *Star*, 4-12-34, p. 1; "Pastors Offer Radicals Bail," *ST*, 4-11-34, p. 1.

Church of the People: "Ousted Pastor Will Hold Independent Service in Theatre," *P-I*, 4-21-34, p. 3; Shorter, "The Pattern of a Modern Church," 1944 pamphlet, *Church of the People Records*.

Russia: "Rev. Shorter Leaves Sunday on Russ Visit," *ST*, 4-3-37, p. 3; *Church of the People Records*, Box 3, File 8; "Shorter to Lecture," *P-I*, 7-12-37, p. 3; "Shorter Returns from USSR; Says Execution of Spies Was Justified," *Sunday News*, 7-3-37, p. 1.

Sinclair: Hachten, "Primary Result Proves Shock to Democratic Chiefs," *P-I*, 8-30-34, p. 1; "California Churches Scored as Tool of Political Parties," *ST*, 11-19-34, p. 1; Pegler, "Merriam Is Sad Alternative for California, Says Pegler," *Star*, 10-30-34, p. 5.

Commonwealthers: Fussell, "State Democratic Candidates Veer to Left after Sinclair Victory," *P-I*, 9-2-34, p. 1; Berner, *Seattle 1921–1940*, pp. 328–329, 371–372; "Statewide EPIC Program Launched" and "Here's Commonwealth Plan for Legislative Action Putting End to Poverty," *Commonwealth Builder*, 8-23-34, p. 1, and endorsement list, 9-8-34, p. 3; "Schwellenbach Urges Plan Like Sinclair's EPIC," *ST*, 11-2-34, p. 22; Acena, *The Washington Commonwealth Federation*, pp. 34–51.

Costigan: Acena, *The Washington Commonwealth Federation*, pp. 39–40.

Schwellenbach: Wood, "Speaking for the Times," *ST*, 1-22-39, p. 6.

Left caucus: Gilbert, "Left Wing Out of Legislature," *ST*, 11-10-40, p. 1.

1935 Legislature: "Governor Martin's Speech," *Star*, 5-2-35, p. 4; Hunt, "Right Wingers Form Block," *P-I*, 1-14-35, p. 1; "Important Bills Introduced Show Liberal Trends," *Commonwealth Builder*, 1-26-35, p. 1; "Milk Business Bill Is Studied," *Star*, 2-13-35, p. 4; Hunt, "Senate Kills Bill for State Gasoline Sale," *P-I*, 2-28-35, p. 1; "Commonwealth Set on Olympia Fight on Security Bill," *Commonwealth Builder*, 12-22-34, p. 1; "Here's What Legislature Did, Did Not, Accomplish," *ST*, 3-20-35, p. 10.

Farquharson: Berner, *Seattle 1921–1940*, p. 372; and "Brief Sketches Introduce Members of Legislature," *ST*, 3-3-35, p. 30.

State AAA: "State," *Argus*, 7-27-35, p. 3.

Pension: "House Approves Old-Age Pension," ST, 3-7-35, p. 1; "Governor Signs Old-Age Pension," *ST*, 3-24-35, p. 8; "Old-Age Pension Announced for First of May," *ST*, 3-6-36, p. 21; "32,839 in State Given Pensions," *ST*, 7-9-37, p. 2.

State finances: "No More Bonds, Says Martin," *P-I*, 10-7-34, p. 14; "Tax Provisions of Revenue Bill," *P-I*, 3-20-35, p. 1; "Sales Tax Has Balanced State's Budget, Governor Martin Says," *Star*, 2-26-36, p. 3; "A Frank Statement on Behalf of Your Retail Tobacconist Concerning the Price of Cigarettes," *ST*, 6-7-39, p. 2; Department of Revenue, "Washington's Tax History," pp. 17–18.

Chain letters: Emahiser, "Need Tax Token or Car? Maybe Chain Letter Will Aid You," *Star*, 5-3-35, p. 1; "Chains and Chains and More Chains," *ST*, 5-12-35, p. 2; "Chain Letter Riches May Be Myth, but Rumors, Oh, My!" *ST*, 5-13-35, p. 1; Moore letter, *ST*, 5-9-35, p. 6; "Chain Letter Motives," *ST*, 5-13-35, p. 2.

Long: "Huey Long and Ted Husing on Radio Program," *ST*, 1-19-35, p. 3; "Money for All, Huey's Plan as He Deserts F.R.," *Star*, 1-10-35, p. 1; "Huey Long Hits at Millionaires," *Star*, 2-7-35, p. 2; "The Tragedy of Louisiana," *Star*, 1-30-35, p. 6; "Kingfish's Seattle Organizer Wonders about Club's Future," *Star*, 9-12-35, p. 2; White, *Kingfish*, pp. 90–91, 196–198, 212–216, 245.

Townsend: "Dr. Townsend Upholds Age Plan in Quiz," *ST*, 2-17-35, p. 8; Gallup, "U.S. For Pensions but Against Townsend Plan," *Star*, 1-13-36, pp. 1, 7; Fullerton letter, *ST*, 1-6-35, p. 6; Siegel letter, *ST*, 1-22-35, p. 6.

Alberta: O'Leary, "Alberta Faces Dire Crisis" and "Social Security Bubble Bursts," *P-I*, 3–7 and 3-9-36, pp. 2, 4.

Wakefield: "U of W Debate Team Wins against Idaho," *ST*, 3-29-28, p. 13; Dennett, *Agitprop*, pp. 25, 39, 47.

Moe: *State v. Moe* (1933); "Four Anacortes Food Rioters to Serve Sentences," *ST*, 10-23-32, p. 3; "High Court OK's Convictions in Anacortes Riot," *ST*, 8-31-33; "The Anacortes Trial at Mount Vernon," Box 1, File 11, *Dennett Papers*.

Weyerhaeuser: "1 vs. 100,000," *Voice of Action*, 6-7-35, p. 4.

Raport: Immigrated 1902. See Ancestry.com.

Not allowed: "UW Bans Reds after Veterans File Protest," *ST*, 3-9-34, p. 13; "Two Men Jailed for Circulating Red Bills at School," *ST*, 11-11-35, p. 11; "Legion Bares Red Support of Youth Meet," *P-I*, 11-16-35, p. 2.

In West Seattle: Tate, "God Dies: An Essay by Frances Farmer," HistoryLink.org essay 4008.

To Russia: "Coed Going to Russia Despite Mother's Fight," *ST*, 3-28-35, p. 1; "Frances Farmer Wins Trip to Russia," *Voice of Action*, 3-29-35, p. 4; Farmer, "Why I Am Going to Russia," *ST*, 3-29-35, p. 2; "Warning against Red Teachers," *P-I*, 3-29-35, p. 1.

Her politics: "Frances Farmer, Career Launched by NW Progressives, Favors Union," *Commonwealth News*, 11-15-36, p. 11; "Frances Farmer Gives Stand on Peace League," *P-I*, 12-3-38, p. 8; Lyons, *The Red Decade*, pp. 294–296.

In Hollywood: "Miss Farmer Enters Movies," *ST*, 9-19-35, p. 9; O'Neil, "Frances Farmer, Film Star, Arrives for Picture Premiere," *ST*, 11-4-36, p. 4.

Her life: imdb.com.

10. The Labor Push, 1934–1937

Registry: Foisie, "Decasualizing Longshore Labor and the Seattle Experience," Waterfront Employers of Seattle, 2-1-34.

Strike issues: "Teamsters Back Longshore Strike of 1,500 Men Here," *P-I*, 5-10-34, p. 1; Bennett, "Dock Situation Related by Workers' Secretary," *ST*, 5-24-34, p. 1; ad, "To the Longshoremen and the Public from the Waterfront Employers of Seattle," *ST*, 5-27-34, p. 20; "Longshoremen Story Told," *Labor News*, pp. 6–29,34; Palmquist, "Labor's Great War on the Seattle Waterfront," UW Labor History project.

Initial tactics: "2,000 Longshore Strikers Raid 12 Ships; Stop Work" and Phil R. Gruger, "Foreman of Dock Relates How Mob Threw Him in Bay," *P-I*, 3-13-34, pp. 1, 6; "Mob Drives Workmen from Piers and Ships," *ST*, 5-13-34, p. 1.

Port closed: "Shipping Tie-Up Most Complete in City History," *ST*, 5-20-34, p. 7; "Seattle's June Exports Total Nothing at All," *ST*, 7-8-34, p. 29.

Mill closures: "Longshore Walkout Forces Fisher Mills to Close," *P-I*, 5-15-34, p. 3; Lovering, "Business News and Views" *ST*, 7-15-34, p. 29.

First offer: "Union Recognized, Open Shop Maintained, in Strike Agreement Terms," *P-I*, 5-29-34, p. 2; "Ryan Here, Urges Men to Accept Compromise," *ST*, 5-29-34, p. 1; "Seattle Vetoes Strike Peace," *ST*, 5-31-34, p. 1.

Alaska: "Strike Causing Food Shortage in Northland," *ST*, 6-28-34, p. 23.

Violence: "Three Men Beaten in New Outbreak of Dock Violence," *P-I*, 6-7-34, p. 1; "Smith Predicts Strike Peace Pact by Tonight," *ST*, 6-13-34, p. 1; "Dock Strike Picket Badly Hurt by Truck," *P-I*, 6-15-34, p. 2; "Armed Police Guard Waterfront," *P-I*, 6-16-34, p. 1.

Second offer: "Text of Dock Strike Peace Pact Outlined," *ST*, 6-17-34, p. 11.

Bridges: "Mystery Man of Longshore Strike Is Now Frisco's Ruler," *Star*, 7-17-34, p. 1; "Bridges, Head of SF Strike, Is Australian," *ST*, 7-16-34, p. 12; "Iron Man," *P-I*, 7-13-34, p. 2.

"Open the Port": "Seattle Shall Not Die," *ST*, 6-10-34, p. 1.

Deputies: "Special Police, on Strike Duty, Are Dismissed," *ST*, 8-19-34, p. 2.

Canisters: "Employers Bought Munitions to Crush '34 Strike," *New Dealer*, 4-1-39, p. 1.

Additional Violence: "Driver Pulled from Car and Beaten by Four," *P-I*, 6-21-34, p. 2; "Man Carried Off by Picket Mob," *P-I*, 6-26-34, p. 1; "Man Shot in Strike Clash," *ST*, 7-1-34, p. 1; "Youth Tells of Fatal Shooting at Point Wells," *ST*, 7-5-34, p. 1; "Criminal Intent in Strike Death," *ST*, 7-6-34, p. 1; "Bannock Aide Slain, Policeman Slugged," *ST*, 7-10-34, p. 1; "Jury Finds Deputy Died in Longshore Riot by His Own Revolver," *P-I*, 7-13-34, p. 3.

General strike: "Workers! Support General Strike," etc., *Voice of Action*, 7-20-34, p. 1; "Lynch Mob of 1,000 Foiled Here," *P-I*, 6-27-34, p. 1; Palmquist, "Labor's Great War on the Seattle Waterfront," depts.washington.edu, accessed 11-24-2018; "General Strike Grave Mistake, Says Green," *ST*, 7-22-34, p. 21.

Police raids: "Arrest Scores in Swift Raids by Police Here," *Star*, 7-18-34, p. 1; "Red Squad Arrests 55; 37 Are Released," *Voice of Action*, 7-27-34, p. 1; "Owner of Paper Sues Mayor Smith for Police Raids," *ST*, 7-28-34, p. 7.

Smith Cove battle: "Chief Howard Gives Up Job," *Star*, 7-18-34, p. 1; "Tear Gas Routs Mob in Smith Cove Riot," *ST*, 7-18-34, p. 1; "Police Launch Raids Here," *P-I*, 7-19-34, p. 1; "Mayor Leads Police in Routing Strikers," *ST*, 7-20-34, p. 1; Bermann, "Mayor Leads Vigorous Drive against Smith Cove Strike Pickets" and "Vessels Here Load Unhindered," *P-I*, 7-21-34, pp. 1, 3; "Police Freed of Blame for Picket's Death," *P-I*, 8-17-34, p. 3.

Winners, losers: "Maritime Strikers Betrayed, Undefeated," *Voice of Action*, 8-3-34, p. 1; "Longshoremen Win More Pay," *ST*, 10-13-34, p. 1; Lundin, "President's Annual Report for 1934," *Seattle Chamber of Commerce Records 1935*, pp. 19–20; "Strike Demands and Offers," *P-I*, 1-31-37, p. 1.

Coastwise service: Brown, "The Culmination and Decline of Pacific Coastwise Shipping, 1916–1936," *Pacific Northwest Quarterly* 7-49, p. 188; "Coastwise Ships Scheduled," *ST*, 11-3-37, p. 24 (contradicts Brown); Wood, "Our Coast Dictator," *ST*, 11-2-38, p. 6.

Fisher strike: "Strike Follows Bitter Fight against Union by Fisher Management," *Labor News*, 10-25-35, p. 2; "Fisher Companies Inc. History," *Funding Universe* web page.

Anti-union: ad, *ST*, 6-5-34, p. 4; ad, *P-I*, 10-2-35, p. 5; "Special Police, on Strike Duty, Are Dismissed," *ST*, 8-19-34, p. 2; "Industrial Group Will Fight Reds," *P-I*, 8-13-35, p. 1; "Fisher Makes Show of Self at Open Forum," *Voice of Action*, 11-15-35, p. 4.

Interview striker: Victor, "What Does Seattle's Most Progressive Employer Pay for Ten Years of a Man's Life?" *Voice of Action*, 10-25-35, p. 4.

New trucking co.: "All Units of Fisher Mills Will Resume," *Star*, 10-18-35, p. 1; "Fisher Product Again Moves to Grocery Stores," *ST*, 10-19-35, p. 1.

Fund-raising letter: *Labor News*, 12-27-35, p. 1.

Notes for pages 153–159 309

Communists: "Fisher Boldly Blames Reds," *ST*, 11-11-35, p. 2. "Fisher Makes Show of Self at Open Forum," *Voice of Action*, 11-15-35, p. 4; "Legitimate vs. Company Unionism," *Voice of Action*, 10-25-35, p. 2; "Red Leaders Ordered Jailed," *P-I*, 11-10-35, p. 3.

Settlement: "Union Crews Man Fisher Mill," *Labor News*, 1-31-36, p. 1.

Hopkins: "We'll Always Have Jobless, Says Hopkins," *ST*, 9-13-36, p. 1.

Projects: "Golf Champ Bosses WPA Work," *ST*, 1-31-36, p. 17; "Boeing Field Improvement Work Halted," *P-I*, 4-8-36, p. 1; "WPA Gives Women Sewing Jobs," *ST*, 2-6-37, p. 3.

Green Lake: "Island May Be Built in Lake," *ST*, 10-30-35, p. 7; "Two Escape as Green Lake Dredge Burns," *P-I*, 5-5-36, p. 1; "Action Postponed on Green Lake Fountain," *P-I*, 6-9-36, p. 19.

Drinking: "WPA Work Crew Admits Drinking, Shirking on Job," *ST*, 3-30-36, p. 1; "WPA Workers Win Jobs Back," *ST*, 4-2-36, p. 13; "State Bans Beer at City Park Picnics," *ST*, 7-20-36, p. 1.

Morale: "Jokes at WPA Ruin Morale, Abel Declares," *P-I*, 5-14-38, p. 1.

Communists: *Workers' Alliance of America Records*, ULS Digital Collections, University of Pittsburgh; Berner, *Seattle, 1921–1940*, pp. 374–375; Lyons, *The Red Decade*, pp. 86–87.

Shoe workers: "Sit-Downers Dropped from WPA Payroll," *P-I,* 7-16-1937, p. 1; "There Will Be Shoes," *Star*, 9-7-37, p. 4.

Brockway: Squire, "Facts on Communism," *Star*, 1-1-38, p. 2.

Strike: "WPA Workers Call Meeting," *P-I*, 12-10-36, p. 6; "Strikes Close Ten Seattle WPA Projects," *P-I*, 1-26-37, p. 1; "WPA Spurns 'Sit' Demands," *ST*, 1-29-37, p. 5; "WPA Dismisses 1,700 Strikers on 30 Projects," *P-I*, 2-6-37, p. 1; "Riot Broken Up at WPA Project," *P-I*, 2-10-37, p. 3; "WPA Strikers Arrested for Chasing Crew," *P-I*, 2-11-37, p. 1; "Bell Frees and Warns 42 in WPA Sit-Strike," *ST*, 2-20-37, p. 1; letter from C.G. Harris, *Star*, 2-20-37, p. 14; letter from Ray Wroten, *Star*, 4-16-37, p. 6.

Settlement: "Peace Plan Is Heavily Supported by Workers," *ST*, 2-24-37, p. 1; "WPA Aids 7,000 in County, Spends $500,000 Each Month," *ST*, 3-19-37, p. 4.

Construction: "Seattle Building Trades Council Scores 'Rivalry' of WPA," *Star*, 12-7-38, p. 2.

Costigan: Canwell hearings, p. 365.

Murders: "Two Men Slain in Café Battle," *ST*, 12-2-36, p. 3; "Union President Murdered," *Philippine American Tribune*, 12-9-36, p. 1.

Cannery workers: Crystal Fresco, "Cannery Workers' and Farm Laborers' Union, 1933–1939," *Seattle Civil Rights and Labor History Project*; Buaken, *I Have Lived with the American People*, p. 199; "Pickets Halt Loading of Alaska Ship," *P-I*, 5-1-37, p. 1; "Labor Strife Halts Alaska Shipping," *P-I*, 5-2-37, p. 1; "Clash of Two Cannery Unions Stops Alaska Ship Sailings," *ST*, 5-2-37, p. 12; "CWFLU Wins Votes for Cannery Workers after Negotiation with Packers," *Cosmopolitan Weekly*, 5-4-37, p. 1; "CIO Wins Salmon Cannery Election," *P-I*, 5-9-38, pp. 1, 4; "Agreement Reached in Salmon Tieup," *P-I*, 5-20-38, p. 1.

11. Dave Beck, 1931–1938

Interview: "America Hunting Security, Not Success, Says Garrett," *ST*, 11-8-38, p. 7; Garrett, "Labor at the Golden Gate," *Saturday Evening Post*, 3-8-39, pp. 12, 13, 39.

Laundries: Summary for Washington Laundry Co., 1165 Eastlake Ave., Parcel ID 216390–0955 / Inv # 0, Seattle Dept. of Neighborhoods; Report on Designation, Troy Laundry Building, pp. 311–329 Fairview Ave. N., LPB 173/95, 8-15-95, Landmarks Preservation Board.

Rise of Beck: Berner, *Seattle, 1921–1940*, pp. 358–359; Sale, *Seattle Past to Present*, pp. 144–149.

1930 fight: "Cleaner Attacked," *Star*, 5-15-30, p. 1; "Police Open War on Rackets Here," *Star*, 6-2-30, p. 1; "Star's Plan Will Aid in Settling Dyer War," *Star*, 6-11-30, p. 1; "Dyers Approve King Dykeman," *Star*, 6-19-30, p. 1; "Two Dye Works Cut Prices to Former Levels," *ST*, 8-4-30, p. 5; "Dyers and Union Workers Patch Up Wage, Price Fight," *Star*, 8-7-30, p. 8; ad, Dixie-Queen Anne Dyers & Cleaners, *ST*, 8-11-30, p. 26.

1932 cartel: "'Cleaners Ask Legal Okeh for Dictator," *P-I*, 2-5-32, p. 1; "Burgunder Says Dyeing 'Czar' Illegal" and "Milk Fight Ruling Citied to Show Dyers' 'Czar' Illegal," *P-I*, 2-6-32, pp. 1, 5; story refers to *State v. Erickson*, 54 Wash. 472, (1909); "Burgunder OK's Plan for Dyers, Cleaners 'Czar,'" *P-I*, 2-12-32, p. 1; "Dyers Halt War as Price Czar Named" and "Dyer 'Czar' Power Bared," *P-I*, 2-13-32, pp. 1, 4; "Independent Shops Fight 'Czar' Plan," *P-I*, 2-16-32, p. 1.

1932 attacks: "Dye Racket Bomb Perils 3 Children," *P-I*, 3-4-32, p. 13; "Victim Bares 3 Years of Terror in Dye Industry," *P-I*, 3-5-32, p. 11; "Cleaners End Warfare; Fix Uniform Rate," *P-I*, 4-26-32, p. 11.

After 1932: "New Cleaner Price Boost Edict Defied," *P-I*, 8-8-35, p. 1; "New Document Bares Threat to Press Shop," *P-I*, 8-11-35, p. 9; "Teamster Head Denies Desire to Fix Prices in Any Seattle Industry," *P-I*, 8-27-35, p. 3; "Dry Cleaners Maintain High Standards Here," *Star*, 11-7-35, p. 8; "Dye Works Wrecked by Bomb," *Star*, 12-18-37, p. 1.

Russian: "Peter Marinoff," *Labor News*, 5-10-35, p. 1.

Strike: "In Fairness to Seattle Brewers and Bottlers," Brewery Workers' Ad, *Labor News*, 7-21-33, p. 4; "Liquor" and J. H. Brown, "State Capital," *Argus*, 9-8-34, pp. 1, 2; "Brew Strike to End Today," *P-I*, 9-5-34, p. 9; "Rifles Quell Mob in Beer Strike Riots," *P-I*, 9-8-34, p. 1; "Beer War Likely as Marinoff Cuts Price $2 Barrel," *P-I*, 9-9-34, p. 19; "Judge Brands Seattle Beer War 'Anarchy,'" *P-I*, 9-11-34, p. 1; "Windows Broken by Rock Barrage in Brewery War," *P-I*, 9-12-34, p. 4; "Marinoff Asks U.S Probe of 'Beer War' Here," *ST*, 9-14-34, p. 4; "Brewery Attorney Accuses Beck of Conspiracy to Boost Beer Price," *P-I*, 9-25-34, p. 2.

Aftermath: "Marinoff Posts Death Case Bond," *ST*, 6-7-35, p. 12; "Marinoff and Union Agreement," *Labor News*, 7-5-35, p. 1; "Twenty Years for Marinoff," *Labor News*, 1-31-36, p. 3; "Tacoma Unfair Beer Dumped," *Labor News*, 7-3-36, p. 1; "Prosecutor Defends Dore," *ST*, 10-16-36, p. 1; "Court Says Teamsters Can Boycott in Limits," *P-I*, 1-21-39, p. 3; Horne, "Plaintiff Testifies in Beck Libel Suit," *ST*, 5-6-81, p. 26; *State v. Hiatt*, 60 P.2d 71 (Wash. 1936); Walter Galenson, *The CIO Challenge to the AFL*, Harvard, 1960, pp. 488–490; files on Marinoff and Northwest Brewing at www.brewerygems.com.

Beck regime: "Industrial Council to Declare War," *Labor News*, 4-17-36, p. 1.

Wrecking a truck: "Showdown Near in Auto Strike," *P-I*, 6-15-36, p. 2; "The Price of Successful Leadership," *Labor News*, 8-21-36, p. 3.

Golden Rule: "Bakery Charges Union with Plot," *ST*, 4-17-36, p. 13; "Union Pickets Overturn Milk Truck at Pier," *P-I*, 5-9-36, p. 3; "W.H. Pemberton, Baker, Is Dead," *ST*, 5-10-36, p. 19; "Golden Rule and Unions End War," *P-I*, 6-3-36, p. 13.

Car dealers: "Labor Lobby Boos Cleric for Urging Strike Curb," *ST*, 6-23-36, p. 1; "Police to Guard Workers," *ST*, 7-2-36, p. 1; *Violations of Free Speech and Rights of Labor*, Vol. 21, p. 24252, Senate Committee on Education and Labor.

Writers and unions: "Statement Explains Newspapers' Stand on Guild Issues," *ST*, 8-13-36, p. 7.

Broun: "Broun Calls Green Barrier to Unionism," *P-I*, 7-20-37, p. 2; Lyons, *The Red Decade*, p. 254.

Shutdown: "P-I Suspends!" *ST*, 8-14-36, p. 1; Ames & Simpson, *Unionism or Hearst*, pp. 74–75, 89–90; "For the Sake of Seattle," *Star*, 9-17-36, p. 1; Russell B. Porter, "Seattle Business Backs P-I in Strike," *NYT*, 8-30-36, p. 16.

Beck: "This Shameful Page" and "A Statement by the Post-Intelligencer," *ST*, 8-14-36, p. 1; "Newspaper Management Says Future Now Is Up to Community," [Hearst statement] *ST*, 8-17-36, p. 1; "The Times Files Its Answer to Dave Beck's Libel Suit," and "Full Text of Dave Beck's Complaint in Suit for $250,000 Damages for Libel," *ST*, 9-15-36, pp. 1, 14.

Violence: *State v. Hiatt*, 60 P.2d 71 (Wash. 1936), "U.S. Board Will Hear Guild Plea," *Star*, 8-14-36, p. 1; "Say Hearst Was Opposed to Guild," *Star*, 9-12-36, pp. 1, 2.

Parade: "15,000 in Seattle Labor Day Parade," *ST*, 9-7-36, p. 1.

Hearst: "W.R. Hearst's Views on Democratic Principles and American Ideals," *ST*, 11-8-36, p. 12C; "Text of P-I Agreement with Guild," *ST*, 11-26-36, pp. 1, 14.

"Royal family": Ames and Simpson, *Unionism or Hearst*, pp. 131–135, 150–153.

Lynch, Armstrong: "P-I Loses in Strike Decision," *ST*, 1-15-37, p. 5; "P.E. Armstrong, Critic, Is Dead," *ST*, 3-19-37, p. 5.

Beck: Boettiger, "Seattle's New Labor Program," *P-I*, 1-25-37, p. 1; Ames & Simpson, *Unionism or Hearst*, pp. 89–90.

Chamber: "G.K. Comstock Heads Chamber," *ST*, 12-23-36, p. 7; "Seattle Labor Leaders Praise C of C Industrial Peace Plan" and Comstock, "Industrial Peace and Expansion Major Goals," *P-I*, 1-23-37, pp. 1, 2; "Labor," *Argus*, 9-11-37, p. 3.

Bridges: "Harry Bridges Forecasts End of Employers," *P-I*, 5-15-37, p. 1; "Communism Bridges' Aim, Says State Labor Chief," *ST*, 5-16-37, p. 1. At his deportation hearing in 1939, Bridges testified that the statement in the *Times* was invented by a college student, but the *P-I*'s version, which uses different words, is substantially the same. See "Bridges Discounts Communist Aid in 1934 Strike," *ST*, 8-3-39, p. 1.

Beck: "No Rackets in Seattle—Beck," *ST*, 2-5-37, p. 3; "Destruction of Labor is CIO Aim, Says Beck," *ST*, 4-2-37, p. 1; "Fight on CIO Urged by Beck," *ST*, 1-27-38, p. 5.

Dennett: "Dennett Raps Teamster Union," *ST*, 12-3-37, p. 11; Dennett, *Agitprop*, p. 1.

Coon Chicken Inn: "Inn Under Guard after Bomb Threat," *ST*, 9-21-30, p. 4; "2 Men Jailed in Odor Bombing," *P-I*, 1-25-37, p. 13; "Inn on Highway Being Picketed," *ST*, 3-8-37, p. 3; "Pickets Withdrawn from Highway Tavern," *ST*, 3-13-37, p. 13.

Builders: "Pickets Halt Magnolia Work," *ST*, 3-15-37, p. 2; "Building Tieup Ended," *P-I*, 3-23-37, p. 1.

Elevators: "Labor," *Argus*, 6-26-37, p. 4.

312 *Notes for pages 171–179*

Hotels: "Hotels Agree to Raise Pay Scale Monday," *P-I*, 4-7-37, p. 2; "Seattle Hotels to Raise Rates," *ST*, 4-12-37, p. 1.

Apartments: "Union Signs Pact with Biltmore Apartments," *P-I*, 3-24-37, p. 17; "900 Apartments to Boost Rents," *ST*, 6-29-37, p. 4.

Restaurants: "Culinary Workers Get Pay Rise," *P-I*, 6-5-37, p. 4.

Food stores: "Grocers Won't OK Hour Plan in Union Pact," *P-I*, 6-12-37, p. 2.

Department stores: "17 Big Stores Sign Contract with AFL Union," *P-I*, 9-5-37, p. 1; "Retail Stores Sign Pact with Clerks' Union," *P-I*, 11-2-37, p. 1.

Beck: Sale, *Seattle, Past to Present*, p. 145–146; Morgan, *Skid Road*, p. 257; Garrett, "Labor at the Golden Gate," *Saturday Evening Post*, 3-8-39, pp. 12, 13, 39.

Beck's Seattle: Cooke, *The American Home Front, 1941–1942*, Atlantic Monthly Press, 2006, p. 178; Morgan, *Skid Road*, pp. 220, 224.

12. John Dore, 1932–1938

Dore: MacGowan, "Dore's Expose Stories in Star Led to Success," *Star*, 7-26-32; MacGowan, "One Year in Law School Enough, Dore Declares," *Star*, 7-27-32; "Early Training as Reporter Aid to Mayor-Elect," *ST*, 3-9-32, p. 9; "Harlin Speaker Gets 'Razz' in Attacking Dore," *ST*, 3-1-32, p. 1.

Pay cuts: "Labor Protests Dore Wage Plan," *P-I*, 6-23-32, p. 3; "Pay Cuts Put Up to City Council in Legal Opinion," *ST*, 7-1-32, p. 7; "City Council Die-Hards May Block Pay Cut," *P-I*, 7-17-32, p. 4; "Council Sustains Dore Cost Cuts in Stormy Session," *P-I*, 7-23-32, p. 1.

Laundries: "Strikers Fight Laundry Girls," *ST*, 8-5-32, p. 1; "Several Injured when Laundry Workers and Strikebreakers Clash," *P-I*, 8-6-32, p. 3; "Mayor Refuses Police Guard for Strikebreakers," *ST*, 8-7-32, p. 2; "Laundrymen, Union Reach Agreement," *P-I*, 8-9-32, p. 1.

Phones: "Dore Demands Telephone Co. Get Franchise," *P-I*, 7-31-32, p. 1; "Dore Seeks Council Aid in Phone Suit," *P-I*, 8-5-32, p. 13; "Dore Clashes with Council in Phone Case," *P-I*, 10-2-32, p. 3.

Streetcars: Blanchard, *The Street Railway Era in Seattle*, pp. 94–111; Fessler, "Flu Fear Helps Transit Sale," *Star*, 12-3-29, p. 3, and "Heh! Heh! Car Line Was Bought on April Fool's Day," *Star*, 12-4-29, p. 3; "Municipal League Tram Report Is Made Public," *P-I*, 1-27-32, p. 2; "Making Trolleying a Pleasure," *Star*, 9-17-29, p. 4; "Street Car Situation," *Argus*, 5-23-31, p. 1.

Finances: "City's Contract for Car Lines Called Impossible," *ST*, 1-26-29, p. 12; *Von Herberg v. Seattle*, 288 P. 646 (Wash. 1930); "Car Line Gets 2-Year Delay in Paying Bonds," *P-I*, 10-29-29, p. 15; "Banks' Refusal to Cash Tram Warrants Precipitates Crisis," *P-I*, 1-16-32, p. 2.

Rainier line: "Purchase of Old Renton Line Hinted in Car Talk," *P-I*, 2-2-32, p. 1; "The Stroller: Street Car Statistics," *Argus*, 8-12-33, p. 2; "Transportation," *Argus*, 12-1-34, p. 2.

Brown: "Brown Given Free Hand to Cure Sick Tram System," Brown, "Out of the Red in Three Months, Brown Predicts," and "Who Is This Man Brown?" *P-I*, 2-3-32, p. 15; "Brown Announces Details of Car and Bus Line Changes," *ST*, 3-20-32, p. 8; "Mr. Brown Is Through," *ST*, 5-4-32, p. 6.

Dore and streetcars: "Dore Issues Ultimatum to Stone, Webster," *P-I*, 3-10-32, p. 1; "Let 'Em Puff on Trolleys, That's Mayor-Elect's Idea," *ST*, 4-5-32, p. 1; "Five-Cent Trolley Fare to Be Dore's First Objective," *P-I*, 6-3-32, p. 1.

Cuts: "City Pay Cuts Held Invalid by High Court," *P-I*, 6-21-34, p. 11; "Mayor Saves Jobs of 38 Policemen by Juggling 1935 Budget," *P-I*, 1-1-35, p. 3; "Policemen and Firemen Draw Down $800,000 in Back Pay," *ST*, 3-21-35, p. 1; "Police," *Argus*, 12-28-35, p. 2.

Beck: Acena interview with Harold Eby, 9-4-67, Eby Papers; "State Session Battles over Union Conflict," *P-I*, 7-16-36, p. 8.

Farmers: "Farmers Form Own Group to Fight Rackets," *ST*, 10-15-36, p. 1; "Dore 'Too Busy' to Hear Racketeer Proof," *ST*, 10-23-36, p. 1.

P-I strike: "Mayor, P-I Chief in Argument," *Star*, 8-19-36, p. 1; "Dore Upholds Labor Radicals in UW Speech," *ST*, 10-18-36, p. 16.

Star strike: "Green Backs Teamsters over Guild," *ST*, 7-6-37, p. 1; "Dore Offers to Ban Star Picket Line," *ST*, 7-7-37, p. 1; "The Star Will Fight for Its Right to Live" (ad), *P-I*, 7-8-37, p. 4; "Dore Assails Lewis Union at Labor Meet," *P-I*, 7-15-37, p. 1; "Teamsters and Pickets Mix at Star," *ST*, 8-11-37, pp. 1, 8; "Violence Flares in Star Strike," *P-I*, 8-12-37, p. 3; "No More Mass Pickets, Dore Tells Strikers," *P-I*, 8-15-37, p. 1; "Teamsters Head Posts Bail for Accused Slugger," *Sunday News*, 11-6-37, p. 2; "NLRB Ruling on Star Upheld," *ST*, 6-15-38, p. 8.

Rainier Valley line: "Council Votes for Rail Removal," *P-I*, 2-11-36, p. 13; "Rainier Valley Rides Buses," *ST*, 1-1-37, p. 7.

Streetcar plan: Blanchard, *The Street Railway Era in Seattle*, pp. 94–95, 197–207; "City Cars May Soon Lead U.S.," *ST*, 1-16-37, p. 2; "Newest Types of Cars, Buses, Called for in City's Plan," *ST*, 1-18-37, p. 5; "Langlie, Dore to Debate Cars," *ST*, 3-2-37, pp. 1, 2; "6,000 Cheer and Jeer Dore and Langlie in Car Debate," *ST*, 3-8-37, p. 1; "Power Co. Sues City on Power Bonds," *ST*, 7-30-37, pp. 1, 4.

Election: "Labor Wins Council; Trolley Plan Loses," *Star*, 3-10-37, p. 1.

Vanderveer: "Council OK's Vanderveer in Car Debt Deal," *P-I*, 7-29-37, p. 1.

Default: "Default on Railway Bonds," *P-I*, 9-2-37, p. 11.

Parades: "Workers Stage Huge May Day Parade Here," *P-I*, 5-2-37, p. 4; "May Day Parade Banners in Seattle Laud Communism," *ST*, 5-2-37, p. 1; "CIO Barred from Labor Day Parade," *ST*, 8-26-37, p. 1; "Marchers Celebrate Labor Day," *ST*, 9-6-37, p. 1; "Seattle Labor Celebrates Day," *ST*, 9-7-37, p. 10.

FDR visit: Gilbert, "Democrat Rift Made Wider by Roosevelt Visit," *ST*, 10-3-37, p. 2; "Police Confiscate War Banners," *P-I*, 9-29-37, p. 8.

Communists: "Dore, Beck United in CIO Battle," *ST*, 6-12-37, p. 3; "Dore Bans Communist Meeting," *ST*, 11-5-37, p. 1; Cooper, "Communists Defy Dore Ban on Auditorium," *P-I*, 11-6-37, p. 1; "Court Upholds Dore's 'Red' Ban," *ST*, 11-9-37, p. 1.

Warrants: Cooper, "Banks to Reject City Pay Warrants," *P-I*, 12-28-37, p. 1; Cooper, "Interest Rate Increased on City Warrants," *P-I*, 2-4-38, p. 1.

City finances: "City's Finances Facing Crisis," *P-I*, 3-12-37, p. 1; "City Hall," *Argus*, 6-12-37, p. 3; "Fussell, "City's Financial Plight Analyzed," *P-I*, 1-23-38, pp. 1, 6; Fussell, "Tax Cut Reduced City's Revenues," *P-I*, 1-24-38, pp. 1, 5; Fussell, "City's Need for Revenue Shown," *P-I*, 1-27-38, p. 10; Winans, "Civic Big-Heartedness Blamed by Many for Financial Impasse," *ST*, 1-27-38, p. 2; Winans, "Seattle's $$$$—What to Do?" *ST*, 1-25-38, pp. 1, 6; "Dore Vetoes New Tax and Water Boost," *P-I*, 1-30-38, pp. 1, 2; Givens, "Report on the Fiscal Affairs of the City of Seattle, Washington, 1939," 5-22-39, pp. 14, 27.

Parking meters: "Mayor Vetoes Park Meter Act," *P-I*, 5-28-36, p. 3; "First Day over Parking Meters," *ST*, 2-5-42, p. 1.

Contra Dore: Hunt, "Langlie Gets Municipal League OK," *P-I*, 2-9-38, p. 1; Menefee, "The Decline of Dave Beck," *The Nation*, 3-26-38, pp. 354–355.

Contra Meyers: Hunt, "Dore Strikes at Vic Meyers' Candidacy," *P-I*, 2-18-38, p. 1; Hunt, "90,000 Expected to Vote Monday," *P-I*, 2-20-38, pp. 1, 2.

Dore's health: "Dore, Recovering, at Desk Monday," *P-I*, 12-4-37, p. 1; "Dore Undergoes Operation," *P-I*, 12-7-37, p. 1; "Mayor Dore Improving Rapidly," *Star*, 1-11-38, p. 5; "Dore Returned to Hospital," *P-I*, 1-18-38, p. 1; "Dore Rumors Blasted by Mayor's Son," *P-I*, 1-28-38, p. 2; Gilbert, "Dore, Due out of Hospital, to Lay Plans for Campaign," *ST*, 2-11-38, p. 1.

Primary election: Hunt, "Langlie and Meyers Win Nomination; Dore Third," *P-I*, 2-22-38, p. 1.

General election: "Complete City Returns," *P-I*, 3-9-38, p. 1.

Dore's death: Hunt, "Mayor John F. Dore Dead" and "Colorful Career Ended by Mayor's Death," *P-I*, 4-19-38, pp. 1, 2.

City finances: "Langlie Details Finance Plan," *ST*, 6-18-38, pp. 1, 3; Cooper, "City Employees to Get Salaries in Cash," *P-I*, 7-21-38, p. 1; Cooper, "Council OK's 1939 Budget of $12,577,684," *P-I*, 10-4-38, pp. 1, 2; "3 More City Funds Reveal Soaring Debt," *P-I*, 12-3-38, p. 2; tombstone, City of Seattle Emergency Funding Bonds, *P-I*, 2-10-39, p. 23; "$3,293,090.19 Warrant Call," *ST*, 3-7-39, p. 2.

Streetcars: Cooper, "RFC Approves Ten Million City Tram Loan," *P-I*, 9-3-38, pp. 1, 2; Cooper, "RFC Increases Tram Loan to $10,200,000," *P-I*, 2-4-39, p. 1; "The Stroller," *Argus*, 3-16-40, p. 2.

13. J. D. Ross, 1930–1939

DeCou: DeCou, Laird & Co. ad, *ST*, 8-29-26, p. 29; obit, *ST*, 11-2-50, p. 29.

Tower project: City Light Building Co. application for permit to sell shares, 1930; Agreement for First Mortgage, 9-25-30; J. S. Moltzner to City Light Building Co., 10-23-30; C. H. Bowen to Mortgage Investment Co., 12-11-30; C. H. Bowen to Dwight D. Hartman, 2-26-31; Charles H. Maybury to Dwight D. Hartman, 4-10-31; L. A. DeCou to C. H. Bowen, 4-13-31; C. H. Bowen to Oliver H. Morris, 6-20-31, all from Box 54, File 1785, Department of Licensing, State Archives; "Time Extension Asked for City Light Building," *ST*, 5-15-31, p. 4; "DeCou Confident of Future Plans for Light Tower," *ST*, 6-3-31, p. 6.

Settlement: "City Light Co. Would Give Up Building Lease," *P-I*, 8-28-31, p. 6; "Accord on City Light Building Release Reached," *P-I*, 9-4-31, p. 15; "City Lacks Cash for Light Tower Pay," *ST*, 1-15-32, p. 7; *Abrams v. Seattle*, 23 P.2d 869 Wash. (1933).

Moltzner: "Loan Executive Given 2 Years," *P-I*, 1-16-32, p. 2.

Charge: "Mayor, in Ouster Statement, Charges 'Willful Neglect of Duty' to Ross," *P-I*, 3-10-31, p. 1; "Mayor Files Ross Charges," *ST*, 3-23-31, pp. 1, 9; "Ross' Answer to Mayor Edwards," *ST*, 4-9-31, pp. 12, 20.

Payoff: Ross to FTC Counsel Robert Healy, 8-12-31, Box 17, Ross Papers.

Hostility: "Mayor Will Launch Probe of City Light," *P-I*, 2-17-29, p. 16; "Is City Light Seceding?" *ST*, 4-20-30, p. 6; "Self-Interest Should Bring Voters to Polls," *ST*, 3-5-31, p. 1.

Ross's shares: Ross to Harry Carroll, 12-9-31, Box 12, Series 9, *Ross Papers*.

"One thought in mind": Ross to Donald Gawne, 1935, Box 16, *Ross Papers*.

Elections: "City Light Ticket Is Victorious!" *P-I*, 3-11-31, p. 1; Fussell, "Edwards Ousted, 35,657 to 21,836," *P-I*, 7-14-31, p. 1.

Ross: Stein, "Ross, James Delmage," *historylink.org*; Dick, "The Genesis of Seattle City Light," pp. 117, 186; Brown, "The Romance of City Light," *Star*, 1-21-37, pp. 1, 7; Sparks, "J.D. Ross and Seattle City Light, 1917–1932," pp. 24–28, 77, 138; "J.D. Ross, City Light Veteran Head, Begins 33rd Year of Service;" *P-I*, 1-4-35, p. 24; Berner, *Seattle 1921–1940*, pp. 49–50; Friedheim, *The Seattle General Strike*, pp. 116–120; "City of Seattle Department of Lighting: An Analysis," Hartley, Rogers & Co, Seattle, 1938, ACC 0838–004, Box 13, *Ross Papers*.

Kitchen ranges: Annual report 1930, p. 41.

"Bitter Competition": Ross, "The Story of City Light's Application for Federal Money," typescript, 2-27-34, p 4, Box 13, *Ross Papers*.

Struggle recedes: Berner, *Seattle 1921–1940*, p. 296.

Bond market: "City Light Is Paying Debts, Economizing," *P-I*, 12-9-31, p. 15; "Bonds of City Light Fail to Attract Bids," *ST*, 2-5-32, p. 1.

Asking feds: Ross, "The Story of City Light's Application for Federal Money," typescript, 2-27-34, Box 13, *Ross Papers*; "Nichols Tells of Loan Fight," *Star*, 12-16-32, p. 1.

Diablo: City Light Annual Report 1931, p. 7, and City Light Budget Files 1932, 200–03, 3/6, Seattle Municipal Archives.

Revenues: Tombstone for City Light bonds, *ST*, 4-23-34, p. 11; Puget Sound Power & Light Co. annual reports, 1930–1933.

Dividends: Puget Power annual reports, 1931–1943.

10 % yield: Hill, "City Light Bonds Jump Two Points on Day's Turnover of $150,000," *P-I*, 5-24-33, p. 16.

Federal loan: "Dill, Bone, Ask for Skagit Project," *Star*, 10-9-33, p. 3; "The Modern Caliph," *ST*, 8-7-34, p. 6; Mallon, "Bone to Win in Fight for Skagit Cash," *Star*, 10-19-33, p. 1; "Ross Home, Hopeful of $7,500,000 Loan," *ST*, 12-23-33, p. 1; "Skagit Lost to Grand Coulee, Asserts Ross," *ST*, 2-18-34, p. 5.

Diablo and Ross: "Diablo Work Seen as City Light Gets $4,600,000 Offer," *P-I*, 4-11-34, p. 9; "Dore Will Veto City Light Bond Bid," *ST*, 5-1-34, p. 5; tombstone, City Light bonds, *P-I*, 4-23-34, p. 15; Duffy, "Bankers Loosening Up on Public Ownership," *P-I*, 5-17-37, p. 20; "Board Approves Ruby Dam Plans," *ST*, 5-27-37, p. 1; "Bond Bid Held Tribute to City Financial Status," *ST*, 2-11-43, p. 11.

City Light HQ: "Light Building Warrants to Be Cashed by City," *ST*, 4-15-34, p. 8; "City Hall," *Argus*, 6-30-34, p. 2.

Future: "Prophet of a New Promised Land of Power," *NYT*, 11-14-37, p. 154.

Proposal: "City Asked to Buy Puget System," *P-I*, 10-4-34, p. 1; Ross to Donald Gawne, 1935, Box 16, *Ross Papers*; Ross, "A Proposal to Acquire the Holdings of the Puget Sound Power and Light Company by the People of Western Washington," 10-3-34, Box 16, *Ross Papers*; Baker, "The Proposed City Light Merger: A Study of Public Opinion."

Opposition: "Let's Not Play Santa Again," *Star*, 10-4-34, p. 1; "Leaders Condemn Proposed Purchase of Puget Power," *P-I*, 10-5-34, p. 13; "Puget Sound Power Deal Doomed, Poll of Voters by Friends of Plan Shows," *P-I*, 2-21-36, p. 13.

Merger: Hartley, "City of Seattle Department of Lighting: An Analysis," *Ross Papers*, Box 13.

Dividends: "Business & Finance," *Argus*, 5-30-36, p. 3.

Recapitalization: Puget Power Annual Report, 1943; "One More Step," display ad, *P-I*, 11-24-43, p. 7.

Takeover: "Here Are Basic Facts of Pending Power Deal," *P-I*, 7-11-50, pp. 1, 3; "Puget Power, Chelan PUD Partners in 2 Columbia Projects," *ST*, 1-6-56, p. 1.

Preferred: Niendorff, "Residential Electric Revenue Sharply Up," *P-I*, 8-7-38, p. 15; "Power Co. to Call Prior Stock," *P-I*, 5-2-50, p. 24.

14. The Popular Front, 1936–1938

47 states: McCarthy, "Circus Politics in Washington State," *The Nation*, 10-17-36, p. 442.

Planned economy: "Economic Security Act of 1937," *Washington Commonwealth*, 4-4-36, pp. 1–3.

Seattle elections: Acena, *The Washington Commonwealth Federation*, pp. 6, 16; "Follow the Lead of the Central Labor Council," *Voice of Action*, 2-28-36, p. 1; "Rescue Seattle Schools from Banker-Lawyer Domination," *Washington Commonwealth*, 2-29-36, p. 4.

Communists: "All Out of Step but Jim," *Washington Commonwealth*, 3-14-36, p. 1; "Communist Leader Refutes Charge that Reds Seeking to Capture WCF Parley," *Voice of Action*, 3-20-36, p. 3; Raport, "Communist Leader Here Boasts About Party's Victories in State," *Star*, 8-3-38, p. 1; Dennett testimony, HUAC, 3-18-55; Costigan testimony, Canwell hearings, 2-2-48, pp. 359–361, and HUAC, 10-3-52, pp. 5977–5980.

1936 convention: Voorhees Jr., "Plans Made by WCF at Meet" *Star*, 4-6-36, p. 1; "Official WCF Convention Record," *Washington Commonwealth*, 4-11-36, p. 3.

Democrats: "Political," *Argus*, 5-23-36, p. 3; "Left Wing Rules State Democrats," *P-I*, 5-25-36, p. 1; Brown, "Under the Capitol Dome," *Argus*, 5-30-36, pp. 3, 8; "State Group Deserted," *P-I*, 6-25-36, p. 1; Acena, *The Washington Commonwealth Federation*, pp. 117–123.

Stevenson: Acena, *The Washington Commonwealth Federation*, p. 27; Hunt, "Commissioner Stevenson Accused of Being Fugitive on Buffalo Larceny Charge" and other stories, *P-I*, 6-6-33, pp. 1, 2, 7; "The Week," *Argus*, 11-4-33, p. 4, and 11-11-33, p. 4; "Commonwealth OK's Stevenson," *P-I*, 7-27-36, p. 1; "Smashing Victory Seen for WCF People's Front," *Washington Commonwealth*, 8-1-36, p. 1; Gilbert, "Martin Assails Stevenson and WCF Tactics," *ST*, 8-12-36, p. 1; "Stevenson Admits Fund Was Aided," *Star*, 10-27-37, p. 1.

"A-weepin": McCarthy, "Circus Politics in Washington State," *The Nation*, 10-17-36, p. 442.

1936 primary: Gilbert, "New Primary May Disrupt Parties," *ST*, 7-26-36, p. 1; Gilbert, "Beat-Stevenson Fight Accounts for Switches," *ST*, 9-9-36, pp. 1, 10; "Stevenson Won but Three Counties," *ST*, 10-1-36, p. 16.

WCF split: Gilbert, "W.C.F. Split Laid to Red Influx," *ST*, 9-20-36, p. 1; Gilbert, "WCF Split to Mean New Unit," *ST*, 9-21-36, p. 4; "WCF Torn by Internal Dissension," *Star*, 9-21-36, p. 1; testimony of H. C. Armstrong, Canwell Hearings, pp. 423–426.

Bouck: "Name Committee to Aid William Bouck," *Star*, 10-13-18, p. 12; Gilbert, "WCF Issue Splits Demos" and "Farmer-Labor Candidate to Talk at Forum," *ST*, 10-18-36, pp. 12, 14.

Production for Use: "Liberal Power," *Western States Technocrat*, 8-30-35, p. 4; Gilbert, "Production-for-Use Means Complete Socialist State," *ST*, 9-21-36, p. 16; Squire, "State Would Be Divided in 4 Districts Under 119," *Star*, 10-26-36, p. 9; Gilbert, "Radical Measures Defeated by Voters," *ST*, 11-4-36, pp. 1, 9; "About Production for Use," *Sunday News*, 11-22-36, pp. 6–7.

Cinema: "The Man in the White House," *Star*, 7-31-36, p. 4.

1936 election: "How the State Cast Its Vote," "Magnuson Wins; State's Solons All Democratic," *ST*, 11-4-36, pp. 1, 9.

Martin: "State," *Argus*, 12-19-36, p. 4.

Faction: Gilbert, "Left Wing out of Legislature," *ST*, 11-10-40, p. 1.

Legislation: Brown, "Under the Capitol Dome," *Argus*, 3-13-37, p. 7; Schoeni, "Martin's Security and Highway Programs Approved," *Star*, 3-12-37, p. 5; Murrow to Martin, 3-16-37, Murrow papers, Box 1; Mixed Marriage Bill Supported," *ST*, 2-23-37, p. 11; Stefanie Johnson, "Blocking Racial Intermarriage Laws in 1935 and 1937," *Seattle Civil Rights and Labor History Project*, UW; "Senate Approves Filipino Bill," *P-I*, 3-11-37, p. 4; "Left Wing Bloc Action Praised," *P-I*, 3-15-37, p. 3.

DeLacy: "Introducing Candidates for the Seattle City Council," *Star*, 2-13-37, p. 9; Costigan testimony, 2-2-48, Canwell Hearings, p. 365.

People's daily: "Incorporations," *ST*, 1-29-36, p. 21; "WCF Resolves to Launch New Daily," *Voice of Action*, 7-31-36, p. 1; "Editor Coming for Daily Deal," *ST*, 8-31-36, p. 5; "The New Daily," *Argus*, 9-5-36, p. 1; "Tyler 'Delays' Morning Paper," *ST*, 10-2-36, p. 15; Minutes, WCF board, 1-18-37, *Dennett Papers*, Box 3, File 11; "Announcing a $2,500 Drive for a Better Sunday News," *Sunday News*, 5-1-37, pp. 6, 7; Costigan, "Sunday News to Be a Daily Liberal Newspaper," *Sunday News*, 10-2-37, p. 1; Ames and Simpson, *Unionism or Hearst*, pp. 89–90; "Harvey O'Connor," *Wikipedia*.

Voice of Action: "To All Supporters and Readers of the Voice of Action," *Voice of Action*, 9-25-36, p. 1; "Our Last Edition," *Voice of Action*, 10-9-36, p. 1.

Tyler: Tyler, "Difference between Technocracy, Communism Shown by Educator," *Western States Technocrat*, 1-22-35, p. 3; "Soviet People Support Purge of Traitors," *Sunday News*, 10-23-37, p. 3.

Costigan's marriage: "Costigan Now a Benedict," *Washington Commonwealth*, 7-18-36, p. 4.

Race to WA: Hunt, "Martin Races to Halt Session," *P-I*, 4-20-38, p. 1; "Court May Rule on Meyers' Call," *ST*, 4-20-38, p. 1; "Court Will Rule on Session Today," *P-I*, 4-23-38, p. 1.

Cabal: Dennett, *Agitprop*, pp. 82–83.

Afterward: "Governor Welcomes 'Vic' Back into Official Family," *ST*, 7-15-38, p. 7.

Relief: "One in Every 8 on State Relief," *ST*, 12-3-37, p. 4; "Martin Assails 'Pump-Priming,'" *ST*, 4-13-38, p. 7; "County Seeks to Restrict Relief," *ST*, 4-6-38, p. 2.

Aid cut-off: "State Halts King County Relief Fund," *P-I*, 3-11-38, p. 3; "WPA to Take Up Relief Slack," *P-I*, 3-24-38, p. 1; "State May Take Over County Relief," *P-I*, 4-29-38, p. 1.

Protests: "300 Jobless Men Occupy Relief Office," *P-I*, 4-2-38, p. 1; "Resign! Angered Relief Group Shouts at Nash," *ST*, 4-18-38, p. 1; "Jobless Stage Sit-Down Strike," *P-I*, 7-12-38, p. 1; "Relief Strike Comes to End," *P-I*, 8-3-38, p. 10.

Outcome: "73 Millions Spent in State on WPA Jobs," *P-I*, 7-31-38, p. 2; "Once-a-Month Relief Ration Inconvenient to Recipients," *ST*, 8-21-38, p. 8; "Most Relief Applicants Are Given Jobs with WPA," *ST*, 8-24-38, p. 9.

Convention: Gilbert, "Left Wing Will Control State's Demo Conclave," *ST*, 7-3-38, pp. 1, 2; Gilbert, "Left and Right-Wing Demos Battle," *ST*, 7-13-38, pp. 1, 2; "Platform Adopted by Democratic Convention," *P-I*, 7-14-38, p. 1; Gilbert, "Demos Split by Row at Convention," *ST*, 7-14-38, p. 1; "Platform of Demos Is Mild," *Tacoma News Tribune*, 7-15-38, p. 1; "Governor Welcomes 'Vic' Back into Official Family," *ST*, 7-15-38, p. 7; Meyers, "Meyers Revokes Rap at WCF, Hits Martin," *Sunday News*, 7-23-38, p. 4.

Communists: Berner, *Seattle 1921–1940*, p. 411; Gilbert, "Dalton Demands Reds Be Ousted," *ST*, 7-29-38, p. 3; "A Job for Democrats: Clean Out the Communists!" *Star*, 8-3-38, p. 1; "Mr. Costigan, Will You Answer These Questions?" *Star*, 8-5-38, p. 1; Costigan, "Costigan Gives His Answer," *Star*, 8-8-38, p. 1; Howard, "Organizer Says Party Strong in WCF Ranks," *Star*, 8-16-38, p. 1; "Three WCF Heads Sue the Star for Libel," *Sunday News*, 8-20-38, p. 1; Costigan testimony, Canwell hearings, 2-2-48, pp. 359–361.

Maxwell: Hunt, "Legislature to Have Its Own 'Dies Committee,'" *Star*, 12-30-38, p. 1; Gilbert, "Solons Shelve Probe of Reds," *ST*, 1-17-39, p. 12.

1938 Election: Gilbert, "Conservative Control Certain for Coming Legislative Session," *ST*, 11-19-38, p. 2; "Legislative Meet Adopts Wide Program," *P-I*, 11-28-38, p. 3; "632,813 Cast Vote on Nov. 8, State Reports," *P-I*, 12-9-38, p. 12; Wood, "Speaking for the Times," *ST*, 1-23-39, p. 6.

15. The Front Shatters, 1937–1939

Nazis in Seattle: Knute Berger, "When Nazis Walked the Streets of Seattle," *Crosscut*, 3-10-2016, and follow-up stories 3–13, 15, 20, 23, and 4–8; Richard T. Forbes, "How Nazi Doctrine Spreads in Seattle," *P-I*, 6-25-39, p. 1, and follow-ups 6–26, 28, 29, 30 and 7–2, 3, 4, 5, 6, 7, 8, 9 and 10.

German Club speech: Cooper, "Council Investigation of Nazis Planned," *P-I*, 11-13-37, p. 1; "Nazi Speaker Scores FDR, Jews Here" and "Investigate the Nazis!" *Sunday News*, 11-20-37, pp. 1, 2; "Seattle's Pro-Nazis Plan Gatherings," *Sunday News*, 4-16-38, p. 1.

Communists: "350 Attend NW Communist Meet," *Sunday News*, 5-28-38, p. 3.

Lane Summers: "Welfare Board to Buy Firewood from Jobless," *ST*, 2-16-33, p. 7.

Thane Summers: "N.W. Men Valiant in Spain, Says Veteran, Visiting Here," *ST*, 2-25-38, p. 1; "Seattle Man Killed on Spain Battlefield," *P-I*, 6-22-38, p. 22.

To Krauses: Letters of 11-13-35, pp. 9–10; 2-4-36, p. 12; 6-3-36, pp. 13, 15, 23; undated, p. 9; 6-21-37, p. 4; 7-14-37, pp. 6–7; 9-18-37, p. 1; 11-28-37, p. 1.

To Elaine and/or Jay: 7-14-37, pp. 9–10; 10-28-37, pp. 9–10. All letters from *Thane Summers Papers*.

Funeral: "Memorial for Youth Killed in Spain Is Denounced by Father," *ST*, 7-8-36, p. 1.

UW professors: Ralph Gundlach to Lee Paul Sieg, 3-2-39, *Pacific NW Historical Documents Collection*, UW; testimony of Lane Summers, *Sixth Report of the Senate Fact-Finding Committee on Un-American Activities*, California legislature, 1951.

Scrap trade: "Japan Buying Huge Total of Scrap Iron from American Firms," *P-I*, 12-22-34, p. 3; "Neutrality Act, If Invoked, Would Curb Scrap Exports," *ST*, 8-26-37, p. 15; "Weir Opposes Scrap Exports," *ST*, 3-22-39, p. 22; "Embargo Scrapiron!" *P-I*, 3-17-39, p. 8.

Seattle protests: "Group Protests Shipping of Iron to Japan," *ST*, 4-2-38, p. 10; Calkins, "From the Crow's Nest," *ST*, 4-6-38, p. 21; "Pickets Halt Scrap Iron Loading Here," *P-I*, 3-23-39, pp. 1, 4;

"Scrap Iron Ship Pickets Hold Lines," *P-I*, 3-24-39, p. 1; "Japanese Iron Still Held Up," *ST*, 3-24-39, p. 13; "Langlie Appeals to Ship Pickets," *ST*, 3-28-39, p. 1; "The Stroller," *Argus*, 3-15-39, p. 2.

Late shipments: "Scrap Rails from Seattle Go to Japan," *P-I*, 10-11-40, p. 3; "Japan to Get Last of U.S. Iron," *P-I*, 12-22-40, p. 27.

The test: "Chelan, Wash., Starts Townsend Plan Trial," *NYT*, 1-18-37, p. 1; "Townsend Plan Test Started," *P-I*, 1-18-37, p. 3; "Spending $200 a Month Is Easy," *ST*, 1-19-37, p. 1; "Pension 'Tester' Eyes Movies," *P-I*, 1-20-37, p. 3; "Pension Burns Hole in Pocket," *P-I*, 1-22-37, p. 6; "Chelan's $200 Pension Tester Down to $1.35," *P-I*, 1-28-37, p. 6; Wood, "Speaking for the Times," *ST*, 2-15-37, p. 6; "Chelan Pension Test Fails," *P-I*, 3-7-37, p. 24.

Critics: Letter from Wm. Worthington, *Star*, 7-19-37, p. 6; "What the State Thinks," *ST*, 2-7-37, p. 6.

Resolution: "More Buncombe," *Argus*, 1-30-37, p. 1.

Workaneat: Weller, "The Workaneaters of Washington," *Free America*, 11–39, pp. 10–12; "Workaneat Garden," *Charles R. Coe Papers*, Box 1, File 8; "Workaneat Seeks 5,000 Gardeners," *P-I*, 11-27-37, p. 6; "Sinclair to Head Production Group," *P-I*, 5-3-38, p. 9; "Incorporations," *ST*, 7-20-38, p. 20; "Workaneaters to Hold 2nd Harvest Festival Tonight," *ST*, 10-20-38, p. 11; Welch, "Workaneaters Earn Their Food," *P-I*, 11-7-38, p. 13; "Workaneaters Asks Use of Big County Farm," *P-I*, 11-15-38, p. 4; "Workaneat Group to Limit Members," *P-I*, 1-20-39, p. 8; "Co-Op Garden Project Closed," *ST*, 12-17-39, p. 20.

Smith: Acena, *The Washington Commonwealth Federation*, pp. 42, 142; "WCF Backs Tom Smith— Fluent," *Washington Commonwealth*, 2-15-36, p. 1; Squire, "Smith Tells Two-Year Rise from Shovel to Desk," *Star*, 12-17-36, p. 2.

Patronage job: "Official Denies Relief, Is Fired," *ST*, 7-7-37, p. 9.

Writers' Project: "State Solon Bares WPA Red Inquiry," *P-I*, 2-16-39, p. 1; "WPA Clears Writers' Group of 'Red' Charge," *P-I*, 2-17-39, p. 3; "Writers' Project 'Riot' Calls Police," *P-I*, 2-18-39, p. 7; "WPA Writers Slur Marcus Whitman and Hail IWW," *ST*, 2-19-39, p. 9; "WPA Director Ends Writers' Project Here," *P-I*, 3-8-40, p. 3; Caldbick, "Federal Writers' Program in Washington Is Terminated after Years of Controversy on March 7, 1940," *historylink.org*.

Butterworth: Farquharson interview by Acena, tape 201A-1, 4-24-75; testimony of Sarah Eldredge, Canwell hearings, 7-22-48, p. 207.

Westman: Westman letter, *Voice of Action*, 8-31-34, p. 2; "Westman Says He Was 'Red,'" *ST*, 1-13-41, p. 4; Markel, "Westman Denied Seat in Senate," *P-I*, 1-25-41, pp. 1, 4; Farquharson interview by Acena, Tape 201A-2, 4-24-75; Clutter, "An American Communist," *ST*, 4-12-90, p. F1.

Meets FDR: Acena, *The Washington Commonwealth Federation, Vol. 2*, pp. 285–287; Pearson and Allen column, *Tacoma News Tribune*, 1-19-39, p. 2.

WCF and Stalin: Rader, "Road to Peace," *New Dealer*, 9-21-39, p 2; DeLacy, "The WCF and War," *New Dealer*, 9-28-39, p. 2; "Subversive Peace," *New Dealer*, 3-4-40, p. 2.

Boettigers: Hunt, "Will Left-Wingers Run Boettiger for Governor?" *Star*, 7-7-39, p. 1; Anna Boettiger to Katherine Littell, 11–17 and 11-30-39, and 4-8-40, *Costigan Papers*, Box 2, Files 12 and 13; Dennett, *Agitprop*, pp. 112–113.

"Naively accepted": "Statement about the Appeal [of] the Original Communist Philosophy," Costigan Papers, Box 2, File 26.

Stalinist: Acena, *The Washington Commonwealth Federation*, pp. 326–327.

Armstrong: His testimony, Canwell hearings, p. 430.

Tyler: Tyler to DeLacy, 5-18-40, Costigan Papers, Box 2, File 13.

DeLacy: "The Stroller," *Argus*, 3-9-40, p. 2; "Second Front Urged at Mass Meeting," *P-I*, 8-15-42, p. 5.

Letters: "Home Building Slump Laid to Working Wives," *P-I*, 1-12-38, p. 3; first name, occupation and camp from 1940 Census; Helen Wales Huron letter, *Sunday News*, 1-22-38, p. 2.

County: "County Acts to Eliminate Working Wives," *P-I*, 1-11-38, p. 3; "Unions Oppose Working Wives," *ST*, 1-13-38, p. 7; "Working Wives to Battle for Equal Rights," *P-I*, 2-13-38, p. 1; "Working Wives' Plea Overridden," *ST*, 2-14-38, p. 1; "Working Wives Group Rebuked by Mrs. Powell," *P-I*, 2-15-38, p. 3.

State: "Ouster of UW Professor's Wife Opposed by Teachers," *ST*, 1-4-38, p. 7.

UW: Palay, "Lea Miller's Protest"; "Ouster of UW Professor's Wife Opposed by Teachers," *ST*, 1-4-38, p. 7; Wood, "Speaking for the Times," *ST*, 1-6-38, p. 6; "Ex-Instructor Hurls Unfair Charge at U," *P-I*, 1-7-38, p. 3; "Professional Women Attack Ouster at U," *P-I*, 1-8-38, p. 1; "Successor and Wife Defend Mrs. Miller," *P-I*, 1-11-38, p. 3; "Labor Council in Endorsement," *Star*, 1-14-38, p. 1; "Conservation Society Will Honor Miller," *ST*, 5-18-38, p. 15; "Dr. R.C. Miller to Quit UW," *P-I*, 7-22-38, p. 3; UW Catalog, Spring quarter 1952, p. 17.

16. The Great Builder, 1930–1939

Canal: "Grays Harbor Canal Survey Is Authorized," *ST*, 3-2-33, p. 21; *Report on Proposed Canals*, Canal Commission, 6-7-33, State Printing Office, 1935; "Against the Canal," *ST*, 2-8-34, p. 6.

Tunnel: Batcheller, "Mammoth Cascade Tunnel Project Revived," *Pacific Builder & Engineer*, 6-6-25, pp. 40–41; *First Report of the Cascade Tunnel Commission*, 1927, Gov. Clarence Martin Subject Files, Highway Dept. 1933 file, Box 2L-1-45, State Archives; "Not Necessarily," *Argus*, 10-25-30, p. 1; Murrow, "Highway Transportation and the Low-Level Cascade Tunnel," presented to the Washington State Planning Council, 3-28-36, Cascade Tunnel File, 1936–37, Toll Bridge Authority Files, Tunnel Files, 1936–62, State Archives; "Pass Highway's Third Link to Be Open Today," *ST*, 8-19-34, p. 5; McDonald, "State May Have World's Longest Tunnel," *ST*, 4-29-45, p. 4.

Seawall: "Sea Wall Work Is Begun under Official's Eyes," ST, 1-15-34, p. 2; "Sea Wall Growing Rapidly," *P-I*, 3-23-36, p. 9.

Names: "Maritime Ave. Name Selected for Waterfront," *ST*, 5-19-32, p. 24; "Cosmos Quay Name Proposed for Waterfront," *ST*, 7-21-32, p. 9; "Naming the Front," *ST*, 8-11-1932, p. 6; "Strolling around the Town," *ST*, 12-15-34, p. 2; 'Interplanetary ships' letter, *ST*, 2-2-35, p. 6; Blethen, "A Name for Front Street," *ST*, 2-17-35, p. 1; "Ex-Sourdoughs Ask Harbor Road Be Named 'Alaska Way,'" *Star*, 4-12-32, p. 7; "Let's Call It Alaska Way!" *Star*, 2-27-35, p. 1; "Wanted—The Right Name!" *ST*, 5-28-36, p. 1; "What's in a Name? Plenty, If It's Pierway," *P-I*, 7-2-36, p. 3; "Alaska Way!" *Star*, 7-3-36, p. 1; "The Stroller," *Argus*, 7-4-36, p. 2; "RR Ave. Now Alaskan Way," *ST*, 7-7-36, p. 5.

Aurora: "Higher and Longer Is Order for Lake Spans," *ST*, 3-12-29, p. 1; "Aurora Bridge Plans Now to Be Completed," *ST*, 3-14-29, p. 2; "Double Deck Bridge Plan Is Abandoned," *ST*, 9-29-29, p. 3; "Margins of Victory at Polls Shown in Unofficial Returns," ST, 3-12-30, pp. 12–13.

University: "State Buys U Bridge Bonds," *P-I*, 12-12-31, p. 4; "New University Bridge Will Be Opened Tonight," *ST*, 4-7-33, p. 3.

Ballard: "New Approaches for Ballard Planned," *ST*, 6-30-29, p. 4; "Ballard Bridge Work Blocked," *P-I*, 6-24-36, p. 3; "U.S. Allots $450,000 to Ballard Span," *P-I*, 10-6-38, p. 1.

Lake Washington: "Mercer Island Bridge Campaign Dates Back Many Years," *Star*, 7-6-38, p. 1; Hunt, "Floating Mercer Span Proposed," *P-I*, 8-12-37, p. 1; "Pontoon Span Called Costly and Dangerous," *ST*, 8-12-37, p. 1; "A Floating Bridge!" *P-I*, 8-13-37, p. 12; Wood, "Speaking for the Times," *ST*, 8-13-37, p. 6; Holt, "Cars Throng Lake Bridge as Tolls End," *P-I*, 7-3-49, p. 1.

Woodland Park: "Save City's Parks," *ST*, 6-5-30, p. 1.

Interurban: Welch, "He's Seen Life from Front of Interurban," *P-I*, 1-22-39, p. 5; "It's Good-By to Everett Interurban," *P-I*, 2-21-39, p. 10.

17. Up, Down, and Up Again, 1936–1939

Real estate: "Local Building Trend Is Upward," *Journal of Commerce*, 1-2-36, p. 1; "Year's Building Permits Increase," *Journal of Commerce*, 1-2-40, p. 5; "Revivified Realty," *Argus*, 5-23-36, p. 1; Niendorff, "Office Building Occupancy Gains," *P-I*, 6-18-36, p. 19; "Apartment Building in Seattle at Standstill," *Star*, 9-12-36, p. 14.

Brooklyn Building: tombstone, Brooklyn Bldg. bonds, *P-I*, 1-2-29, p. 21; Niendorff, "Big Realty Deal in U District," *P-I*, 2-6-36, p. 1; "Big Neon Sign Now Flashing in U District," *ST*, 3-10-37, p. 8.

Hotels: Niendorff, "Seattle Hotel Income Curve Continues up," *P-I*, 4-29-36, p. 15; Niendorff, "Meany Hotel Plan Submitted to Court," *P-I*, 2-16-37, p. 19.

Marriages and Suicides: *Seattle Department of Health and Sanitation Report, 1939–1943*, pp. 22, 124.

Stocks: Anderson, *Economics and the Public Welfare*, p. 440; "Full Text of Morgenthau's Speech," *ST*, 11-11-37, p. 16; Forbes, "Capital Apprehensive," *P-I*, 3-2-37, p. 20; Forbes, "Speculation Lags," *P-I*, 6-17-37, p. 21; "Market Breaks as War Fears in U.S. Mount," *ST*, 9-7-37, p. 1; Wall, "Stocks Run Range from Boom to Panic in 1937," *P-I*, 1-2-38, p. 17.

Strike of capital: "Big Business Strike against U.S. Charged," *P-I*, 12-30-37, p. 1; Wood, "Speaking for the Times," *ST*, 12-31-37 p. 6; Thompson, "On the Record," *P-I*, 1-5-38, p. 6.

Rebound: "Defeat of Shake-Up Bill May Speed Adjournment" and "Stocks Soar as Traders Rush to Buy," *ST*, 4-9-38, p. 1; Dickson, "Senate Passes Five-Billion Tax Bill" and "Stock Prices Soar in Brisk Trading," *P-I*, 4-10-38, p. 1.

Lumber: "Save State's Lumber Industry, Martin Asks Hull," *ST*, 5-14-38, p. 1; Niendorff, "Empire Pact Hits Port Hard, says S.M. Wilson," *P-I*, 5-11-38, p. 16.

Real estate: "Residential and Business Vacancies Show Decrease," *ST*, 2-27-38, p. 18; "City Housing Crisis Told Councilmen," *P-I*, 5-20-38, p. 7; "Report of Department of Buildings 1936–1937," pp. 12–13.

1930s construction: "Seattle Building Permit Figures Year by Year," *Journal of Commerce*, 1-31-40, p. 3.

Edgewater: "Huge Madison Park Project Paves the Way," *P-I*, 6-19-38, p. 8C; "Rental Project to Be Launched," *ST*, 6-26-38, p. 21; "Edgewater Park Apartment Project Open for Inspection," *P-I*, 4-16-39, p. 11.

Labor: "Unions Reject 8-Hr. Day Bid," *ST*, 1-22-38, p. 2; "N.W. Contractors Rap Six-Hour Day," *P-I*, 1-30-38, p. 6; "Bankers, Unions Differ on Hours," *ST*, 2-17-38, p. 3; "Union Fights Eight-Hour Day," *P-I*, 2-18-38, p. 10; "Builders Offer 3-Yr Labor Pact," *ST*, 2-20-38, p. 9; Letter from Norbert

Cormier, *P-I*, 4-7-38, p. 10; "Building Labor Pact Is Signed," *ST*, 10-13-38, p. 20; "Trades Adopt 8-Hour Day for Emergency Jobs," *ST*, 9-28-40, p. 1.

Plasterboard: "Plan to Amend Building Code Raises Issues," *P-I*, 4-6-38, p. 1; "Langlie OK's Plasterboard," *ST*, 6-16-38, p. 5.

Rents: Classified ad, *ST*, 1-26-39, p. 28.

Not built: "Plans Revealed for $1,000,000 Seattle Hotel," *P-I*, 3-8-39, p. 3.

Shortage: Williams, "City Housing Shortage Rapidly Nearing Crisis," *ST*, 11-30-41, pp. 1, 20.

Permits: "Seattle Building Permit Figures Year by Year," *Journal of Commerce*, 1-31-40, p. 3.

Houses: "100 New Homes a Month Going up in Seattle," *P-I*, 7-1-39, p. 1; "Grade of Homes Here Improves," *ST*, 7-13-39, p. 3.

Alvensleben: Lazarus, "Vancouver's Flamboyant Entrepreneur," *Vancouver Historical Society Letter*, 3–2013; Nagler, "Enemy Aliens and Internment in World War II," *Utah Historical Quarterly*, Vol. 58, No. 4, 1990; "Alvensleben, Long Resident, Now a Citizen," *ST*, 3-28-39, p. 5; "Alvo von Alvensleben, 86, Son of a German Count," *P-I*, 10-23-65, p. 3.

Normandy Park: "Seattle: Schwabacher & Co.," tracingthetribe.blogspot.com; Kershner, "Normandy Park Thumbnail History," *historylink.org*; Helen Kludt, *Wonderful World of Woods and Water: A History of Normandy Park*, Emerald City Graphics, 1991; "3 Tree Point Tract Is Sold for $450,000," *P-I*, 8-15-26, p. 1; tombstone, land co. bonds, *P-I*, 4-8-28, p. 6; Normandy Park ad, *P-I*, 5-18-28, p. 4; "Normandy Park House," *ST*, 5-12-29, p. 24.

Fobes: Born 8-17-1899 (1930 Census); "Fobes to Build at Normandy," *P-I*, 5-16-29, p. 9; "Business Man Kills Himself Over Worries," *P-I*, 6-13-31, p. 1; "Demand Continues for Fine Homes," *P-I*, 10-18-31, p. 20; "Davies Gives Chevi Outlook," *ST*, 4-5-36, p. 25.

Work-out: Niendorff, "Water Front Bonds Jump as Tracts Sell," *P-I*, 1-25-39, p. 17.

Stadium: Eskenazi, "Seattle First Citizen Emil Sick," and "Hutch—a Man and an Award," *SportsPressNW.com*, 4-17-2000, and 1-24-2012; "Ball Fans Hail Opening of New $350,000 Park," *ST*, 6-15-38, pp. 1, 19; Boren, "Society Attends Opening of New Baseball Stadium," *ST*, 6-16-38, p. 18.

Arson: "Man Owns Up to Setting 70 Seattle Fires," *P-I*, 5-7-35, p. 1; "Dugdale Ball Park Fire Laid to Driscoll," *P-I*, 5-10-35, p. 1.

Construction: "Church First Unit Planned by St. Mark's," *P-I*, 8-29-26, p. 3; "Church Asks City to Approve Tower," *ST*, 9-8-28, p. 2; "Cathedral Ground to Be Broken Today," *ST*, 9-30-28, p. 5; "$2,000,000 Edifice," *P-I*, 1-4-29, p. 1.

Foreclosure: "$185,000 Paid for Cathedral," *P-I*, 5-19-40, p. 3; Williams, "Bank to Take Possession of St. Mark's," *P-I*, 4-28-41, p. 1; "Means to Save Church Sought," *ST*, 4-28-41, p. 1; Welch, "Mortgage Holders Take Over Church," *P-I*, 5-1-41, p. 1; Rue, "Dean Lays Loss of St. Mark's to Disinterest," *P-I*, 5-5-41, p. 5; "Dean Opposed by Eddy in St. Mark's Rift," *P-I*, 5-16-41, p. 1; "Rev. McLaughlan Estate $51,336.85," *P-I*, 11-14-46, p. 4; "A Brief History of St. Mark's," saintmarks.org.

18. Enterprise, 1933–1939

Ferries: Shrader, "The Black Ball Line, 1929–1951," Shorey, 1980, pp. 2–14; Stein, *Safe Passage: The Birth of the Washington State Ferries*, WSF, 2001.

Pacific Car: Burdick, "Building a Box Car Every 30 Minutes," *ST* Sunday supplement, 6-15-30, p. 9; "Pigott Group Buys Pacific Car Foundry Control," *ST*, 2-17-34, p. 1.

500 workers: "$25,000 Loss in Renton Fire," *ST*, 7-27-36, p. 5; "Pigott, Paul," *HistoryLink.org* essay No. 3193.

Aircraft Plywood: Perkins, "Aircraft Plywood Company" monograph; "New Plant in Aircraft Production Is Planned," *ST*, 7-1-29, p. 1; "Plywood Offers High Yield Issue of Convertibles," *ST*, 7-3-29, p. 17; "Three Seattle Men Named on Board of Washington Veneer," *ST*, 10-24-29, p. 33; Burdick, "Ribbons of Gold from Washington Logs That Girdle the Globe," *ST*, 5-11-30, Sunday supplement, p. 9; "Local Plywood Plant to Open with 100 Men," *ST*, 7-31-32, p. 1; "AF of L Will Picket CIO Plywood Plant," *ST*, 9-24-37, p. 16; Niendorff, "Aircraft Plywood to Effect Merger," *P-I*, 4-16-37, p. 25; offer to redeem bonds, *ST*, 11-26-37, p. 28.

Congress, mail contracts: "Boeing Made Millions from $259 Investment," *Star*, 2-6-34, p. 1; "Boeing Bares High Salaries Paid to Agents at Capital," *P-I*, 2-7-34, pp. 1, 4; Lewis, "Roosevelt Cancels Air Mail Contracts, Orders Army to Take Up Air Mail Schedules," *P-I*, 2-10-34, p. 1; Serling, *Legend & Legacy*, pp. 23–27.

Bone: "Bone Will Ask U.S. Factories for Aircraft," *P-I*, 2-27-34, p. 2.

Egtvedt: Thomas, "Claire Egtvedt of Boeing, Developer of B-17, Is Dead," *NYT*, 10-21-75, p. 40.

Prototypes: Serling, *Legend & Legacy*, pp. 18–19; "Monomail Plane Built by Boeing Displays Speed," *ST*, 5-23-30, p. 11; "Cigar-Type Plane Swoops Like Swallow," *P-I*, 6-30-31, p. 2; "Boeing Bomber Rated Fastest by Corps Expert," *ST*, 1-25-32, p. 15.

United Air: "Four Boeing Air Transport Lines Merged," *P-I*, 6-1-31, p. 14.

The 247: "New Boeing Transport Will Be Fastest Big Airplane in World," *P-I*, 3-26-33, p. 15; Boeing ad, *Star*, 11-27-33, p. 9; Serling, *Legend & Legacy*, pp. 20–22.

B-17: "First Bombers Ready by Fall," *ST*, 12-23-35, p. 9.

Plant Two: "Boeing Plant Expands, Buys 28-Acre Plot," *P-I*, 3-8-36, p. 1; "Completion of Boeing Field Work Assured," *ST*, 5-3-36, p. 1.

Finances: Niendorff, "New Boeing Stock Offering at $23," *P-I*, 6-2-37, p. 22; Niendorff, "Boeing Declares First Dividend," *P-I*, 11-18-37, p. 19; "Boeing's 1937 Profit 51 Cents Per Share," *P-I*, 3-27-38, p. 18; Niendorff, "Boeing Reports on 1938 Record," *P-I*, 4-2-39, p. 24; Niendorff, "Boeing Research," *P-I*, 5-26-39, p. 29.

Quote: Boeing, "Selling of Speed to Travelers of U.S. Necessary," *P-I*, 8-25-29, p. M1.

Clipper: Serling, *Legend & Legacy*, pp. 38–41; "World's Biggest Clipper Nears Completion in Seattle," *P-I*, 2-14-38, p. 5; Van der Linden, "How World War II Killed the Flying Boat," Smithsonian Air and Space Museum.

Flight test: "Thousands Gaze as Giant Clipper Warms Up," *ST*, 6-3-38, p. 7; Bermann, "Mishap Mars Trial Run of Boeing Clipper," *P-I*, 6-4-38, p. 1; Bermann, "Maiden Flight Planned for Clipper Today," *P-I*, 6-5-38, p. 1.

The company: Serling, *Legend & Legacy*, pp. 20–27; "Boeing Plants Make Seattle Aviation Hub," *P-I*, 7-25-37, progress section, p. 4.

Bigger Clipper: "Boeing Designs 100-Place Plane," *ST*, 6-23-38, p. 1.

Stratoliner: "Boeing Plant Builds 'Stratoliners,'" *ST*, 3-13-38, p. 7; Bermann, "Stratoliner Taken Aloft on Test Flight," *P-I*, 1-1-39, p. 1; "10 Die in Stratoliner Crash," *ST*, 3-19-39, p. 1; "Stratoliner

324 *Notes for pages 257–267*

Structure Described," *Star*, 4-5-39, p. 2; McClary, "Boeing S-307 Stratoliner Prototype Crashes near Alder in Pierce County, Killing 10, on March 18, 1939," *historylink.org*.

B-17: "Boeing Begins Mass Output of Huge Bombers for Army," *ST*, 5-31-39, pp. 1, 11.

Plant: "Aircraft Plan Boosts Payroll," *P-I*, 7-12-36, p. SF-7; "Boeing to Spend Quarter-Million for Expansion," *ST*, 3-28-37, p. 1; "Big Planes Can Be Handled," *Star*, 6-8-38, p. 12.

Jobs: "Boeing: Company One of U.S. Leaders in Its Field," *P-I*, 7-23-39, p. P-3; "Boeing Facilities Increased with Record Orders on Hand," *Journal of Commerce*, 1-31-40, pp. 9, 12.

Shipyard: "Board Named to Act in City Shipping Crisis," *P-I*, 6-5-38, p. 1; "Seattle Shipbuilding Co. Launched," *P-I*, 12-10-38, p. 1; Blethen, "All Hands on Deck!" *ST*, 12-18-38, p. 1; "Shipyard Drive Gets $150,000 in Pledges," *P-I*, 12-21-38, p. 1; "Advantages for Shipyard Here Listed," *P-I*, 12-15-38, p. 3; "Business Men Called on to Aid Shipyards," *ST*, 12-28-38, p. 1; "Answers Given to Questions on Proposed Shipyard Here," *P-I*, 12-30-38, p. 8; "An Open Letter to Capital and Labor on Shipbuilding," *Star*, 1-11-39, p. 1; "Chamber Head Sounds Plea for Civic Unity," *P-I*, 1-15-39, p. 5; "4 New Ships Ordered for Seattle Line," *ST*, 1-27-39, p. 1.

Revival: "Seattle Yard Gets Five U.S. Ships in $10,000,000 Bid," *Star*, 9-16-39, p. 1.

Linden: Whitehouse, "Linden Comes Back!" *Star*, 4-28-38, p. 1

Mall: "Drive-In Market to Open Tomorrow," *P-I*, 3-26-31, p. 14.

New products: "Sales Speeded by Name Stamp," *P-I*, 7-19-36, p. 9; "Eba's Groceries Extends Service," *P-I*, 12-18-36, p. 13; "Public Acclaims New Paper Milk 'Bottles,'" *P-I*, 3-16-38, p. 12; "New Treatment Improves Milk," *P-I*, 4-5-40, p. 12.

Phones: Pacific Telephone ad, *ST*, 11-29-38, p. 11; Niendorff, "Telephones in Use on Pacific Coast Hit All-Time High," *P-I*, 2-16-39, p. 17.

Air travel: Bird, "100 Daily Take Planes from Seattle," *Star*, 10-15-37, p. 5; "Radio Landing-Control Now Operating at Boeing Field," *ST*, 6-19-38, p. 12.

19. Forward from Hard Times

Marshall: "The Stroller," *Argus*, 6-26-37, p. 2; Marshall, "Panay Crew Praised by Jim Marshall for Bravery under Fire," *ST*, 12-14-37, pp. 1, 9; "Jim Marshall's Surgeons Find Many Wounds," *ST*, 12-16-37, p. 1; "Panay Bomb Victim Now Recovering," *P-I*, 1-29-38, p. 3; "Japanese Army Boasted Destruction of Panay, Says Jim Marshall," *ST*, 2-12-38, p. 1; Welch, "Marshall, Back from China, Bares Inside Story of War," *P-I*, 2-13-38, p. 1.

Military: "Exchange Bldg. Gets Navy Plaque," *P-I*, 6-29-46, p. 9; "City Postwar Plans Urged," *P-I*, 3-21-44, p. 3; Higgs, *Depression, War and Cold War*, pp. 111–118.

Northgate: Fussell, "$12,000,000 Business Center North of City Is Planned," *ST*, 2-22-48, p. 1; "Met Tract Pioneer's Son Heads Northgate," *ST*, 5-11-49, p. 23.

Legislators by party: Web pages of Washington Senate and House.

Union density: Bureau of Labor Statistics news, 1-28-2025.

Co-op Books: Schwartz, "Somewhere out There Is a Bookstore for You," *ST*, 7-9-77, p. B1.

Technocrats: Duncan, "Technocrats Survive, Offer Ideas for 90s," *ST*, 2-20-90, p. C3.

"Soft on capitalism": Scates, *Warren G. Magnuson and the Shaping of 20th Century America*, p. 59.

DeLacy: Niendorff, "Demos' Headache over DeLacy Grows," *P-I*, 9-24-44, pp. 1, 6; Niendorff, "Harlin Hits DeLacy's Record," *P-I*, 9-27-44, pp. 1, 6; Niendorff, "Truman Hints GOP Would Close Coulee," *P-I*, 10-20-44, pp. 1, 6; "Seattle May Have Soviet Consulate Soon, Says DeLacy," *P-I*, 3-9-45, p. 5; Hanson, "Mission to Soviet Embassy Detailed," *P-I*, 10-14-55, pp. 1, 6; Williams, "DeLacy Attacks Hoover, Denies Reds Run Policy," *ST*, 4-7-46, p. 2; HUAC testimony, 9-14-54, pp. 6886–6887; Evans, "Whatever Happened to Hugh DeLacy," *P-I*, 6-6-76, p. A2.

Costigan: Note to Howard Costigan Papers and Guide to DeLacy Papers, UW Special Collections; "Costigan Tells Probe How He Aided Reds," *P-I*, 10-20-55, pp. 1, 5.

Woodward: *Journal of Proceedings*, California State Grange, 1948, p. 109.

Farquharson: Licata, "Farquharson, Mary," historylink.org; interview by Albert Acena, 4-24-75, Farquharson papers; "Educators Assail Peacetime Draft," *NYT*, 7-9-40, p. 4; display ad by Post War World Council, *NYT*, 7-25-45, p. 10.

Tyler: "R.G. Tyler, Ex-UW Dean," *ST*, 8-5-67, p. B12.

Wakefield: "Witness Charges Red Spy Ring in Alaska," *P-I*, 9-15-49, p. 1; Page, "Alaska King Crab Boom," *P-I*, 8-16-64, Sunday pictorial, pp. 1, 10, 11; Patty, "Alaska," *ST*, 7-27-75, p. 25; Patty, "Alaska," *ST*, 10-2-77, p. 64; Mancel G. Blackford, "Small Business in America: Two Case Studies," *Business and Economic History*, pp. 11–13; Sharon Alvarez, "How Lowell Wakefield Made Crab King," *Entrepreneur & Innovation Exchange*, 10-11-2016; B. L. Brynko, "Lowell A. Wakefield," The Free Library, Alaska Business Publishing, 1-1-90; "Lowell Wakefield and the Birth of the Alaska King Crab Fishery," Kodiak Maritime Museum, 9-21-2022; Klehr, *The Millionaire Was a Soviet Mole*, p. 15.

Duck Island: "Swans in Green Lake," *P-I*, 4-26-37, p. 4.

Horton Building: Niendorff, "Dexter Horton Bldg. Reorganization Plan Assailed in Court," *P-I*, 3-11-36, p. 19; "Business and Finance," *Argus*, 3-14-36, p. 4; "Dexter Horton Plan Upheld," *ST*, 3-18-36, p. 24.

Appendix: Seattle Dailies and Their Biases

P-I, Times bias: Haarsager, "Choosing Silence: A Case of Reverse Agenda Setting in Depression Era News Coverage," *Journal of Mass Media Ethics*, 1991, pp. 35–46.

Propaganda: Lovering, "Trend of the Times," *ST*, 12-24-29, p. 16.

Optimists, pessimists: Forbes, "Stock Market Recovery Will Exceed Expectations—Forbes," *P-I*, 1-3-30, p. 2F; "Forbes on Way Here, Escape East's Gloom," *P-I*, 7-18-30, p. 1; Forbes, "In This Spirit Enter New Year—You'll Win," *P-I*, 1-2-31, p. 16; Lovering, "Trend of the Times," *ST*, 1-19-30, p. 28; 2-16-30, p. 28; 4-1-30, p. 27; 6-30-30, p. 24; Hill, "Andrew Price Finds Seattle Banks Strong," *P-I*, 10-25-30, p. 16.

Lidablanche Robe: "Beginning Her Adventure," *P-I*, 1-24-32, p. 9, also 1-11-32, p. 9; 1-12-32, p. 11; 1-13-32, p. 13; 1-14-32, p. 13; 1-15-32, p. 13; 1-16-32, p. 11; 1-17-32, p. 9; 1-18-32, p. 9.

Angelina: "Weeds Kill Starving Child," *ST*, 5-4-34, p. 1; "Baby's Fatal Meal of Weeds Laid to Hunger," *P-I*, 5-5-34, p. 1; "Father's Pride Made Him Delay Relief Request," *ST*, 5-6-34, p. 1.

Curriers: Heise, "Evicted Family Waits for Time Dad's Job Can Start," *Star*, 4-11-39, p. 1; "Seattle Opens Heart to Needy Family," *Star*, 4-12-39, p. 14; Heise, "Roofless Family Forced Out of Second Home," *Star*, 4-15-39, p. 1; Census report, 4-17-40.

Dole: "Costly By-Product," *ST*, 8-15-31, p. 6; Hearst, "Employment, Not Dole, Should Be America's Program for Needy," *P-I*, 2-6-31, p. 1; "Failure," *Star*, 10-13-30, p. 6; "Relief a Government Duty," *Star*, 2-17-31, p. 6; "Charity, When Needed," *Star*, 11-21-31, p. 2.

P-I: "Bar the Radicals," *P-I*, 5-7-36, p. 8; "'Red' Congress Barred by School Board," *P-I*, 5-23-36, p. 1; "United Front Policy of American Reds Explained," *P-I*, 12-22-35, p. 12; "Radicals" *Argus*, 2-8-36, p. 3.

Gareth Jones stories: "Russia, Land of Starvation," *P-I*, 1-12-35, p. 2; "There Is No Bread," *P-I*, 1-13-35, p. 2; "Fate of Thrifty in USSR," *P-I*, 1-14-35, p. 2.

Times: Wood, "Speaking for the Times," 9-4-36, p. 6.

Star: "Guns and Billies Are Not the Answer to Parade Like This; It's Pay Checks!" *Star*, 3-6-30, p. 1; "Seattle Must Stay United," *Star*, 5-7-32, p. 1; "Who Runs the University, Anyway?" *Star*, 5-26-33, p. 8; "A One-Way Ticket," Star, 11-11-37, p. 4; "A Job for Democrats: Clean Out the Communists!" *Star*, 8-3-38, p. 1.

Court packing: "After Some Reflection," *Star*, 2-23-37, p. 1.

Anti-Communism: "What Happened to the Star?" *Sunday News*, 12-4-37, p. 2.

Principal Works Consulted

Books
Ames, William E., and Roger A. Simpson, *Unionism or Hearst: The Seattle* Post-Intelligencer *Strike of 1936*, Pacific Northwest Labor History Association, 1978.
Anderson, Benjamin M., *Economics and the Public Welfare: A Financial and Economic History of the United States, 1914–1946*, Liberty Fund, 1979.
Asaka, Megan, *Seattle from the Margins*, University of Washington Press, 2022.
Berner, Richard C., *Seattle 1921–1940: From Boom to Bust*, Charles Press, 1992.
Blanchard, Leslie, *The Street Railway Era in Seattle: A Chronicle of Six Decades*, Harold E. Cox, 1968.
Dennett, Eugene V., *Agitprop: The Life of an American Working-Class Radical*, SUNY, 1990.
Eichengreen, Barry, *Golden Fetters: The Gold Standard and the Great Depression, 1919–1939*, Oxford University Press, 1995.
Friedheim, Robert L., *The Seattle General Strike*, University of Washington Press, 1964.
Gravelle, Randal, *Hooverville and the Unemployed: Seattle During the Great Depression*, Self-published, 2015.
Higgs, Robert, *Depression, War and Cold War: Studies in Political Economy*, Oxford University Press, 2006.
Hopper, Mary E., *A Frontier of the Spirit*, Seattle, self-published, not dated.
Hughes, John C., *Pressing On: Two Family-Owned Newspapers in the 21st Century*, Washington State Legacy Project, 2015.
Klehr, Harvey, *The Millionaire Was a Soviet Mole*, Encounter Books, 2019.
Knight, Neil Roy, *Gold Horizon: The Life Story of Manson F. Backus*, Seattle, Dogwood Press, 1937.
Lyons, Eugene, *The Red Decade*, Bobbs-Merrill, 1941.
Morgan, Murray, *Friend of the Family*, Washington Mutual, 1989.
Morgan, Murray, *Skid Road*, University of Washington, 1982.
Mullins, William H., *The Depression and the Urban West Coast, 1929–1933*, Indiana University Press, 1991.
Pierce, J. Kingston, *Eccentric Seattle*, WSU Press, 2003.
Porteous, Jeffrey, *Taking Stock: A True Tale of Seattle's Investment Community*, Northwest Center for Research Journalism, 1989.
Ramsey, Bruce A., *The Panic of 1893*, Caxton, 2018.
Sale, Roger, *Seattle, Past to Present*, University of Washington Press, 1976.
Serling, Robert J., *Legend & Legacy: The Story of Boeing and Its People*, St. Martin's Press, 1982.
Straumann, Tobias, *1931: Debt, Crisis and the Rise of Hitler*, Oxford, 2019.
White, Richard D., Jr., *Kingfish: The Reign of Huey Long*, Random House, 2006.

Dissertations
Acena, Albert A., "The Washington Commonwealth Federation: Reform Politics and the Popular Front," MA, History, University of Washington, 1975.
Baker, Miner, "The Proposed City Light Merger," MA, Sociology, University of Washington, 1938.
Branom, Robert T., "Against the Hun: Anti-Germanism at the Seattle Public Schools and the University of Washington, 1917–1918," History, University of Washington, 2006.
Dick, Wesley Arden, "The Genesis of Seattle City Light," MA thesis, University of Washington, 1965.

Longnecker, Justin, "History of the University Book Store, 1900–1955," PhD, Business, University of Washington, 1956.
Roy, Donald Francis, "Hooverville: A Study of a Community of Homeless Men in Seattle," Sociology, University of Washington, 1935.
Sparks, William O'Dell, "J. D. Ross and Seattle City Light, 1917–1932," MA, University of Washington, 1964.
Willis, Terry R., "Unemployed Citizens of Seattle, 1900–1933: Hulet Wells, Seattle Labor and the Struggle for Economic Security," PhD, Philosophy, University of Washington, 1997.

Articles

Aguado, Iago Gil, "The Creditanstalt Crisis of 1931 and the Failure of the Austro-German Customs Union Project," *The Historical Journal*, Vol. 44, No. 1, 2001.
Alvarez, Sharon, "How Lowell Wakefield Made Crab King," *Entrepreneur & Innovation Exchange*, 10-11-2016. Retrieved December 21, 2024, from https://eiexchange.com/content/231-how-lowell-wakefield-made-crab-king
Blecha, Peter, "Linden Records: Seattle's 'Lost' Postwar Music Company," historylink.org essay 7772, 6-8-2006. https://historylink.org/File/7772
Brown, Giles T., "The Culmination and Decline of Pacific Coastwise Shipping, 1916–1936," *Pacific Northwest Quarterly*, Vol. 40, No. 3, July 1949.
Caldbick, John, "Federal Writers' Program in Washington Is Terminated after Years of Controversy on March 7, 1940," historylink.org essay 21271, 7-12-2021.
Chesley, Frank, "Seattle City Council resolution establishes the Seattle Housing Authority on March 13, 1939," historylink.org essay 8992, 4-22-2009.
Cole, Harold L., and Lee E. Ohanian, "New Deal Policies and the Persistence of the Great Depression: A General Equilibrium Analysis," Working paper 597, Federal Reserve Bank of Minneapolis, Research Department. May 2001. https://doi.org/10.21034/wp.597
Cooper, Matt, "The Elephant in the Room," *Oregon Quarterly*, Spring 2014.
Edwards, Katharine, "'Anti-Nepotism' Policies at the University of Washington in the Depression (Part Two)," University of Washington, 2009. https://depts.washington.edu/depress/women_uw_working_wives.shtml
Eskenazi, David, "Seattle's First Citizen Emil Sick," and "Hutch—A Man and an Award," sportspressnw.com, posted April 17, 2000, and January 24, 2012.
Eskenazi, David, and Steve Rudman, "Genesis of Husky Stadium," 8-27-2013, and "The Washington Athletic Club," sportspressnw.com, 10-29-2013.
Flom, Eric, and John Caldbick, "5th Avenue Theatre (Seattle)," Historylink.org essay 3750, 3-17-2012; "Paramount Theatre (Seattle), essay 3973, 5-11-2012; and Flom, "Orpheum Theatre," essay 4267, 12-12-2003.
Flynn, Gary, "Northwest Brewing Company Inc. 1931–1937," www.brewerygems.com.
Garrett, Garet, "Labor at the Golden Gate," *Saturday Evening Post*, March 18, 1939.
Goss, E. Lyle, "University Book Store: A Personal Overview." University of Washington Special Collections, 1979.
Haarsager, Sandra, "Choosing Silence: A Case of Reverse Agenda Setting in Depression Era News Coverage," *Journal of Mass Media Ethics*, Vol. 6, No. 1, 1991.
Iwamoto, Gary, "Rise and Fall of an Empire Furuya," *International Examiner*, Vol. 32, No. 16, 8-30-2005. https://iexaminer.org/rise-fall-of-an-empire-furuya-imm-1890-2/
Jorgensen, Erika, and Jeffrey Sachs, "Default and Renegotiation of Latin American Foreign Bonds in the Interwar Period," Working Paper No. 2636, National Bureau of Economic Research, June 1988.
Kemezis, Kathleen, "Edmond Meany Hotel (1930–1931)," historylink.org essay 9163, 9-19-2009.

Kersher, Kate, "Normandy Park–Thumbnail History," historylink.org essay 10759, 4-3-2014.
Leuchtenberg, William E., "A Klansman Joins the Court: The Appointment of Hugo L. Black," *University of Chicago Law Review*, Vol. 41, No. 1, Fall 1973.
Licata, Eleanor, "Farquharson, Mary," historylink.org essay 10264, 12-6-2012.
Macey, Jonathan R., "Double Liability for Bank Shareholders," *Wake Forest Law Review* Vol. 27, No. 31, 1992.
Marquis, Ralph, and Frank Smith, "Double Liability for Bank Stock," *American Economic Review*, Vol. 27, No. 3, September 1937.
McClary, Daryl, "Boeing S-307 Stratoliner Prototype Crashes near Alder in Pierce County, Killing 10, on March 18, 1939," historylink.org essay 2230, 3-4-2022.
McDonald, Judith A., Anthony Patrick O'Brien, and Colleen M. Callahan, "Trade Wars: Canada's Reaction to the Smoot-Hawley Tariff," *Journal of Economic History*, Vol. 57, No. 4., December 1997.
Novak, Matt, "Musicians Wage War against Evil Robots," *Smithsonian Magazine*, 2-10-2012.
Palay, Claire, "Lea Miller's Protest: Married Women's Jobs at the University of Washington," University of Washington, 2009. https://depts.washington.edu/depress/women_uw_lea_miller.shtml
Palmquist, Rod, "Labor's Great War on the Seattle Waterfront," Waterfront Workers History Project, University of Washington.
Patch, Buel W., "Soviet-American Political and Trade Relations," *CQ Researcher*, 2-24-1933.
Perkins, Nelson S., "Aircraft Plywood Company," monograph, Plywood Pioneers Association, November 1975.
Pinar, William F., "The Communist Party/NAACP Rivalry in the Trials of the Scottsboro Nine," *Counterpoints* (New York, N.Y.), vol. 163, 2001, pp. 753–811.
Richardson, Gary, "Banking Panics of 1930–31: November 1930–August 1931," Federal Reserve Bank of Richmond, https://www.federalreservehistory.org/essays/banking-panics-1930-31.
Schneider, John, "Seattle Radio History: KJR and KOMO," theradiohistorian.org.
Spitzer, Hugh D., "A Washington State Income Tax—Again?" *Seattle University Law Review* 515 (1993). https://digitalcommons.law.seattleu.edu/sulr/vol16/iss2/1/
Stein, Alan J., "Ross, James Delmage," historylink.org essay 2557, 7-22-2002.
Stein, Alan J., historylink.org essays 5294, 5295, 5296, 5081 on the Black Ball Line and Washington State Ferries, posted 2003.
Tate, Cassandra, "Ehrlichman, Ben Bernard," historylink.org essay 7861, 8-6-2006.
Tate, Cassandra, "Farmer, Frances," and "God Dies: An Essay by Frances Farmer," historylink.org essays 5058 and 4008, 1-17-2003 and 11-6-2002.
Weller, George, "The Workaneaters of Washington," *Free America*, Vol. 3, No. 11, November 1939.
White, Eugene Nelson, "State-Sponsored Insurance of Bank Deposits in the United States, 1907–1929," *Journal of Economic History*, Vol. 41, No. 3, September 1981.

Papers

Associated Students of the University of Washington, University of Washington Special Collections.
Burke, Robert E., Papers, University of Washington Special Collections.
Coe, Charles R., Papers, University of Washington Special Collections.
Costigan, Howard G., Papers, University of Washington Special Collections.
Dennett, Eugene, Papers, University of Washington Special Collections
Eby, Edwin Harold, Papers, University of Washington Special Collections.
Farquharson, Mary, Papers, University of Washington Special Collections.
Murrow, Lacey V., Papers, Washington State Archives.
Ross, James D., Papers, University of Washington Special Collections.

Shorter, Fred, Church of the People Papers, University of Washington Special Collections.
Summers, Thane, Papers, University of Washington Special Collections.
University of Washington Board of Regents, University of Washington Special Collections.
University of Washington President's Office, University of Washington Special Collections.
Washington Emergency Relief Administration Papers, Washington State Archives, Olympia.
Wells, Hulet, Papers, University of Washington Special Collections.
Zioncheck, Marion A., Papers, University of Washington Special Collections.

Documents and Reports

Arnold, Claude, "Review of Emergency Relief Activities of King County Welfare Board, February 1933 to April 1935," Department of Public Welfare, 1935, Welfare Department Reports 1933–1949, Series 1715, Box 1.
"Bank Histories 1907–1937," Washington Division of Banking, V4-E-13-1, Box 5, Washington State Archives, Olympia.
"City of Seattle Department of Lighting: An Analysis," Hartley, Rogers & Co, Seattle, 1938. ACC 0838–004, Box 13, Ross Papers, University of Washington.
"Constitution of the Unemployed Citizens League," Seattle Public Library, 1932.
Gordon, Karen, "Landmarks Preservation Board Report on Designation," Washington Athletic Club, LPB 129/08, March 11, 2008.
"Marion Anthony Zioncheck, Late a Representative from Washington," House Document No. 352, 75th Congress, 1938. https://www.govinfo.gov/content/pkg/SERIALSET-10123_00_00-005-0352-0000/pdf/SERIALSET-10123_00_00-005-0352-0000.pdf
Senate Committee on Banking and Currency, "The Pecora Investigation: Stock Exchange Practices and the Causes of the 1929 Wall Street Crash," 1934.
House Special Committee on Communist Activities in the United States, "Investigation of Communist Propaganda," Hearings, 71st Congress, Second Session, Part 5, Vol. 1, Seattle, October 3, 1930, and Portland, October 4, 1930.
House Committee on Un-American Activities, 83rd Congress, October 3, 1952; March 16, May 28, June 2 and 9, 1954.
"Report of Department of Buildings, 1936–1937," City of Seattle, May 17, 1938.
"Report of Joint Legislative Fact-Finding Committee on Un-American Activities Established by the Thirtieth Legislature Under House Concurrent Resolution No. 10" (Canwell Hearings), Olympia, 1948.
Seattle Chamber of Commerce Records, Seattle Public Library, 1935.
Seattle Department of Health and Sanitation, Reports of 1932–1935, 1937–1938 and 1939–1943. Seattle Public Library.
Seattle Municipal Street Railway Annual Reports, 1930–1933. Seattle Public Library.
Seattle Stock Exchange, Annual Reports, years ended 2-28-30 and 2-28-31. Seattle Public Library.
Spencer, R. D, "Report of First Examination, Public Welfare Department, King County, 1933–1936," File 407-6-40, Box 6, King County Municipal Audit Reports.
Summary for 814 2ND Ave. (Mehlhorn Building), Seattle Historical Sites, Seattle Department of Neighborhoods, posted at Seattle.gov, accessed April 25, 2019.
"Washington's Tax History: A Brief Overview of the Development of State and Local Taxes In Washington," Department of Revenue, Olympia.
Wells, Hulet, and Wray M. Lewis, "Minutes of the State Convention of Delegates from the Unemployed Citizens League," Tacoma, May 29–30, 1932.

Court Cases

Abrams v. Seattle, 23 P.2d 869 Wash. (1933).
Conant v. State, 197 Wash. 21 (1938).

Culliton v. Chase, 174 Wash. 363, 25 P.2d 81 (1933).
Denny v. Wooster, 175 Wash. 272, 27 P.2d 326 (1933).
De Jonge v. Oregon, 299 U.S. 353 (1937).
Griffiths v. Robinson, 181 Wash. 438, 43 P.2d 977 (1935).
King County v. Superior Court, 199 Wash. 591, 92 P.2d 694 (1939).
Osner & Mehlhorn, bankruptcy 31248, U.S. District Court, Seattle (1930–1937).
Ridder Bros. v. Blethen, 142 F2d 395 (9th Cir. 1944).
Ridder v. Blethen, 166 P.2d 834 (Wash. 1946).
State v. Comer, 17 P.2d 643 (Wash. 1932).
State v. Comer, 28 P.2d 1027 (Wash. 1934).
State v. Hiatt, 60 P.2d 71 (Wash. 1936).
State v. Linden, 171 Wash. 92, P.2d 635 (1932).
State v. Matson Co., 182 Wash. 507 (1935).
State v. Moe, 24 P.2d 638 (Wash. 1933).
State v. Pierce, 175 Wash. 461, P.2d 1098 (1933).
State ex rel. Stiner v. Yelle, 174 Wash 402, 25 P.2d 91 (1933).
Von Herberg v. Seattle, 288 P. 646 (Wash. 1930).
Washington Loan & Securities Co. bankruptcy 31992, U.S. District Court, Seattle (1931–1936).
Willamette Valley Lumber Co. v. Watzek, 5 F. Supp. 689 (1934).

Index

Abel, Don G. 84, 155, 223
Aberhart, William 141
Acena, Albert 226
Aircraft: Boeing 247 254; Boeing B-9 254; Boeing B-17 254–55, 257–59; Boeing Clipper 255–56, 258; Boeing Model 80 8; Boeing Stratoliner 257–58; Dornier Do-X 255–56; Douglas DC-3 254; Hughes Spruce Goose 256
Aircraft Plywood Corporation 249–52
Al G. Barnes Circus 74
Alaskan Way 231–32
Albertson, Abraham 9
Allen, Edmund T. 256
Allen, Robert S. 225
Alvensleben, Alvo von 242–44
American Broadcasting Company (ABC) 43–45
American Federation of Labor (AFL) 117, 149, 152, 154, 156, 158–59, 167, 169, 180, 184, 214
American Legion 183
American Mail Line 258
Ames, Harry 241
Amtorg Trading Corporation 5, 30, 31
Anderson, Marian 44
Anhalt, Frederick 20, 57, 58
Arai, Clarence T. 158
arboretum 154–55
Argus, The: anti-radicalism 134, 185, 206; cable car appeal 185; dismissive of *P-I*'s "Red horrors" 279
Armstrong, Everhardt 131, 166, 168
Armstrong, Harry C. 213, 226–27
Auburn National Bank 35
aviation 5–8, 11, 250–56, 261

Backus, Manson II 240
Backus, Manson F. 18
Bailey, William C. 251
Baker, Miner 1–2
Banks: depositors 34–36, 40, 46–51, 76, 104–5, 188; closures, temporary 104–5; failures 20, 34–35, 46–47, 103–5; regulation and regulators 34, 41–46, 49–51, 104; runs 46–48, 104–5; warrants, redemption of 90, 178, 183, 185
bankruptcy 9, 25, 38, 44–45, 71, 126, 237, 271, 273
Bannick, Claude 28
Barber, H. C. 74–75
Bartell Drugs 126, 127
baseball 21, 147, 244–45
Bastheim, Arthur 19
Bayley, Frank S. 123
Beck, Dave 147, 149, 153, 161–72, 175, 179–81, 245, 247, 266, 267
Beeler, John 182
beggars and begging 27–28, 71, 77
Bellamy, Edward 136
Benjamin, Herbert 155
Bennett, Richard B. 30
Bickford, Willis 75
Black, Hugo 239, 252–53
Black, J. C. 94
Black Ball Line 249–50
Blanton, Thomas 112
Blethen, Clarance 21, 23–24, 102, 189, 232, 259, 280
Boeing Field 8, 20, 154, 222, 255, 261
Boeing Air Transport 25
Boeing Aircraft Company 30, 104, 253; Plant 2 255
Boeing, William E. 25, 252–53
Boettiger, John and Anna 168, 198, 224, 226
Bogolawlenski, Nicholas 5
Bon Marché 9, 33, 265
bond market 3, 61–62, 70, 90, 92, 107, 194–95, 233
Bonds: Associated Students 59–61; City Light revenue 194, 196; corporate 23, 43, 50, 59–61, 250
  defaults: real estate 38, 58, 126, 237, 244, 273; foreign 15, 56, 141; industrial 251; streetcar 181, 182

333

foreign 14–15, 18, 56, 61–62, 69–70, 141;
  public general obligation 92, 106–7, 233;
  real estate 12–13, 25, 38, 50, 58, 59, 97,
  126, 128, 237, 243, 265, 273; streetcar 176,
  178–82, 185; toll-bridge 13, 22, 62, 235
Bone, Homer T. 102–3, 111, 195, 219, 253
Boren, Virginia 245
Boronzoff, Ivan 132–33
Bouck, William 204
boycotts 153, 164
Brannin, Carl 87, 88, 91, 93
bread and bakeries 6, 77, 123
breweries 109, 163–65, 179, 244
Bridges: Aurora 20, 271, 232–33; Ballard 95,
  233–34; Lake Washington 16–17, 22, 62,
  232–35; Longview 13; University 233;
  West Seattle 20
Bridges, Harry 147, 149, 151, 169, 170, 185,
  218, 267
Brinton, Wilmer 94
Brisbane, Arthur 105
Brockway, Harold P. 155
Broderick, Henry 72, 240
Brooklyn building 237
Brown, J. H. 202, 206
Brown, Walter F. 252
Brown, Walter M. 178–79
Bull, Milton 74–75
Burgunder, Robert 50, 123, 163
Burke, Thomas (estate) 240
Burkheimer, John E. 260
buses *see* transit
Butterworth, Dorothy 223

Camlin Hotel 9, 32, 41–43, 54, 272
Campbell, Edmund 41–43, 45, 49, 51–54,
  265
Canada and Canadians 29–30, 62, 68, 141, 191,
  239, 242, 244
Caples, D. Elwood 212
Carnation Farms 120, 124, 261
Cascade tunnel proposal 231
Case, Otto 204
Centennial Mills Company 21, 247
Chadwick, Harry A. 54, 134
chain letters 139
Chapman, Horace P. 259
Chase National Bank 47
Chelan, Washington 220–21

China and Chinese Americans 218–19,
  263–64, 268
Chittenden, Hiram 231
Church of the People 135, 136, 153, 201
Churchill, Winston 267
City Light Building Company 187–89, 196
Cleanwell Dye Works 163
Comer, William D. 13–14, 20, 45–46, 49, 52,
  54, 60, 264
commodity prices 24, 30, 32, 55, 69, 107
Commonwealth Builders 136–38, 201
Communist Party: and Democrats 210,
  212–13, 223–28, 267; and elected officials
  210, 226–27; and election campaigns 155,
  201; and Hitler-Stalin Pact; invasion of
  Finland 225–28; and labor 149, 169–70;
  and press 131, 142–43, 149, 207–8; and
  Nazis 216, 225–26; and racism 142; and
  Spain 217–18; and Unemployed Citizens
  League and Washington
Commonwealth Federation 87, 90–92, 136;
  and University of Washington 2, 31, 207,
  217, 225; and WPA 223–24; demonstra-
  tions 24, 76, 142, 182, 183, 211; ideology
  and strategy 24, 201; opposition to 31, 91,
  142, 149, 183, 184, 201, 213
Comstock, George K. 169
Congress Against War and Fascism 278–79
Congress of Industrial Organizations (CIO)
  158, 159, 167, 169–70, 180, 182, 184–85,
  214, 225
Continental Mutual Savings Bank 34
Cooke, Alastair 172
Coon Chicken Inn 170
Costigan, Howard G. 136, 156, 202–3, 208,
  210, 212, 213, 223–26, 267
Cove Mid-City Market 260
crab industry 270
Crane, Elmer 122
Currier, Leon and family 277

D'Ambrose, Angelo and Angelina 276–77
Daffron, Shelvy S. 148
dairy industry 120–21, 123–25
DeCou, Lorenzo A. 187–88
deflation *see* prices
DeLacy, Hugh 207, 210, 215, 224–29, 267–68
Democratic Party: 1932 election 101–3; 1934
  election 135–38; 1936 election 167,

Index 335

202–11; 1938 election 212–14; and
    Communists 210, 212–13, 223–28, 267;
    long-term gains 265
Dennett, Eugene 142, 170, 210, 226
deficit finance (state, city) 90, 92, 106–7, 138,
    183, 185
Dent, Hawthorne K. 237
department stores 9
Dexter Horton building 10, 273
Diablo Dam 194–96
Dill, Clarence C. 29, 137, 174
Dimond, John E. 18–19
Dix, Irving F. 88–90, 175
Dixon, C. L. 77
Donnelly, J. C. 64
Dore, John F.: 1932 election, political style
    173–74; pay cuts, 1932 68–69, 174–75,
    179; rescue of Tusko 173–74; role in
    strikes 164, 175, 180–81; telephone
    franchise 175–76; streetcar finances
    176–79, 181–82; support of Dave Beck
    179–82; anti-communism 182–84; city
    financial crisis 183–84; City Light-Puget
    merger 198; defeat and death 184–85
Douglas Aircraft Company 254
Dornier, Claude 255–56
Driscoll, Robert 244
Duncan, James A. 175
Duranty, Walter 279
Duyungan, Virgil 157

Eba's Supermarket 261
Eby, Harold 213
economic planning 111, 117, 133–35, 201, 269
Eddy, John W. 55, 247
Edgewater Apartments 240–42
Edmond Meany Hotel 38, 59, 237, 260
Edris, William 59
Edwards, Frank 110, 188–91
Egtvedt, Clairmont 253–54
Ehrlichman, Ben B. 10–13, 122, 196, 264–65
Elections
    ballot measures, city: Light Department
        recall 187, 189–92; streetcars 176, 181–82;
        telephone franchise 175
    ballot measures, county: relief bond 92
    ballot measures, state: income tax 69, 138,
        214; liquor 108, 110; property tax limit
        92, 205, 214; production for use 204–5;

public utility districts 196; strike
    restrictions 214
blanket primary law 204; Canada 30, 141
city offices, mayor: 87, 173–74, 178–79,
    184–85, 209
city offices, council: 182, 201, 207, 227
federal 102–3, 137, 205, 213, 267; labor
    union 147, 152, 158–59, 170, 241; recall
    189; school district 201; state legislature
    102–3, 137, 205, 213, 269; statewide
    office 102–3, 137, 155, 203–5; student 61
Elfendahl, Victor 59
Elinor, Alice 79
Epstein, Jesse 84
Ernst, Charles F. 211, 212, 277
Esse, Jay 40
Evans, Don G. 90
Exchange building 12, 25–26, 126 264

Farley, James 112, 253
Farmer, Frances 143–44
farming and farmers 28, 179
Farquharson, Burt 137, 201
Farquharson, Mary 137, 206, 223–24, 229, 269
Fascism *see* Mussolini
Filipinos 28, 79, 156–59, 206
Finland and Finns 132, 226
First National Bank of Auburn 34–35
First National Bank of Sedro-Woolley 15
First National City Bank 15
Fish, Hamilton 31
Fisher Body 250
Fisher Flouring Mills 145–46
Fisher, O. D. 153
Fisher, O. W. 153–54
Fleming, Curtis and Elizabeth 220
Fletcher, Jess 267
Fobes, Leon 244
food aid, diet 77, 83, 87–96, 98, 211–12,
    221–22, 276–77
Forbes, Bertie C. 8, 24, 32, 101, 107, 128
Forbes, Richard T. 215
Forbus, Willie 228
Ford, Henry 5, 6, 20, 119
Ford Motor Company 4, 5, 20, 64–67, 250, 272
Ford, Sherwood 14
foreclosures *see* real estate market
Fox, William 44–45
Frandsen, Frank 76–77

Frandsen, Orlan 76, 83
Frankland, Charles 61
Fraser, A.G.M. 33–34
Fraser-Paterson Company 33
Frazier, Raymond 21, 34, 47–48
Frederick, Donald E. 25, 27
Frederick and Nelson 127, 261
Friends of the Soviet Union 5, 87, 135
Fuller, Richard E. and Margaret McTavish 64
Fullerton, James T. 141
Furse, Roy E. 89
Furuya, Masajiro 39–40

Garrett, Garet 161, 171–72
General Insurance Company (Safeco) 237
Geraghty, James M. 69
Gerard, James W. 56
German American Bund 215
German Americans 37, 215, 242–44
Germany 14, 56, 61, 70
Gill, Hiram 193
Gitlin, Todd 275
Goebbels, Joseph 56
gold standard 30, 61–62, 106–8
Gold Star Creameries, Everett 261
Golden Rule Dairy and Bakery 165
Gowman, Harry 21
Graham, John 9, 25, 33, 64, 240
Graham, John Jr. 265
Green, Joshua 55, 129
Green Lake 154, 270–71
Green, William 149
Griffiths, Austin E. 232
Griffiths, Austin E. Jr. 123
Gromyko, Andrei 267
Gundlach, Ralph 217

Haarsager, Sandra 275
Hadley, Homer 233–34
Hall, H. D. 226
Hanson, Harold C. 30
Harborview Hospital 20, 37, 68
Harlin, Robert H. 178, 191, 267
Hartley, Roland 31, 32, 42, 44, 55, 64, 90–91, 101–2
Hawley, Willis 15
Hearst, William Randolph 101, 167–68, 278–80
Hemphill, Wylie 31, 55

Henry, Ed 226
Henry, Fred H. 14, 45
Hiatt, Harold E. 167, 180
Hill, L.E. 19, 39, 276
Hinkle, J. Grant 43–44, 50, 103
Hoffman, H. J. 46
Holcomb, Oscar 69
Home Savings and Loan Association 47, 49–50, 76
homeless persons, camps 77–83, 86, 126, 271
homicides 136, 149, 151, 157, 164
Hoover, Herbert 15, 18, 20, 29–30, 61, 101–2, 265
Hoover, J. Edgar 112
Hooverville, *see* homeless persons, camps
Hopkins, Harry 99, 154
Horr, Ralph 45, 102
Houston, David F. 193
Howard, George F. 150
Howard, Ralph 213
Humane Society 74
Hunt, Lester M. 185, 203

Ickes, Harold 122, 123, 195
immigration 28–29
Industrial Council of Washington 152–53, 164, 167, 169
international trade 30, 62, 64, 132, 258
interurban rail closures 178, 235–36
investment, long-term 128, 172, 249

Jackson, Robert H. 239
Jamieson, Frank T. 21
Jamison, H. E. 82
Japan 70, 183, 185, 218–20, 227, 257, 263–64
Japanese Americans 28, 39–40, 85, 93, 157–59, 179, 269
Jermane, W.W. 30, 101, 122
Johnson, Albert 28
Johnson, Hugh S. 117
Johnson, Philip G. 25
Jones, Gareth 279
Jones, Homer R. 267
Jones, Jesse H. 194
Jones, Wesley L. 29, 102

KJR Radio 43, 49, 139, 184
Kalakala 249, 250
Kahn, Albert 5, 64

Keaton, Buster and Natalie 24
Kennedy, Robert F. 172
King County government: commission 22, 92, 203, 211, 229; bonds 92, 107; relief 82, 88, 90–96, 211–12; superior court 49, 61, 76, 95, 123–24, 163, 183; women employees 229; warrants (debt) 90, 92, 94, 107
King County Labor Council *see* Seattle Central Labor Council
Knudson, Gus 74
Kraft, Vincent I. 43
Kristoferson, August 124

Labor: hours 6–8, 171, 175, 240–41; pay cuts (percent) 59, 68, 69, 175; pay increases (percent) 121, 171; wage rates 20, 28, 32, 69, 88–89, 233; *see also* unions
Lake Forest Park project 97–98
Lake Washington bridge 22, 62, 233–35
Lamb, Isom 220–21
Landes, Bertha K. 8, 66, 68
Langlie, Arthur B. 184, 198, 209, 219
Lasser, David 155
laundry industry 162–64, 175
Lehman, Herbert H. 203
Levine, David 215
Lindbergh, Charles 6
Linden, Adolph F. 40–46, 49, 51–54, 260, 265
Lippmann, Walter 117, 125
liquor 49–50, 79, 82, 101, 108–9, 155
Littler, Anson A. 57
Long, Huey 139–40
Longview bridge 13
looting 142
Lovering, Paul 20, 25, 276
loyalty oaths 31
lumber and wood products 121, 132, 146, 239, 250–52
Lundin, Alfred 148
Lustig, B. B. 74
Lynch, Frank M. 166, 168, 208

MacGowan, Howard 173
Maged, Jacob 122
Magee, John 154
Magee, Thornton 259
Magnuson, Warren G. 37, 51 96, 103, 107, 115, 144, 202, 219, 267
Marcantonio, Vito 111

Marinoff, Peter 163–64, 179, 245
marriage and divorce 63, 126, 206, 238
Marshall, Jim 97, 263–64
Martin, Clarence 69, 76, 93, 102, 109, 138, 149, 183, 198, 202–06, 209–12, 228, 231, 233
Masterson McNeilly, Mildred 62
Matanuska project 96–97, 99
Maxwell, Earl 206, 213
McCarthy, Mary T. 201, 203
McDonald Act 93, 103
McFarland, Sarah 96
McIlroy, Doris 83
McKay, William O. 5, 41, 55, 119
McLauchlan, John and Adelaide 245–46
McNary, John Hugh 121
Medical Dental Building 10, 21
Mehlhorn, August and Else 36–37
Meisnest, Darwin 58–59, 110
Menefee, Selden 80, 184
Meridian Electric Bakery 123
Merriam, Frank 137, 148
Messelheiser, Otto 228–29
Meyers, Victor A. 103, 183–84, 209–11, 213, 229
milk *see* dairy industry
Miller, Lea van Puymbroeck 228–29
Moe, Iver 142
Moen, Martin 81–85
Moltzner, Jay S. 188
Moody's Investors Service 56
Morgan, Murray 172
Morrill, Madge and May 18
Morrison, Earl W. 187
Mortgage Investment Company, Portland 187
Mullins, William H. 88
Murray, William H. 92
Murrow, Lacey V. 205, 231, 234
Mussolini, Benito 105, 118

Nash, Louis 94, 211, 229
National Bank of Commerce 18, 31, 35
Nazi party and Nazis 56, 134, 215–16
Neal, M.T. 226
Neuberger, Richard L. 114–15
New Deal effects 265–66
Newhall, Charles 89
Newhaven project 97
New York Stock Exchange 104–5
Nicely, Wallace L. 41, 43–46, 49, 52

Nichols, Ralph 88–89, 194
Niendorff, Fred 244
Nix, Rubye 112–13
Nolde, George 132–33
Nordstrom, Everett, Elmer, and John 32
Normandy Park 242–44
Northern Life Tower 9–10, 16
Northern Radio Company 243–44
Northgate mall 265
Northwest Peoples Publishing Company 207
Northwest Radio Service 43–45, 50
Norton building 25

O'Connor, Harvey 207
O'Neil, Paul 180
Oeconomacos, Nicholas 71–73
Olympia Brewing Company 109
Olympic Hotel 9, 24, 58, 75, 103
Oregon Museum of Natural and Cultural History 75
Osner and Mehlhorn 36–37

Pacific Car and Foundry Company 249
Pacific Coast League 244
Pacific Commercial Bank 39–40
Pacific National Bank 35, 61
Pacific Telephone and Telegraph Company 88–89, 175, 261
Pan American Airways 256
Parades: Communist 24, 142, 279; German American Bund 215; Labor Day 167, 182; May Day 182; NRA 118–19; Unemployed Citizens League 93
Parker, Emmett 69
Patron, Placido 157
Peabody, Alexander M. 249
Pearson, Drew 225
Pemberton, W. H. 165
Penney, J. C., Company 34, 57
Pennock, William J. 213
pensions 138, 141, 212, 220–21
Phinney, Russell H. 243
Pierce, Ahira and Kay 49–51, 53–54, 264
Pierce, Albert 181
Pigott, Paul 249
Pilgrim Congregational Church 13, 134, 225
planned economy *see* economic planning
plasterboard 241

plywood 250–52
Port of Seattle 75, 219
Ponzi schemes 35, 50
Powell, Mildred 229
Pratt, Cornelia Atwood 14
Prices: goods and services 15, 55, 58, 60, 71, 107, 120, 122–25, 128; land and capital 44, 56, 70, 238, 242–44, 249, 251; price-fixing 117–18, 133, 161–65, 170, 172, 184
Prison sentences: financial crimes 35, 37, 52–54, 188; looting 142; tax evasion 172; violence 76, 164; welfare fraud 16
"Production for use" 135–36, 138, 201–05, 221–23
Prohibition *see* liquor
protests 24, 56, 66, 76–77, 91, 93–94, 101–2, 142, 211, 218
Public Utility Districts 196–97, 199
Puget Sound Bridge and Dredging Company 22, 62
Puget Sound Canal proposal 231
Puget Sound Navigation Company 249
Puget Sound Power and Light Company 176, 182, 185, 192–99
Puget Sound Savings and Loan Association 41–52, 187
Puget Sound Shipyard Company 259

Qualitee Milk Products 120–21

racism 28, 29, 39, 170, 206
Rader, Melvin 225
radio, political use of 43, 104, 136, 210
Rainier Brewing Company 109, 244–45
Raport, Morris 143, 227
Reagan, Ronald 268
Real estate market: abandoned, torched 57, 75, 126; apartments 64, 126, 237, 240; foreclosures 71, 76, 127, 246–47; ; hotels 9, 13, 126, 237; houses 127, 240, 242; mortgage rates and terms 127, 242; offices 9–10, 126, 237; retail 239; teardowns 126–27; theaters 128
Relief: food banks 90–94; income, asset requirements 90, 93, 96; resettlement 96–99; residence requirements 90; work requirements 94–95; *see also* King County and Washington state

Republican Party 29–30, 101–2, 137, 204, 213, 265
retail stores 9
Ridder, Bernard, Joseph, and Victor 23
Robe, Lidablanche 3, 62, 276
Robinson, Walter J. 123–24
Ronald, James T. 163
Roosevelt, Franklin D.: daughter Anna Boettiger 168, 198, 224; meets Howard Costigan 224–25; handicap not shown 103, 106, 184, 266; political rhetoric 95, 104, 128–29; support for J.D. Ross 196, 198; visits Seattle 174, 183
Roosevelt Hotel 20, 37
Rosellini, Albert D. 137
Ross, James D.: City Light Tower, Ross fired 187–91; rivalry with Puget Power 192–93; financing Diablo Dam 194–96; merger plan rejected 196–98; posthumous victory 198–99
Ross Dam 196
Roy, Donald Francis 79, 82
Rukeyser, Merryle S. 128
Russia: Americans to Russia 31, 131–32, 135, 143–44, 208, 267; trade with Russia 30, 31, 132; Russians to America 5, 132–33; Russian fishing in Bering Sea 270
Ryan, Joseph P. 14

Sale, Roger 171
salmon canneries 157–58
Safeco General Insurance Company 237
Schmitz, Dietrich 120
Schwabacher Brothers 243
Schwellenbach, Lewis B. 137, 202–03, 212, 219, 258
Schwinn, Herman 215
Scott, Howard 132, 134, 269
Scottsboro Boys 142
scrap metal export 185, 218–19
scrip currency 89, 104, 136
Seattle Art Museum 64
Seattle Building Trades Council 241
Seattle Central Labor Council: dominated by Dave Beck 166; married women workers 66, 229; May Day v. Labor Day 182; opposes city pay cuts 89; strikes, pro and con 153, 156, 166, 180

Seattle Chamber of Commerce: opposes private-sector pay cuts 31; home ownership campaign 127; open-shop campaign 148–53, 169; president heads relief effort 88; tourism campaign 55; shipyard campaign 258–60 welcomes Russians 5
Seattle Citizens' Emergency; Committee 148–49
Seattle, City of: budget 69, 183, 185; building permits 57, 64, 126, 237, 239, 242; City Light 3, 104, 111, 187–99; plan to buy Puget Power 196–98; council 66, 89, 148, 182, 183, 185, 196, 215, 231–32; employee pay, hours, layoffs 68, 69, 104, 174–75, 179, 193; fire department 69, 179
Police: arrests 18, 96, 113, 135, 143, 180; demos, suppressed 24, 183; burnouts of shacks 77; escorts 5, 158; raids 31, 149; interrogations 111; strike action, pro-union 145, 165, 175; strike action, anti-union 147–49, 158, 176, 180–81
parades 167, 182; relief 88–89; street railway 89, 176–79, 182, 185; warrants (debt) 68–69, 104, 179, 183–85, 188, 194, 196; water department 89, 104; waterfront 231–32; zoo 73–74
Seattle-First National Bank 1, 23, 48, 272–73
Seattle Housing Authority 84–85
Seattle Maritime Association 231
Seattle Post-Intelligencer
Opinions: 1932 endorsements 101–2; Dave Beck 167; City Light 189; Lake Washington bridge 234; New Deal 105–6, 124, 168–69, 280; tariff, trade 29, 219; unemployment relief 278; radicals 278–79
publishers 101, 168, 198, 224, 226; reporters, editors 1, 14, 39, 62, 79, 83, 119, 131, 173, 185, 221, 244; strike 165–70, 180; syndicated columnists 8, 101, 105, 128
Seattle and Rainier Valley Railway 178, 181
Seattle Schools 69, 120–21
Seattle Star
Opinions: 1932 endorsements 101–2; Alaskan Way name 232; City Light, Puget Power 195–98; FDR, New Deal 105–6, 121–24; optimism, boosterism 20, 25, 38, 260; radicals 90, 137, 213, 279; tariff, trade 129; unemployment relief 278; women at work 66
reporters, columnists 18, 125; strike 180–81

Seattle Stock Exchange 20, 25, 69, 128
Seattle Symphony 71–72
Seattle Tacoma Land Company 243
Seattle Times
    Opinions: 1932 endorsements 101–2; City Light 189, 193; economy, optimism 25, 27, 33, 55, 80–82; FDR, New Deal 104–7, 118, 121, 124; Filipino immigration 28; radicals 90, 102, 147, 167–68, 279; liquor regulation 69; roads, bridges 234–35; tariff, trade 29, 132; unemployment relief 96, 155, 278; women at work 67, 229
    reporters, editors 2, 20, 101, 180, 245, 270; Ridder Brothers' investment in 23–24
Seattle Trust and Savings Bank 63–64
Shank, Corwin 41
shipyards 249, 258–60
Shopping Tower 11–12, 171, 272
Shorter, Fred 114, 134–36, 153
Sick, Emil J. and Sick's Stadium 244–45, 247
Simon, Aurelio 157
Sinclair, Upton 135, 137–38
Skinner, Gilbert 59
Sloan, Alfred P. 129
Smith, Charles L. 148, 149, 154, 179, 183
Smith, Jurie B. 226
Smith, Michael 226
Smith, Roscoe E. 124
Smith, Tom E. 211, 222, 229
Smith Tower 16
Smoot, Reed 15
Snell, Bertrand H. 111
Socialist Party 134, 136, 137
Soviet Union *see* Russia
Spanish civil war 144, 161, 216–18
Spaulding, Lester 80–81
spies against unions 153
St. Mark's Cathedral 245–47
Stalin, Solomon 163
Standard Oil Company of California 148
Steinbrueck, Victor E. 128
Steinert, William J. 51–52
Stevenson, John C. 93–94, 203–04
Stock: dividend cuts 195; double liability 35–36; market 18–20, 25, 28, 56–57, 62, 69–70, 105, 128, 238; public offerings, failed 21, 44, 187; public offerings,
successful 109, 250, 252, 255; private offerings, successful 43, 265, 270
streetcars *see* transit
Strikes: auto mechanics 165; Fisher Flouring Mills 152–54; general strikes 149, 154, 192, 207; Inlandboatmen 249; laundry workers 175; longshore 145–52, 154; Marinoff Brewery 163–64; *Post-Intelligencer* 165–70; *Star* 180–81; Works Progress Administration (WPA) 155–56
Strong, Anna Louise 207, 208
Strong, Sydney 207
Stuart, Bert 75–76
suicides 14, 19, 49, 63, 114, 238, 244
Sullivan, James T. 226
Summers, Thane 216–18

Taxes and fees: business revenue 69, 139, 184; cigarette, liquor 138–39; garbage pickup 183; income 69, 138, 212, 214; parking meters 183; property 69, 138–39, 183, 205, 214; retail sales 138–39, 206; undistributed profits 129, 239; utility 184
Taylor, Jack 229
teachers *see* Seattle schools
Technocracy 132–33, 135–36, 155, 201, 208, 269
telephone lines 126, 261
Textile Tower 20, 187
theaters 8–9, 71
Thomas, Paul G. 226
Thomsen, Charles M. 21, 247
Thomsen, Moritz 21, 247
Todd Dry Docks 260
Townsend plan 141, 204, 220–21
Trans World Airlines 257
transit 21, 181–82, 185
trials 51–52, 54, 164, 188
Truman, Harry 264, 267
Tugwell, Rexford 122
Tusko the elephant 73–74
Tyler, Richard G. 133–34, 207–08, 227, 269

U.S. Government: Bonneville Power Administration 196; Civil Works Administration (CWA) 94, 195; Courts, District and Supreme, 121, 125, 204, 206, 238–39; Federal Deposit Insurance Corporation (FDIC) 105; Federal

Emergency Relief Administration 96; Federal Housing Administration 127, 240; Federal Writers Project 223–24; Home Owners Loan Corporation 127; Maritime Commission 258; National Labor Relations Board 154, 168, 181; National Recovery Administration (NRA) 117–29, 171, 251; Public Works Administration (PWA) 195–96, 233; Reconstruction Finance Corporation 185, 194, 270; Securities and Exchange Commission 196; Resettlement Administration 96; Un-American Activities Committee 224, 268; War Department 232–33; Works Progress Administration (WPA) 84, 95, 154–56, 212, 255, 270–71

U.S. Laws: Air Mail Act 253; Bonneville Power Act 197; National Industrial Recovery Act 117–19, 145; National Labor Relations Act 158, 166, 265; Sedition Act (disloyalty) 87; Social Security Act 111, 138, 141, 205, 220; Smoot-Hawley Tariff 15, 18, 29, 239 Trading With the Enemy Act 104, 106,

U.S. Plywood Corporation 251

Unemployed Citizens League (UCL) 87–94, 101–2, 110, 136, 222

unemployment rates 24, 57, 62, 93, 94, 125–26, 128, 238, 239, 261

Unions: Auto Mechanics 165; Aero Machinists 268; Brewery Workers 163–64; Building Service Workers 171, 267; Building Trades 170–71; Cannery Workers and Farm Laborers 156–59, 182; Cereal Workers 152, 153; ; Inlandboatmen 170; Laundry and Dye Workers 162–63; Longshoremen 145–47, 154, 159, 182; Newspaper Guild 166–70, 180; Plasterers 241; Retail Clerks 171; Teamsters 122, 147, 153, 158, 163, 169, 179, 180, 182, 222; Weighers and Warehousemen 152; Workers' Alliance 154–56, 202, 211

union organizing 162–65, 170–71, 179

United Aircraft and Transport Corporation 252–53

United Air Lines 252, 254

United National Corporation 11, 20, 21, 56–57, 62, 70, 128, 238

University of Washington: anti-nepotism policy 228–29; anti-smoking policy for coeds 8; Associated Students (ASUW) 2, 58, 60–61, 110; ban on Communist speakers 31; bookstore 58, 60; radical professors 133, 207, 213, 217, 225; professors' pay cut 69; sports and athletes 58–59, 110, 148; tuition cut 69

Usatalo, William 164, 167

Vanderveer, George 166, 182
Van Soelen, Anton C. 175, 176
Vanguard, The 87, 90, 93
veterans' organizations 66, 101, 135, 143
Violence, labor related: by labor 145–48, 149, 151, 156, 162–67, 170, 175, 180; by owners 146, 148, 157, 164, 170; by government 149–51
Voice of Action, The 143, 149, 153, 154, 201, 207–08

Wakefield, Jessie London 2
Wakefield, Lowell A. 2, 141–43, 207, 269–70
Wallace, Henry A. 268
Wallin, Carl F. 32
Walters, Charles E. and Ralph 34–35
warrants (debt) 68–69, 90, 92, 94, 107, 178–84, 188, 194, 196
Washington Athletic Club 14, 20, 37, 58–60
Washington Commonwealth Federation (WCF) 182, 183, 185, 201–08, 212–14, 218, 221–27, 229, 267
Washington Loan and Securities Company 50
Washington Mutual Savings Bank 34, 37, 47–48
Washington State Federation of Labor 175
Washington State Grange 201, 206
Washington, state of: Agriculture Department 122–23, 138; bank regulators *see* Nicely, Hoffman; bonds, 106–7; Canwell hearings 156, 213, 225, 268; criminal syndicalism law 138, 143, 206–7; ferries 249; governor *see* Hartley, Roland and Martin, Clarence; housing, public 214; Emergency Relief Administration 138; legislature 137–38, 224; liquor control 109–10, 155; relief programs 76–77, 92–93, 98–99, 106–7, 211; securities regulators 43–44, 50, 97, 188; Supreme Court 90, 107, 125, 163, 167, 179, 233

Watson, Richard 247
Watson, Steve S. 149
Welch, Doug 73, 103, 119, 221–22, 235
Wells, Hulet M. 37, 87–93, 111
West Coast Lumbermen's Association 121
Western Hotels 32
Western States Technocrat 204
Westman, Lenus 224
Weyerhaeuser, George 142–43
Willamette Valley Lumber Company 121
Williams, Walter 247, 259–60
Wills, Ellsworth 226
Wimmler, Norman L. 30
Winkenwerder, Hugo 2
Withington, Wilfred 201
women and work 8, 65–68, 228–29

Wood, Gardner 18–19
Woodland Park and Zoo 73–74, 235
Woodward, Cyrus E. 201–2, 204, 221–22, 269
Workaneaters 221–23
World War I: influence on 1930s 101, 104, 117, 119, 150, 233; German reparations 14, 56, 61, 70
World War II and postwar adjustment 263–64
Wurdemann mansion 42

Yesler Terrace 128
Young, Ray 223

Zioncheck, Marion 59, 93, 102, 189, 110–15
Zwarg, Henry O. 97

About the Author

Bruce A. Ramsey came to history through journalism. Born in Seattle, he grew up along Puget Sound. At the University of Washington in Seattle, he studied business, and at the University of California, Berkeley, journalism. For 16 years he was a business reporter and columnist at the *Seattle Post-Intelligencer*, where he won a national award for his coverage of the failure in 1982 of the Seattle-First National Bank. For 14 years, he was an editorial writer, columnist and book reviewer for the *Seattle Times*. Most of the 150 books he reviewed were of 20th century history, as were many of the books he kept on his shelves.

As a hobby, he edited two books of family history from taped interviews. He also researched the life of Garet Garrett, a writer for the *Saturday Evening* Post in the 1920s and 1930s, and wrote a biography, *Unsanctioned Voice* (Caxton, 2008). In retirement, Ramsey undertook to research the depression of the 1890s, mainly by digging through old newspapers. The result was *The Panic of 1893: The Untold Story of Washington State's First Depression* (Caxton, 2018). Using the same method, he has produced *Seattle in the Great Depression*.

Ramsey lives in Seattle with his wife, Anne, a former vice president of Citibank.

Cover image credits

Front cover, background image: Looking north on Broadway, Seattle, 1934. Item 8760, Engineering Department Photographic Negatives (Record Series 2613-07), Seattle Municipal Archives. Wikimedia Commons CC BY 2.0

Back cover, background image: University Bridge under construction, 1931. Item 139494, Fleets and Facilities Department Imagebank Collection (Record Series 0207-01), Seattle Municipal Archives. Wikimedia Commons CC BY 2.0

Back cover, left inset: The corner of Fourth Avenue and Blanchard Street during second Denny Regrade, 1930. Seattle Municipal Archives. Wikimedia Commons CC BY 2.0

Back cover, right inset: Railroad Avenue (now Alaskan Way) and Pier 14 (now Pier 70), Seattle, Washington, ca. 1935. Seattle Municipal Archives. Wikimedia Commons CC BY 2.0